More Praise for The Permanent Revolution

"*The Permanent Revolution* is an example of the kind of theological work that is urgently needed to 'equip the saints for the work of ministry' apostolically, prophetically, evangelistically, pastorally, and instructively."
—From the Foreword by Darrell Guder, *Winters Luce Professor of Missional and Ecumenical Theology*

"*The Permanent Revolution* by Hirsch and Catchim is a timely reminder that Jesus founded a dynamic missionary movement. This is a well-researched and thoroughly engaging study of the dynamic that Jesus planted at the heart of the church and now calls us to rediscover."
—Steve Addison, Australian director, Church Resource Ministries; author of *Movements That the Change the World*

"C. S. Lewis believed the ultimate compliment you could give a book was to reread it. As I read *The Permanent Revolution* for the first time, already I was anticipating the opportunity to reread it! How often does that happen? I knew it would be one of those few books that would become a reference point for my entire life and ministry from then forward. Outside the New Testament, in this one man's humble opinion, *The Permanent Revolution* is the seminal work on apostolic ministry."
—Rob Wegner, pastor, Life Mission Granger Community Church; lead catalyst, EnterMission; experience director, Future Travelers; author, *Missional Moves*

"A very PROVOCATIVE and INFORMATIVE book! Readers are invited to give careful consideration of reclaiming the Ephesians 4:11 gifting of apostles, prophets, evangelists, shepherds, and teachers (APEST) as the foundational framework for exercising and structuring Christian leadership. It is an argument worth serious consideration given the problems associated with the clergy/laity dichotomy that continues to exist in so many of our churches today."
—Craig Van Gelder, professor of congregational mission, Luther Seminary

"'Jesus has given the church everything it needs to get the job done.'" This statement reverberates throughout this book. There is no greater job in the world, and belief in this statement with action reflecting it will no doubt reform the western church. This truly is the capstone to all of Hirsch's work. Every church leader must consider this Permanent Revolution as Jesus intended."

—Tammy Dunahoo, vice president of U.S. operations/general supervisor, The Foursquare Church

"Clearly, practically, and with much love for the church, Alan Hirsch and Tim Catchim redress the imbalance brought about by the exiling of the apostle, prophet, and evangelist from the leadership of the local church. There is a challenge here that must be listened to. *The Permanent Revolution* is a must-read for every leader who seeks to recover the apostolic heartbeat that drives the church into God's mission."

—David Fitch, B. R. Lindner Chair of Evangelical Theology, Northern Seminary; author, *The End of Evangelicalism?*

"Hirsch and Catchim are architects of the future. Their goal is not to dismantle today's church, but to help re-engineer its future by realigning around the five-fold gifts. Every other solution currently being offered is simply a façade. Cover to cover this is a truly worthy read."

—Linda Bergquist, church strategist; coauthor *Church Turned Inside Out: A Guide for Designers, Refiners, and Re-Aligners*

"Alan Hirsch and Tim Catchim have written a book that all church leaders should read as we consider the church's mission and movement into the twenty-first century. There is a growing, and often confusing, dialogue concerning apostolic ministry in the church, and *The Permanent Revolution* offers both clarity and a compelling argument. If you have a heart for 'sent' ministry, read this book."

—Ed Stetzer, president, Lifeway Research

"The crisis of the Western church cannot be adequately addressed merely by working harder or smarter. We need a fresh paradigm for the church in order to frame and direct our efforts. Hirsch and Catchim contend that Ephesians 4:1–16 provides just such a "back to the future" paradigm.

For too long the church has depended almost exclusively on the gifts of pastor and teacher, but now we must cultivate the full range of Christ's gifts to the body. The greatest need for our day, the authors believe, is to reactivate apostolic giftedness. At stake is the success of the missional movement and the renewal of the evangelical church. This is an important book that needs to be widely read and broadly debated. But watch your toes . . . they will be stepped on!"

—David G. Dunbar, president, Biblical Theological Seminary

"There is desperate need for what Alan Hirsch and Tim Catchim have designed this book to be: '. . . *a single, comprehensive reference text promoting the ongoing role of the apostolic person in the life of the church.*' It is a long overdue conversation of critical importance. The stakes are high, particularly in the West. A new generation of apostolic leaders is essential if the Church is to ever regain the initiative that we have lost by ignoring this essential biblical function."

—Sam Metcalf, president, Church Resource Ministries

"An exhaustive exploration of the dynamics of apostolic ministry, interweaving biblical, historical, and contemporary material, presenting a persuasive argument for the recovery, recognition, and release of this neglected ministry as a crucial component in the emergence of missional churches. The Christian movement in post-Christendom needs to reappropriate the ministries of apostles, prophets, and evangelists alongside pastors and teachers. This book offers a wealth of resources to help us."

—Stuart Murray, author, *Post-Christendom* and *The Naked Anabaptist*

"In matters of mission—especially in the West—there are no simple solutions and no magic bullets. There are some key starting points and the debate about leadership is just such a point. Hirsch and Catchim have opened up the difficult issue of leadership, imagination, and gifting with no holds barred. This is a text that will inform the controversy around this issue for some time to come. If you care about leadership and mission you will want to grapple with this book."

—Martin Robinson, president, Springdale College; National Director of Together in Mission

"This book, written by one of the foremost missional thinkers of our day, addresses what I believe to be *the* most necessary and neglected of subjects in the New Testament—the equipping gifts of Ephesians 4:11. Once again Alan Hirsch (now with the help of Tim Catchim) has opened the Pandora's box of missional inquiry so the rest of us can try and get our minds around a subject of wide consequence that will not likely settle back down. This book will be the first of its kind, but I guarantee not the last."

—Neil Cole, founder, Church Multiplication Associates; author, *Organic Church, Organic Leadership, Search & Rescue, Church 3.0,* and *Journeys to Significance*

"In *The Permanent Revolution* Alan Hirsch and Tim Catchim gift us with a weighty tome that befits the epic adventure unfolding in these days of the collapse of Christendom. Church leaders are increasingly aware that the big shift for us is to move from managing an institution to leading a movement. Our learning curve is steep. We need help in reimagining and redesigning our leadership beliefs and practices. Nothing less than reconnecting with our apostolic roots will do. This volume helps us do exactly that."

—Reggie McNeal, author, *The Present Future, Missional Renaissance,* and *Missional Communities*

the permanent revolution

Apostolic Imagination and Practice for the 21st Century Church

ALAN HIRSCH AND TIM CATCHIM

FOREWORD BY
DARRELL L. GUDER

WITH

CONTRIBUTIONS FROM MIKE BREEN

JOSSEY-BASS
A Wiley Imprint
www.josseybass.com

iblication

Published by Jossey-Bass
A Wiley Imprint
One Montgomery Street, Suite 1200, San Francisco, CA 94104-4594—www.josseybass.com

Jossey-Bass books and products are available through most bookstores. To contact Jossey-Bass directly call our Customer Care Department within the U.S. at 800-956-7739, outside the U.S. at 317-572-3986, or fax 317-572-4002.

Wiley publishes in a variety of print and electronic formats and by print-on-demand. Some material included with standard print versions of this book may not be included in e-books or in print-on-demand. If this book refers to media such as a CD or DVD that is not included in the version you purchased, you may download this material at http://booksupport.wiley.com. For more information about Wiley products, visit www.wiley.com.

Credits are continued on p. 326.

Library of Congress Cataloging-in-Publication Data

Hirsch, Alan, date
   The permanent revolution : apostolic imagination and practice for the 21st century church / Alan Hirsch and Tim Catchim ; foreword by Darrell L. Guder ; with contributions from Mike Breen.
      p.   cm.—(Jossey-Bass leadership network series ; 57)
   Includes index.
   ISBN 978-0-470-90774-0 (hardback); 978-1-118-17357-2 (ebk); 978-1-118-17358-9 (ebk); 978-1-118-17359-6 (ebk)
      1. Church development, New.   2. Mission of the church.   3. Missional church movement.
      I. Catchim, Tim.   II. Breen, Mike, Revd.   III. Title.
   BV652.24.H57   2012
   262.001'7—dc23   2011039901
Printed in the United States of America

FIRST EDITION

HB Printing   10 9 8 7 6 5 4 3 2

LEADERSHIP NETWORK TITLES

The Blogging Church: Sharing the Story of Your Church Through Blogs, Brian Bailey and Terry Storch

Church Turned Inside Out: A Guide for Designers, Refiners, and Re-Aligners, Linda Bergquist and Allan Karr

Leading from the Second Chair: Serving Your Church, Fulfilling Your Role, and Realizing Your Dreams, Mike Bonem and Roger Patterson

In Pursuit of Great AND Godly Leadership: Tapping the Wisdom of the World for the Kingdom of God, Mike Bonem

Hybrid Church: The Fusion of Intimacy and Impact, Dave Browning

The Way of Jesus: A Journey of Freedom for Pilgrims and Wanderers, Jonathan S. Campbell with Jennifer Campbell

Cracking Your Church's Culture Code: Seven Keys to Unleashing Vision and Inspiration, Samuel R. Chand

Leading the Team-Based Church: How Pastors and Church Staffs Can Grow Together into a Powerful Fellowship of Leaders, George Cladis

Organic Church: Growing Faith Where Life Happens, Neil Cole

Church 3.0: Upgrades for the Future of the Church, Neil Cole

Journeys to Significance: Charting a Leadership Course from the Life of Paul, Neil Cole

Off-Road Disciplines: Spiritual Adventures of Missional Leaders, Earl Creps

Reverse Mentoring: How Young Leaders Can Transform the Church and Why We Should Let Them, Earl Creps

Building a Healthy Multi-Ethnic Church: Mandate, Commitments, and Practices of a Diverse Congregation, Mark DeYmaz

Leading Congregational Change Workbook, James H. Furr, Mike Bonem, and Jim Herrington

The Tangible Kingdom: Creating Incarnational Community, Hugh Halter and Matt Smay

Baby Boomers and Beyond: Tapping the Ministry Talents and Passions of Adults over Fifty, Amy Hanson

Leading Congregational Change: A Practical Guide for the Transformational Journey, Jim Herrington, Mike Bonem, and James H. Furr

The Leader's Journey: Accepting the Call to Personal and Congregational Transformation, Jim Herrington, Robert Creech, and Trisha Taylor

The Permanent Revolution: Apostolic Imagination and Practice for the 21st Century, Alan Hirsch and Tim Catchim

Whole Church: Leading from Fragmentation to Engagement, Mel Lawrenz

Culture Shift: Transforming Your Church from the Inside Out, Robert Lewis and Wayne Cordeiro, with Warren Bird

Church Unique: How Missional Leaders Cast Vision, Capture Culture, and Create Movement, Will Mancini

A New Kind of Christian: A Tale of Two Friends on a Spiritual Journey, Brian D. McLaren

The Story We Find Ourselves In: Further Adventures of a New Kind of Christian, Brian D. McLaren

Missional Communities: The Rise of the Post-Congregational Church, Reggie McNeal

Missional Renaissance: Changing the Scorecard for the Church, Reggie McNeal

Practicing Greatness: 7 Disciplines of Extraordinary Spiritual Leaders, Reggie McNeal

The Present Future: Six Tough Questions for the Church, Reggie McNeal

A Work of Heart: Understanding How God Shapes Spiritual Leaders, Reggie McNeal

The Millennium Matrix: Reclaiming the Past, Reframing the Future of the Church, M. Rex Miller

Your Church in Rhythm: The Forgotten Dimensions of Seasons and Cycles, Bruce B. Miller

Shaped by God's Heart: The Passion and Practices of Missional Churches, Milfred Minatrea

The Missional Leader: Equipping Your Church to Reach a Changing World, Alan J. Roxburgh and Fred Romanuk

Missional Map-Making: Skills for Leading in Times of Transition, Alan J. Roxburgh

Relational Intelligence: How Leaders Can Expand Their Influence Through a New Way of Being Smart, Steve Saccone

Viral Churches: Helping Church Planters Become Movement Makers, Ed Stetzer and Warren Bird

The Externally Focused Quest: Becoming the Best Church for the Community, Eric Swanson and Rick Rusaw

The Ascent of a Leader: How Ordinary Relationships Develop Extraordinary Character and Influence, Bill Thrall, Bruce McNicol, and Ken McElrath

Beyond Megachurch Myths: What We Can Learn from America's Largest Churches, Scott Thumma and Dave Travis

The Other 80 Percent: Turning Your Church's Spectators into Active Participants, Scott Thumma and Warren Bird

Better Together: Making Church Mergers Work, Jim Tomberlin and Warren Bird

The Elephant in the Boardroom: Speaking the Unspoken About Pastoral Transitions, Carolyn Weese and J. Russell Crabtree

We thank you, our wonderful Lord Jesus. We humbly offer these words to you; we trust that you might sanctify them, cleanse them of sinful motivations, and witness the truth and/or falsity of what is being said, so that you might ultimately use them in the extension of your purposes in our lives and through your people.

To Jesus, Paul, Peter, St. Patrick, John Wesley, and the myriad apostles who have gone before us and trailblazed the ground on which all of us stand. We humbly and gratefully stand on your shoulders.

To Mike Breen, Neil Cole, Martin Robinson, Mike Frost, Felicity and Tony Dale, Tim Keller, Steve Addison, Dick Scoggins, Bob Roberts Jr., Dave Ferguson, Reggie McNeal, Chris Wienand, Milton Oliver, Rob Wegner, Caesar Kalinowski, Hugh Halter, Jeff Vanderstelt, and the many other contemporary practitioners who ably demonstrate what apostolic ministry is all about. What an honor it has been to be a part of your worlds.

To the seminal apostolic thinkers who have kept alive the tradition of apostolicity, especially Darrell Guder, and the late Leslie Newbigin and David Bosch.

Brave souls all.

This one is for you!

—Alan

To my wife, Tiffany, who was a constant source of encouragement during the process of carving out time to press forward through the challenges of writing. To my dear friend David Noles who provided spiritual counsel, and to Jason Gayton who provided key reflections at various stages of writing. To the 3DM crew who have been a beacon of light in the landscape of discipleship and mission. And to our local Christian community, Ikon, which provided the context, support, and patience for the implementation and refinement of this material.

—Tim

CONTENTS

PART ONE
Ephesians 4:1-16: Frameworks for Ministry

PART TWO
Apostolic Ministry

PART THREE
Apostolic Leadership

ABOUT THE JOSSEY-BASS
LEADERSHIP NETWORK SERIES

LEADERSHIP NETWORK'S mission is to accelerate the impact of OneHundredX leaders. These high-capacity leaders are like the hundred-fold crop that comes from seed planted in good soil as Jesus described in Matthew 13:8.

Leadership Network . . .

- explores the "what's next?" of what could be.
- creates "aha!" environments for collaborative discovery.
- works with exceptional "positive deviants."
- invests in the success of others through generous relationships.
- pursues big impact through measurable kingdom results.
- strives to model Jesus through all we do.

Believing that meaningful conversations and strategic connections can change the world, we seek to help leaders navigate the future by exploring new ideas and finding application for each unique context. Through collaborative meetings and processes, leaders map future possibilities and challenge one another to action that accelerates fruitfulness and effectiveness. Leadership Network shares the learnings and inspiration with others through our books, concept papers, research reports, e-newsletters, podcasts, videos, and online experiences. This in turn generates a ripple effect of new conversations and further influence.

In 1996 Leadership Network established a partnership with Jossey-Bass, a Wiley Imprint, to develop a series of creative books that provide thought leadership to innovators in church ministry. Leadership Network Publications present thoroughly researched and innovative concepts from leading thinkers, practitioners, and pioneering churches.

Leadership Network is a division of OneHundredX, a global ministry with initiatives around the world.

To learn more about Leadership Network, go to www.leadnet.org.

To learn more about OneHundredX, go to www.100x.org.

FOREWORD

ONE OF THE MOST intriguing pieces of evidence that Western Christendom is over, or is rapidly disintegrating, is the emergence of a broad spectrum of initiatives to plant untraditional, postdenominational congregations in the Western cultures once self-defined as Christian. These initiatives are enormously diverse, although they all share a commitment to experiment with forms and styles of community life that are clearly not beholden to the received traditions of the Western churches. In terms of the practices and patterns of their gathered life, they are decidedly countercultural. Although no defined theological consensus guides them or serves as their common ground, many of these initiatives are generating a biblical and theological engagement that is challenging and encouraging. *Convergence* may be too strong a term for what is happening, but there is clearly a mutually constructive theological conversation emerging among theologians like Alan Hirsch, Michael Frost, Tim Catchim, and the participants in the missional church conversation. This book is an important resource for that discussion and a motor to advance it further.

The term *missional* came into broad use after a small group of missiologists published *Missional Church: A Vision for the Sending of the Church in North America* in 1998.[1] The term immediately became a cliché that today means everything or nothing. Its original sense, focusing on the essential purpose and character of the church as the called and sent instrument of God's mission in the world, has been recognized and enriched by the work of such pioneer planters of post-Christendom Western indigenous churches (my term) as the authors of this book. Alan Hirsch neatly summarized the thrust of the missional church proposal when he wrote in his *The Forgotten Ways: Reactivating the Missional Church*:

> A missional church is a church that defines itself, and organizes its life around its real purpose as an agent of God's mission to the

world. In other words, the church's true and authentic organizing principle is mission. Therefore when the church is in mission, it is the true church. The church itself is not only a product of that mission but is obligated and destined to extend it by whatever means possible. The mission of God flows directly through every believer and every community of faith that adheres to Jesus.[2]

In *The Permanent Revolution*, Alan Hirsch and Tim Catchim propose a revolutionary missional ecclesiology shaped by the New Testament account of the apostolic missionary strategy. From the outset, the Christian mission focused on the calling and forming of communities that would continue the witness to the person and work of Jesus Christ that had brought them into being. To reclaim that strategy, Hirsch and Catchim argue that the functions of Word ministry in Ephesians 4:11ff—apostolic, prophetic, evangelistic, pastoral, and teaching—are essential for the formation of authentic and faithful witnessing congregations. This emphasis is linked with a strong critique of Western Christendom's reduction of these essential functions to the last two: pastoral (or shepherd) and teaching. The problem of clericalism that results from that reduction is certainly one of the major and most daunting challenges that the Western Christian movement faces as it moves out of the protections of established Christendom. Especially crucial for the missional ecclesiology today is the recovery of the apostolic function in the church. It is this ministry that ensures that the church is always centered on its calling to be the agent and instrument of God's mission and that everything it is and does relates to and demonstrates that calling. I share this conviction and have argued that the Nicene marks of the church need to be interpreted in the reverse order—apostolic, catholic, holy, and one—so that apostolicity defines every aspect of the life and action of the church. Only when apostolicity functions in that way can God's mission be served obediently.

In the missional church discussion, this conviction has been linked with the critique of Western ecclesiologies that replace the central and decisive theme of mission with various theologies of institutional maintenance. This book's focus on apostolicity clearly converges with this insistence that mission defines the church, and the authors' exposition of the practice of apostolicity broadens and deepens the discussion in truly generative ways.

Hirsch and Catchim persuasively argue their proposal of a revolutionary ecclesiology from many perspectives, exegetical and theological as well as organizational and sociological. To flesh out the practice of apostolicity, they turn to diverse insights from the world of organizational behavior and leadership in Western cultures. This approach can be understood as an exercise in contextualization. It expounds the way in which apostolic ministry ought to work in Western cultures by calling on the research and analysis of corporate organizational behavior, which constantly generates new theories and interpretations. This leads to their "interesting conclusion that underscores the purpose of this book: it seems that the degree to which a system is willing to acknowledge and legitimize apostolic ministry is directly proportional to the ability to be entrepreneurial and have higher levels of entrepreneurial intensity."[3] This claim will undoubtedly trigger a range of responses from critical to laudatory.

That may well be one of the primary merits of the bold proposal of this missional ecclesiology: it will generate questions that need to be debated passionately and thoroughly. And it should. The lasting value of this theological proposal will be measured by the quality of the debate that it evokes. It speaks to a number of issues that have dogged the missional church process since it started—for example:

- The character and role of leadership in the missional church
- How Jesus's own formation of the disciples (described in the four gospels) and the apostles' formation of their churches (continued in the epistles) define our formation today
- The dialectical tension between the church's dependence on the empowering work of the Holy Spirit and the intentional actions of Christians in obedience to the biblical mandate
- The appropriate reception of the Christendom legacy with both critique and gratitude
- The faithful translation of the gospel and the formation of witnessing communities in diverse cultures, without being assimilated into those cultures and becoming ultimately their captives

It is significant that the theological process represented by this book (and its predecessors) is shaped by the hard challenges of secularized post-Christian cultures such as Australia, the United Kingdom, and the United States. It is just as significant that some of the most intriguing examples of post-Christendom Western indigenous churches have emerged in the midst of the most advanced, even hostile, secularization. Health-giving theology should emerge from the crucible of such faithful, radically obedient mission. *The Permanent Revolution* is an example of the kind of theological work that is urgently needed to "equip the saints for the work of ministry" (Ephesians 4:12) apostolically, prophetically, evangelistically, pastorally, and instructively.

Darrell L. Guder
Henry Winters Luce Professor of Missional
and Ecumenical Theology
Princeton Theological Seminary

PREFACE: A BRIEFING FOR THE JOURNEY

THOUSANDS OF YEARS AGO, and well before mass publishing, Ecclesiastes wryly commented that of the making of books, there is no end (Ecclesiastes 12:12). We cannot imagine what he'd say today. So what are we doing writing *one more book*?

Why We Wrote This Book

Given the fact that so little of substance has been written on the subject of Ephesians 4 (which speaks of the roles of apostles, prophets, evangelists, shepherds, and teachers—APEST) in general, and the apostolic ministry and person in particular, the sin in this case actually lies in the deficiency of thinking and reflection in these matters, not in their excess. This is a big statement, but we hope to show that it is entirely justifiable. Here are some of our guiding objectives and reasons.

To Change Some Minds and Strengthen Others

First, in relation to those unaware, the not yet convinced, or even those who harbor antipathy to the idea of the fivefold ministry in general and the apostolic in particular, our aim is nothing less than to change minds about the importance of these for the church today. We cannot shake the conviction that nothing less than the future viability of the Western church is involved in the revitalization of its ministry along more biblical lines. And so if we fail to somehow shift any readers' paradigm, even a little, then we consider that we will have failed at least in part. This is no small task: we fully recognize that we are going against the inherited grain of thinking in this matter. Nonetheless, we think that the Western church has been wrong on this, and it is high time for a thorough reassessment, along with some significant change, in this regard.

Second, for those who are already convinced of the need for a broader, apostolically focused ministry in the church—either because they come

from traditions where the typology of Ephesians 4 is accepted or have
become more aware of the power of APEST because of their immersion
in missional thinking and practice—we hope to strengthen your case,
calibrate your thinking and practice, correct possible misperceptions, and
equip you with a deeper and significantly sturdier justification of these
particular aspects of the biblical ministry than has been given to date.
Our hope is that this work will encourage and equip others in their ministry and help them better fulfill their calling as part of God's people in
his kingdom.

To Rectify the Poverty of Thinking in Relation to Ephesians 4 and Apostolic Ministry

From our research, it appears that most standard thinking actually dele-
gitimizes the apostolic role by either replacing it with the canon of scripture (as in Protestantism) or by transferring apostolicity to the bishops and
the institution of the church itself (as in Roman Catholicism and Eastern
Orthodoxy). There seems to be no space between biblicism and institutionalism for any contemporary activation of the apostolic role. This
seems utterly strange to us given the central role that apostolic ministry
plays in the New Testament itself, as well as in every movement that has
achieved significant missionary impact throughout history.

And although there are some good academic studies exploring the
role of the original apostles in the New Testament church and in the first
three centuries, most of these are scholarly and inaccessible to the average
reader and have little to say to the concerns of contemporary apostolic
mission and ministry.[1] In fact, when they do comment on the possibility
of ongoing ministry, they tend to take the standard line that apostles (as
well as prophets and, to a lesser degree, evangelists) have not featured in
the church's ministry mix since Constantine. As we shall see, this is not so.

The other school of thought and reflection on Ephesians 4 and the
apostolic ministry tends to have a distinctly charismatic, pragmatist, and
fundamentalist perspective. It also is loaded with the type of dominion
theology that effectively equates the apostolic with a kind of superpastor—
the hotshot CEO type in the organization. And while most quote the
Bible a fair bit, they tend to lack any theological depth and end up being
one-dimensional in approach and perspective. In many ways, these
approaches provide the easy straw man that academics and clergy find
all too easy to reject. At best, these writings are highly unlikely to con-
vince the unconvinced, and at worst, they hinder the cause in the broader
church.

Neither of these approaches—the scholarly New Testament studies theorists and the one-dimensional charismaniacs—is much help as we seek to rediscover our missional calling and purpose. And as far as we are aware, there is at this time no single, comprehensive reference text available promoting the ongoing role of the apostolic person in the ongoing life of the church. Consider this book at least the beginnings of a much-needed remedy.

To Change the Frameworks

As you will soon discover, *The Permanent Revolution* is mainly a work of theological (re)imagination and (re)construction. We have drawn deeply from biblical studies, theology, organizational theory, leadership studies, and the key social sciences to substantiate our claims about Ephesians 4 and the ongoing legitimacy of the apostolic role. All of this points to our fundamental claim: that insofar that it depends on human agency, the church's capacity to embody and extend the mission and purposes of Jesus in the world depends largely on a full-intention to provide robust theoretical foundations with which to relegitimize and restructure the ministry of the church as fivefold and to reembrace the revitalizing, intrinsically missional role of the apostolic person.

We are in fact attempting to rescript the very codes that shape our view of ministry—nothing less than a shift in our thinking. We have intentionally sought to construct a substantive text, not only because there is precious little positive material on the subject, but also because the holism of Ephesians 4:11 has effectively been discarded, marginalized, or deliberately ejected almost entirely from our thinking and practice.

Reframing paradigms is difficult work. It goes against the grain of acquired thinking and exposes many blind spots, and it is likely to meet with resistance from those deeply invested in the prevailing paradigm. Nonetheless, we feel constrained to submit this for reflection in the hope the Spirit will awaken ancient energies largely dormant within the Western church.

To make the truth of *The Permanent Revolution* unavoidable, we have deliberately used an interdisciplinary recipe of theology, sociology, leadership studies, psychology, and the organizational sciences because we believe that they all point us in the direction originally given in the New Testament itself. All truth is God's truth, and we believe that nowhere else is this more evident than in this area of New Testament ecclesiology. The church, rightly conceived as an organic movement, was well ahead of its time in relation to best thinking and best practices on organizations and leadership. Everything in contemporary literature and research on these issues confirms the ingenious design built into the ecclesia that Jesus intended.

Our primary audience for this book remains the key leaders in the churches and other organizations that make up the heartland of biblical Christianity—from Conservative evangelical to Pentecostal, from missional to traditional, and anything in between. We are both evangelicals in the broad nonsectarian sense of the word.[2] Alan has roots within the Pentecostal tradition, has a Reformed theological training, and has worked with all the major evangelical churches for most of his time in ministry. Tim is a grassroots church planter with a restorationist heritage and training.

We both love, and are deeply committed to, the church, but some readers are going to be tempted to think of us as fervent anti-institutionalists. And although we offer a critique of institutionalism, we are not against structure and organization in any way. In fact, the reader will find a plethora of material that relates to organization and systems thinking laced throughout the book. And certainly we see ourselves as servants of God's people in all the forms in which they express themselves.

Furthermore, although we accept the role of tradition in guiding and sustaining the church in any age, we will admit that in our view, institutionalism and traditionalism almost invariably involve reliance on past formulas and thinking, tend to be reactionary, snuff out creative thinking and solutions, and are self-referential and bureaucratic. We ask questions in this book that go to the leadership paradigm, and when doing this, it is impossible to avoid the twin issues of traditionalism and institutionalism—both well represented in the Bible. From a prophetic concern with the corrupt and corruptible institutions of the king, judge, and priesthood; to Jesus's railing against the oppressive religious institutionalism of the scribes and pharisees of his day; to Paul's doctrine of the powers entrenched in human institutions and people: the Bible sustains a thorough and consistent critique of religious institutionalism. Without wanting to sound self-righteous, we really do feel that we are in good company here.

As uncomfortable as critical appraisals tend to make us feel, we do well to remind ourselves at this point that despite the towering effect that institutions have on us, they have to be seen for what they truly are: mere products of human activity. As human constructs, institutions cannot adequately reflect back to us our own intrinsic worth. Jesus's own rejection by the religious and political establishment of his day bears witness to the tendency of institutions to develop their own metrics and categories for what should and should not be valued or deemed essential. It is in Jesus himself that we can find the higher authority—one that transcends the towering effect of the institutions—with which to speak the corrective word into our context.

To Stimulate Apostolic Imagination, Leading to Missional Action

Because not much has been written on the subject of apostolic ministry and because it has not been a historic model, we did not have a lot of constructive material to work with. That is why in some parts of this book, we have had to exercise a fair bit of theological imagination mingled with ideas gleaned from the social sciences. We hope readers find our thinking stimulating, but we ask them to remember that at some points, we are engaging in educated guesswork and theological intuition and to give us some space to be playful. Engage these sections with an open mind, and do not assume we are being prescriptive. Rather, we are offering spiritual prods, or suggestive thought-experiments, aimed to stimulate thinking and action. Rest assured that we never make wild conjectures. Even our guesses are informed and weighted with a lot of reflection. And we will let you know when we are making intuitive leaps.

The book is intentionally loaded with challenging concepts and replete with fertile ideas that carry rich possibilities for new learning and action. We did not intend to produce a praxis-oriented work; we hope to leave that to a possible future workbook based on this book. Our aim is to empower the church as movement and not to simply add another book to a seminary curriculum and library. We hope it will help leaders become the leaders God intended them to be in the first place. Like any other good revolution, the aim is to liberate your minds as well as your vocations from the constraints currently imposed on them.[3]

Who Wrote What?

This book is a collaboration between the two of us. In addition, 3DM leader Mike Breen assisted in the construction of Part One, on Ephesians and APEST, contributing some key ideas and doing some editing and commenting. Mike is a long-term practitioner of Ephesians 4 ministry. He is a highly respected international leader, a genuinely seminal thinker and practitioner, and one of the most prolific Christian leaders to emerge from Great Britain in a decade or more. We are very grateful for Mike himself and what he represents to the missional movement of our day.

He is a genuine permanent revolutionary, and we are honored that he is willing to put his name on this material.

Most of the book is a work of our own collaboration. Tim has played the role of primary researcher and resident maven. He did his job all too well, because in order to get the book to a reasonable size and focus, we had to delete about half of what he researched and wrote. Alan's primary role has been to shape the material and direct the project and, of course, add his own writing along the way—his aim being to elaborate on previously written material as well as add new insights on the topic.

We write in the first person wherever it is appropriate and where personal biography is involved. But for the most part, we use the second person *we* and speak in common voice.

On issues of examples, we have certainly provided them where we could, but we have generally chosen to bolster the ideas with numerous figures. What we lack in stories we certainly make up for in illustrations. Partly this is a personality thing because we are conceptual thinkers and tend to think more in pictures and less in narrative, and partly it is because we believe that diagrams better convey the ideas we hope to communicate.

A Word to the Wise

It was the ancient philosopher Epictetus who stated that it is impossible for a man to learn what he thinks he already knows. And that could be true for all of us who think that we know what church and ministry is. Most of us have been raised in, trained in, and thoroughly coded by the prevailing paradigm.[4] Therefore, initial responses to this material that come readily to mind generally arise directly out of the deep scripting we have assumed to be true. This is the very scripting that has led us inexorably to the decline of the church in the West.

Because of this, we ask that you allow yourself to reimagine ministry as we are presenting it, even if it does not square with the prevailing scripts and invites repentance and change. We suggest that you try to restrain any somewhat reflexive defenses for a while, so that you might look afresh at a core issue of ecclesiology. If we are right about this, changing the primary scripts will completely revolutionize the way we conceive of being and doing church in a very good way. To be able to learn anything new, we have to be willing to think differently about ourselves and approach ideas from a different angle, which will allow new possibilities to arise. Remember that Albert Einstein, the great paradigm buster, wisely said, "The only thing that interferes with my learning is my education." Please do not let your education interfere with your learning on this matter. Way too much is at stake.

Size Matters

This is an unusually large book because it explores a big and strategically critical issue. We fully realize that for various reasons, including issues of time and patience, weighty books might put off some readers. But we suggest that the importance of the subject and the critical situation of the church at this time require that we delve deep and do not shortchange the intellectual and spiritual engagement required to change the game now.

We encourage you to read this book carefully and, if you can, do this with others and discuss it as you go. If you are already convinced of the need for apostolic ministry in the church and are pressed for time, you can skip Chapter Six and the Appendix at the back of the book. That will reduce the text by about 15 percent.

A View from the Top

The only thing left to do in this Preface is to describe the logic and the flow of the book itself.

Part One, on Ephesians 4:1–16, provides the basis for a fuller understanding of biblical ministry, as well the context for an exploration of the apostolic ministry. This is where Mike Breen collaborates with us.

Part Two is about apostolic ministry. Chapter Five is a key chapter: it provides the basic definitions of apostolicity that we use throughout the book. Chapter Six suggests some largely unexplored, and we hope fruitful, ways in which to understand the nuances within the apostolic ministry itself. We contrast Pauline and Petrine apostolic ministry and their contributions to creating missional impact. And because of these distinctions, Chapter Seven looks beyond the purely pioneering function normally associated with the apostolic role to see how the apostolic ministry facilitates ongoing renewal in the life of the church.

Part Three focuses on apostolic leadership. Rather than ranging far and wide, we focus on leadership in relation to missional innovation and entrepreneurship. Elaborating on the pioneering functions, along with those of custodian, designer, and architect, we look at how apostolic leadership can provide new and missionally creative ways forward.

Part Four focuses on apostolic organization. Clearly, issues of how we structure and organize are critical to being translocal and movemental. Being ignorant about the issue of social structures generally hands

dynamic movements over to the human default of increasing institutionalism. This final part of the book examines the nature of organization as
reframed through the lens of apostolic ministry and leadership, particularly that of being a movement. And then we look at essential characteristics of apostolic movements and how to restructure in a way that more
consistently aligns with them.

The Appendix is in effect an essay that we feel is important enough to
include in the book but not necessary to the flow of the book itself. We
felt that the issues of how and why the apostles, prophets, and evangelists
(the APE functions in APEST) were exiled warrant further understanding. They bring needed insights and provide clues to our own thinking in
these matters.

We ask that you be patient with us as we seek to (re)construct a holistic understanding of an all-but-lost imagination. We address some of the
more practical questions about organization in Part Four. And given that
we do not have a rich heritage of thinking and acting on which to draw
from, we beg readers' indulgence in using examples that are clear-cut
illustrations of apostolic ministry. We love Patrick, John Wesley, William
Booth, Aimee Semple McPherson, and others: they provide lights that
we can all walk by, and so they become our primary models. This is not
to say there are not countless others who express apostolic forms, only
that they might lack the profile needed to substantiate this kind of work.

By emphasizing human agency and our responsibility to make the leadership decisions to shift the paradigm, it is not our intention to diminish
the sovereignty of God in all affairs and that we live in and through his
grace. The survival of the church is surely a testimony to the grace of
God who has not forsaken us as much as we have forsaken him. It is suf-
ficient to say that we submit this book to our readers in humble trust that
the Holy Spirit will use it for the furtherance of the cause of our Lord
Jesus in this broken world.

To God be the glory, and *Viva la revolución permanente!*

INTRODUCTION

THE CRISIS OF INFERTILITY AND
WHAT TO DO ABOUT IT

*The illiterate of the future are not those that cannot read or
write. They are those that cannot learn, unlearn, relearn.*
Alvin Toffler

*People in any organization are always attached to the obsolete—
the things that should have worked but did not, the things that
once were productive and no longer are.*
Peter Drucker

*He who cannot change the very fabric of his thought will never
be able to change reality, and will never, therefore, make any
progress.*
Anwar el-Sadat

IN THE MOVIE *THE CHILDREN OF MEN*, there is a plague of infertility, and
no one knows why. Diego Ricardo is the youngest person in the world:
eighteen years, four months, twenty days, sixteen hours, and eight min-
utes old. He was the last human being to be born on earth, and since his
birth, women everywhere have been unable to reproduce. When he suddenly dies, his demise is repeatedly broadcast and is viewed as a not-so-
subtle reminder of the slowly creeping disaster that has undermined hope
and created political disorder, social decay, radical doubt, and universal
despair. The aging population is edging toward the end of the human race.

In the story, Great Britain is one of the only places in the world that has
managed to maintain a limited sense of order, and people from everywhere
have fled there, only to be rounded up as illegal refugees and transported
to holding bins where they await deportation to the anarchy of Europe.
Amid this chaos, Theo, a British citizen grown cynical and despairing in
the surrounding hopelessness, is paid by a band of revolutionaries to escort
Kee, a young woman, out of Britain and hand her over to an underground
organization called the Human Project.

Theo soon discovers that his mission is much riskier than he had expected, and he faces, and courageously evades, all kinds of traps to guard her from danger. But Theo is not told why his charge is so controversial. Clearly she has become the focus of militant groups, and his association with her has made him a prime target for violent attacks. It is not until he gets halfway to their destination that he finds out exactly who this woman is and why she is so important: Kee is pregnant, and the revolutionaries want to use her as a tool, a symbol of hope, a powerful weapon in a high-stakes political game to incite a revolution that would overthrow the government.

Whatever sense of responsibility Theo felt toward his assignment in the beginning is now amplified as he realizes that the very future of humanity is in his custody. This is no ordinary assignment. He is to cross danger-ous terrain, through uncharted territories, so that Kee can regenerate the human race. Theo is a custodian of life in a world of infertility.

The Children of Men provides a parabolic pointer to a similar fruit-lessness in the church throughout the West. To explain it, some have said that the vinedresser is simply pruning his vine or that he is judging some supposed unfaithfulness on our part, and that it will pass and our fertility will return. However we may want to figure it, we have to acknowledge that after almost twenty centuries of Christianity in Western contexts, we have generally not seen the kind of transformation implied in the gospel. Neither have we often approximated the vibrancy of the gospel movements that somehow manage to structure their ecclesial life much closer to the kind of church that Jesus designed it to be in the first place: that of an apostolic people movement; the kind of dynamic, fluid, viral, ecclesiology we see in the pages of the New Testament and throughout history. The early church, various movements over the centuries, and the developing world now (especially India and China) have displayed this same vitality. These are all great expressions of apostolic movement.

Our situation today is not that dissimilar to the one described in *The Children of Men*. All of the statistical indicators show serious infertility in Western Christianity, and so we too are caught in a despairing spiral of trended numerical and spiritual decline in just about every context in the Western world.[1]

A Permanent Revolution? Really?

In this situation, we are forced to ask ourselves what the church is all about. What are God's original purposes in and through his people? Is the gospel capable of renewing the world and transforming the hearts of all human beings? Did God really mean for the ecclesia to be the focal point for the wholesale renewal of society? Are we really called to be a colony of a much-disputed kingdom, or did Jesus intend that we become the chaplains of a so-called Christian civilization in the West? These are questions that take us to the core of our self-understanding and purpose, and we must be willing to ask them again and again.

It was seminal missiologist Ralph Winter who said, "Every major decision you make will be faulty until you see the whole world as God sees it."[2] Seeing things from God's perspective is what lies at the heart of what it means to have a biblical perspective, and certainly it matters when it comes to thinking about the church, its mission, its leadership, and its intended impact. The two of us fully believe that the ecclesia that Jesus intended was specifically designed with built-in, self-generative capacities and was made for nothing less than world-transforming, lasting, and, yes, revolutionary impact (see, for example, Matthew 16:18). And we certainly do not believe that Christianity was ever meant to become a domesticated civil religion. As far as we can tell, Jesus intended us to be a permanent revolution—an outpost of the kingdom of God no less. And if we are not actually being that, then we have to take stock.

When the embarrassing issue of falling short of being somewhat infertile is brought out into the open, it raises all kind of questions about the nature and function of church, the influence of various types of leadership, and ultimately the intended impact of the gospel. And while clearly unprecedented global economic, social, and cultural shifts are taking place in our time, we believe that the current decline of Christianity cannot be blamed on these external factors alone. That is just a dodge, and a dangerous and irresponsible one at that. As significant as external factors are, much of our infertility arises from *within* the community of faith: in the dynamics of our human sin and unfaithfulness, our lack of audacious faith, and a historical, all-too-human penchant for doing things according to our own preferences when it comes to running the church.

Acknowledging that we are not all that God intended us to be is not meant to simply create guilt and endless self-recriminations in God's people. Rather, acknowledging our shortfalls gives us an opportunity to repent. And it is repentance that allows us to be forgiven for our infertility and intransigence, to recalibrate, and so start again. The gift of repentance allows us to seek new solutions for the way we can reconceive of and restructure our life in God and in accordance with his eternal purposes in the gospel. This is sheer grace, and we should embrace it wholeheartedly in our common life as much as in our personal one. And it should certainly be a living aspect of what it means to be a believing church full of faith.

Doubt and the Permanent Devolution

If believing the gospel (under guidance of the Spirit) means to align ourselves with God's purpose, form the ecclesia, and provide a guiding principle to plot our way forward, then it is what we call missional doubt (doubt that affects the mission and purposes of God through the church) that will undermine that belief. In matters of spirituality, doubt and unbelief change everything; they affect the way we see ourselves and how we go about being the kind of people we were intended to be. Under the corrosive influences of missional doubt and unbelief, there is no permanent revolution; instead we devolve into a self-focused, missionally reticent, risk-averse institution, inching our way ever closer toward our own demise.

Sociologists of religion have long acknowledged that decline in the church is associated with ever-encroaching doubt. Because entrenched doubt prevents us from aligning with God's design and intent, it heralds inevitable infertility and decline in the people of God. Witness the cycles of disintegration and renewal in the stories of Israel in the Old Testament. Whenever Israel refused to follow God's distinctive ways, it led to decline and judgment. And renewal, brought about by repentance, inevitably involved a realignment with his purposes and ushered in a period of blessing. It is no different in the church.

As you can see in Figure I.1, the first, and seemingly innocuous, form of doubt in the life cycle of movements is referred to as operational. It

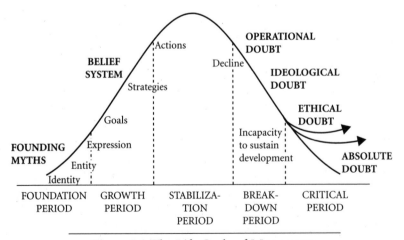

Figure I.1 The Life Cycle of Movements

Source: Adapted from L. Cada, R. Fritz, G. Foley, and T. Giardino, Shaping the Coming Age of Religious Life *(New York: Seabury Press, 1979), 53, 78.*

involves a struggle in the organization to keep pace with its missional functions and objectives. In other words, organizational doubt is first experienced as a problem of wineskins—the situation where prevailing organizational systems and designs originally used to host and transmit the founding ideals no longer get the job done. It goes like this: "We very much believe our message, but we can't seem to deliver it as effectively as we used to, and we feel bad about it." Operational doubt will become caustic and destructive unless the church's organizational expressions are appropriately realigned to more adequately suit its purposes and mission. Unless it is properly resolved, this doubt will become entrenched and gnaw away at the soul of the ecclesia.

We have all seen this process: If the problem of wineskins is not resolved through the renewal of structures, the community will proceed to the next stage of ever-increasing cynicism and unbelief. Unresolved operational doubt leads to ideological doubt, where we begin to no longer believe the message itself, and from there the organization devolves to ethical doubt, where we begin to behave badly because there is no good reason not to. This life cycle eventually ends with absolute doubt, which precipitates closure: the death of the original movement. Theology, history, and sociology affirm the truth of this progression. It is plainly evident in the long-term trajectory of decline of the mainline denominations (most of which are predominantly theologically liberal in orientation). All of them, without exception, have inexorably declined over the past 150 years.[3] In the end, systematic, structural, ethical, and ideological doubt, of both liberal and fundamentalist varieties, involves a failure to be the people God intended us to be: a radical, hard-core, fully engaged, living movement of people loved and redeemed by Jesus, committed to his causes on earth.

A doubt-filled church inevitably lacks the spiritual resources needed to empower dynamic movements. Instead of gathering a growing number of disciples, developing leaders, and adapting the organization, it will tend, rather slothfully, to rely on tired solutions arising from a worn-out, traditionalist paradigm of church—one that has patently failed in Christendom Europe, the very context that gave us that paradigm in the first place.

This lack of growth, development, and adaptation is a call for repentance and change. We can be sure that more of the same will not deliver fundamentally different results. It is time to reappraise the way we think about ourselves as ecclesia and how we go about fulfilling our calling. This needed audit must include how we think about and practice ministry and leadership. In other words, we need to rescript by returning to the original script. It is time to recover the power of Ephesians 4:11 ministry in general and the missional potencies of the apostolic in particular.

Of Black Swans, Algorithms, and Revolutions

We have already hinted at an idea that we reassert repeatedly in this book: Jesus has given the church everything it needs to get the job done. The church is equipped by Spirit and gospel to fulfill whatever tasks the Lord has set for us to do: evangelism, discipleship, church planting, serving the poor, worship, healing, and much more. We are designed to be the world-transforming agents of the kingdom. We are meant to be a permanent revolution, not one that came and went, leaving a codified religion in its wake. That we only seldom realize this truth can be attributed to a bad case of recurring theological amnesia, one that has some seriously detrimental consequences on our capacities to get our mission done. Every now and again, we recover something of the original potencies associated with apostolic movements. Perhaps most times we are forced into this discovery through situations that require us to adapt or die. For example, it took the death of the institutional forms of church in China for it to become a dynamic people movement again. But every now and again, we do it for the best possible reasons: out of our desire to be authentic and faithful to what the Lord of the church requires of us.

Part of the amnesia comes from the way we conceive of, and subsequently configure, the church and its ministry. We create a paradigm—a way of perceiving our world, of filtering out what is considered real and unreal, of creating mental models of how things should be. Once established, paradigms in many ways do our thinking for us; that is their purpose. They in turn comprise clusters of what creative thinking expert Roger Martin calls algorithms.[4] An algorithm is a predetermined formula that will produce reliable outcomes when it is consistently applied. Although paradigms help us make sense of our world by giving us ways to interpret it, they also create what is called paradigm blindness: an incapacity to see things from outside that particular perspective or paradigm. And this can account for how people fail to see certain important things that might be glaringly obvious to others. It can also account for many of the problems we in the church now face. But there is another serious downside to algorithms, as Martin so effectively articulates: "What organizations dedicated to running reliable algorithms often fail to realize is that while they reduce the risk of small variations, . . . they increase the risk of being overpowered by the various cataclysmic events that occur, situations when the future no longer resembles the past and whatever algorithm one has used is no longer relevant or useful."[5]

Paradigms and algorithms are good only as long as they match and interpret external conditions. When the context shifts significantly, algorithms can become problematic because they can prevent an organization from readily seeing its way beyond them. Now this should be beginning to sound all too familiar to us. The Bible tends to call this a stronghold—a mental or spiritual trap. For instance, well-worn formulas are used to define what it is to be a church (referred to as the marks of the church): that the church exists where the sacraments are rightly administered and where church discipline is seldom submitted to critical review. And yet without some serious theological gymnastics, they are patently deficient, especially in making space for the tasks of mission, discipleship, and human community.[6] They are assumed to be true, just the way denominational templates are.

Nassim Nicholas Taleb refers to the impact of unforeseen occurrences as "black swan events": events that the prevailing models could never have foreseen, let alone predicted, and yet they account for just about every major shift in human history.[7] In other words, game-changing events are outliers—phenomena that deviate markedly from what is expected and seen as normal. The 2008 financial crisis is one such event; others are the terrorist attacks of September 11, 2001; the rise of the Internet; the 2010 British Petroleum spill in the Gulf of Mexico. In the same way, our inherited algorithm of church, ministry, and leadership is now being seriously challenged. It has no way of engaging the escalating bombardment of black swan–level events that our increasingly complex, globalized context seems to usher in regularly.

This crisis is not just in the church. In many ways, the crisis is universal. Joshua Cooper Ramo, managing director of Kissinger and Associates, a major geostrategic advisory firm, has written a rather prophetic book, *The Age of the Unthinkable*.[8] As Ramo would have it, many of the problems we face today arise from applying outmoded nineteenth-century thinking to twenty-first-century problems. He suggests that we live in a "revolutionary age," defined by problems whose complexity, unpredictability, and interconnectedness increasingly defy our efforts at control: terrorism, global warming, pandemics, and financial meltdowns, for example. States no longer dominate, new actors abound, and the day belongs to the agile and adaptive. In other words, we live in a situation defined by an increasing frequency of black swan events. These threatening new dynamics demand, in Ramo's view, nothing less than "a complete reinvention of our ideas of security," even the reversal of "a couple of millennia of Western intellectual habits." We must innovate and keep learning, and we must become resilient and adaptive.[9]

The penalty for nonadaptive behavior is severe. Unforeseen events happen more regularly and challenge the formulas and responses gleaned from a retrospective glance at history. As writer and social observer Malcolm Gladwell tells us, black swan events play a much bigger role in shaping success and failure than we tend to think.[10] Generally planning and good management do not determine success; rather, success comes from being able to respond well to forces out of our control that push us to innovate and adapt. For instance, if you are taking a leisurely stroll in a forest, everything seems fine until you get hopelessly lost. Then everything changes. When you are lost, the forest takes on a menacing aspect. Mere objects in normal life now become a potential threat, a tool, or perhaps something to ingest. When this happens, we see our world in a different light and so behave differently; we find ourselves in a learning mode. It is not too presumptuous to say that the church in the West appears to be lost in the forest, a menace indeed, but this is equally an invitation to ongoing learning, something fundamental to our calling as disciples of Jesus.

A model's success is always dependent on a certain level of congruence between that model and its environment. What Martin, Ramo, Taleb, and Gladwell are highlighting is the limited capacity of a successful organizational model to endure beyond a specific time or survive a climactic event. The reality is that in a complex world with an ever-increasing rate of discontinuous change, we can use an existing approach only until the environment shifts, or a black swan requires an adaptive solution. A simple improvement in current practices will no longer do in these circumstances. When strategy and environment are radically incongruent, innovative strategies have to be explored in order to reengage that environment.

The old Christendom algorithm in the church is failing as Christianity in the West begins to adjust to the increasing decentering it has experienced over the past few decades. This has created a great sense of anomaly that has precipitated a much-needed paradigm shift in the Western Christianity. But if we do not change at this point, we must expect Christianity to continue in its long-term, seemingly inexorable decline in every Western setting. Our ability to adapt and respond to this failure of algorithms will determine the future viability of Christianity in Western cultural contexts. The two of us think the signs of a serious rethinking are promising, but we must all be willing to change the algorithms when and where appropriate or face the consequences.

What is exciting about the crisis—and it is that—is that we are being forced to wake up from our institutional slumbers, shake off our complacencies, and rediscover the apostolic movement. Marx rightly called organized religion the opiate of the people. Like all other drugs, it dulls us to the realities we must face. Our situation today requires that we renew our covenants with the Lord of the church, trust his Holy Spirit, dig deep into our own self-understanding, and in this way recover our purpose as well as our latent and unused potentials as God's people.

We were never meant to settle down and become a civil religion; there is no indication of that in our primary scripts. It is time to become again the permanent revolution that we are meant to be in the first place.

Two Algorithmic Shifts

Two major algorithms need a thorough reformulation: the ways that we think about church and the ways that we envision ministry and leadership. The two are inextricably tied together, and the natural link is found in the term *apostolic,* the key theme of this book.

Ecclesia as Apostolic Movement

We have already hinted at an assumption that underlies the writing of this book: that many of the problems the church now faces can be resolved simply by thinking differently about it and its God-designed mission in the world. By changing our metaphors, or paradigms of church, we can change the game. The name we give to this different paradigm of church is simply *apostolic movement.* It is not new—in fact, it is ancient—and it is the only way to describe the fluidity and dynamism of the spiritual phenomenon we see evidenced in the New Testament itself. In short, apostolic movement involves a radical community of disciples, centered on the lordship of Jesus, empowered by the Spirit, built squarely on a fivefold ministry, organized around mission where everyone (not just professionals) is considered an empowered agent, and tends to be decentralized in organizational structure.

We have spent much of our adult years trying to understand and unlock the dynamism inherent in apostolic movements. I (Alan) have written extensively on various aspects of it. But in many ways movemental ecclesiology—the church reconceived as movement—can be located, and summed up, in the primary term for *church* in the New Testament: *ecclesia.* If we understood *ecclesia* properly and began to reappropriate its various levels of meaning, then many of the problems we now face can be resolved. For instance, our more concrete, institutionalized idea of church must be redefined in the much broader, more fluid meaning used in the Bible. And as we generally use the term throughout this book, here we set out some of the levels of meaning inherent in it.

We can discern four ways, in four ascending levels, in which the word *ecclesia* is used (Figure I.2):

1. Paul uses the term to describe the people who met in the various places of their city—primarily the home (called an *oikos* in the Greek), but riverbanks, markets, and other places as well. For example, Paul addresses the ecclesia that happens to meet in so-and-so's house. This is the most local, or basic, reference of the term.
2. Then Paul (and the other apostles) talk of an ecclesia in a particular city, knowing that there might in fact be many house churches scattered throughout the area. In fact, most of the letters are addressed to churches at this level. So here we have the regional application of the term—a citywide ecclesia that is in fact made up of many ecclesias.

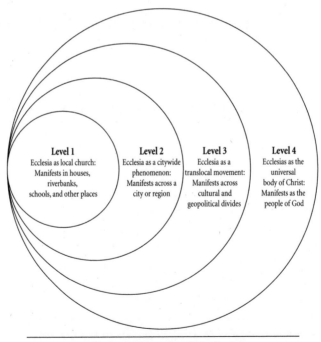

Level 1
Ecclesia as local church:
Manifests in houses,
riverbanks,
schools, and other places

Level 2
Ecclesia as a citywide
phenomenon:
Manifests across a
city or region

Level 3
Ecclesia as a
translocal movement:
Manifests across
cultural and
geopolitical divides

Level 4
Ecclesias as the
universal
body of Christ:
Manifests as the
people of God

Figure I.2 Levels of Ecclesia

3. The next level up is that it is used to denote the movement across a larger geopolitical region—in this case, the Roman Empire, or Asia. Here the word is used to identify the Jesus movement in the various parts of the world known in the apostles' time. We still use it to refer to a historical phenomenon.

4. The final, and the most symbolic, level is where the apostles can address the people of God as the church of Jesus Christ, meaning, of course, the universal invisible church, that is, the body of Christ on earth. This is the more theological, metaphorical meaning of the term as the redeemed new covenant people of God.

To put this concept in the framework of algorithms we have been discussing, the biblical algorithm being communicated through the word *ecclesia* represents God's people as a dynamic, translocal, social force that manifests in multidimensional ways. Jesus advances this vision of the ecclesia as movement when he maps out the trajectory of the church going from Jerusalem, to Judea, to Samaria, and ultimately to the ends of the earth.[11] Ecclesia is a movement or, more technically, an apostolic movement. By engaging this distinctly movemental view of ecclesia, we can no longer limit it to a local church with a distinctive building and a certain denominational preference and style. That is the institutional algorithm. The apostolic movement is far more wide-ranging. Just as the ecclesia as apostolic movement in the New Testament spanned the Roman Empire, so too our notion of the church must expand to biblical proportions.

This new, yet also ancient, ecclesia as apostolic movement algorithm will allow us to unlock the meaning and potential of church in our day. We have to think differently, and more broadly, about ourselves for everything else to fall into place.

Apostolic Leadership for Missional Movement

Thinking like a movement instead of an institution has massive implications because an authentic missional church should exist and express itself at all four levels to be the kind of church that Jesus envisioned. This expands the equation of church and in so doing forces us to completely rethink our understanding of its associated ministry, leadership, and organization. No longer can leadership be limited to the local. It must include that but go beyond it to be able to include the other three levels: city, region, and symbolic. And to do this, we cannot apply the age-old shepherd-teacher algorithm that has prevailed in the church over the past seventeen centuries. This formulation cannot provide the impetus for the kind of movement that is needed now—the kind of movement we were meant to be in the first place.

Clearly we think that Ephesians 4 provides the way forward by giving us a direct link backward into the ministry that infused and led the early church. In other words, we are convinced that we are dealing with the most foundational genetic codes of ministry in the ecclesia of Jesus Christ. In APEST (the acronym we use for Ephesians 4:11 ministry: apostles, prophets, evangelists, shepherds, and teachers), we touch base with the primary algorithm of ministry in ecclesia. And we can certainly say with confidence that in the New Testament itself, ministry was at least fivefold in form. There can be no refuting this. As a burgeoning apostolic movement, the original church had a built-in, highly dynamic ministry that included the holistic collaboration of the ministries of apostle, prophet, evangelist, shepherd, and teacher. Together these provided an appropriately expansive ministry for an expanding movement. In Part One, we discuss reestablishing this ministry algorithm into the twenty-first-century church.

From that fuller discussion, we then focus on what we believe is the catalytic ministry of the apostle. The apostle is the quintessentially missional form of ministry and leadership. The apostolic role provides the key that unlocks the power of New Testament ecclesiology insofar as its ministry is concerned. In the power of the Holy Spirit, apostles are given to the ecclesia to provide the catalytic, adaptive, movemental, translocal, pioneering, entrepreneurial, architectural, and custodial ministry needed to spark, mobilize, and sustain apostolic movements. Apostolic ministry is the appropriate form for missional movements. In fact, we doubt whether there can be significant movement in the church without it. Nothing less than the renewal of the church and its mission is bound up with the rediscovery and reappropriation of this type of ministry.

Along the lines of the idea of *reformata et semper reformanda* (that the church reformed ought always to be reforming) we use the phrase "the permanent revolution" to connote the idea that the church that Jesus designed has built-in capacities for the ongoing renewal of its theology and practice, and that short of the return of our Redeemer King, we never arrive at a perfected state. In other words, we ought to be in a state of a permanent, ongoing, transformative revolution. We argue in this book that the apostolic ministry (and beyond it, all ministries described in Ephesians 4) is an intrinsic aspect of the ministry of the church in all ages. Apostles are literally given to the ecclesia by Jesus (Ephesians 4:7, 11) to drive the permanent revolution that we are meant to be.

If the church is indeed called to be a permanent revolution, then it is APEST in general, and the apostolic in particular, that are called to be its permanent revolutionaries.[12] Revolution and revolutionaries are inexorably bound together; the two go hand-in-glove; we cannot have one without the other. If we have chosen to narrow the ministry of the church, then we have in that same choice chosen to limit the possible impact of the church. And in so doing, we have messed with the design for impact. We need apostolic ministry in order to foster the apostolic ecclesiology so needed in our day.

It is time for learning again what we should already know. It is time to discover some of our most potent potentials that have been dormant for way too long. It is time to become again a permanent revolution. So it is back to the future we go.

the
permanent
revolution

•

ephesians
4:1-16

Frameworks
for Ministry

1

Activating the Theo-Genetic Codes of APEST Ministry

It is difficult to get a man to understand something when his salary depends upon his not understanding it.
Upton Sinclair

Those who make history are those who submit to the One who orchestrates it.
John R. Mott

Every viewpoint is a point from a view.
Richard Rohr

THE REASONS THAT SISYPHUS WAS APPARENTLY CONDEMNED BY THE GODS are not entirely clear. What is clear is that his terrible punishment was to roll a huge rock up a steep hill, and then just as he reached the top of the hill, it would roll back to the bottom. One can almost feel the sense of futility and frustration that this created. Wretched Sisyphus is condemned to repeat again and again the same meaningless task—one that requires continual effort that never quite pays off.

We start this chapter with a reflection on the nature of futility because we believe that in many ways, the historic church has been engaged in a Sisyphean task. The history of movements of mission and renewal seems to indicate that as soon as we appear to be making significant progress, we bungle it and have to start all over again. At times we have been our own worst enemy. We are so divided against ourselves, how can we stand? Clearly much of our struggle, being not against flesh and blood, can be put down to our participation in the kingdom's struggle against evil. In a fallen world, evil does not give up without a fight. However, if we were honest, we would have to admit that much of our struggle to extend the mission of Jesus into the world arises from our own sinful attempts to do it our way, willfully or otherwise going against the grain of God's original design and purposes in and through the church. The result is that we seem to be unable to get the job done when everything in our scriptures indicates that we can—and in fact should.

The capacity of God's people to fulfill our very purposes is implicit throughout all our theological codes. For instance, the command to obey implies the possibility of some form of realization through actual obedience, and the injunction to love God and people implies the possibility of fulfilling that command. If that were not true, that is, if we were being given commands that we cannot possibly fulfill, God would be rather capriciously toying with us, and the Bible becomes not the word of God that we are called to believe and lovingly obey, but something that takes on the nature of a cosmic, and rather nasty, prank.

The same potential for fulfillment is also implied in our ecclesiology (the New Testament teachings about the nature and purposes of the church) itself. We are called to believe that Jesus has given us everything that we need to be the kind of church that he intended us to be. We must take our Lord at his word. And if we are not being that kind of Jesus-shaped church, then we should look to our own practices and see whether we conform to the original intention and design. To do otherwise commits us to the Sisyphean struggle of rolling the boulder of the church up the hill, only to have it roll down again, and having to repeat the procedure over, again and again, producing only more toil and frustration.

It stands to reason that to mess with the DNA of the church (that is, its original design and function) means to seriously damage our capacity to actually be ecclesia. In fact, this is exactly how all genetic mutations occur. If we believe that the New Testament codes are authoritative and function in the same way genetics does in biological systems, then we must be sure to align with those codes. We believe that the church's lack of adherence to the teachings of Ephesians 4 is a clear case of how we have altered the genetic codes and paid the price. It is time to correct this egregious flaw in our ecclesiology.

This chapter introduces the foundational dimensions of Ephesians 4, which will provide the context to explore and understand the specific nature of the apostolic ministry. Ephesians 4 is the foundation and context of everything we say about the apostolic ministry in the rest of the book.

Almost a Silver Bullet

In presenting Ephesians 4:1–16, we are tempted to say that it is one of those rare things—a silver bullet: a simple, guaranteed solution for a difficult problem. Of course we do not believe that, but over time we have come to think that it is *almost* a silver bullet. We believe that a full appreciation and application of Ephesians 4 typology will unleash enormous energies that will awaken now-dormant potentials in the church that Jesus built.

As far as we can discern, every observable, highly transformative apostolic movement that achieved exponential missional impact has operated with *some* expression of fivefold ministry.[1] We are absolutely convinced of this: it is clear in the explicit teachings of scripture, evidenced in mission's history and in contemporary apostolic movements in the global church, and confirmed by the best thinking in the social sciences. The rediscovery and reapplication of this one piece of Pauline ecclesiology has massive consequences in our time and place.

The Devil Made Me Do It

We fully recognize that in writing this book, we go directly against the grain of inherited assumptions of the church and its ministry. Perhaps we should instead use the phrase "the institutional church in the West" because there are literally hundreds of millions of believers, hundreds of thousands of churches, and thousands of movements throughout the world today that do believe in and appropriate the teachings of this text, and with great effect. In fact, viewed from the global perspective, our inherited Western views are the minority.

The reality is that the Ephesians 4 typology (the fivefold ministry that we call APEST: apostle, prophet, evangelist, shepherd, and teacher) is a major piece of Pauline ecclesiology. Although there have been bits and pieces of affirmations, we have not been able to find a single theologically substantial published book dedicated solely to this topic. To be sure, some books have emerged from the twentieth-century charismatic and Pentecostal wings of the church, but these are largely one-dimensional and fundamentalist, lack depth, and are front-loaded with domination theology with its overly hierarchical and elitist notions of leadership, the kind of which our Lord expressly forbids (Matthew 20:25–28). We suggest that many of these books are part of the reason that APEST ministry is not embraced as widely as it ought to be in the broader church: they have instead provided the straw man that the others so easily reject.

These books aside, readers should consider how many theological books there might be in the history of the church. We guess that must be numbered in the tens of millions. Yet in the many millions of theological books that have ever been written, we cannot find serious explorations of the topic of fivefold ministry as a living and vital piece of the church's genetic coding. In theological libraries, you will find hundreds of thousands of books that explore some of the most obscure concepts conceivable—from interpretations of matters of ecclesiological polity, the meaning of conjunctives in Lukan grammar, and the eschatological prognostications of the Hittite peoples, to four-hundred-page studies on the finger of God in Luke 11:20, not to mention countless contemporary books of theological bubblegum, and yet there is no open-minded and focused thinking on Ephesians 4 even though it contains a concentrated piece of deeply foundational Pauline ecclesiology.[2] Mostly we have silence, misunderstanding, and a deeply ingrained belief that somehow Ephesians 4 no longer applies to the church. This is not just a tragic omission; it constitutes a direct indictment against our integrity, our love of truth, our pursuit of the things of God and our scholarship.

How can we explain this? How did it come to be such a profoundly unexamined teaching? The only conclusion we can reach is that this must ultimately be the work of the Devil. And as extreme as that sounds, it makes complete sense: surely if the Devil wanted to strike a blow against our capacity to be the church that Jesus intended us to be—the gospel's agency for world transformation no less—then this would be as good a place as any. It is a classic divide-and-conquer strategy: divide the foundational ministry of the church, completely delegitimize some of the players, and overlegitimize the others by institutionalizing them, and the ministry of the church, along with its leadership, is thus rendered largely ineffective.

As with any other form of deception, truth telling always disarms the power of a lie and positions us for an embrace with reality. By looking into Ephesians 4, we will be confronted with another reality, one that has been there all along.

"Perfectly Designed"

We are perfectly designed to achieve what we are currently achieving. As a certain tree bears specific fruit, so too the organizational systems we inhabit are biased toward achieving certain outcomes. This axiom is hard to dispute and cuts two ways. One meaning is that if we are in decline, there are likely to be some identifiable, and to varying degrees controllable, reasons for that decline. The task of good leadership is to constantly ask, "What is our core purpose?" and to make sure that the organization makes the right choices to remain true to that purpose. There is nothing fatalistic about this; unwanted outcomes can be corrected with the right leadership vision along with the political will to do so. The whole notion of leadership actually assumes that this must be the case: we are response-*able*. If we are not doing what a church should be doing, then the task of its leaders is to direct it to be the church that it should be. And if leadership is unwilling to do this, then we suggest that they are abdicating their calling before God.

The other meaning in the idea of being perfectly designed is where our hope lies. In light of the clear New Testament teachings on the church, we are called to believe that we really are perfectly designed by God to be everything that he intended for us to be and do. In other words, if we take our Lord and the scriptures themselves at face value, then we already have everything we need to get the job done. The ecclesia is perfectly designed to achieve its distinctive mission, but to do so means that we must build according to code. We must work with Jesus in the power of the Holy Spirit to be the church that makes the difference that only we were designed to make. Only this idea of inherent design can explain why dynamic apostolic movements in history can have massive impact and growth with apparently very few of the resources we in the West think we need to get the job done. We are designed for world transformation; impact is built into the idea of ecclesia itself.

A Missional Ministry for a Missional Church

Clearly one of the biggest issues in the church today is the discussion about what it means to be missional. We believe that how we deal with this will determine the future viability of the church in the West. But we fear that so many of these vital conversations are doomed to frustration because the people in them are unwilling or unable to reconfigure ministry to suit the missional context. Although many buy into the concept, they are unwilling to recalibrate the ecclesiology. Christendom church has been run on a largely shepherd-teacher model, and because it has had a privileged position in society, it has been inclined to dispense with the more missional or evangelistic ministry types (apostle, prophet, and evangelist).

These inherited forms of church are not equipped for the missional challenge because they refuse to recalibrate their ministry along the lines suggested in Ephesians 4. We believe that in order to be a genuinely missional church, we must have a missional ministry to go with it, and that means putting this issue of the apostle, prophet, and evangelist roles back on the table. If we do not, we believe that there is no real possibility of becoming truly missional.

We devote entire chapters to defining the APEST ministries, but here are some brief working definitions of each of these gifts:

- The *apostle* is tasked with the overall vigor, as well as extension of Christianity as a whole, primarily through direct mission and church planting. As the name itself suggests, it is the quintessentially missional ministry, as "sentness" (Latin *missio*) is written into it (*apostello* = sent one).
- The *prophet* is called to maintain faithfulness to God among the people of God. Essentially prophets are guardians of the covenant relationship.
- The *evangelist* is the recruiter to the cause, the naturally infectious person who is able to enlist people into the movement by transmitting the gospel.
- The *shepherd* (pastor) is called to nurture spiritual development, maintain communal health, and engender loving community among the people of God.
- The *teacher* mediates wisdom and understanding. This philosophical type brings comprehensive understanding of the revelation bequeathed to the church.

We represent these five roles symbolically in Figure 1.1. All five are needed if we are to be the authentically missional church as Jesus intended us to be.

The Order of Creation and the Order of Redemption

Our friend and colleague Andrew Dowsett, who has worked extensively with Mike Breen, maintains rather intriguingly, and we think correctly, that APEST is reflected in the orders of creation (as part of the general

Figure 1.1 The Five APEST Ministries
Source: Reprinted by permission of Nathan Freeberg,
leadershipvisionconsulting.com.

human experience) and not simply in the orders of redemption (the church). In other words, these apply in some way to all people, not just Christians.[3]

Dowsett came to this understanding by reflecting on the image in verses 8 and 9, which picture Jesus as liberating people—people who were by creation naturally apostolic, prophetic, instructive types—from the dominion of Satan, and subsequently giving these now-liberated captives to the church as gifts, for the very purpose of enabling the church to be an effective community in the world. This certainly makes sense of the ascension narrative used here. In other words, Jesus redeems what is already present in the world and realigns it, giving it a new theological significance and function within the church.

In this light, one can see how perhaps society in general can be interpreted through the APEST grid:

- Apostles in the generic sense are those sent to pioneer something new—for example, teachers who are called in to turn failing schools around, along with people who start movements of sorts, architect systems, or start entrepreneurial business ventures. Can we see non-Christian people who fit this category? Definitely.

- Prophets tend to be visionaries, but in a very different sense; they often have a keen interest in issues of justice, environmental responsibility, or the creative arts. Are there such people outside the church? Of course.

- Evangelists are particularly gifted at enthusing others about what they stand for, selling the significance of their work, company, or product outside the group itself. These are easy to spot. The United States is full of them.

- Pastors are those with a special concern for seeing and affirming what is human within structures. They might not be the most appropriate people to put together a policy for addressing drug abuse, but if they are not part of delivering the policy, the addicts are in trouble. Are there people who create community and bring healing to others in the non-Christian world? Indeed.

- Teachers are those who are effective trainers and inspirers of learning. They are philosophers, thinkers, people who understand ideas and how they shape human life. Do such non-Christians exist? No brainer.

Viewing APEST sociologically allows us to demystify the overly fraught language of the Bible and approach the meaning of Ephesians

4:11 without the polemics that have accompanied it in the past. When we see it this way, we can see how powerful these roles really are. Of course, any healthy leadership team in any context (corporate, non-profit, or anything else) would benefit from such a complex of influences. It also gives us insight into why having only two of the types in the mix leads to dysfunctions. Finally it is very helpful because it helps us to appreciate the sheer movemental power of the redemption won in and through Jesus Christ. People who are naturally inclined to one of the other APEST types are redeemed, set apart, focused, and legitimized in the church. In fact, they are Christ's ascension gifts (Ephesians 4:8–10).

A Letter for Everyone

We can tell a lot about a letter from whom it is addressed to. Ephesians is not addressed to a president of a organization, theologians, seminarians, or a group of leaders; rather it is addressed to the regular people of God who inhabited the various house churches throughout the city of Ephesus. We must keep in mind that the church in Ephesus was made up of ordinary people—including women, slaves, people of different races, class, and socioeconomic status. This is a letter for the church about the church, and it must be read as such. Furthermore, it is a general, or generic, letter, intended for wide use and distribution among the various churches, including beyond Ephesus itself.[4] The Ephesian text is not what scholars would call a highly contextual document. Letters like Galatians, or 2 Corinthians were crafted for a particular community facing a particular problem. Ephesians has universal significance beyond merely local concerns. Recognizing the cosmic, universal nature of Paul's ecclesiology in Ephesians repositions us to approach the pivotal text of Ephesians 4 from a new angle. This has direct implications for how we digest the entire letter, not to mention our focus on Ephesians 4:7–16.

The Constitution of the Church (with No Amendments Allowed)

This universal significance also means that Ephesians functions as something of a constitutional document of the church as Paul sees it. In fact Markus Barth calls this section "The Constitution of the Church" and considers verses 11 and 12 to be the means of operationalizing it.[5]

We can apply the metaphor of constitution to the whole letter itself. For instance, if you were to say to Paul, "Tell me your best thinking about the church," he would without doubt slap the book of Ephesians on the table. Although he no doubt says other things about the church elsewhere, they tend to be incidental to the other issues his letter is addressing. In Ephesians, he is specifically talking about the ecclesia as God intended it to be. In fact, no other book in the Bible deals so specifically, and so authoritatively, with the nature of ecclesia. There is a certain distinctly constitutional weight to this document, and like any other good constitution, it sets the criteria about how we must think about the church and provides all the essential frameworks by which it was intended to operate ever since.

This is exactly why we locate the lever for change here in Ephesians, and especially in 4:1–16. It is also why we think the APEST configuration, as opposed to the other possible lists of gifts, operates as the interpretative center for how we conceive of ministry. Imagine trying to act according to a constitution when more than half the leadership provisions provided for by the constitution itself were annulled or dismissed. It would be like having to run government with no executive powers. Yes, that is precisely what we have done.

Language Matters

In a chapter in *Organization at the Limit*, a book dedicated to analyzing the organizational dynamics that contributed to the *Columbia* space shuttle disaster, William Ocasio discusses the unique connection between language and organizational activity. Applying an analysis of the language used and how it points to deficiencies in thinking, Ocasio points to the subtle yet powerful capacity of language to focus our attention as well as to blind us to seeing problems when they occur. The language we commonly use can greatly influence what gets noticed and what gets ignored. He says, "It's not that language determines what can be thought, but that language influences what routinely *does* get thought."[6] In other words, as G. K. Chesterton noted about institutionalized insiders, it is not so much that insiders cannot see the solution. It is that they cannot see the problem itself because they have no language for it.

To illustrate, the fact that we tend to experience blind spots in vehicles is not so much an engineering problem as it is a linguistic one. When we refer to "rear-view mirrors," we use those mirrors to look at the rear view alone, in essence, creating the blind spot on the side. When we refer to the external mirrors as "side-view mirrors," then we will use them to view what is happening on the side of the vehicle. Words matter big time.

Taking his cue from the official report of the *Columbia* disaster, Ocasio and his team of organization consultants concluded that simply putting it down to individual error does not solve the issue of what caused the crash. The problem instead lay in the way NASA actually conceived of and articulated organization and management itself. Their language indicated that they did not have the categories to help them even see the problem coming, let alone resolve it. He calls this phenomenon of organizational blindness the "vocabulary of organizing."[7]

In an effort to describe its core practices and procedures, organizations develop a vocabulary that helps describe, as well as prescribe, organizational activity. Realizing this inherent connection between organizational vocabularies and activity is insightful because it helps explain why some issues receive more attention and become more prominent than others. Ocasio says, "The vocabulary of organizing serves to provide the organizational categories which designates what constitutes a problem or issue to be attended to as well as what type of solutions and initiatives are to be considered."[8] Essentially a vocabulary of organizing plays a significant role in determining what practices will be considered normative and what practices are literally unheard of. Thus, the linguistic categories that an organization uses can shape how it conceives of core tasks.

By applying these ideas to the Western church, we can easily see how our most generative forms of ministry—the apostle, the prophet, and the evangelist—have been edited out of our organizational vocabulary. They are no longer considered to be legitimate descriptors for leaders of ministries in most churches. The result is that we are scripted not to see or pay attention to issues related to apostolic, prophetic, and, to a lesser degree, evangelistic concerns, even when they are staring us in the face. Again we are shown how we are perfectly designed to achieve current outcomes.

Because APEST supplies the church with the essential linguistic categories to form a complete vocabulary of organizing, reinserting the very language of apostle, prophet, and evangelist into organizational discourse will revolutionize our conception of the church and its core tasks. Instead of seeing the church as an extension of the seminary (teacher) or as a place to merely get fed (shepherd), we can rightly conceive of the church within the broader framework of Christ's ministry. For instance, if we persist in using the standard shepherd and teacher frameworks for church planting, then we will inevitably see that the primary purpose of the new plant will be to run worship services and Bible studies.

Adopting a broader APEST understanding and vocabulary brings other insights about the functions of the church into play. New possibilities will present themselves. It will reinstate the possibility of the permanent revolution by giving us a broader range of options and opening us up to a multidimensional way of seeing. Try it: extend your ministry vocabulary, ensure you have a good understanding about the five APEST roles and functions, and watch how the analysis of the situation as well as the capacity to problem-solve will improve.

Getting into the Text (or, Allowing It to Get into Us)

When we consider the text itself, we discern three movements within the overall unity of verses 1 to 16: unity (verses 1–6), diversity/APEST (verses 7–11), and maturity (verses 12–16).

Unity in the One God: Verses 1 to 6

The text at the beginning of Ephesians 4 flows out of the famously lofty Pauline prayer for the church in Ephesians 3:14–21. Here Paul prays that they might attain the knowledge of God in Jesus Christ and grow up into being the fullness of Christ (a key theme in the letter) in the world. Immediately he goes on to appeal to the Ephesians (and to all other Christians everywhere) to live consistently with who God is and what he has done in Jesus.

Ephesians 4 is the pivotal section of the letter where Paul moves from theology to praxis. And like any good preamble to a constitution, Paul first condenses the core theological essentials into seven theological axioms relating to the oneness of God, faith, and church.

This was a strategic move that Paul made because any movement experiencing spontaneous expansion will encounter, and therefore become vulnerable to, competing systems of meaning:

> As a prisoner for the Lord, then, I urge you to live a life worthy of the calling you have received. Be completely humble and gentle; be patient, bearing with one another in love. Make every effort to keep the unity of the Spirit through the bond of peace. There is one body and one Spirit—just as you were called to one hope when you were called—one Lord, one faith, one baptism; one God and Father of all, who is over all and through all and in all [Ephesians 4:1–6].

Much like the nature of the Ephesian letter, the seven "ones" (one body, one Spirit, one hope, one Lord, one faith, one baptism, one God and Father of all) are its universal truths. They provide the necessary theological coordinates to maintain unity within a burgeoning and increasingly diverse movement. Here Paul, true to the apostolic calling, is essentially ensuring the theological integrity of the church. Formulating it in this manner was a clever way for Paul to clarify the boundaries of orthodoxy yet package it in a reproducible form.

The elevated speech in these verses reflects both the theological significance and the inescapably foundational nature of the text.

Diversity in APEST: Verses 7 to 11

Having laid out the basis of ecclesial unity, Paul proceeds directly to affirm the God-given, or to be more accurate the Christ-apportioned, nature of the ministry of the ecclesia:

> But to each one of us grace has been given as Christ apportioned it. This is why it says: "When he ascended on high, he led captives in his train and gave gifts to men." (What does "he ascended" mean except that he also descended to the lower, earthly regions? He who descended is the very one who ascended higher than all the heavens, in order to fill the whole universe.) It was he who gave some to be apostles, some to be prophets, some to be evangelists, and some to be pastors and teachers [4:7–11].

Putting aside the meaning of the ascension reference here, Paul clearly states that Jesus has "given" (*aorist*, indicative) certain "charisms" (what we will variously call *ministries*, *callings*, or *vocations*) to the church, distributing them among all the people as he (the giver) sees fit.[9] These gifts are clearly and unequivocally stated as being in the fivefold expressions of apostle, prophet, evangelist, shepherd, and teacher; they have a Christological source and basis and approximate what can now be called *the* constitutional ministry of the church and—following our metaphor of constitution—its legitimate executive.[10]

Growing Up into Christ: Verses 12 to 16

While it is a false break to split verse 12 from verse 11, we can discern a shift in Paul's argument from a prescription of APEST in verse 11 to a description of the expected results in the church in verse 12. Here we gain insight into why APEST is given in the first place:

> To prepare God's people for works of service, so that the body of Christ may be built up until we all reach unity in the faith and in the knowledge of the Son of God and become mature, attaining to the whole measure of the fullness of Christ. Then we will no longer

be infants, tossed back and forth by the waves, and blown here and there by every wind of teaching and by the cunning and craftiness of men in their deceitful scheming. Instead, speaking the truth in love, we will in all things grow up into him who is the Head, that is, Christ. From him the whole body, joined and held together by every supporting ligament, grows and builds itself up in love, as each part does its work [4:12–16].

The charisms of APEST are given that the body of Christ might grow and mature, that we may live out the unity described in verses 1 to 6, that we might achieve true understanding and not be capricious people given to theological illusions, and to find our organic wholeness in Christ and each other, that is, to be the people Jesus intended us to be. We represent these in Figure 1.2.

The logic of this text is integrated and sound theologically. It makes clear that the church's capacity for reciprocity and maturity is based on orthodox understandings of God and church and the constitutional ministry expressed as APEST. A mature and healthy church lives out of its confession as well as into it; it is a self-reinforcing system. If we ignore the inner logic of the text, we should not expect to produce the outcomes it foresees.

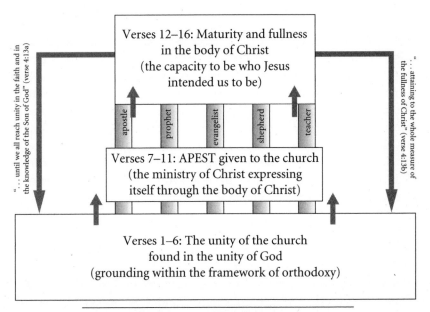

Figure 1.2 APEST Charisms

According to Paul, a fully functioning fivefold APEST ministry is the Christ-given defense mechanism against heresy and false doctrine. There is something about APEST as a whole that moves the church past theological naiveté and anchors it in a more integrated understanding of its central message and core doctrines.[11] Oddly enough, it is the very diversity contained within APEST that aids the church in attaining to the "unity of the faith."[12]

Can We Mature with a Twofold Ministry?

Actually if we take the text plainly (inductively) and without prior theological prejudice (deductively), it is not hard to discern that we cannot be a healthy movement without the necessary APEST ministry. Verse 13 explicitly says as much, but the logic of the entire text aims at this. So, for instance, we can ask whether there is any doubt about the universal significance of verses 1 to 6 for any church in any time and place. We seriously doubt that anyone reading this book would suggest that they do not still have abiding authority over us. They were clearly not intended just for the Ephesian Christians.

So if both sections on either side of verses 7 to 11 are true and binding on the church for all time, then by what form of theological trickery have we come to believe that verses 7 to 11 would be any less abiding and universal, especially when grammatically and thematically they are placed at the heart of the same piece of scripture? As far as we can discern, it is simply not possible to be the church that Jesus intended if three (APE) of the five constitutional ministries are removed. According to the explicit teaching of Ephesians 4:1–16, it cannot be done. But in fact it has been done, and the tragic consequences are dramatically demonstrated in and through the history of the Christian church through the past seventeen centuries. We have been condemned to Sisyphean frustration in this matter ever since (Figure 1.3). Every time we seem to develop some semblance of movement and get the missional boulder up the hill, it rolls back down again, only to initiate the next cycle of seemingly futile efforts all over again. Seldom (and maybe never) have we stopped to correct our misunderstandings at this point.

And to be clear, the kind of maturity Paul is talking about here reaches beyond psychological wholeness and moral behavior.[13] These are certainly involved, but what is ultimately at stake is the church's capacity to embody and extend the mission and purposes of Jesus in the world. When Paul says that APEST is given to "equip" the saints, he uses the Greek word *kataptismo*, which, among its various nuanced meanings, is

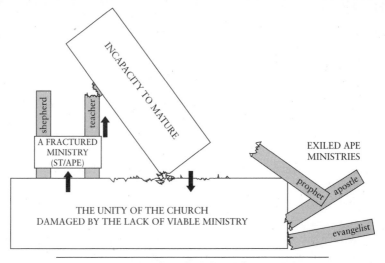

Figure 1.3 The Church Without APE

applied to the act of setting a broken bone.[14] APEST helps us mature so that the "body" can "walk" and ultimately "stand" against the principalities and powers that dehumanize and then crush humanity (Ephesians 6:10–16). Our capacity as a movement to engage the spiritual powers that be is at stake when APEST is not fully operative.

The Exiling of the APEs

Much of this book seeks to redress the imbalance brought about by the disastrous exiling of the APE types from the equation of ministry. We suggest a thorough account as to why it happened in the Appendix, explore many of the results, and make what we believe ought to be a convincing case as to why they should be included again. But to do this, we must ask readers to be patient because we are going against the inherited grain of thinking and have to be thorough. What we are certain of is that we are dealing here with something that has nothing less than paradigmatic significance as to how we might fulfill our distinctive mission in the world. By effectively exiling the apostolic, prophetic, and evangelistic ministries, we have meddled with the very mechanism Jesus intended for us to be a fully functioning ecclesia. The result is that all ministry has been forced to fit into the predetermined formats of shepherd and teacher, pastor and theologian, and nothing else has legitimacy. In the end, when all is said and done, we are perfectly designed to achieve what we are currently achieving. It stands to reason that if we have found it expedient to ignore the ministry formula revealed in Ephesians 4, we should not expect to achieve the desired outcomes that this same passage promises.

The Bed of Procrustes

Procrustes, whose name means "he who stretches," was arguably one of the most intriguing characters in all Greek mythology. Like a serial killer in the TV series *Criminal Minds*, he was a devious villain who kept a house by the side of the road where he would offer hospitality to passing strangers. The guests were invited in for a pleasant meal and a night's rest in his very special bed, a bed Procrustes described as having the magical property in that its length exactly matched that of anyone who lay down on it. What Procrustes did not volunteer was the method by which this one-size-fits-all was achieved: as soon as the guest fell asleep Procrustes went to work on him, stretching him on the rack if he was too short for the bed or chopping off his legs if he was too long—a rather unfortunate way of making everyone conform to his one-size-fits-all bed.

Procrustes' infamous but profoundly allegorical activity found its way into our language as *procrustean bed* or *procrustean effort* or simply calling something "procrustean." It means setting a standard or set of conditions, determined arbitrarily, to which everyone and everything is subsequently forced to conform. It means asserting a set of assumptions and subsequently forcing everything to fit those assumptions even when they do not fit. Similar to this is the idea of the narrative fallacy (also called illusory correlation): our tendency to construct stories around facts. This may serve the purpose of illustrating the facts, but when people begin to believe the stories and accommodate facts into the stories, they are likely to err.

We suggest this is what we have done with ministry. Having exiled the APE types within the first three centuries of Christian history and having subsequently defined ministry according to the remaining two types, shepherd and theologian, we have effectively practiced what is called reflective equilibrium: the tendency to retrofit facts and evidence into preexisting categories in order to resolve apparent categorical tensions. In essence, we have forced all other possible forms of ministry to conform to this twofold standard.

This anachronistic, procrustean reading is the approach that the overwhelming majority of interpreters take—for instance, a random grab at a commentary produced by Arthur Patzia. Patzia, a New Testament scholar based at Fuller Theological Seminary, rightly acknowledges that "what is certain . . . is that Christ gave (appointed) these offices to the church for the specific function of having the church attain its full maturity in him (4:12–16)."[15] But then he rather arbitrarily goes on to deny any subsequent function of APE in the ongoing life of the church. Parroting the inherited scripting, he says these were replaced by the canon of scripture and the role of shepherd and teacher. Yet nothing in the text itself suggests that this is the case. To the contrary, all evidence points in the other direction. He is not alone in this: the vast majority of commentaries follow the same predetermined, lock-step approach. Rather than taking the text as the starting point of doctrine, they have anachronistically forced it to fit later, and decidedly deductive, conclusions.

Darrell Guder exposes the self-same procrustean tendencies in John Calvin:

> Calvin devotes much attention to the relevance of Ephesians 4:1–16 for the formation and structuring of the church. But after centuries of Christendom, he has some problems with Christ's gifts of some to be apostles, prophets, and evangelists. So, he argues, "These three functions were not established in the church as permanent ones, but only for that time during which churches were to be erected where none existed before." He acknowledges that there might be special situations in which these offices become necessary again, but they will remain, in his view, "extraordinary." But, he goes on, "Next come pastors and teachers, whom the church can never go without."[16]

More surprising perhaps is when some of the best thinkers in missional church circles perpetuate the same basic errors. For instance, Alan Roxburgh certainly acknowledges the missional significance of the Ephesians 4 typology, but he then modifies the terminology so as not to offend prevailing ecclesiological sensibilities. Even as he acknowledges that the current decline of the church in the West requires the apostolic function, he nonetheless subsumes the function itself to that of the pastor. He rather skittishly comes up with the names *pastor/poet* (ST), *pastor/prophet* (P), and *pastor/apostle* (A), and he does not even mention the evangelist.[17] The apostolic, as well as all the others, are thereby forced to fit that of the pastor. In fact, it ends up that there is no stand-alone, fully legitimized, apostle or prophet at all, only the apostolic pastor or prophetic pastor and the like.

All these interpretations amount to hermeneutical gymnastics and demonstrate how deeply biased the Christendom system is toward interpreting the APE modes of ministry through an ST lens. The truly puzzling thing is that no one can clearly state why this is the case, except to give the embedded, traditionally scripted answer that the functions of apostles and prophets just seemed to have passed away with the canon of scripture. And so the traditional interpretation, that is, the pastor-teacher model, has become the false standard by which all subsequent ministry is assessed. Rather than assessing ministry in light of a fivefold form, we have forced the New Testament to fit our assumptions. As a result, the pastor (shepherd) (and perhaps, to a lesser extent, the teacher) becomes the catchall title, the procrustean office, on which all subsequent ministry is built.

Just to press the point a little more, how many times do you think the word *shepherd/pastor* (*poimein*) is used in the New Testament for people in ministry? The answer is completely astonishing given the universal use of the term—*once!* Yes, once—here, in Ephesians 4:7 no less. Although it is a biblical term in that it is used in the New Testament, that one use hardly justifies having everything from pastors of technology to pastors of administration, and pastors of anything in between. And although the word *teacher* is used much more extensively in the New Testament (around ten times), we are unambiguously warned in scripture that not many of us should seek to become teachers because this vocation is judged more strictly by God (James 3:1). Yet we have made teaching a standard criterion for all ministry. Now Procrustes and Sisyphus join together.

One Aorist *Rules Them All*

Just one more thing on this issue of the integrity of the APEST ministry as a whole unit: it is very important to note that the verbs for *given* (*edothe*) in verses 7 and 11 are aorist indicatives, that is, adamant verbs with no room for subtle reinterpretations. These are given, once and for all but with clear and abiding significance, to the church. They have the ring of constitutionality with no possibility of amendments about them, once again highlighting the foundational implications of these verses.

What is more, all five APEST ministries come together under the power of the ruling verb—*edothe*. The verbs govern the objects to which they refer—in this case, all five ministries as a self-contained grammatical unit of speech. We cannot eliminate or downplay one of these ministries without undermining the legitimacy, significance, and vitality of the others.

To Each One of Us

Even when these verses are taken seriously by various churches and denominations (for example, the Vineyard, Assemblies of God, and Foursquare), by far the most common way that APEST has been read is to identify it as the leadership of the church. As the idea states it, Jesus has equipped *some* in the body in order to train all the *others* to do ministry. At first glance, this seems to make a lot of sense: the church staff equips the members to do ministry. Unfortunately, this interpretation of the text is a by-product of the institutional ways we organize ourselves and fails to recognize the movemental nature of ecclesia in the New Testament.

This misunderstanding can be rectified by reading the text organically at verse 7 instead of reading verse 11 as a stand-alone. Paul says in verse 7, "But, to *each one of us* [Greek *hekasto*] grace was given, according to the measure of Christ's gift."[18] *Hekasto* literally means "to each and every person."[19] He intends that we understand it quite literally to mean every person, that is, all believers hearing these words both then and now. Rather than gifts being given to an elite few and for the benefit of the many, these gifts are given to all and are for the benefit of all; it is the saints who equip the saints.

Remember that the letter is written to, and intended to be read out in, the gathered ecclesia (the various house churches) in Ephesus and not to a leadership conference. It is addressed to all of the people of God as a whole, including women and slaves, and in all their nonprofessional glory. Furthermore, the hearers came from across the racial, social, economic, and gender spectrum. This means that every believer fits into the APEST typology! This is a deeply radicalizing text that has huge ramifications for how we both recognize and unleash the ministry of every believer. This is a massive paradigm shift that in itself will take us to the core of what it means to be an apostolic movement.

Seeing APEST through the lens of the ministry of all believers leads us to believe that Ephesians 4 is not primarily a leadership text but rather a ministry text. Paul is setting forth a reflexive paradigm where each part of the body gets access to, influences, and ministers to all the other parts of the body. In organizational language, Paul is describing a cross-functional team where every person comes to the table with his or her own gifts and contributes to the ongoing development of the body, and thus to the movement.

We therefore suggest that calling and ministry are different from leadership only by matter of degree and capacity.[20] Leadership embodies a particular APEST ministry but extends and reorients it to fit the distinct functions of leadership. In other words, there is a certain flow from gifting to ministry to leadership.

Everyone may have a gifting, and therefore a possibility of a maturing ministry, but not everyone functions as a leader within his or her

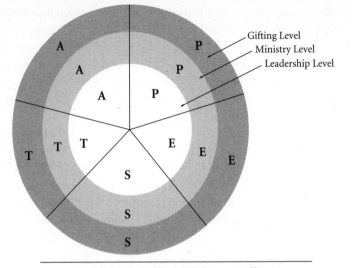

Figure 1.4 Calling Within a Calling

scope of ministry. This shift radically changes the way we see God's people. Everyone is gifted and called to operate out of his or her vocational energies, but not all are leaders. Some people are designed to function prophetically, for example, but not all prophetic people will function as leaders. And some people who are gifted in pastoral care are not necessarily gifted or skilled in leadership. The same is true in all the ministries. Ministry does not a leader make. Leadership must be conceived as a calling within a calling (Figure 1.4). It encompasses a set of skills that enhance the basic calling and influences others from within that call.

APEST is a part of the DNA of all God's people, making it a universal feature of all communities in Christ.

The Ministry of Christ in and Through the Body of Christ

We can say that APEST is part of the DNA of the church because we are absolutely sure that Jesus himself is. Verse 11 is nothing less than the *ministry of Christ expressing itself in and through the body of Christ.* Consider this. Is Jesus an apostle? The sent one? Yes, clearly he is the archetypal apostle. Is he a prophet? Yes, and the greatest one. Is he the evangelist of evangelists? Yes, clearly he is. Shepherd? Yes, he calls himself that many times. Teacher? Of course. So if we are the body of Christ, then it is hardly surprising that we should reflect these many dimensions of Christ's ministry. In fact, it would be surprising if we do not reflect a fully orbed extension of what Jesus was about. The spiritual gifts find their proper role in relation to God's purposes in this world through his people. Eugene Peterson rightly says that "each [APEST] gift is an invitation and provides the means to participate in the work of Jesus."[21]

A twofold ministry can never hope to reflect a complete and comprehensive ministry of Christ to the world, and neither can it ever hope to fulfill his purposes through the church. Anything less than a fivefold ministry is a misrepresentation of the ministry of Christ, and by consequence, that leads to a misrepresentation of Christ in the world.

This Christological basis of APEST can be reinforced with the help of the social sciences. According to seminal sociologist Max Weber, when a charismatic leader of a movement is "removed" by death or other means, the various roles that leader played, along with the tasks he or she performed, are now left open. This vacuum poses a dilemma for the followers because typically no one person can step into the founder's shoes and provide the same level of charisma and leadership. What happens next is what Weber called "the routinization of charisma." The function and activities originally performed by the founder are now distilled into roles and distributed through the organization to the various adherents and followers. These roles and activities evolve into routine practices that essentially perpetuate the founder's influence.[22]

In many ways, this is exactly what has happened with the church. Jesus parses out the core elements of his ministry into five distinct categories and plants those ministries deep within the church. What we have here is "root-in-ization of charisma"—the ministries of APEST are rooted in, and consequently extend, the original ministry of Christ. Through his ascension, Jesus distributes the vocational elements of his ministry to the church to mature and equip it for the task of being the fullness of Christ in the world. Christ's ministry is thus routinized into his ecclesia. The question of how the church functions as the fullness of Christ in the world is given a concrete answer here.[23] Visually, it could look something like Figure 1.5.

APEST perpetuates the ministry of Christ so that the church is endowed with the same capacity for movement as the founder. Contained within APEST are the core elements of a full-blown movemental ecclesiology.

Did We Miss Something?

Only one more foundational issue needs to be explored here before we move on to discussing the content and texture of each APEST profile. In our various talks on APEST, people invariably ask us, "Why this list

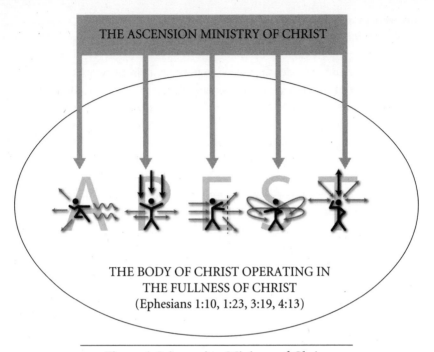

Figure 1.5 Ascension Ministry of Christ

Table 1.1 Contrast of Key Terms

	Key Word in Greek	English Translation	Implication
1 Corinthians 12:7	*Phanerosis*	Manifestation	Situational
Romans 12:4	*Praxis*	Action	Practical
Ephesians 4:1	*Kalesis*	Calling	Vocational

alone? Why not include the other lists of gifts (for example, those in Romans 12 or 1 Corinthians 12)?" It is a legitimate question.

Although we are not going to offer a detailed taxonomy of those giftings here, we do assert what we believe to be important distinctions among them. If we look closer into Romans 12 and 1 Corinthians 12, we notice each of the lists is prefaced by a key word that frames the nature of the gifts (Table 1.1). The list in 1 Corinthians seems to be mostly associated with the Christian gathering, and that in Romans 12 seems to be more concerned with practical activities done by members of the community.[24]

We believe that what is being referred to in Ephesians 4 is something more substantial, more permanent, and more decisive—something that touches on the idea of a vocation or calling. We are explicitly introduced to the vocational nature of APEST when Paul begins Ephesians 4 by saying, "I, therefore, the prisoner of the Lord, beseech you to walk worthy of the calling (*kalesis*) with which you were called (*kalesis*)." Perhaps most convincing is the way Paul uses nouns to present APEST in verse 11: "He gave some to be apostles, and prophets, and evangelists, and pastors and teachers." Instead of listing activities that exist separate and apart from the individual, he connects the being with the doing: task and person are the same. It becomes a matter of vocational identity. By rooting APEST in our sense of identity and calling in Christ, we believe Paul is affording them a gravitas and permanence not afforded to the other giftings.

So where does this leave these other giftings in Romans and 1 Corinthians? Think about it this way. If each believer has received a specific APEST calling in some form, then that person fulfills that calling by living into it. However, functioning successfully in one's vocation requires drawing from additional capacities to execute and carry out the task in various contexts. Every assignment is different and presents unique challenges. Because of this, God gives various gifts to carry out the work he has assigned each person to do. In our view, Ephesians 4:11 is the interpretative center, or the organizing principle, around which the other gifts listed in scripture are organized.

Consider this illustration from the field of construction. Let us say someone has a particular calling to build houses. That is, his vocation is to be a carpenter and builder. To accomplish this job, this person needs more than one tool: a hammer, a sledgehammer, a drill, pliers, and so on. At some point, he will need all of these to accomplish the work of building the house, but he will use them only as needed.

Similarly, the gifts in Romans and 1 Corinthians can be viewed as a kind of tool belt. If I am a prophet, I will always be a prophet, but the context in which I function prophetically necessitates that I use the different tools on my belt: insight, prayer languages, dreams, and foresight. It is not uncommon to see an apostle with a natural bent for the gift of visionary leadership, but there are times when an apostle will need the gift of healing, administration, or encouragement to accomplish the task at hand. And the evangelist can draw from the gift of faith, miracles, encouragement, and so on.

Paul seems to be saying that each of us has a fixed vocation, but to live out this calling, we need different tools in different situations to accomplish the task. The Spirit supplies us with those tools to help us get the job done: these are the charismatic giftings. What is important to recognize is that it is the Spirit who gives these gifts as they are needed and in the ways they are needed.

The artist Henri Matisse was reputed to have said that to look at something as though we had never seen it before requires great courage. That much might be true, but to look at something and recognize its truth and not be willing to change would amount to simple cowardice. For leaders in God's church, this kind of cowardice takes on dimensions of sinful defiance against the purposes of the Lord. In this book, we challenge the church to respond in ways that bring us closer to what Jesus intended in and through us in the first place. If it is repentance that is needed, then we suggest that this is exactly what should be done, and now. The time is critical now, and when it comes to recovering the transforming power of being an apostolic movement again in the West, it is impossible to travel north without turning one's back on the south.

Facing a new direction not only opens us up to new and untapped resources of human capital; it also positions us to once again be enriched by the full spectrum of collective intelligence that Jesus has placed within his people. Once we see the rightful place of APEST within the framework of biblical ministry, we see the church in a new light and full of potential and possibility. Unlocking this can be likened to unleashing the power released in nuclear fission. To this we now turn.

An Elegant Solution

DISTRIBUTED INTELLIGENCE IN THE BODY OF CHRIST

There are only two ways to live your life. One is as though nothing is a miracle. The other is as though everything is a miracle.
Albert Einstein

When a paradigm shifts, everyone goes back to zero.
Joel Barker

Learning to observe the whole system is difficult. Our traditional analytic skills can't help us. Analysis narrows our field of awareness and actually prevents us from seeing the total system.
Margaret J. Wheatley

EINSTEIN ONCE REMARKED THAT WHEN THE SOLUTION IS SIMPLE, God is speaking. What he meant by "simple" was not simplistic and one-dimensional, but a solution that unlocks the mystery of complex problems—something ingenious. His $E = MC^2$ is a classic example of simplicity unlocking complexity. Similarly, when scientists refer to something as an elegant solution, they are referring to situations where the maximum desired effect is achieved through the smallest, or simplest, effort. An elegant solution is also likely to be accomplished with appropriate methods and materials, so, for instance, duct tape is not likely to be part of an elegant solution unless, of course, the problem involves taping ducts. When we look at Ephesians 4, we are no doubt looking at the rare blessing of an elegant solution. It has an implicitly beautiful symmetry that mirrors in a direct way the ministry of Jesus Christ, especially in comparison to the inelegant twofold shepherd-teacher approach that has dominated Christian history.

Having laid out some of the theological foundations for an APEST model, we now turn to giving some definition and meaning to the vocations as we see them. Given the predominance of the shepherd and teacher understandings of ministry, we trust that most people reading this book already have a reasonably clear comprehension of these roles. In addition, the chapters in Parts Two through Five explore the nature and function of the apostolic ministry, so we will give only the briefest of definitions here and leave the rest to later. The main emphasis in this chapter is on the prophetic and the evangelistic ministries.

Get Smart

Approaching APEST from the angle that each ministry carries a certain intelligence, especially as a complement to the deeply biblical idea of calling or vocation, yields helpful insights. We refer not only to IQ but also to emotional intelligence (EQ): the ability, capacity, and skill to perceive, assess, and manage one's emotions. Some aspects of EQ are personality based, and certainly some can be learned and developed. This concept of having special aptitudes, or intelligences, also spans a wide variety of human capacities. Clearly some people have a knack for business, others in seeing systems, and yet others in organization. There are now widely used tests that gauge people's political intelligence, social intelligence, creativity index, and so forth.

This idea of intelligences (or aptitudes) provides a valuable metaphor for unlocking the power and functionality of APEST: each particular ministry brings a unique vocational bias, a certain sensibility, and a heightened receptivity to issues that others cannot see. Above all, each brings an enhanced capacity to the multidimensional tasks of the church. We also suggest that each ministry is characterized by a type of intelligence: apostolic intelligence (AQ), prophetic intelligence (PQ), and so on. The combination of these five APEST intelligences creates a synergistic, heightened intelligence in the people of God as a whole. Individually and collectively, this intelligence directly strengthens the church's capability to process and interpret information, be more agile and adaptive to changing conditions, communicate its core message in multiple settings, empower people into being whom God intended them to be, as well as to organize both locally and regionally.

Before we can look at this collective intelligence as a whole, we describe the aptitudes and characteristics of each APEST type.

Apostolic Intelligence: Custodian of the DNA

The apostle is the custodian of the core and founding ideas (that is, its DNA) of the ecclesia. The ministry is characterized by the following interrelated components:

- Extension of Christianity as a whole onto new ground
- Developing and maintaining systemwide health
- Mobilizing for movement and broad impact
- Maintaining glocal (a combination of global and local) networks and relationships[1]

Not surprisingly, apostolic types tend to favor the entrepreneurial edges of the church and have a natural capacity for adventure and risk. They are systems-sensitive types who possess a keen intuition of the systemic dimensions of people movements (ordinary people mobilizing for extraordinary impact on society) and what it takes to initiate and maintain them. Hence we generally use the term *apostolic movements* to refer to highly transformative, exponential people movements that shape the extension and mobilization of Christianity into new frontiers. A contemporary example is the various movements that make up the underground Chinese church with its rapid expansion through mission, church planting, and radical discipleship. With this simple working definition in mind, we can turn to the other ministries in the Ephesians 4:11 mix, especially the prophetic and evangelistic ministries. (See Chapter Five for a comprehensive description of these functions.)

Prophetic Intelligence: Guardian of Faithfulness

Prophets have always been perceived as those who are in the know. In the Old Testament, where the roots of any biblical understanding of prophetic ministry lie, they are seen to be the God-intoxicated, biblical existentialists, calling all to live faithfully in covenant relationship with God and consistent with his kingdom and rule in the world.[2] The effect of prophetic ministry is to bring our world into divine focus.

Although prophets have a futuristic orientation, their real focus is a call to live in the existential here-and-now of faithfulness and obedience. It is certainly a caricature to see them as fortune-tellers, because even when they do predict or refer to the future, their primary concern is to motivate their listeners to live faithfully in light of that possible future. In his classic work on prophets, Abraham Heschel rightly characterizes the prophet's essential task as "declaring the word of God to the here and now; [disclos-ing] the future in order to illuminate what is involved in the present."[3]

On the Edge of the Inside

Obsessed with the idea of covenantal faithfulness, prophetic ministry can be said to revolve around two questions:

1. Who is God? (What is his nature?)
2. What does God require of us in this particular place and time? (How then shall we live?).

These questions provide the focal point of prophetic sensibility or intelligence. This fusion of God's values and reality forms the first essen-tial component of prophetic intelligence.

The prophet's intimate connection with God and his concerns will almost always cause him or her to experience the divine pathos, or the suffering of God as he experiences the world. They feel God's intense pain, his longing, and his anger, and because of this, they tend to be pas-sionate and spiritual people. Like God, they feel strongly and deeply. And because of this primary concern for God, his values, and his vision for the world, they seem to be able to sense situations where those values are not reflected. They feel the sin and dysfunction in the world. In this way, they function like canaries in the coal mine that because of their sensitivity to toxic environments keel over long before anyone detects something has gone wrong. They notice what goes unnoticed: injustice, unfaithfulness, indifference toward God, and cruelty, for example.[4]

This experience of encountering two contradicting realities causes the prophet to passionately call into question the existing order of things. Heschel again sheds light on the prophet's unique ability to experience these two realities simultaneously: "The prophet's eye is directed to the contemporary scene; the society and its conduct are the main theme of his speeches. Yet his ear is inclined to God. He is a person struck by the glory and presence of God, overpowered by the hand of God. Yet his true greatness is his ability to hold God and man in a single thought."[5] Holding these two realities together creates tension within the prophet. The prophet identifies the gaps between God's reality and our own. By forcing us to face up to these gaps in our faithfulness, the prophet creates a context that allows us to perceive the truth of our situation. It is in this space that prophetic intelligence (or sensibility) plays its most critical role (see Figure 2.1).

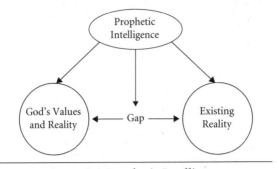

Figure 2.1 Prophetic Intelligence

The prophet's recognition of this gap often requires a confrontation with personal and collective idolatry, especially in contexts where the institution has legitimized its particular worldview that makes some ideas possible and others unthinkable.[6] The institutionalization of racism within the church leading up to and after the civil rights movement in the United States is a case in point. Treating African Americans as equals within the church, much less in society, was literally unthinkable in most denominational practices. As a result, people, and the institutions they inhabit, can find themselves being held hostage by their own logic and systems of justification. In such situations, we need prophetic imagination to deconstruct and dismantle these systems of justification that so often conceal our fears and selfishness. Recognizing the prophet's distinct, focused role to awaken our imaginations partly explains why the prophetic person can often have an aversion, even disdain, for strategy and structured planning.

As a result of all the work of bridging God and humanity, prophets generally are not content with the status quo. They tend to be always calling God's people to greater degrees of faithfulness. They question everything that does not seem to be God honoring and force us to face up to the distance between us and God. They stir up the pot, rock the boat, move our cheese, harp, nag and agitate us until we pay attention to the areas of our individual and communal lives that do not reflect the values of the gospel and God's kingdom. As such they often evoke the darker, more self-protective human responses. No wonder they tend to be killed, exiled, or simply marginalized. (See Matthew 14:1–5, 23:29–36; Hebrews 11.) God's people have always struggled to hear and integrate prophetic messages, which is why so many prophets are rejected and isolated from the ministry of the church.[7] But without them, it is hard to see how we can remain a faithful, covenantal people.

Criticize and Energize

Prophets generally draw attention to the gap by calling into question the current social, political, or theological arrangements. And in this lies an important, even unique, gift to the church as an adaptive community. Learning systems theory maintains that organizational learning takes place when programs are subjected to questions. As the quintessential questioners, prophets play a critical role in developing a community's capacity to adapt to its environment.

In his practical book *Leading with Questions*, human resource expert Michael Marquardt could well be speaking about the prophetic role when he says: "The failure to ask questions . . . allows us to operate with a distorted sense of reality." He refers to organizations that are unable to question their prevailing view of reality as zombies. A zombie organization, he says, is a walking corpse that does not yet know that it is dead "because it has created an insulated culture that systematically excludes any information that could contradict its reigning picture of reality."[8] If a community receives only positive feedback, it will never be able to discover its weak points or failures. Prophets initiate the process of critical feedback that is necessary for organizational learning. We need to give permission to prophets and their dissenting voices. Stifling holy dissent is a guaranteed way to create bigger problems down the line. "Turn off your radar and you will eventually hit the side of a mountain."[9]

The prophetic function is more than a purely critical one; it can also play an animating, profoundly revitalizing role. In fact, in calling us to repent and change, the prophet opens us up to the ever-renewing encounter with God. Walter Brueggemann therefore rightly characterizes the role of the prophet as one who both criticizes and energizes.[10] These two categories suggest a continuum between criticizing and energizing on which prophetic ministry can be located, which points us to an important distinction: criticizing and energizing are not always given equal attention. Genuine prophetic ministry will always include both, but with different degrees of emphasis. Some who are called to function prophetically may have a more energizing effect to their ministry, while others may operate in a more critical fashion.

A Few Conditions

Because of the challenging nature of the prophetic ministry, it is important to maintain some biblical criteria for discerning the ministry of a prophet.

First, the role of the prophet is to call people back to God. If the God they call us to is made known in Jesus Christ, then faithfulness must be defined as being faithful to Jesus and his mission. To be sure, this includes ethics and social concerns, but it goes beyond that to be fully resonant with God's heart for the nations. Prophets in the new covenant not only call us back to God; they also call us forward to God's preferred future for the world—one defined by the ministry and work of Jesus the Messiah. In other words, it is messianic as well as missional in nature.

Second, criticism is not a license for cynicism. Cynicism denies the possibility of future transformation and keeps prophets from engaging their context. All faithful prophetic ministry should both criticize *and* energize, even if one of those functions receives more emphasis than the other.

The third important qualifier for prophetic ministry is love. Because prophets are the guardians of the covenant, they must maintain a deep-seated, covenantal love for God's people no matter where and in what state they are in. In other words, they live on the edge of the inside.[11] Martin Luther King Jr. was fond of saying that those whom you would change you must first love, and given his specific context in so doing, he demonstrated a profoundly biblical, deeply covenantal, spirit so characteristic of the authentic prophet.

Fourth, critical distance should not translate into permanent distance.[12] The prophetic vocation sometimes has to learn how to be the loyal opposition of remaining connected to the system while consistently challenging and prodding the system toward greater faithfulness.

Fifth, prophets are not infallible, and we are encouraged to always test the prophet's message to see if it is from God. As highly intuitive types, prophets have an uncanny knack for seeing things others cannot, but intuition can be right or wrong. Collective discernment by the community needs to be applied to prophetic insight.

Finally, prophets need to be aware of their humanity and the possible ways that they might actually be contributing to the crisis they so passionately address. Spending time away from the community and inhabiting God's reality through prayer and meditation and identification with those on the margins can blind prophets to the ways in which their own lives and choices may be perpetuating problems within their own context. The mystics were susceptible to an other-worldly ethic that detached them from the life of the everyday. Mediating revelation does not absolve participation in today's reality. Prophetic ministry stands in the gap for sure, but it does so with one foot in God's reality and one foot firmly anchored in the existing reality.

Good Reasons to Get it Right

Mike Kim, a self-confessed "former traditional pastor" in the Evangelical Free Church of America, went on a deep journey of discovery into the power of APEST ministry. These are some of his insights about why prophetic ministry is so necessary:

- *Without the prophetic voice*, we become overly pragmatic and mechanistic in our orientation towards effectiveness and success as a church. From the prophetic perspective, the goals are wrong, and therefore the methods and metrics are too.[13]
- *Without prophetic witness*, most Western Christians don't expect God to speak to us. His voice remains stuck on the pages of a book that only a professional can access and then spoon feed to us.
- *Without prophetic imagination* to show us the possibilities, we don't expect God to perform miracles in our midst and in our present era. There is a concomitant loss of the sense of the God who is Lord of, and who intervenes in, history.
- *Without prophetic urgency*, we don't question status quo and are afraid to disturb social and traditional equilibrium—something that the prophetic consistently did to a stagnating people of God in the Old Testament.
- *Without the prophetic perspective*, eschatological living (where past, present, and future are held together) has also been lost. Eschatological living is the kind that asks "what kind of people should we then be?" (e.g. 2 Peter 3:10–14). The future, as a meaningful concept and motivation, is relegated to a distant reality, not a present one. And thus we function primarily from the past rather than the future in how we live out the present—which slows the pace and flattens the peaks of what can really happen.
- *Without prophetic modelling*, we lose our transformational and radical edge: Prophets always model an alternative Reality. They call us to live differently, to choose God's ways over the ways of the world.
- *Without prophetic spirituality*, our spirituality becomes intellectual, predictable and segmented. We don't embrace mystery and the mysterious aspects of spirituality and of communal life. Faith takes on less and less risk and more and more intellectual assent in pursuit of "certainty" and orthodoxy.

- *And without prophetic longing*, we are content with God being a distant Savior and Creator but lose the sense of him as Lover, Friend, Judge, Comforter, etc. Spirituality becomes about right belief or even right practice—not right relationship [italics added].[14]

Evangelistic Intelligence: Recruiting to the Cause

From what we can gather from observation and scripture, evangelists are always looking to create a positive encounter between people and the core messages of the church, especially the gospel. Generally they spread the message and enlist others to the cause.

The Genius of Evangelists

Their genius—their specific intelligence—is therefore indicated in at least three ways.

EXCEPTIONAL RECRUITERS. The most obvious outcome of the ministry of evangelists is that people are enlisted to the cause of Christ. In other words, the church grows. Evangelists have the capacity to get significant buy-in from their hearers. Although the concept of "salesmen" has negative connotations, Malcolm Gladwell's category of the "salesmen" is highly applicable here: persuasive, viral-type people with seemingly infectious personalities.[15] In terms of the diffusion of ideas and the spread of movements, salesmen are the persuaders—people with significant negotiation skills. They tend to have an indefinable trait that goes beyond what they say and makes others want to agree with them. For this reason, evangelists are agents of conversion.

SOCIAL CONNECTORS. It stands to reason that evangelists are great socializers—the kind of people who can link the rest of us up with the world: "They have a special gift for bringing the world together," Gladwell says, and they "are the "handful of people with a truly extraordinary knack [for] making friends and acquaintances." Gladwell is useful here again in describing these kinds of people as connectors who have the kind of intrinsic confidence, curiosity, sociability, and energy that propel them into new relationships.[16] They seem to have a capacity to make connections with people in a way that demonstrates what organizational psychologist Daniel Goleman calls social as well as emotional intelligence.[17] In many ways, their function is therefore genuinely priestly in that they mediate between God and people as well as between people and people.

Yet the evangelistic ministry goes beyond their priestly capacity for relational engagement. Evangelists also have an affinity for the gospel that makes them adept at applying it to people's unique experience and circumstance.

SHARERS OF GOOD NEWS. This is the obvious function of evangelistic people, but their sharing of good news is an inextricable part of their capacity to understand people and make connections. In effect, evangelism involves making the connections between God and people as well as between people and people. As ministers who work with what John Wesley called "prevenient grace"—the belief that God is involved in everyone's life, calling them to himself in and through Jesus—evangelists help people see God's love and calling in Jesus in their lives and so precipitate the conversion process. This too is an intrinsic aspect of priestly ministry: mediating the knowledge of God.

A Deeper Appreciation, a Wider Application

Of all the APEST vocations, perhaps no other is more subject to caricature than evangelists: obnoxious Ramboesque street evangelists with their sign-here, make-the-deal, bait-and-switch methodology. But this is a one-dimensional parody of evangelists that distorts an irreplaceable ministry and needs to be overcome in order to come to grips with the biblical function.

In his book *Conversion in the New Testament*, Richard Peace provides the useful clue to broadening our understanding when he says that "how we conceive of conversion determines how we do evangelism."[18] According to Peace, the American church has typically understood the nature of conversion through the lens of Paul's instantaneous conversion on the road to Damascus. Consequently, evangelistic ministry for the most part has sought to reproduce that instantaneous, sudden experience of conversion by orchestrating events where people can encounter Jesus for the first time. In many ways, this informs the rationale behind the seeker-sensitive model of church that looks to draw people into a controlled environment so someone (usually a charismatic speaker) can deliver a dynamic message.

Process and Event

Peace expands our understanding of evangelistic ministry by uncovering an additional paradigm of conversion in the New Testament, one that often goes unnoticed because of where it is located and who is being "converted." He demonstrates a paradigm of conversion in the gospel of Mark where the twelve apostles undergo a gradual, incremental process of conversion where they arrive at the true identity of Jesus, and its implications for discipleship, only after a lengthy process of discovery.[19]

John Finney, in *Recovering the Past: Celtic and Roman Mission,* sums up these two paradigms of conversion and their corresponding types of evangelism by using the phrases "road to Emmaus" and "road to Damascus."[20] The road to Emmaus involves process: walking with people through life, eating meals together, discussing Jesus and the meaning of scripture. The road to Damascus looks to provide an event—that critical moment of persuasion and conviction to move people beyond their current place in the journey toward a decision to enter into covenant.

Although process and event are two entirely different approaches to evangelizing, they are both nonetheless legitimate methods of bringing people to a point of conversion.

Recovering a process-based paradigm of conversion expands our view of both evangelism and the ministry profile of an evangelist. If evangelism can also be framed around metaphors of journey, pilgrimage, and quest, then an evangelist is not just a witty communicator who can set people on edge or a verbal jouster who specializes in confrontational, argumentative encounters. The broader, more general portrait of the evangelist is a person who finds great satisfaction in being strategically instrumental in helping someone else move closer to Jesus, no matter what phase of the journey he or she is in.

Those more inclined to engage in process evangelism are likely to be energized by the thought of investing a lot of time, energy, emotions, and sometimes even financial resources in people over an extended period of time. They will have a certain affinity for helping people assess where they are on their spiritual journey, asking thought-provoking questions and providing accurate metaphors and language to talk about God and spirituality.

Presence and Proclamation

Widening our perception about evangelistic ministry to include both process- and event-based approaches raises questions about how the gospel is transmitted from person to person. Just as some evangelists gravitate more toward a process approach, there is also room to differentiate between methods of communicating and delivering the message, between proclamation and presence. Proclamation does not simply mean preaching in the popular sense, it has more to do with bringing something out into the open with our words. This can take place by seeding an idea through metaphors or a story. It can be polished rhetoric or casual conversation. Basically proclamation can take on any form of verbal communication.

One of the reasons evangelism has been routinely narrowed down to the proverbial sales pitch or elevator speech is that the usual approach to sharing the gospel has yet to be refined by the Incarnation (not to mention that it is still based on an overly simplistic understanding of the gospel itself). This is where the prophetic ministry is poised to enrich and broaden our understanding of evangelistic ministry. Some evangelists demonstrate a knack for proclamation, and others take a more incarnational approach by simply being present with people.

Presence is about participating in situations and relationships with the intent of provoking interest in God, spirituality, and the gospel. Presence evangelism has a lot in common with an incarnational impulse: being with people in tangible ways so they can get an idea of what it would be like to hang out with God and Jesus.

Would evangelism have taken on an opportunistic and sometimes pushy dynamic if it had been informed by the logic of the Incarnation? What if evangelists enjoyed frequent, close proximity to the people they were trying to evangelize? Would evangelistic ministry be solely characterized by confrontational encounters if evangelists knew they would see those same people the next week or even the next day? These two categories of presence and proclamation present a continuum of necessary yet obviously different modes of engagement.

We must make an important qualification about presence evangelism. Being present with people can nurture an openness to Jesus, but it cannot by itself communicate the particulars of the founding story of Christianity: an incarnated, crucified, risen, and ascended messiah. Without proclamation, the soil that was cultivated, tilled, and weeded through presence evangelism is left fallow, with no seed to bring forth fruit.[21] This is what demarcates an evangelist who engages in presence evangelism from, say, a prophet, who leans toward incarnational forms of ministry. The difference between the prophet and the evangelist is that the evangelist is not satisfied until the seed of the gospel makes it into the soil and converts are produced. In fact, evangelists see the sharing of the gospel as a climactic point of the relationship.

The Evangelistic Ministry

Just as the prophetic ministry can be located along continuums of different yet equally legitimate features, the evangelistic ministry also carries

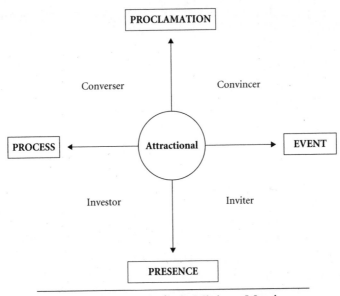

Figure 2.2 Evangelistic Ministry Matrix

within it a degree of complexity that resists a one-dimensional under-standing. These four basic dimensions of evangelistic ministry—process and event, presence and proclamation—come together to demonstrate a variety of vocational dimensions with corresponding evangelistic roles.

This evangelistic matrix shown in Figure 2.2 does not account for the complexity and variety contained within the evangelistic vocation. It does, however, provide a more complex, varied understanding of what evangelistic ministry can look like and therefore a deeper and wider view as to the nature of the evangelistic calling. We need presence and proc-lamation, process and event, and everything in between if we are going to relegitimize this profoundly generative form of ministry. These four continua, when cross-sectioned with each other, suggest four types of evangelistic people with corresponding approaches to evangelism.

INVESTORS. The investor sees evangelism as walking with people through the entire process of conversion, from the beginning of their friendship all the way through conversion and beyond. They gravitate toward a more extended process of exposing people to Jesus. Their tagline is, "Let's walk together." They enter into relationships with people ready to walk with others through all of life's ups and downs. Because they are willing to devote lots of their own time, energy, and emotion in other people, they typically go deep with a few people rather than spreading themselves out with a lot of people. This kind of evangelism demonstrates facets of the gospel related to faithfulness and sacrificial love.

Evangelists of this type are tempted to think they are not evangelistic because of a focus on the more event-based paradigm of conversion. Nevertheless, the staple quality of evangelists is their passion to help lost people move closer to Jesus. Investors do this gradually and methodically through their willingness to pour their life into someone else.

INVITERS. Unlike their more process-oriented counterparts who take a more incremental approach to exposing people to Jesus, inviters woo others to accompany them into strategic environments that allow them greater exposure to Jesus. Investors are more comfortable mediating the gospel primarily through a relationship. They are more prone to triangulate the delivery of the gospel by routing it through other people or events. In this way, inviters are quite catalytic: they bring people and the gospel together by arranging strategic encounters between people and events designed to present the gospel in meaningful ways.

Entreating people to leave their comfort zone and enter into a somewhat foreign environment can be unsettling for most people. But evangelists are often energized by meeting new people. It is this quality that makes them so effective in getting people whose social bearings steer them away from new experiences and relationships to literally walk with them into new environments. They have the unique ability to make the often intimidating experience of being introduced to new people and environments appealing and enjoyable.

Going along with this form of evangelism is the somewhat intuitive ability to soften the potentially abrasive pathway of entering a new group of people. Inviters specialize in the art of inclusion, making them invaluable to any missional venture. Because they know how to attract people, they also intuitively know what can potentially repel people.

Two scriptural figures who operated as inviters were Andrew and the women at the well (John 1:40–41; John 4). They all had a "come-and-see" quality to their evangelistic ministry that brought others into closer proximity to Jesus. Inviters are especially good at gathering people together for common social activities like meals, parties, recreation, and even community projects and service. They generate traffic and direct it to social spaces where relationships can be formed.

CONVINCERS. Convincers are particularly adept at making persuasive and compelling presentations of the gospel. They have confidence in the gospel and champion its power to change people. They believe that exposure to the gospel can, and will, radically transform people.

In contrast to evangelists who gravitate toward more of a style of presence, convincers are less likely to shy away from situations that require explaining and even defending the gospel. They are energized by the task of persuading and convincing others of their point of view. They find great satisfaction in debunking false notions of the gospel, effectively removing the cultural stigma that is often attached to Jesus and the church.

Apollos is a good example of someone who was naturally drawn toward proclaiming the gospel in convincing, and even confrontational ways (Acts 18:24–27).[22] He refuted people in public debate, convincing various Jewish people that Jesus was the Messiah. On a more persuasive yet less argumentative side of things, Phillip the evangelist serves as a model of a more event-based proclamation style of evangelism. His time in Samaria and encounter with the Ethiopian Eunuch demonstrate an entrepreneurial, itinerant, compelling, and obviously persuasive kind of evangelistic ministry (Acts 8).

Convincers have a capacity to proclaim the gospel within a limited, focused period of time. When we use the term *event*, we are not necessarily referring to a church gathering. An event is a specific time frame in which the message of the gospel is poured out with dynamic force, prompting a decision to move closer to Jesus. These moments could be during Bible study, a conversation, a meal, or a random divine appointment where a convincer perceives someone is ready to hear about Jesus.

Convincers' capacity to deliver the gospel in concise presentations is tied up in their ability to formulize the gospel and package it in ways that hone its accessibility and practicality. James Choung's four circles are a good example of how a convincer will compress the meaning and significance of the gospel into metaphors, illustrations, and diagrams that allow people to grasp some of the essential thrust of the gospel and communicate it in focused, concise ways.[23]

This tendency of convincers to formulize and effectively codify the gospel often leads them to develop evangelistic training materials.[24]

CONVERSERS. Not everyone is ready to have an intense, concentrated encounter with the gospel. Some people need to be exposed gradually to the message in ways that allow them to process and internalize its meaning and significance for their lives. Conversers are especially equipped for this because, like investors, they are more comfortable with helping someone discover the meaning of the gospel in an incremental fashion.

Conversers are most comfortable talking about Jesus when the dialogue is shaped by the other person's interests and context. They are more comfortable with dialogue than monologue, with offering sound-bites about Jesus rather than an entire album or Jesus CD. Conversers are sensitive to the contingencies of people's lives and feel most natural in sharing the gospel when they are navigating the emergent dynamics of conversation. They are often good at asking questions and listening, and they prefer to let the needs and interests of the other person decide what particular feature of the gospel they will emphasize or introduce into the conversation. Their ability to expose people to the gospel incrementally often prolongs the relationship and allows people to learn at their own pace. A biblical example of the converser is Jesus with the women at the well (John 4).

The Evangelist's Orbit

Although evangelists are usually based in a local community, they also reach out from there into the broader society. They have more direct social contact with not-yet-Christian people than the other types, except perhaps Pauline-style apostles, a topic we discuss in Chapter Six. At the very least, the evangelistic engagement is much more deeply personal than that of the apostolic engagement.

The orbit of evangelists is generally in and around a local or regional church, but certainly a case can be made for roving, translocal itinerant evangelists. Philip, George Whitfield, Charles Finney, and Billy Graham come to mind.

Whatever the range of operation, evangelists have to work with local communities because although they are adept at bringing new people in, they typically struggle to integrate them into the community. This is partly due to their more theologically and socially outgoing (generative) orientation. They are not wired for the more integrative functions of the shepherd, whose primary orientation is to foster a sense of community and belonging. Evangelistic people specialize in recruiting, but they are not designed for retention. This function falls more to the shepherding vocation.

Shepherd Intelligence: Creating Empathic Community

With the rise of the pastoral theology movement in the 1970s, along with millennia-old traditions of practice, perhaps more is understood about the pastoral ministry than all the others. The only other contender for first place is the teaching ministry. In the light of this, we will not try to give anything but the most basic of definitions here to be able to explore how the shepherd role relates within the APEST system.

The term *shepherd* is used throughout the Old Testament to categorize various types of leaders (kings and priests) and, significantly, that of Yahweh himself—he being the Shepherd of Israel. Along with its metaphorical quality, the concept of shepherd comes to us with a rich interpretive framework that can easily fund the imagination and provoke almost endless analogies and insight about leadership and followership. The oddity, though, is that while the word *poimen* (shepherd) is used eighteen times in the New Testament, only once does it describe the ministry function of Christians; rather, it refers mainly to the person and work of Jesus. Despite this strong restriction of the term, it has pretty much captured our thinking when it comes to church leadership and other organizational arrangements. This means that contrary to the APE types, which require us to reconstruct a sound comprehension of these ministries, we probably have to do a lot of deconstruction here to arrive at a biblical understanding. The catch-all nature of the term obscures the central functions of shepherd, especially considered in relation to the other roles.

Formation in Christ: Local and Communal

At its core, the shepherd is tasked with creating a healthy community, with nurturing people in the faith, and caring for the welfare of the people. Perhaps one of the best ways to articulate the essence of the shepherding function is summed up in the word *formation* in the way of Christ, lived locally and communally. This impulse to nurture and protect the community leads us to say that shepherds operate primarily out of a communal impulse. They are invigorated by a sense of cohesion, inclusiveness, and stability. In a sense, they are the ecclesial equivalent of an organization's human resource department.

Shepherds pay close attention to their immediate environment, noticing details about people and the state of the community. They necessarily have strong empathic aptitudes and heightened capacities for meaningful friendship and relationships. For instance, drawing on what is called Dunbar's rule, which states that relational networks are maxed out between 120 and 150 people, Neil Cole says that a pastor's ministry is likely limited to around 120 people. To be a good shepherd in any sense of the word, pastors have to know all the names and the stories of the people in their care.[25] Although this does not exclude a broader shepherd-of-shepherds (*pastor et pastorium*) role that allows a larger pastoral organization, it does highlight that calling oneself a pastor or shepherd yet not knowing the personal details of the people in one's orbit probably disqualifies one from being a shepherd in any meaningful sense of the term. This alone should cause concern in the way we tend to use the term.

Because of their great sense of and need for cohesion and unity, shepherds will find it disheartening when people leave the community—for good or not-so-good reasons. In many ways, this echoes the heart of our Lord when he goes in search of the one (Luke 15:4–5). People, even (or perhaps especially) the most unlikely, most vulnerable, and most insignificant ones, matter to shepherds. The dark side of the sense of, and need for, harmony is that shepherds/pastors can often avoid conflict in the name of keeping the peace. (There is a difference between peacekeeping and peacemaking.) They also tend to be passive-aggressive because they are generally expected to be "nice," civil people. Hence when this need to impose harmony manifests darkly, it creates a stifling need for conformity with little patience for dissenting voices.

Although this book is largely dedicated to the recovery of the APE, especially the apostolic function, it is not our intention in any way to sideline the two functions of shepherd and teacher. As far as we are concerned, it is hard to see how a local church can sustain itself without shepherds over the long term. In fact, without the vital role of shepherds, it is hard to see how to sustain Christian witness at all. But shepherds who exclude other forms undermine their own capacities in the process. Therefore, the role must be limited to its biblical proportions lest it overreach itself.

The Missional Shepherd?

We are often asked what the role of the shepherd is in the missional church. If their ministry is primarily focused on the people of God, do they have a part to play in the broader purposes of the church, especially now that the church in the West is having to be recalibrated along missional lines? Can there be a missional shepherd/pastor? The answer has to be a definitive yes.

Not only is the church itself the product of the mission of God, but it can never hope to be the church that Jesus intended if it does not exist to participate in what God is doing in the world. Therefore, the term *missional* can be used to describe the faith itself, as in "missional Christianity." It is an important term that ought to be comprehensively applied. So, for instance, the function of mission (God's purposes in the world, especially in and through the church) must determine various forms in which ecclesiology must manifest. The term *missional* qualifies the role of the shepherd as much as it qualifies the other APEST functions.

Shepherding, like any other ministry, can never function in isolation or as an end in itself. It fulfills itself in relation to God's purposes and by realizing its role within the body of Christ. A shepherd's role in relation to the flock is to ensure that the sheep are healthy, to be sure, but in the end, health must ultimately be measured in terms of numerical increase. A sheep farmer that does not ensure healthy reproduction of sheep (the natural measure of fruitfulness) will not be long in the business of farming.

Another way is for the shepherd to participate in and through the extension ministries of the other members of the body—particularly those of apostle and evangelist. Ephesians 4:16 says as much: "From him the whole body, joined and held together by every supporting ligament, grows and builds itself up in love, as each part does its work." Trying to be all things from within one role is likely to lead to failure in the very task one is actually called to. Not only is this a recipe for burnout, but it is likely to lead to being unfaithful to what Jesus has determined in the first place: each of us has received our callings "as Christ apportioned it" (Ephesians 4:7), and in Christ's ecclesia, none is greater than the other. Overreaching our roles amounts to being untrue to our proper vocation. That is, once again, a reason to circumscribe the pastoral role to its biblical definitions to make vocational space for the others Jesus has called and gifted.

Teacher Intelligence: Bringing Wisdom and Understanding

Much is known about the art of teaching and the role of the educator in the various domains that make up life in the world. Education is basic to life in the West, and we are indelibly shaped by its power. In the church, theologians and preachers have long held a privileged status and have a powerful impact on our collective imaginations. Nevertheless, the historical impact of doctrinal theological controversies throughout our history, along with the countless associated schisms and conflict, is ample evidence that teachers have not always had a good impact on the people of God. Of course, many have, but we cannot deny that some of the most toxic religion has come from bad teaching and from people who want to engage in mind-control tactics. Truly does St. James warn, in no uncertain words, of the power of ideologues to bring demonic destruction in human life (James 3:1–5).

The warnings here should give us a direct clue to the central importance of mediating ideas in the church, as well as a good reason that the teaching ministry needs to be brought into biblical perspective. We need to adopt the same deconstructive approach to teachers as we have taken with shepherds if we are to demarcate the role in ways that the Bible itself intends.

At its core, the teaching function is about mediating a particular type of wisdom and understanding nuanced by the biblical worldview. As teaching expresses itself in church circles, it is about helping people gain insight into how God wants them to see and experience their world. As such, it is concerned with theological truth and shaping the consciousness of God's people to be consistent with that truth.

In many ways, teachers are similar to prophets, and apostles, in that they all deal with ideas that shape life. The difference perhaps is that teachers are concerned more about broad comprehension and systematic understanding as opposed to faithfulness to the covenant (prophets) and the nest of more foundational and formative ideas that apostles hover over with a strong sense of custodial responsibility. Besides, a sure sign of the difference is that teachers do not have that sense of urgency that instills the apostolic and the prophetic ministries. Teachers are not concerned with how long learning takes; their main aim is that learners come to a fuller understanding, and that such learning can only be conceived as a lifelong process. (We think that if it were solely up to teachers, the seminary process, now around four years, would likely extend to ten years.)

But because of its primary commitment to ideas, of all the ministries the teacher is probably the most susceptible to being ideological—something that almost always privileges ideas at the expense of people. In the New Testament, the scribes and pharisees (the resident ideologues in Jesus's day) come in for some severe criticism. (See, for example, Matthew 15:1–16.)

We believe it is necessary to make a distinction here between the teacher in the more philosophic Hellenistic tradition and in the more existential Hebraic one so that we can understand how to transfer faith in a meaningful, life-oriented way.

For the Hebrews, and by extension the Bible itself, ideas are not important in themselves. Hebraic sensibilities do not allow for mere speculation on ideas divorced from life and ethics; it is impossible to find any such speculation on the nature of being (ontology) in all the scriptures. The teaching ministry as the Bible intends it is more inclined to be oriented toward life and obedience than toward ideas divorced from life and context. For instance, endless discourse on why "kingdom of heaven" is used in Matthew and "kingdom of God" in the other gospels may be intellectually stimulating, but if it does not lead us to be more open to the rule of God in our contexts, we cannot really say we stand-under (understand) the text.

For biblical teachers, their lives are to be their primary messages, and they speak with the authority of people who can live what they speak; these are the true rabbis. Teaching is not about speculation of ideas in themselves (idealism); rather, it is about the ministry of ideas in action (ethos), that is, discipleship or formation. We cannot teach what we do not know, and we cannot lead where we will not go. Therefore, biblical teachers must have real participation in the ideas they propose.

If this is true (and from a biblical perspective, we believe that arguing against it is hard), then it should raise significant questions about the legitimacy of what goes by the name of the teaching ministry in our churches. This is not to deny a need for serious scholars to engage the deeply philosophical issues of our day or to maintain the primacy of the pulpit. But to make speculative capacities the standard form of theological reflection, as well as an immutable basis for ministry, moves us away from discipleship to ideology and can account for our nearly systematic failure to produce disciples in Western churches. As Dallas Willard says, we are educated way beyond our own capacity to obey.[26] The Celtic movement, started by Patrick, Columbanus, Aiden, and others, combined mission, learning, and discipleship in a profoundly biblical way is rightly credited with "saving civilization," evangelizing Europe, and founding liberal arts education rooted in the Hebraic worldview.[27]

All this has significant implications for our methods of formation—our pedagogy. Methods matter. We are perfectly designed to achieve what we are currently achieving—the fruit of the tree speaks volumes about the nature of the tree itself. If we remove action from the equation of learning, we end up with an academic understanding of the faith and little by way of genuine discipleship. And if the people teaching cannot actually do what they are requiring of others, they will exacerbate the problem.

We have been somewhat critical here because once again, we believe that theologians have pretty much monopolized how we have defined ministry and think about God and faith, and we believe that this accounts for many of the problems the church in the West now faces: immaturity and trended decline. We suggest that the current arrangement that champions the didactic role at the expense of the other ministries needs to experience a decentering, with a subsequent recentering around the other life-giving vocations in the APEST typology. Teaching is indispensable to the health of the community, but contrary to what is happening today, the teacher should not be the axis around which the community revolves.

Jesus never intended it to be so dominant in the mix—a fact attested to its being mentioned last in Ephesians 4:11.

We need vibrant and engaging teaching that should be resituated within a field of practice and with a keener concern to training in context. Mastery is bound up not in those who can expound ideas but in reflective practitioners who engage in their disciplines accompanied with guided reflection. Perhaps one of the critical roles of teachers in a missional community is to provide the environments and processes for this reflection to take place. For instance, Forge Mission Training Network, the missional movement started by Alan and others in Australia, is built squarely on these principles—in context, action reflection, and led by practitioner-teachers, for example.[28] Ideas come alive when put into practice.

The Genius of the Church

Having given some definition to the various APEST ministries and aptitudes, we can now see the spiritual power of these as they are brought together to create a corporate intelligence in the church. (See Table 2.1 at the end of this chapter.)

Looking at the various forms of APEST intelligences as a whole and in systemic relation to each other makes it possible to see the importance of having them all in the ministry mix. It is hard to see how we could possibly survive, let alone thrive, without a fivefold APEST ministry.

In fact, serious dysfunction will inevitably occur when one form of ministry becomes hegemonic. Partly this is because one form cannot possibly represent the whole ministry of Christ in the world, but partly because there will be no balancing in the leadership equation, and all the dysfunctions will come to the fore. For example, when one form of APEST leadership is dislocated from the others, it will tend to monopolize the culture and have a negative effect in the long run. The one-leader type of church is most at risk in this case, but we can recall organizations that demonstrate the truth of this—for instance:

- A/PEST: If an apostolic leader dominates, the church or other organization will tend to be hard-driving, autocratic, with lots of pressure for change and development, and will leave lots of wounded people in its wake. It is not sustainable and will tend to dissolve with time.
- P/AEST: If the prophetic leaders dominates, the organization will be one-dimensional (always harking back to one or two issues), will likely be factious and sectarian, will have a "superspiritual" vibe, or, somewhat paradoxically, will tend to be either too activist to be

sustainable or too quietist to be useful. This is not a viable form of organization.

- E/~~APST~~: When an evangelistic leader dominates, the organization will have an obsession with numerical growth, will create dependence on effervescent charismatic leadership, and will tend to lack theological breadth and depth. This type of organization will not empower many people.

- S/~~APET~~: When pastoral leadership monopolizes, the church or other organization will tend to be risk averse, codependent and needy, and overly lacking in healthy dissent and therefore creativity. Such an organization will lack innovation and generativity and will not be able to be transfer its core message and tasks from one generation to the next.

- T/~~APES~~: When teachers and theologians rule, the church will be ideological, controlling, moralistic, and somewhat uptight. A rationalistic, doctrine-obsessed, Christian gnosticism (the idea that we are saved by what we know) will tend to replaces reliance on the Holy Spirit. These types of organization will be exclusive based on ideology like that of the pharisees.

Once again, it might be useful to use more creational, nonecclesiastical terms to reconsider the power of an integrated, multidimensional leadership team (Figure 2.3).

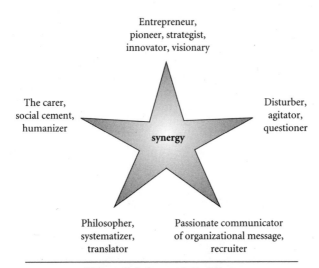

Figure 2.3 Synergistic Team

Any organization that is able to bring together, encourage, and capture the energies of a team comprising all the intelligences will succeed in whatever it is seeking to achieve. If this is true for the secular world, it is even truer for the church. Each of the APEST vocations adds a necessary ingredient to the overall missional fitness and maturity of the church, but each needs to be informed and shaped by the others in order to anchor the church in the fullness of Christ's nature and mission.

In many ways, we are talking about a theological and practical reality found in two biblical metaphors. The theological reality is that the bride of Christ is called to be holy and pure, and this bride must be ready, complete, pristine, and unsullied. The second metaphor is that of the body of Christ. The church is the manifestation of Jesus, allowing the world to see who Jesus was and how he functioned when we have all parts of the body working together. However, for far too long, the church has been offering an incomplete picture of who Jesus is because the picture has become so weighted to teachers and shepherds. By exiling APEs within this metaphor, we are jettisoning Jesus from our midst and all the things that Jesus was able to do in those APE ministries.

Can you imagine Jesus not pioneering new frontiers and innovating new ways of being on mission together? Can you imagine him not speaking truth to power or questioning the religious status quo? Can you imagine him not calling new people into the kingdom? Yet those elements are largely missing from churches' understandings and practices of ministry in the body of Christ.

It's about holiness and purity.

It's about presence and functioning as Jesus functioned.

It's about being who God created us to be as both his body and bride.

Table 2.1 The APEST Ministries

	Apostle	Prophet	Evangelist	Shepherd	Teacher
Core vocation	Custodian of DNA Pioneer Entrepreneur Architect	Guardian of the covenant Questioner of the status quo	Connector to cause Recruiter Entrepreneur Raconteur	Nurturer Humanizer Sustainer Social integrator	Mediator of wisdom and understanding Trainer-educator Theological formation
Impulse	Missional	Incarnational	Attractional	Communal	Instructional
Effect	Propagate	Incarnate	Aggregate	Integrate	Explicate
Focus	A viable future and expansion of the Christian movement	God orientation: Keeping the movement aligned with God	That people come to know God and join the movement	The community living healthily in the love of the triune God	Awareness and integration of truth, especially revealed truth
Spirituality-character complex	Adventurous and futuristic Has anarchitectural/systemic sensibility, with an emphasis on risk	Transcendent and existential Has a strong intuition of what is right and wrong and emphasizes integrity, obedience, and mystery	Relational and communal Emphasis on novelty, sociality, playfulness, and celebration	Nurturing and communal, with an emphasis on healing, wholeness, and community	Intellectual and philosophical, with an emphasis on curiosity, learning, knowledge, and the intellect

(Continued)

Table 2.1 The APEST Ministries (Continued)

	Apostle	Prophet	Evangelist	Shepherd	Teacher
Leadership style	Decisive Design focused Strategic	Demonstrative Motivational	Persuasive Motivational	Inclusive Collaborative	Prescriptive Analytical
Overriding concerns when making decisions	Will this help increase our capacity for mission?	Will this help us embody God's concerns?	Will this help us bring people to a point of conversion?	How will this affect the organization and people in the community?	How does this line up with theology and scripture?
Metrics for success	Healthy and systematic extension of Christianity within and beyond cultural boundaries Church multiplication	Faithfulness to God's values through visible and tangible actions and consciousness of God's character and presence	Growth through individual and group conversion and in increasing the number of adherents in the movement	People's experience of a sense of belonging, intimacy, and personal transformation	Adequate engagement with, comprehension of, and consistency with truth in all its forms
How it contributes to the health of a movement	Ensuring consistency with core ideas Laying new foundations and designing systems around mobilization and extension	Anchoring the movement in God's values and providing critical feedback for constant realignment	Explicitly valuing the gospel as our core story Adding new people Sharing the message in the local vernacular	Cultivating and integrating people into a socially cohesive community that fosters relational health and discipleship	Systematizing and articulating the multidimensional aspects of truth Optimizing operational efficiency

	Driven, demanding, and insensitive to others	Ideological and demanding, short-sighted, simplistic	Anything to "make the deal" Not demanding enough	Obsessive need for harmony and aversion to risk	Demand for ideology conformity and lack of urgency
Shortcomings					
Slogan	Onward and upward	Repent and believe	Join the party	Love one another	Take time to know God
Likely Meyers-Briggs personality typing	ENTJ, INTJ, INTP, ENTP	INTP, INFP, ISFP	ENFP, ENFJ	ISFJ, ESFJ	ISTJ, ESTJ
Historical exemplars	Jesus, Paul, Peter, Patrick, John Wesley, Aimee Semple McPherson	Jesus, Jeremiah, James, St. Benedict, Martin Luther, Dietrich Bonhoeffer, Martin Luther King Jr.	Jesus, Phillip, George Whitfield, Billy Graham, Rick Warren	Jesus, St. Francis, Jean Vanier, Mother Teresa, Eugene Peterson	Jesus, Apollos, Augustine, Aquinas, John Calvin, Henri Nouwen

3

Better Together

THE SYNERGY OF DIFFERENCE

Man is not a mere individual but is his community. The man in Christ is ontologically bound to the ecclesial reality.
Urban Holmes

Fear of difference is fear of life itself. It is possible to conceive of conflict as not necessarily a wasteful outbreak of incompatibilities but a normal process by which socially valuable differences register themselves for the enrichment of all.
Mary Parker Follett

The idea of a life-sharing community which is much more than a human association of the like-minded, a mutual insurance of common interest, and more too than the sum of its several parts and members, is essential to Christianity.
R.E.O. White

MARK CONNER, A FRIEND AND A LEADER OF CITI LIFE CHURCH in Melbourne, Australia, is deeply committed to building his leaders into a team that appreciates and values each other's differences and unique perspectives. Here is one of the team exercises he uses illustrates the importance of diversity: he places an object (say, a statue) in the middle of a round table and asks people to share what they see. He notes that three things happen. First, everyone sees the object differently. Second, no one sees it accurately because each one sees it from where he or she sits. And finally, the only way everyone can see it accurately is when each person listens to everyone else's perspective. Without multiple perspectives, this exercise shows, we cannot develop an accurate view of the challenges and opportunities in front of us. This is true in every area of life and ministry—for problem solving, decision making, vision creation, and strategic planning.

It was the pioneering leadership studies guru W.C.H. Prentice who once noted that leaders succeed because they have learned two basic lessons: people are complex, and people are different. That is precisely the reason it is important to enlist the motivation and active participation of everyone in an organization.[1] Honoring diversity positions the leader to tap into the vast unused, largely dormant reservoirs of human capital.

This point applies directly to the APEST model. To function primarily out of a constricted shepherd/teacher (ST) model ignores a vast surplus of spiritual and human capital contained within the apostolic/prophetic/evangelist (APE) ministries. If we reactivate the potential of APEST, it will not just revolutionize our understanding of the church; it will position us for the permanent revolution that Jesus intended (Ephesians 4:12–16).

The Multifaceted Gospel

In Chapter One, we made a case that APEST is in fact an extension of the ministry of Christ through the body of Christ. So it should not be surprising that each of the APEST typologies brings out different aspects of the gospel itself. For instance, prophets tend to gravitate toward definitions of the gospel that focus on covenant faithfulness, justice, and restoration. Shepherds highlight forgiveness, healing, and perhaps the communal aspects of the work of Christ. Teachers likely focus on the implications for worldview and ideological perspective. Evangelists, true to their calling to be recruiters, catalysts, and the bearers of good news, emphasize the call to trust in Jesus, be saved, and to give one's life to his cause. Apostles highlight the seminal nature of the gospel and how it informs and motivates the church.

Each ministry vocation acts like a facet of the gospel's diamond, and each brings a unique perspective, insight, and contribution to the life of the church. While our understanding of the gospel is enriched by our various vocational perspectives, it will also be constricted by the narrowing concerns and perspectives of each individual calling. The ministry of the church is meant to be multifaceted; when each perspective is taken on its own, divorced from the rest, and perceived to be the whole, a one-dimensional and incomplete understanding of the gospel will result. Many of the battles of the church can be understood as stemming from this inability to see a theological issue from a broader perspective.[2]

Each ministry brings its own unique contribution to the task of the church; it can also be said that each brings out the different qualities of the other. In dealing with issues related to foundational ministries, we need to note that there are particular relationships and synergies latent in the partnerships between the apostolic and the other two marginalized ministries: the prophetic and the evangelistic. This explores the uniqueness of these connections. We begin by looking at the close association of the prophet and the apostle.

Prophetic Intelligence for Apostolic Architecture

Paul declares in both explicit teaching and implicit modeling (which is the way he operates) that the church is built on the foundation of the apostles and prophets (Ephesians 2:20).[3] As you will no doubt guess, for similar hermeneutical reasons used in Ephesians 4, we reject the traditionalist, procrustean interpretation that this applies only to the original apostles and prophets.[4] There is clearly a partnership between the two that moves beyond a random pairing to something essential for the ongoing, foundational health of the movement itself. Two obvious questions come to mind. Why this is the case? And how do these two ministries relate to one another?

Edge Workers Inc.

We can see an essential as well as functional relationship between apostles and prophets in the New Testament:

Acts 13:1–4	Indicates the role that prophets played in key apostolic decisions.
Acts 15:32	Prophets affirm what God is doing in the Gentile mission in Antioch.
Acts 15:40	Paul partners with the prophet Silas.
Acts 21:8–11	Paul receives prophetic guidance and warning (Agabus).
Ephesians 2:20	Paul's central affirmation that the church is "built on the foundations of apostles and prophets" substantiates what was common practice and observation in the Jesus movement.
Ephesians 4:11	Affirms the essentially fivefold nature of the church's ministry.
1 Corinthians 12:28	Indicates the foundational role of apostles and prophets (listed first) in relation to the other gifts.

We think that part of the explanation for this persistent link between prophets and apostles is found in their similar roles of being generators of new forms of thinking and doing: both are generative forms of ministry. And both end up raising uncomfortable questions about the status quo but for different reasons. Their respective visions differ in nature; one is grounded in holy discontent and arises out of the demand of faithfulness to God, the other grounded in the urgency arising from the *missio Dei* (that is, the missionary God, the sent and sending One) and the integrity of the church as its key agency.

As we shall explore in great detail later in the book, there is an intrinsically entrepreneurial orientation in the apostolic calling—an aptitude that enables apostles to generate innovative ways to resolve problems and exploit new opportunities. But theologically, there is a world of difference between simply pursuing a great idea for the wrong reasons and pursuing a good idea for the right reasons. This is where the prophetic function so naturally complements the apostolic function: because of their spiritual sensitivity, prophets provide the necessary guidance and accountability so that the apostolic person might engage in authentic missional innovation and not simply entrepreneurialism for its own sake. This squares completely with our own experience in the broader church as well as personally. For instance Debra, Alan's wife, is constantly bringing a prophetic challenge and viewpoint to Alan's more apostolic ministry. It certainly is foundational to movements like New Covenant Ministries International in setting up what they call apostolic-prophetic teams.

Recall what we said in the Chapter Two about the nature of prophetic intelligence (see Figure 2.1): that prophets sense the gap between God's vision for the world and the status quo, and they call us to narrow the gap in the name of faithfulness to God and his cause.

Just as prophets have a high level of intolerance for gaps between value and reality, so apostles are intolerant of passivity in the face of the challenge to fulfill their calling as church in the world. This makes them want to work to help close the gap that the prophets intuit (see Figure 2.1). Add to this their natural aptitudes for pioneering and their sense of sentness, and it is clear that they are distinctly missional entrepreneurs.[5] This apostolic-entrepreneurial connection with prophetic intelligence is illustrated in Figure 3.1.

Apostolic people naturally pursue the opportunities, but prophets ensure that they take the right pathway to get there. The prophet, in other words, provides the necessary intelligence to guide apostolic decision making, direction, and design. By asking the right questions and calling for faithfulness to God's intent, purpose, and design, prophets play a crucial role in keeping the church on track.[6] This type of relationship is confirmed through countless conversations we have had with partnerships between

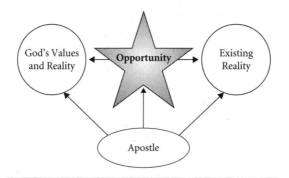

**Figure 3.1 Apostolic Entrepreneurialism Triggered by
Prophetic Intelligence**

apostolic and prophetic people. Certainly it is true to my (Alan's) experience with Debra. Her prophetic intuition and warnings to me have been profound in helping guide my apostolically leaning ministry. Tim has similar experiences with his wife, who is also prophetic in nature.

No leadership function is designed to function alone. Because of their catalytic role in the system, apostles especially need the other ministry vocations to be able to operate in a humble, mature, and efficient way. And prophets, because they are sensitive to God and his values, are best equipped to play this unique role with apostles. They serve to call apostolic entrepreneurialism away from pragmatism toward true faithfulness.

This is clearly evident in the New Testament itself, and it squares with experience in both historical and contemporary movements.[7] New Covenant Ministries International places the apostle-prophet relationship at the heart of the movement's approach to mission.[8] For instance, it requires that all new church planting projects be started by a team of apostles and prophets. It is also a methodological cornerstone for members of the Order of Mission, the international missional network of which Mike Breen is the senior guardian. By building APEST into its lifeshapes system—a formation process that lies at the very basis of the organization's approach—it ensures that these relationships are rightly understood and honored.[9]

Going Out, Going Deep

There is another way to understand the nature of the apostolic and prophetic as being foundational and in inextricable partnership. As we have seen, prophets reproach all forms of superficiality, especially when it comes to God and the things he is concerned with. A major characteristic of prophetic ministry therefore is a call to go deep, to identify with culture and place through participation in the local rhythms of that context. It is because of this call to depth that the prophetic ministry is best associated with the incarnational aspects of mission. Incarnational approaches also require that we go deep, take culture seriously, and go to the heart of the matter. Furthermore, incarnational ministry requires prophetic patience and attentiveness to what God is already doing in neighborhoods and people's lives, and it honors the need for justice and shalom among peoples. This is the very stuff of biblical prophecy.

As the person delegated with guardianship over the missional (sent by God and sending agency) impulse, the apostolic is vocationally responsible for maintaining the outgoing impulses of the church. These two impulses—the missional (going out) and the incarnational (going deep)—associated as they are with the respective ministries of apostles and prophets provide two vital dimensions for a foundation for ecclesia (Figure 3.2). One demands breadth and extension, and the other requires depth and rootedness. They are the warp and woof of mission

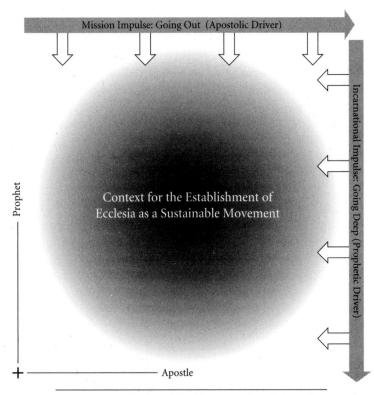

Figure 3.2 Missional and Incarnational Impulse

and together create the foundations on which movements are built. The connection between the apostolic and prophetic goes beyond their vocational chemistry as outliers: they combine to provide the movement with its most basic support structure: the foundation.

As the apostle goes forward, the prophet helps keep the apostle grounded in God's reality and provides critical feedback through questions and observations. As the prophet goes deep, the apostle reminds the prophet of the grander missional objectives of extension and multiplication. Without the apostle, there would be no real movement or extension, and the church might drift into a socialized gospel that has little regard for the missional objective of catalyzing movements, disciple making, and church planting. But without the prophet, the movement might tend to become shallow and lack the spiritual funding required to transform its host environments radically. Apostles and prophets are both foundational and work best in reflexive environments where each is supported and challenged by the other. The dialectic between the two ministries is thus vital for the health and sustainability of ecclesia as movement. The new monastic movement associated with Shane Claiborne, Jonathan Wilson Hartgrove, and Scott Bessenecker, for example, tends toward the prophetic-incarnational, while the church planting movements associated with Mike Breen of 3DM, Neil Cole of Church Multiplication Associates, and Jeff Vanderstelt of Soma Communities, among others, tend to the apostolic-missional. Missional-incarnational movements seek to combine the two impulses' understanding that each is a correlative of the other.

Ensuring Growth: Avoiding the Iron Law of Involution

Having explored something of the special relationship of the apostolic and the prophetic, it is necessary to probe into the largely unexplored relationship between the two ministries that are most responsible for church growth and movement extension: the apostolic and the evangelistic. How are they similar, how are they different, and how can we tell them apart?

One of the concepts in social movement theory is the iron law of involution, which maintains that because social movements (religious or otherwise) are strongly ideological and radical in nature, they need to achieve tangible outcomes in terms of their perceived mission or else face inevitable disintegration into sects and splinter institutions.[10] Involution thus happens when a revolution recoils back on itself because it does not have the impact it seeks. By fostering growth and achieving desired outcomes in their own ways, the apostolic and the evangelistic ministries work against the forces of social disintegration. Instead of involution, which a system dominated by shepherds and teachers will likely produce, they maintain the impetus needed for a permanent revolution.[11]

There can be no doubt that the so-called church growth movement was one the greatest movements of God in the past century, and it remains so. Almost single-handedly, it has reversed the hemorrhaging of the church that had resulted from the loss of the evangelistic ministry and the stifling conservatism of mid-twentieth-century evangelicalism, and it has given the church a way through the corrosive effects of the secular, death-of-God theology of the 1960s. The profoundly seminal thinking of missiologist Donald McGavran led to a thorough restructuring of the church by the many theorists and practitioners who came after him.

In effect, McGavran's work was instrumental in reorganizing the church around the lost function of evangelism. For instance, the "seeker-sensitive movements" of the 1980s and 1990s put evangelism at front and center of the church's purpose in the world. Gone was the church conceived purely as a teaching and pastoral center. Gone was the outsourcing of evangelism to the many parachurches that had popped up in the twentieth century—Youth for Christ, Navigators, Campus Crusade, and the like.[12] The local church took evangelism seriously again. The age of the evangelist-leader was upon us, along with contemporary worship, the megachurches, and church outreach. And it has been a remarkable phenomenon: tens of millions of people have been evangelized as a result.

The reason we raise this bit of history is to highlight not only the vital link between the two ministries (and there clearly are similarities) but also the important differences. In our experience it appears that the two distinct ministries of apostle and evangelist, even when and where they are taken seriously, are almost always confused. Loss of clarity in strategically important times and issues is always a problem. So when evangelism is thought to be synonymous with apostolic ministry, not only is apostolic ministry effectively co-opted to the evangelistic (which is the more understood), but the possibility of the much-needed apostolic impact is seriously diminished by default. This is not to minimize the critical ministry of the evangelist; rather, we mean to help contribute to the church's understanding of apostolic ministry, which is devastatingly underdeveloped. Clearly this confusion needs to be cleared up if we are to reengage apostolic ministry in our churches.

Understanding the Differences Between Apostles and Evangelists

To truly understand the meaning and impact of both apostolic and evangelist ministries and their interrelationship, we need to understand how they are different. Here are some of the main differences as we see them.

The core apostolic task (not an office) is to extend Christianity as a whole. As the primary custodian of the DNA of the church, apostles are called to advance the cause as an integrated faith system, as well as establish it in new contexts. Evangelists, on the other hand, are recruiters to the cause: they are gifted with the ability to catalyze faith in Jesus and thereby gain new adherents to the movement. Apostles and evangelists are therefore different in motivation and outcome.

Apostles almost always catalyze movement primarily through mission and church planting, whereas evangelists create church growth by adding people to the movement through conversions. The impact is clearly different. For instance, when Bill Hybels is on record as stating that Willow Creek does not do church planting, he is indicating that his primary vision and motivation is evangelistic, not apostolic. This certainly does not diminish his leadership and influence; it simply qualifies it. He is possibly one of the greatest evangelistic leaders of our age and leads one of the most influential movements, but that does not mean he is apostolic. One of the clearest pointers of authentic apostolic ministry, particularly Pauline versions, is church planting.

Organizational Design—Addition or Multiplication?

Although both evangelistic and apostolic leadership are growth oriented, they tend to design the systems they lead differently because of the differences in calling, motivation, and technique. The evangelistic person tends to design an organization that will transfer the message en masse as well as well incorporate additional converts to the community. The apostolic person will likely design in order to mobilize converts into the ongoing mission and to extend the church's reach. Viewed in terms of orientation, the one is centripetal and the other centrifugal. Furthermore, if evangelistic ministry (because it primarily focuses on winning individuals to faith a decision at a time) is by nature additional, then it can be said that an apostolic ministry (because it is concerned with movement) is by nature exponential.

For instance, we believe that the American megachurch is largely the result of evangelistic approaches and leadership because it was the direct result of the church's taking evangelism seriously. It has brought millions of new converts into the church, but then it did not quite know what to do with them once they were baptized, so it simply reframed previous notions of the size of the local church and then managed the outcomes.[13] Willow Creek's Reveal study, which understood through research into the capacity of Willow Creek Association to produce mature disciples, pretty much admits this. Seeker-sensitive approaches have a huge evangelistic impact, but it is not as effective in terms of maturing and releasing disciples into the missional purposes of God for their lives.

Those in the church growth movement came under more distinctly apostolic influences when they became inspired by the concept of exponential growth and multiplication and reproducibility. In other words, multisite thinking and church planting movements were a direct result of more apostolic approaches to ministry. Having chosen that math of multiplication, the trajectory is set in a decidedly apostolic direction when the church is conceived of as a genuine people movement where everyone is empowered (discipled) as an agent of the church's mission. In apostolic perspective, effectiveness is measured not by weekend attendance (as in contemporary churches) but by the church's capacity to multiply its impact by church planting as well as activating the APEST gifts and human capital inherent in the church. An example of this shift became evident in a conversation that I (Alan) had with a senior leader in a church with five thousand members. He said that rather than simply adding one new location or campus to the church, the leaders' job was to help every member see that he or she *is* a location. This is multisite thinking conceived in a completely different light.

Mike Breen can recall the exact moment his world shifted from an evangelistic design to an apostolic one:

> I was in a time of prayer, leading a megachurch at the time and one of the largest in the country, and God seemed to visit me in a very specific way. He was able to show me the whole of the community and he seemed to say, "You know, you can have the whole megachurch thing. Or you can have something else." That something else was that the Lord gave me this vision for a continually reproducible network of lightweight and low-maintenance communities (which led to the innovation of lay-led, midsized missional communities). We wouldn't simply grow by adding people to worship services; we'd grow by multiplying disciples who could then multiply missional communities, who could multiply worshipping campuses who could multiply churches and into other networks and cities. We wouldn't be seeing new people come to faith

and discipling them by addition but by multiplication. What I've seen with St Thomas Sheffield in the U.K. and the churches we've begun to work with in the United States with 3DM is this dramatic shift from adding to one place to multiplying everything on every level. I remember thinking that I'd never seen anything like it and I wouldn't even know what we'd call such a thing. It was something completely new and innovative. It was so different from the other "models" of church that I had seen or embraced.

An example of this shift from evangelistic to apostolic design is demonstrated by our friend and collaborator Dave Ferguson and the New Thing Network. As a multisite megachurch and a church planting movement, they are reconceiving the whole system from an apostolic perspective. It also describes what is happening in the many megachurches involved in the Future Travelers' learning journey: using existing platforms to launch movements that have global reach.[14]

Orbits of Influence

Another difference between apostolic and evangelistic ministry can be detected by observing their natural orbits, or zones, of influence and impact. Although a historical case can be made for itinerant evangelists who roam far and wide, it seems that most evangelists operate in close relationship and proximity to a local congregation or movement. Remember that evangelists are basically recruiters to the cause; they have to have a strong relational link and commitment to the cause they so ardently promote. They also have strong relational links to non-Christian people in the broader community. Their gift exists in making the connection among gospel, converts, and the local community of believers. In this way, they act somewhat like worker bees, collecting pollen and bringing it back for processing in the hive. Evangelists are by nature attractional: they act as doorways for new people to come into the ecclesial community. In order to maximize the impact of their ministry and calling, evangelists are unlikely to wander too far from home base; they are what we call supralocal.

The Entrepreneurial Twist

Because of a lack of a meaningful theological thinking on the topic, most American church leaders make the mistake of associating being entrepreneurial with apostolic ministry, that is, someone who is entrepreneurial is also apostolic. Certainly evangelists can also be highly entrepreneurial and culturally inventive. Entrepreneurialism is a skill that can serve all the APEST functions, but it does not take the same form in all of them. It is a categorical mistake to assume entrepreneurial people are automatically apostolic. Both mice and elephants have four legs, a tail, and a mouth, but they are clearly not the same animal. Apparent similarities can be deceptive.

Culture Creators, Engagers, and Redeemers

At first glance, it would seem that all the church needs to do in order to address the decline of Christianity in the West is to reactivate its evangelistic people. And as we have seen, evangelism certainly has brought renewal and growth to the church over the past forty years. But given that evangelists usually function in an attractional way within the cultural orbit of the church, their effectiveness decreases the further they move from their cultural base. This has some serious implications for a church that finds itself increasingly stranded in a context that now requires a distinctly missional approach. Using an evangelistic strategy in a missional situation can create as many problems as it resolves.

In *On the Verge*, Dave Ferguson and I (Alan) suggest that for most of history, churches in the West have perceived themselves as the privileged religion of Western civilization—effectively a civil religion. The church-state alliance in Europe and the associated church-culture alliance in the United States have granted Christianity a privileged status. It has created the situation where, except for some dissenting minorities, most people are automatically considered to be Christian and have some direct, albeit nominal, association with the church. In other words, these countries have had a churched culture for almost seventeen centuries.

In such a situation, the church can assume that most people have a relationship with it, and all they need to do is some convincing to appropriate the claims of Christ more thoroughly. If people are not coming to church, all we need is to do some evangelism, and they will. We have not seen the need to do any cross-cultural translation of the gospel normally required of missionaries going to completely non-Christian cultures.

The problem is that the Western church now finds itself in an increasingly dechurched, and now genuinely unchurched, society. We can no longer assume that simple evangelistic outreach will work. In fact, this may well be the source of much of our crisis in the church. Given that we are now in a missionary situation in the West, we have to employ missional (that is, apostolic) approaches to resolve a distinctly missionary problem.[15] Simply applying an evangelistic solution to a missionary problem will be a big category error, especially in a time that requires theological clarity and decisive strategy. One can't heal a broken leg with a flu vaccination.

Table 3.1 Differences Between Apostolic and Evangelistic Ministries

	Apostolic	Evangelistic
Missional impact	Extension	Growth
Primary metaphor	Missionary	Messenger
Primary thrust	Missional (go to them)	Attractional (come to us)
Key fruit or sign	Church planting	Soul winning
Their passion	Movements	Conversions
Mathematical growth	Multiplication	Addition
Cultural competency	Multicultural (E2–E4)	Monocultural (E0–E1/2)[a]
Cultural orbit	Translocal (glocal)	Supralocal
Constructive role	Architect	Builder
How they are often viewed by the institution	As agitator for development	As asset for growth
Focus/perspective	Macro/systemic	Micro/personal
What they feel called to	Nations (translocal)	Local and regional (supralocal)
What it initiates	Ventures	Relationships

[a]*The numbers indicate cultural distance from a meaningful understanding of the gospel.*

To help resolve the problems, we need to incorporate apostolic imagination and practice back into the churches' self-concept and strategies, one that goes beyond the more evangelistic approach of addition to include the more exponential approach of the apostolic. Table 3.1 highlights some further differences between the apostolic and evangelistic ministries.

The Spatial Profiles of APEST

We believe that it is important to explore the range of influence normally associated with each type of ministry. What is the natural orbit of influence for each ministry, and how can we ensure that this influence is focused and maximized to benefit the overall mission of the church? These questions will have importance in understanding the distinction between generative and operative forms of leadership later in this book. We suggest that shepherds and teachers are most at home within a definite cultural and geographical locality. We have already noted that good shepherds will likely experience diminished influence to the degree that they cannot recall the names and stories of the people in their care. Shepherds therefore must be very attentive to the local and the particular.

Although perhaps somewhat less localized than shepherds, teachers are best suited to situations that encourage attentiveness and personal engagement. At least organizationally, they have tended to prefer stable environments suited to educational purposes such as the seminary.

Evangelists typically operate within the broader cultural and geographical boundaries of the organization (that is, they are supralocal). This means that they are often found venturing out of the strict confines of the local ecclesia. This distance has geographical dimensions, but it is best seen in cultural terms. Evangelists go in and out of the community, but they typically do not venture too far beyond their base cultural framework.[16] They are seldom cross-cultural missionaries but rather act as doorways into the local community of faith.

The very nature of the prophetic ministry requires some spiritual distance from the more parochial interests of the local community so that it can be addressed and called to repentance and change. Prophets need critical distance from the community in order to speak and act objectively.[17] Withdrawing from the center and moving toward the edge does more than create space for listening to God; it also affords prophets a certain level of objectivity that those who are more absorbed in the life of the community do not enjoy. As covenant people, however, prophets feel bound to the people of God in love and can never be too distant lest they damage their capacity to speak with love and commitment. Richard Rohr says that prophets are at their best "on the edge of the inside."[18]

Apostles, because of the missionary calling, are the most distant from the epicenter of a movement. Their pioneering and adventuresome nature propels them beyond the cultural and geographical boundaries of the local community into new contexts. Although not always cross-cultural, they are likely to deal with the engagement of Christianity at the edges of the church. Peter and Paul are a case in point. (In Chapter Seven, we compare and contrast the ministries of these two archetypal apostles and show how these in turn are exemplary for other forms of apostolic ministry.)

Because the vocations of shepherds and teachers are appropriate for an established community, they are best characterized as being integrative and operative. They are natural integrators who help with the assimilation of people and information throughout the community.[19] They are also operative because they are more inclined to drive the routine aspects of running and maintaining the community or organization than charting a new course. They optimize efficiency and resourcefulness rather than generate new forms.

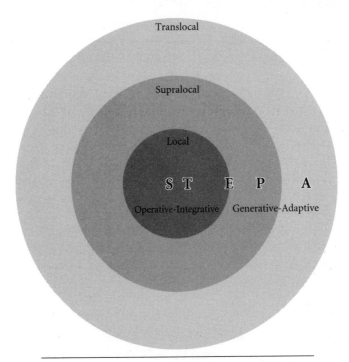

Figure 3.3 Generative and Adaptive Ministries

Because evangelists, prophets, and apostles typically function within and beyond the more parochial interests of the local ecclesia, we suggest that these ministries are best characterized by the terms *generative* and *adaptive* (see Figure 3.3). They are generative because of the effect they have on both the local community and the development of Christianity as a whole. As ministries that operate toward the edge, away from the center of the organization, they provide the center with new insights necessary for organization learning and for an authentic missional encounter with their environment. They are adaptive because their capacity to function effectively away from the center demonstrates an innate ability to adapt to diverse, chaotic, and often complex environments. The center is significantly more routine and predictable than at the edges.

Pioneers and Settlers

A good way to understand the spatial and relational dimensions of APEST is to use the metaphor of pioneers and settlers. If we view the church as the primary agent of God's purposes in this world, his elect community that is called to both embody and extend the kingdom of God in human affairs, then we can see why we need the activities of both pioneers and settlers.

Pioneers by nature take on the challenge to go to places and contexts that others have not explored. In many ways, this tracks the work of the kingdom of God as it expresses itself far beyond the confines of Christianity. Seen in this light, God is the archetypal pioneer: He is involved in the lives of all people, seeking to call them to himself in and through Jesus. The church, specifically the pioneer, joins him in this mission. Pioneers seek the journey. However, hard-core pioneers particularly are more likely to keep on moving, continuing to open up new territory than to stop and build. Unless they are accompanied by people more given to settling new territory, much of the gain can be lost.

Settlers, on the other hand, care deeply about guarding and maintaining the ground that the pioneers have gained, thus making sure it stays under the reign of God. Settlers ask and seek to answer a number of questions:

- It is good that new ground has been gained and that people have come to know Jesus, but will the lives of these people be better?
- Will there be transformation?
- Will they be living into the reality of the kingdom?
- Will the Word become incarnated into their lives?

However, settlers by nature can become so settled that they are resistant to moving forward or embracing change. If we do not learn to manage the inherent tensions between pioneering and settling, we can end up damaging the missional fabric of the church. Pioneers will look to move forward into the frontier, while the settlers will look to stay behind and maintain the establishment. What can ensue from this tension to go in different directions is a breaking away of the pioneering types from the settler types, fracturing the organic structure of the body (Figure 3.4).

In many ways, maintaining APEST dynamics, with built-in biases toward either pioneering or settling, is vital to the missional fitness of the movement as a whole. Both forces are necessary. Leadership must learn to manage, and even harness, these tensions to deliver effective mission.

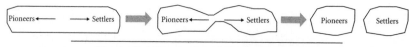

Figure 3.4 Pioneer and Settler Dynamics

We often think that church ought to be a place with no tensions. But this sentiment creates a false sense of harmony that works against the purposes of God and his kingdom: to gain and then maintain the ground won through pioneering and settling. In fact, a false sense of peace, based as it is on passive aggression, will eventually create more conflict and will threaten the church's capacity for fulfilling its task, as we can see in most church splits. Organizational psychologists Kenwyn Smith and David Berg say it this way: "It is indeed a paradox that while the *existence* of conflict and opposition threatens a group's life, the *absence* of the same forces is also a serious threat. Emotionally, a group that does not provide room for the conflicting and ambivalent reactions evoked by group life is not a place where either the individuals or the group as a whole can thrive."[20]

Contained within APEST are competing values and interests. Therefore, left to their own impulses, each of the ministries will seek to delegitimize the others. They will seek to alleviate tension by eliminating its perceived source or isolating themselves from the others. The historical pattern (see Chapter Six and the Appendix) is that the more destabilizing, generative forms of ministry (the APEs) end up getting edited out of the equation by the more stabilizing ST types. There is no conspiracy theory here. Homeostasis ensures a tendency to oversimplify and ignore the inherent complexity that comes with diversity. There is a part of us that finds shelter in overly simplified understandings of people, organizations, and the world.

This is very true when it comes to the pioneer-settler tension inherent in APEST. Without pioneers, we rarely, if ever, gain new territory. Without settlers (what 3DM now calls "developers") we rarely, if ever, keep the new territory. We need to allow the tension to be creative, not destructive. By placing a high value on both and ensuring that both groups learn to operate together to advance the kingdom, we develop missional fitness that can extend the kingdom and maintain health along the way.[21]

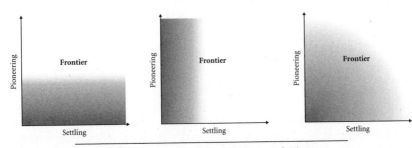

Figure 3.5 Maintaining Missional Fitness

In the left diagram of Figure 3.5, we see settlers leading out but they never reach the frontier. In the middle diagram, the pioneers are pushing toward the frontier, but because settlers are not there to develop the new ground, they end up losing it. The right diagram of the figure indicates a better congruence between the two forces of pioneering and settling: as they work together, both are able to penetrate and maintain a new frontier.

A Missional Dialectic

This chapter has sought to draw out some of the rich relationships and differences that exist within the APEST typology of ministry. It has not been exhaustive by any means. In fact, an exploration of the various possibilities that arise with different combinations opens up new vistas on ministry in and through God's people. But unlocking these potentials must begin with a viable acceptance of the legitimacy and space of the other.

Perhaps a good way to close this chapter is by highlighting the profoundly adaptive potentials inherent in a fully fledged APEST ministry. Progress in any arena of life always involves a tension between the forces of progression and the forces of conservatism. Thesis leads to antithesis and then to synthesis. Every automobile needs both brakes and accelerators—to have only one would render it ineffective. In fact, life itself requires stability (but not too much) and adaptation to changing environment (but not too much) in order to be healthy, invigorating, and sustainable.

Clearly these tensions exist with the fivefold typology of Ephesians 4:11. The healthy, mutually enriching, but always tense relationship between the prophet and all the others is vital for spiritual health. As we have seen, the partnership of apostle and prophet is important in the Ephesians 2:20 dynamics of laying the right foundations in the church. Both need to collaborate, as well as tussle at times, in helping the church to grow in adherents and extend to new territory. In the church, the pioneer needs the settler, and vice versa, if we are going to live under the Lordship of Jesus and be the kind of movement that he intended in the first place.

Truly we are better together than we are apart. Therefore, we must seriously strive for the unity of the Spirit in the bond of true peace (Ephesians 4:3), recognizing that we are very different and that Jesus intended that we should be (Ephesians 4:7–11) and so become the mature and transformative church that lives under the rule of Jesus (Ephesians 4:12–16).

4

missional ministry for a missional church
A CHURCH WHERE EVERYONE GETS TO PLAY

In the New Testament no individual Christian is specifically identified as a priest. Jesus is called a priest, and the church as a whole is called a royal priesthood, but there was no particular group of priests in the New Testament church.
Raymond Brown

The ways and means promoted and practiced in the world are a systematic attempt to substitute human sovereignty for God's rule.
Eugene Peterson

The clergy-laity dichotomy . . . is one of the principal obstacles to the church effectively being God's agent of the Kingdom today because it creates a false idea that only "holy men," namely, ordained ministers, are really qualified and responsible for leadership and significant ministry.
Howard Snyder

IN THIS CHAPTER, WE EXPLORE MORE DEEPLY HOW WE MIGHT INTEGRATE APEST into the very fabric of the church. This integration is factored in at the most foundational level of discipleship through to leadership development and team dynamics. We hope the reader will be able to see the power of Jesus's gifting at work throughout the church or other organization—the church of the permanent revolution.

Between Differentiation and Integration

As we noted at the end of Chapter Three, one of the tasks of leadership is to negotiate the tension that arises naturally within communities and organizations. We believe the process of negotiating the inherent tensions within APEST is best framed around the concepts of differentiation and integration.

Differentiation is the process of recognizing and legitimizing the unique features and qualities that comprise each of the individual APEST vocations. Each has its own unique language, aptitudes, and skills that distinguish it from the other vocations. This entails the development of conceptual and linguistic categories that demonstrate how one's vocation is not only separate and unique but also how it uniquely contributes to the whole. For instance, the apostle's distinct differences actually enhance the life and ministry of the shepherd, and vice versa. Similarly, the shepherd contributes to the apostle's ministry by humanizing the people in the system and affording them adequate space and time to adjust to the pioneer's entrepreneurial ventures. The apostle contributes to the shepherd's ministry by drawing it out of purely inward concerns of belonging and stability.

A significant level of differentiation has been achieved when people in the group (whether leadership or the church in general) are not only able to explain how they are different from one another, but also why those differences stand to enrich and contribute to the growth and effectiveness of both individuals and the group. So, for example, when an apostle is able to explain his or her role and function to a shepherd, and why it stands to complement and enhance the shepherd's vocation and the overall well-being of the system, differentiation has begun.

Because we tend to avoid complexity and desire homeostasis, this kind of social intelligence does not emerge on its own. It takes strategic, intentional efforts to make it a viable part of the organizational culture. A good way to start the practice of differentiation is by deliberately using the language of APEST to develop a corporate understanding of the nature and function of each APEST ministry and its impact on the life of the community.

Integration is the process of creating access and understanding among the individual roles so that meaningful interaction can take place. Often this requires overcoming personal barriers to interaction and communication. It is not surprising that Paul prefaces his writing on APEST with a plea to live in a way worthy of one's calling and to be patient and bear with one another in love (Ephesians 4:1–2). Navigating diversity requires an other-centered spirituality, something counterintuitive to our more selfish, egocentric natures.

Striking the right balance between differentiation and integration is the challenge. Communities typically fall to one extreme or the other: high on differentiation and low on integration or high on integration and low on differentiation. Drifting into one to the neglect of the other has consequences for a group's capacity to mature and effectively engage in mission. These are the outcomes (Figure 4.1):

- *Competing:* Differentiating among the various roles within the group without integrating them into a whole creates an environment for competition. Recognizing diversity requires affirming the value of the others in relation to the whole.
- *Congregating:* Ignoring variety and failing to foster a sense of cohesion translates into a group of people occupying the same space for a selected period of time.

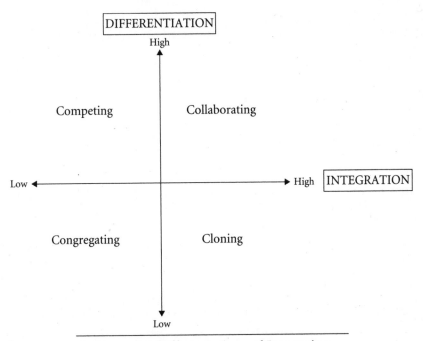

Figure 4.1 Differentiation and Integration

- *Cloning:* This may be one of the most common scenarios within the church. Without a way to recognize and affirm diversity, the operational needs of the organization end up determining the roles that people play. If the organization is not proactive in differentiating and integrating, then charismatic leaders will become the primary point of reference for what constitutes legitimate forms of ministry. In essence, either the organization or influential people end up defining the ministry culture of the community.
- *Collaborating:* Reaching a point where a community celebrates diversity yet manages to hold together a sense of community and common mission is where collaboration happens. Like the enormous amounts of energy released during the process of nuclear fission and fusion, when differentiation and integration find a healthy balance, the potential is there to revolutionize a Christian community.

Whereas differentiation is about valuing our distinctions, integration is about organizing in ways that facilitate the flow of information, skills, and human capital among the various parts of the community. The principal issue with integration is creating access to each of the APEST ministries so equipping can take place. Mike Breen and the 3DM team call the differentiation-integration dynamic "base and phase." We believe that it is a key to activating APEST throughout the system.

Base and Phase: The Pathway to Maturity

Figure 4.2 shows a person with the base calling of teacher; the base is what comes most naturally to us; it is what we were created and designed to do. A sense of needing to bring wisdom and understanding to others is woven in and throughout his own personality, story, and context. His ministry is bound to be unique, expressing itself through unique insights that benefit the community. That is what makes this person different. But to integrate and mature as a member of the broader body, he will need to access the other four ministries in the APEST matrix.

If the local church is operating on the APEST dynamic, this teacher will have direct access to all the other ministries and can be encouraged to expose himself to their particular intelligences: the ways they operate, their motivations, their impact, and so forth. In this way, he becomes increasingly aware of the differences and moves toward understanding and integration.

This pathway of development is entirely consistent with Ephesians 4:12, when Paul says that APEST is given for the "equipping of the saints for works of ministry." Even the word *equipping* (*katartismo* in the Greek) carries with it the idea of creating access by linking together disjointed parts. It was often used in reference to the act of weaving, knitting torn nets, and even setting a broken bone. Paul is letting us know that without access to the other APEST ministries, we simply cannot mature and develop.

Modern leadership theory confirms these ancient insights. For instance, management experts Monica Higgins and Kathy Kram have developed a concept they call developmental networking.[1] Blending social network theory and mentoring concepts, they show how relationships, characterized by strong ties of frequent interaction and reciprocity with various people from different vocational domains, contribute to personal and vocational development.

The purpose of being equipped by the other ministries is to increase our ability to operate in those ministries. For example, Mike Breen is fond of saying that not everyone is a teacher, but everyone is called to share what they know from the scriptures; not everyone is a shepherd, but we are all called to care; not everyone is an evangelist, but we are all called to share the good news; not everyone is a prophet, but we are all called to listen to God; not everyone is an apostle, but everyone is called

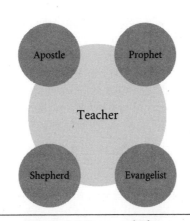

Figure 4.2 Base and Phase

to live a sent life. As we alluded to in Chapter One, maturity is defined not just in moral terms; it must also encompass the capacity to represent the fullness of Jesus to the world, and this includes the capacity to operate out of the various ministries within APEST.

If access to the other ministries is paramount to our own maturity, then we can safely say that our level of growth and maturity will be directly proportionate to the level at which we can inhabit, participate, and receive from the various environments created by the different ministries.

In practice, we should therefore start by recognizing that just as maturity is an incremental, lifelong affair, it takes time for adequate exposure and training to take place around a particular APEST vocation. Mike Breen developed the concept of base and phase to account for this reality. One way of understanding base and phase is to say that our base ministry is something that we cannot help but do, and a phase ministry is something we feel that we cannot do without help.

In a phase ministry, we enter a season of life where we learn some basic competencies and skill sets from another ministry. When you are operating outside your base ministry, you are outside a place of your natural talent and gifting. This is not your ideal environment, and yet it is the reason that it is critical to the maturing process. In order to learn and develop beyond our current state, we have to journey to the edge of our comfort zones and enter into what developmental learning pioneer Lev Vygotsky called the "zone of proximal development."[2] This is the pivotal place where we are forced to acknowledge our own inadequacies, thereby opening us up to receiving guidance and training from someone who is more competent than we are in that particular practice.

For example, if your base ministry is teaching and you enter a phase of prophetic ministry, you may learn how to recognize God's voice, discern his activity with greater clarity, or practice seeing things from God's point of view. Will you be as skilled and efficient as someone else who has the prophetic as his or her base ministry? It is unlikely. But although you may never be as naturally gifted as someone who has a prophetic base, when you enter into a phase of prophetic ministry, you can learn to do some of the basics of what it means to function, think, and maybe even lead prophetically. As time passes, your season of equipping in prophetic ministry will phase out, perhaps leading you to enter a different phase of APEST ministry, but always returning to your base ministry of teaching (Figure 4.3).

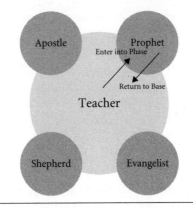

Figure 4.3 Entering into Phase and Returning to Base

Understanding base and phase helps guard us from the faulty assumption that we should operate only out of a place of absolute strength and familiarity when it comes to ministry. If I say, "I'm apostolic; therefore, I'm going to do only things that reflect that ministry," then I have seriously misunderstood Paul's logic in relation to APEST. When he says, "and become mature," in Ephesians 4:13, he is referencing the individual arriving at a threshold of maturity where he or she is equipped to operate with some competency in each of the APEST ministries.

Phasing in, Phasing Out

When Mike Breen was in his twenties, he experienced different seasons of trying new things. After a year or two in a season of immersion into evangelism, it seemed that the grace he was given for this season seemed to dissipate, and he would have to go and start something new again. Then he sought to apprentice himself to someone who was very prophetic and learned a lot about what it is to act out of that prophetic ministry—only to move on again. This happened over and over: God would lead him into a season of learning a different APEST ministry, where he spent a good amount of time in that phase, but kept returning to starting new things, his base ministry. He notes that he could not seem to help himself. As it turns out, there was a reason for that: he is apostolic to the core.

Mike's general observation from these experiences is that disciples enter into phases for one of two reasons. First, they have a clear sense that God is asking them to learn a ministry in which they are not yet competent. In his case, he is apostolic in nature, but it was crucial that he also learn to function evangelistically. Being apostolic is not an excuse for not sharing the good news. He admits that he may not be as good as a base evangelist, but after spending a season of time in a phase of evangelistic ministry, he had a deeper insight into how it works and even some level of competence in evangelism.

Or we enter into a new phase when circumstances require us to operate outside our base ministry. Sometimes in order to accomplish the work God has called us to, disciples have to access skills and competencies that are uniquely located within the other ministries. For example, someone with a base ministry of shepherd who has been serving as a small groups pastor at a local church needs to step into a teaching role because the senior pastor stepped down. So at one level, people can enter a phase by exposing themselves to literature and environments that constitute a particular APEST ministry or by directly subjecting themselves to people or environments where that ministry takes place. Perhaps a more intense way of being equipped to function in any of our phases is to be mentored by someone who excels in that area of ministry. This can happen through internships—high levels of formal and structured relationships that provide opportunities to experiment with a particular ministry, coupled with opportunities to process focused feedback.

When we understand the role of APEST in the equipping process, we begin to grasp what Paul means when he says that each one of us has been given grace "according to the measure of Christ's gift." The word *measure* in the original language is *metron,* which is where we get our word *metric.* Paul seems to be saying that not everyone receives the same measure of gifting when it comes to the distribution of APEST. The capacity to operate out of a particular APEST vocation is measured out differently to each person. This has two implications.

The first has to do with base capacity. For example, two people may have an apostolic base, but one of them may have a greater capacity to function apostolically than the other. Some apostles will be more effective and have a greater impact through their ministries than other apostles. Observation and experience readily confirm this. Some people have been given a greater measure of grace and, consequently, a greater impact with their ministries. This capacity, as the text reveals, is a grace that has been given, which automatically voids boasting or pride.

The genius of the basing and phasing approach is that it structures APEST into discipleship itself and gives us a clear pathway to develop from there into mature ministry and leadership. When APEST happens at the discipleship level, the entire church gets involved. This was built into the very rhythms and structures at St. Thomas Crookes Church (where Mike was the senior leader at the time) in Sheffield, England, and the results were nothing less than transformative. The church exploded with energy and contributed significantly to its becoming an international movement. The Order of Mission grew directly out of this experience and was set up to be able to transfer these ideas and practices into the international scene.

It's All in the Genes

One of us (Alan) developed and articulated an approach to understanding how APEST is distributed within the body.[3] After studying the phenomenology of high-impact apostolic movements, I became increasingly convinced that every believer contains the full potential for the whole. Each believer is in a real sense a seed of an ecclesia, and an ecclesia is the seed of a movement. But the full potential is already fully contained in the seed. The same is true of any living cell. The DNA that codes the life of the whole organism is contained in every part, even though that particular cell might need access to only a tiny portion of the genetic information contained in the full DNA code. So, for instance, a kidney cell accesses only the genes it needs to be a kidney cell, but it contains the full genetic coding for brains, eyes, hands, and so on in the DNA resident in its nucleus. This turns out to be true for the body of Christ no less than it is true for organisms—and this is not surprising, since the Creator is the designer of both.

So, for instance, if someone becomes a Christian, then even 10 percent of the 120 meaningful relationships in his life, when redeemed in Christ, can legitimately constitute an ecclesia as the Bible defines it. In other words, this person is an ecclesia-in-the-making. In fact, phenomenologically speaking, God could use him to start a whole movement, and that church in turn could start other churches in a pay-it-forward style of movement. In fact, this is what God has done in the Bible and throughout history. The conversions of Paul, St. Patrick, Sadhu Singh, and countless other saints generated entire movements. Each part carries the potential for the whole, including the full coding of APEST.

I will use myself as an example. My APEST profile is ATPES. Visually it looks like Figure 4.4. My primary gifting is A. This is my base gift, my primary vocation; my sense of purpose is bound up with the apostolic vision of the church as movement. I feel a deep sense of obligation arising from our sentness as a people. I feel in my bones the profound challenge of our context in the West today and am constrained to call and enable the church to respond and become a movement again. Also, I can see the issues of systemic design and interconnectedness and where systemic wholeness

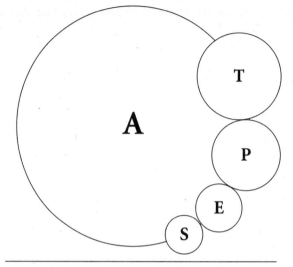

Figure 4.4 Alan's APEST Profile

is violated. Although my teaching gift is secondary, it is significant in my ministry complex. I love and collect ideas, and this plays itself out in all that I do. All my friends know that; my writings are clear evidence.

In psychographics theory, the primary aptitude or gift appropriates the secondary one and expresses itself through it. So people receiving my ministry get apostolic thinking expressed through teaching. As a result of this combination, I tend to produce a lot of new phrases and terms that allow people to see ancient apostolic truths in a new light. The most common response by far to my ministry is something like this: "I feel that you are not saying something that I don't already know, but I feel you're giving new words to what I already think." People thus feel that the truth belongs to them, because as inheritors of the apostolic faith, the truths *do* belong to them. The prophetic is also very strong in me, but currently in third position. It does come into play, and when it does, I can get a bit demanding and confrontational. My top three ministries are dominant, and the others significantly less so. So although I love to evangelize and do so when I can, it is not my strength. I can shepherd people and did it for years. And so you can see how all of the APEST ministries are some-how in me, just as they are in you as well.

Try constructing your own profile, and you will see this is the case. Seen in this light, basing and phasing are not so much about exploring foreign things but in exploring and activating potentials already present or latent in us. This should not be surprising because Christ lives in us. You can take the test at www.apest.org to help you identify your bases and phases. The APEST test provides a profile of those who take the test at the first two ministry vocations, with a supplementary three layers because the psychographics are more complex the further down you go (see Figure 4.5). We suggest therefore that although you should identify your base vocation and undergo the various phases, you also seriously assess the impact that each layer of APEST has on your particular ministry and how it makes you unique.

You can also try to do this assessment yourself. Better yet, to avoid some inevitable self-delusion, work it through with a group of people who really know you. We are always known and experienced in community as part of the body of Christ. Make sure that everyone in the group understands the terms and that you are working from a common understanding. Then start by identifying your base (number 1), then the secondary, tertiary, and so on. You will find that even the category in fifth position, where you are weakest, is still accessible to you.

The truth is that human beings are never one-dimensional; we are never simply apostles or shepherds or whatever else. Our ministries arise from the layered interplay of these vocational dynamics. When personality, history, and culture are added to the mix, we bristle with marvelous complexity and particularity. When we recognize that each of us contains the entire spectrum of APEST within us, then we begin to see why Paul makes the extraordinary claim that APEST equips the body to be the fullness of Jesus in the world. Contained within each of us is the potential for world transformation because we host within us, at varying degrees, the full vocational spectrum of Christ's earthly ministry.

Variety for Adaptivity

We believe that one of the major implications of the Ephesians 4 text, with its associated motifs of grace, body life, and maturity, is to help the church be a living organism—a spiritually empowered, profoundly adaptive, always maturing, missionally fit community of God's people. Clearly APEST plays a significant part in that equation, seen in the law of requisite variety, a central principle arising from the study of living systems (cybernetics). It states that for any system to adapt and thrive in its environment, the level of complexity within the system has to be greater than or equal to the level of complexity in the environment itself.

This theory of the law of requisite variety teaches that the system (an organization, biological system, or society) with the widest possible repertoire of solutions, behaviors, and choices will have a greater chance of thriving in its environment.[4]

This is where the genius of APEST comes in. The fivefold ministry matrix contains the optimal level of diversity to account for and engage the complexities of our environment.[5] A cramped ST model does not contain enough variety to cope with increasing complexity in our cultural context and rapidly changing environment. As a divinely designed system, APEST provides all the diversity we need—and not too much. A full portrait of all the possible primary and secondary combinations of APEST reveals some twenty-five possible profiles (Figure 4.5).

The requisite variety keeps mounting when one adds levels 3, 4, and 5. And considering that each one of us contains all five gives each of us access to a rich repertoire of potential intelligence. Anyone who draws back at the idea of APEST because it sounds too simplistic or puts people into a box has nothing to fear from the APEST typology. If we take into

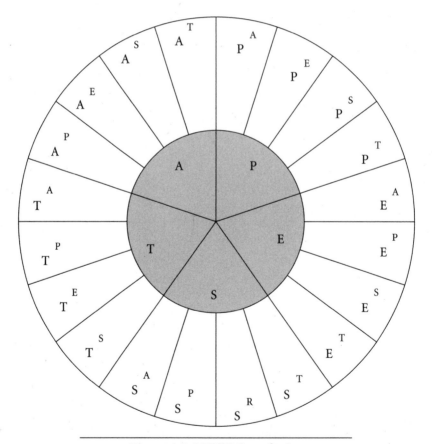

Figure 4.5 APEST Complexity

account all possible variations, we arrive at 120 possible combinations in the APEST system alone. Although it is good to know one's weakest aspects and ensures one learns from and about it, we think the dynamic interaction of the first two or three is what delivers real insight into how one is designed to operate.

And so to engage the unique challenges that are particular to each context, we need to draw on an equally unique variety set of skills and aptitudes. Recognizing that APEST is located at varying degrees within each individual, and therefore the entire community, bolsters our confidence that we can access the needed intelligence and aptitudes to engage our environments effectively for missional impact.

The tri-perspectival leadership model of prophet-priest-king popularized by Drew Goodmanson and David Fairchild is a creative attempt to move beyond the restrictions of the purely binary dimensions of the ST model, but in our opinion it falls short in recognizing the full range of Christ's vocational ministry. As such, we believe it lacks the requisite variety needed to sustain a fully orbed ministry. In addition, although it draws inspiration from the ministry roles of the Old Testament, it lacks the same direct New Testament mandate given in Ephesians 4.

APEST ensures what we like to call a *quantum vision*. Complex perspectives brought about from the vigorous integration of the five vocations will ensure a dynamic, shifting, and profoundly adaptive perception of problems and solutions. If you need a more dynamic, theologically nuanced, less linear approach to the issues, engage apostles, prophets, evangelists, shepherds, and teachers in the process and watch a more creative conversation emerge. If you want an unsurprising, less risky interpretation of the situation, invite everyone who thinks like you do to the table and bask in the security of groupthink—something that reactionary churches (as well as cults) are known for. Remember that according to the first law of cybernetics, if you always do what you have always done, then you will always get what you have always gotten. Flexibility, as well as variety, increases choice.

The APEST ministry matrix is a remarkable tool built into the foundational (constitutional) ecclesiology itself. This is in fact the very thing Paul asserts when he says that the fivefold giftings ensure that we are no longer tossed around by faddish ideas about church and leadership coming from the corporate world. According to Paul, we need to have access to all of the APEST ministries to grow up *in all things*. Depletion of the requisite variety inherent in APEST will lead us to marginalize the essential components that contribute to the church's capacity to mature and represent Jesus to the world.

Embedding the Codes

The most effective way to engage the full power of APEST in a local church or organization is to embed it into the very life of the church. The Ephesians 4 callings include the whole people of God—that is, every disciple rather than just leaders. The aim is to ensure that the whole church and culture has access to the vocations given to them by Christ and are permitted and encouraged to grow in them. The aim is to help everyone discover their vocational energies and motivations by discovering their base and then entering into phases where they are exposed to one of the other four ministries. This helps ensure a clear formation process of discipleship all the way through to senior levels of leadership—all through APEST thinking. In the church I (Alan) was leading in the early 2000s, we did it as shown in Figure 4.6.

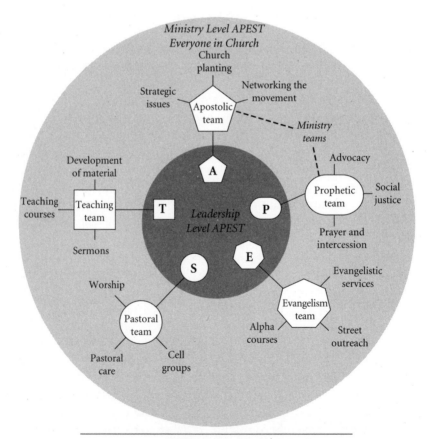

Figure 4.6 APEST Levels of Leadership

We first ensured that everyone was well informed about the ideas of Ephesians 4, especially the levels of leadership. We all understood our function (and the differences among them) and gave everyone permission to be who God made them to be (so that they could be integrated). We then ensured that all the APEST vocations were well represented on the leadership team, with at least one person representing each of the APEST types. Everyone on each team shown in Figure 4.6 was clear about his or her own base gifts, which formed the basis of their job description on the team. Each senior leadership team member was then encouraged to identify, recruit, and develop people within the community to form a team made up of others who fit the same base profiles.

So, for instance, the prophetic leader developed a prophetic team comprising the prophetically inclined disciples in the church. Their job was to do what prophets were designed to do: pray a lot, bug everyone else in matters of faithfulness, discern God's will (and help others to do so), call for justice, and work for spiritual renewal. The shepherding, or pastoral, team, normally the standard understanding of the core of church leadership, became just one of the many teams in the church. The team members did what shepherds do: create community, develop liturgy and worship, do counseling, give spiritual direction and soul care, and run the cell groups.

Mike Breen has used this in several ways with 3DM and the various teams he has been a part of, and they saw unbelievable energy and spiritual momentum released. They started what was the equivalent of an APEST school for each of the five base ministries. Then they took two or three mature prophets (using prophets as an example of one type of school) and had them lead training and practical courses for a group of maturing prophets. The mature teachers did this with the maturing teachers, and so on.

Eventually they released all of them as missional community leaders, each of them leading midsized groups of twenty to fifty. For example, if they were a teacher, they were leading through the lens of their teaching gift.

Here is how 3DM has seen it playing out in practice:

- *Prophets leading a missional community.* Prophets tend to focus on the mission but are not particularly evangelistic. They often seek high visibility, since they desire an incarnational approach to presenting the gospel. Generally this means that they and their groups are radical, often placing the highest demands on members. If you know a group in a tough urban context where there is lots of talk and action about reclaiming the city by their very presence and engagement, then that is probably a group with strong prophetic leadership. Such groups can grow by multiplying, but often they keep the core team and allow new work to branch off into a new context.

- *Evangelists leading a missional community.* Almost certainly evangelists love to go straight after the people of peace—those whom God has specifically prepared to receive the gospel and are gatekeepers to wider networks, as, for example, in Luke 9 and 10, Mark 6, and Matthew 10. They build relationships and through them reach a whole neighborhood. Eventually they want to hand the group on and move into a new context or send out others in pairs to do similar work elsewhere.
- *Teachers leading a missional community.* Frequently teachers go into an existing context where the witness for Christ is struggling or almost extinguished. They give themselves to model how to live the Christian life in worship, community, or mission. Mature teachers do this humbly, so this work does not seem like teaching to them much of the time. They tend to stay for a lengthy season, but many eventually begin to look for a fresh context for their work and then hand their group to another leader. The new groups they send out are thoroughly prepared with a clear model of how to do this work.
- *Pastors leading a missional community.* Pastors long to bring community transformation by establishing and then building on long-term relationships. They highly value the integrity of becoming fully embedded into their context. This means that they have a slower and longer approach to mission. We have noticed that often this model works especially well in suburbs. Because relationships are at the heart of everything they do, it can be more difficult for them to multiply, but they do find it easier to grow with a small group of people and perhaps take what they are doing into a neighboring area or even neighboring street.
- *Apostles leading a missional community.* Apostle-led missional communities usually orbit around someone who has the ability to gather and attract others. The group is innovative and pushes into new missional frontiers. Frequently these are the fastest-growing groups. Their mode of multiplication is often to split down the middle as a result of the pressure of the speed of growth. A mature apostle should have the skills to manage such a maneuver, even though it can be fraught with pastoral land mines, since multiplying a

missional community can be relationally difficult. When you gather specific ministry groups and offer training, deployment, and coaching through the lens of mission, spectacular things begin to happen. People who have been trained to lead how God has uniquely shaped them lead far more naturally.

Literally hundreds of churches are now beginning to apply the APEST model in some way, and to great effect.[6] For instance, recently Christian Fellowship Church, a megachurch in Virginia, has undertaken a radical restructuring of its entire ministry, along with appropriate constitutional changes, along APEST lines.[7] Similarly, the pioneering Bob Roberts Jr. has led the restructuring of his home church, Northwood Church in Keller, Texas, along similar lines.[8] They started by ensuring that each cell in the church engaged all the APEST functions. Rather than seeing their roles as vocational, they articulated them as core tasks and then encouraged each cell to explore those tasks together to allow various members to lead with their vocational strengths when the task called for it. It was a rather novel way to go about embedding the APEST code but seems to be working. Bob says that the result has been nothing less than revolutionary in that it has released previously untapped potentials in communities. He says they are now planting more churches than ever before.

Surfing the Edge of Chaos

Leading a church with a full-fledged APEST model will create far more high-powered energy than the somewhat less generative ST model will allow. Having more viewpoints around the table heightens the likelihood of conflict. Nevertheless, well-handled conflict can be highly creative. It also brings the possibility of newly found creativity. Following is a process that Alan has used to great effect.

A Model for Creatively Managing Conflict

Management guru Richard Pascale rightly notes that highly innovative organizations by nature are exposed to a greater amount of real and potential conflict and that the truly successful ones learn the art of creatively managing it and focusing it on generating outcomes.[9] Pascale's model squares well with what is implied in the Ephesians 4 text. The model for creatively managing conflict involves a process of moving between two dialectical poles: fit and split, contend and transcend.

- *Fit* refers to a team's affirming the characteristics that hold them together: their love and respect for each other, their love for God's church and his mission through it, and their commitment to the city, for example. In many ways this correlates to Paul's teaching in Ephesians 4:1–6, where we are called to strive for the unity of the Spirit in the bond of peace and to base our faith in the one God, faith, or church.

- *Split* is Pascale's term for intentionally legitimizing, acknowledging, and allowing for a great diversity of expression in the team. Here the team acknowledges that we are all different and that God has given each their particular calling. This corresponds to Ephesians 4:7–11, where we are told that the church's ministry is expressed in fivefold diversity.

- *Contend* is what Pascale tells us happens when everyone steps into their distinctive roles and contributes what they think. It requires permitting, even encouraging, disagreement, debate, and dialogue around the core tasks of the organization. This corresponds to Ephesians 4:15, where we are encouraged to speak the truth in love, giving each other respect based on our APEST distinctives.

- *Transcend* means that all collectively agree to overcome disagreement in order to find new solutions. We are committed to finding the mind of Christ through the unity and diversity he has given his people. Transcend happens when we creatively manage contend. In Ephesians 4:12–16, we eventually are enabled to reach unity in the faith and the knowledge of the song of God, to maturity, to the measure of the full stature of Christ. We are told we must grow up in every way into Christ.

APEST Thinking Hats

Another way of approaching team dynamics and problem solving is something I (Alan) have recently developed called the APEST thinking hats. My source of inspiration is a problem-solving tool called the six thinking hats developed by creative-thinking specialist Edward de Bono.[10]

In de Bono's model, the six hats represent six modes of thinking. Most people tend to opt for one or another of these hats because we usually see things from a single perspective and tend to reject other types of thinking. The approach requires that everyone change hats, and when a certain color hat is on, everyone has to think in accordance with that color. People can thus contribute under any hat even though they might have supported an opposite view. Approaching this exercise as a game means that no one needs to get defensive (it's a game after all); each type of thinking will eventually be heard. Here are the various "hats":

- *White hat:* Think of white paper. It is neutral and carries information. The white hat has to do with data and information and therefore asks what information we have, what information is missing, what information we would like to have, and how we can get that information.
- *Red hat:* Think of red fire and warmth. This has to do with feelings, intuition, hunches, and emotions. "Putting on my red hat, this is what I feel . . ." "My gut feeling is . . ." "My intuition tells me prices will soon fall . . ."
- *Black hat:* Think of a judge wearing black robes who comes down heavily on wrongdoers. This is the caution hat. It prevents us from making mistakes, arriving at decisions hastily, or doing silly or illegal things. It points out why something cannot be done or why it will not work.
- *Yellow hat:* Think of sunshine. The yellow hat is for optimism and a positive view. It looks for feasibility and how something can be done. It looks for benefits, but they must be logically based: "That might work if we . . ."
- *Green hat:* Think of vegetation and rich growth. The green hat is for creative thinking, new ideas, additional alternatives, possibilities, and hypotheses. This requires creative effort: "We need some new ideas here." "Are there any alternatives?" "Could we do this differently?" "Could there be another explanation?"
- *Blue hat:* Think of the sky and an overview. Blue hat thinking is visionary thinking. It looks at things from the broadest possible vantage point. "If we had a blank check and anything was possible, what would we do?" "How will we do this? What process can be used?" "What are the implications for our overall strategy?"

Now apply the same idea to APEST, where each role is a hat. You can define a problem facing the team and work your way through the hats in trying to solve it. By putting the A hat on, everyone has to try to see the problem (and the solution) from the apostle's perspective—for example, the interests for missional extension, guarding of DNA of the church and gospel, the multiplication of disciples. Then put another hat on and see it in the light of, say, evangelistic intelligence and sensibilities, and so forth. This exercise helps people use their bases and phases without even realizing they are doing so.

All elements are already resident and latent in everyone; they might have to dig to touch base with some of them, but they are there. We guarantee that the team will have better results for having adopted this approach.

The Importance of Apostolic Ministry

We have come to the end of Part One, which has introduced the context and the basis of what will follow—a thorough exploration of apostolic vocation, intelligence, and practices.

We have chosen to focus this book primarily on the nature and function of the apostolic ministry for good reason; we believe that in many ways, the apostolic plays the catalytic role in activating a fully fledged ministry appropriate for apostolic movement, maintaining the sending-purposive (missional) impulses that we organize around, and cultivating the ongoing adaptive aspects that the church needs to grow and achieve its purpose. In terms of the ministry and leadership of Jesus's people, the apostolic is the permanent revolutionary needed to sustain the permanent revolution that is the ecclesia.

We believe that out of all the APEST ministries, the apostolic is the most generative and catalytic of them all, and because of this, it carries the most promise in helping to reverse the decline of the church. If this is correct, then the apostolic both initiates and maintains the permanent revolution at the root of the constant reformation of the church. This is also the reason that we believe that the apostolic is the key to unlocking Ephesians 4 and therefore all other New Testament forms of ministry. It is not that prophets, evangelists, pastors, and teachers cannot function independently from the apostolic; rather, as far as we can discern, they are designed to function interdependently with it and each other. It is through their relationship with the apostolic calling that they will come into the fullness of their own role and purpose in Jesus's church.

Activating the diversity within APEST necessitates the activation of an equal or greater force that can hold them together in dynamic tension. Apostles are so critical to this inherent dilemma because they are the ones most naturally prone to cultivate a compelling missional focus around which those potentially polarizing forces within APEST can gather. Without the unifying force of a common mission, the diversity within APEST will drift toward fragmentation. By initiating missional ventures, the apostolic provides the cohesive framework in which the other ministries can focus their seemingly disparate interests in collaborative ways. In essence, the apostle is the one who is most likely to facilitate the emergence of communitas, a particular kind of community that is shaped and formed around a challenge or compelling task.

Like all other catalysts, the apostolic vocation initiates a reaction that changes a system. However, we do not wish to suggest that it is the best, or the most important, or that it can act independent of the other ministries in the body of Christ. For one, we believe that following in the way of Jesus Christ means that we are never allowed to conceive of power relations in the church in a hierarchical way (Luke 22:25–27; Philippians 2:4–11). Jesus fundamentally alters the way we view leadership and followership forever; we can never lord it over people in the way of the Gentiles. The apostolic person, although always a likely contender for the position of first among equals, is not to be conceived of as the New Testament equivalent of a boss.

Second, in the same way that the ST model is inadequate, clearly the apostolic model in itself does not have all that is needed to get the job done. The ministry of all five APEST vocations is required to develop the kind of church that Jesus intended us to be. It's never onefold, twofold, or anything less than fivefold. For some, they might even expand ministry to twenty-fold (good luck to them!), but once again, it ought never to be less than fivefold. We ask readers to keep these in mind as we move into the substance of this book.

PART TWO

•

Apostolic ministry

5

custody of the codes
MAPPING THE CONTOURS OF
APOSTOLIC MINISTRY

The great Christian revolutions came not by the discovery of
something that was not known before. They happen when
someone takes radically something that was always there.
H. Richard Niebuhr

One aim of missiology is a more adequate understanding
of the apostolic task of the Church.
Paul Minear

There is no other way to retain continuity with the
apostles than to keep on doing what they did.
Carl E. Braatens

WILLIAM BLAKE WROTE IN "THE EVERLASTING GOSPEL":

This Life's dim windows of the soul
Distorts the heavens from pole to pole
And leads you to believe a lie
When you see with, not thro' the eye.

He was reflecting an insight that philosophers, scientists, poets, and
mystics have long known: that in order to truly understand something
(or someone), we must be willing to see it, acknowledge its presence, and
be surprised by what insights arise from its otherness. And if we could
truly see the miracle of a single flower clearly—as it really is—our whole
life in all likelihood would change.

All advances in knowledge and science are in some sense predicated
on this kind of radical seeing and openness. They are in fact revelations.
This is no less true of theology, especially when theological exploration

takes us to the core of our ecclesial codes, as does any exploration of the apostolic.

If we are willing to lay aside our historical and all-too-habitual prejudice and be willing to fully comprehend the role and function of the apostle, we would be amazed at how the Western church has been able to sustain itself for over seventeen centuries without a fully legitimized form. As we hope to show in the chapters in Part Two, and indeed the rest of this book, the apostolic ministry vibrates with energies that take us directly to the core of what it means to be an authentic Jesus movement. So much of the early codes of Christianity were formulated from within apostolic sensibilities. They seem to be resident in the very theological consciousness of Christianity itself. It is no coincidence that it was the apostles who wrote the canon of scripture, the original and originating codes of the New Testament church.

Perhaps it is for this reason that talk of the apostolic function in the church today makes many of us apprehensive. Is the contemporary apostolic vocation identical with that of Paul and the twelve, or are they in separate categories? Is there continuity between them? And if so, what can we discern about the qualifications, function, and role of contemporary apostles in the church? Because of the close association of the apostolic with the founding of Christianity, all of these questions are laced with hidden curiosities about spiritual power and authority. These questions have important implications for how we conceive of leadership, ministry, and organizational structures.

Little "a" and Big "A" Apostles?

Those who generally oppose the apostolic role in the church seem to suggest that contemporary apostleship might somehow impinge on, replace, or expand the role of the original twelve apostles. The unambiguous response to that concern, however, is an outright "no" . . . it does not. The original twelve clearly played a unique, unrepeatable, irreplaceable role in the establishment of the original church. But we believe that an ongoing apostolic function extends itself throughout the history of the church. The issue that we face is discerning the degree to which later apostles draw on and reflect the functions of the original twelve without superseding their unique role in the history of the church.

Nevertheless, any ongoing apostolic role has to reflect some of the original, and intrinsic, aspects of apostolic ministry. The same is true for the other roles in the APEST typology: they should all draw their vocation from the biblical archetypes that precede, inform, and inspire them.

For instance, a shepherd must have some continuity with the Bible's teaching on the matter. There is nothing new and sinister in suggesting that we maintain continuity with the original archetypes. We simply have to extract the function of little "a" apostles—those mentioned as apostles outside the circle of the twelve—from the big "A" Apostles—the original twelve. We do this in the same way that we have extrapolated the little "t" function from the big "T" function of the teacher. The same standards should apply across the board.

We believe that the standard concerns expressed about apostolic ministry (concerns about the nature of authority and power in the church) are based largely on the false assumption that the primary role of the original apostles was simply to write the Bible. Having done so, such thinking goes, they serenely passed the apostolic baton (in the form of the canon of scripture) over to the ascendant shepherds and teachers to manage and interpret it in the ongoing life of the church. But this is quite clearly wrong. The apostles were not simply Bible writers and scribes. Clearly not all of the original twelve wrote canonical material.

We can say with confidence that whatever the roles of the original apostles were, it went way beyond creating scripture. Apostles, then and now, have an irreplaceable purpose in maintaining ongoing missional capacities, generating new forms of ecclesia, and working for the continual renewing of the church, among many other vital functions. As central and important as scripture is, it was never meant to replace the dynamic missional function of the apostles in Jesus's church. The writings were created to witness a sequence of events so that they continue to happen as the gospel witness moves from Jerusalem to Judea to Samaria to the ends of the earth. In effect, they captured and extended the foundational ideas of Christianity so that all could access them in different times and places. (See the Appendix on how APE was exiled.)

It is also useful to note that both the term and the category of apostle precede the original twelve and extend beyond them to other people in the New Testament. Although the unique work of these twelve does alter the meaning of the term and shapes how Christians think of it, the word *apostle* has a much broader application. It was initially a secular word, used primarily as a verb, with strong functional overtones to indicate the people sent as commercial or diplomatic agents and with a particular purpose or to fulfill. It even applied to the sending of cargo by way of seafaring voyages.[1] It also included the idea of being agents or ambassadors for kings and or others with political and commercial interests. This is important to recognize because it establishes the flow of meaning. The original twelve apostles did not determine the meaning of the word;

rather the word's earlier historical meaning determines the meaning (and function) of the twelve apostles. They were the "sent ones."

Although the word *apostle* is clearly reframed in the light of the original twelve, it retains a significantly broader meaning and function in Jesus's ecclesia. It is this generic quality that allows us to see that the word *apostle* enjoyed a much wider application than to that of the ones whom Jesus personally commissioned. Furthermore, this generic function comes to the fore when other people outside the circle of the twelve and Paul are included in the apostolate in the New Testament.

The Other Apostles

While Paul and, to a lesser degree, Peter stand in the spotlight of scripture as the archetypal apostles, they were not the only ones doing apostolic ministry. The word *apostle* appears around eighty times in the New Testament, and many times it refers to people other than Paul or the original twelve. For instance Paul, himself an apostle beyond the original twelve, casually mentions a cross-section of eight other people who are viewed by himself and his communities as apostles (Table 5.1).

There were undoubtedly numerous other apostolic people who are not named as such but were behind the missionary growth of Christianity in the early part of the first century. The movement across the empire could not have been built solely on the work of twelve people. Although they certainly played the determinative and founding role, they must have enlisted the help of other apostolic types within the body of Christ.

Table 5.1 The Other New Testament Apostles

Name	Reference
Barnabas	Acts 14:4, 14
Andronicus	Romans 16:7
Junia[a]	Romans 16:7
Unnamed apostle of the churches	2 Corinthians 8:23
Epaphroditus	Philippians 2:25
Silvanus	1 Thessalonians 1:1, 2:6
Timothy	1 Thessalonians 1:1, 2:6

[a]*In modern scholarly understanding, Junia is a woman.*

The function (as well as the language) of the apostle is thus clearly applied to people outside the circle of the twelve and Paul, indicating a dynamic functional apostolate within the early movement. The presence of this apostolate throughout the movement also provides an interpretive framework for understanding the nature and function of contemporary apostolic ministry.

Gifted and Empowered

There is a natural curiosity about whether *apostolic* refers to a certain kind of personality, a gifting, or a vocation, or whether it is just a term used in the Bible to describe what we could call entrepreneurial people. Clarity in this area is crucial if the apostolic ministry is to be reactivated. But our exploration into this issue must begin with the language of scripture itself.

In the New Testament, *apostolic* refers variously to one of the spiritual gifts (*charismata*) and vocations (*kleseos*) that God gave to his people so that the ecclesia can directly extend the ministry of Christ in the world. They involve expressions of God's manifest presence in our midst, in concrete and individual form, and of the power of God's grace, which takes hold of his people and leads them to their appointed service. If mission is the organizing principle of the church (and we believe it is), then the apostolic person aids the church in participating in its highest calling.

As one of the five ascension ministries from Ephesians 4, apostles give believers a unique involvement in the reign of Christ. By extending the gospel of the kingdom across cultural and geographical boundaries, they embody and catalyze the expanding rule of God that will encompass the entire cosmos eventually. Like all other ministry, which incorporates and sanctifies natural gifting and acquired skills, apostolic ministry is in the end dependent on the Holy Spirit and comes to us in the form of a spiritual grace, or *charis*. That is why, as theologian Hans Kung said, the church's ministry is always fundamentally charismatic in nature.[2]

Furthermore, the New Testament clearly teaches the rather radical notion that every believer is uniquely gifted for ministry. The New Testament knows nothing of a separate class of believers who are specially endowed with the Spirit to minister. Ministry flows out of gifting, and because God has distributed these gifts to everyone in the body, ministry is the responsibility and privilege of every member of the community.[3]

In fact this is why the idea of apostolic succession, a fundamental assumption of Roman Catholic, Eastern Orthodox, and certain

Anglo-Catholic forms of church, breaks down. It is built on the assumption that the church, not the Spirit, confers grace in apostolic succession from Peter. We see this practice as short-circuiting the charismatic, God-generated nature of all true apostolic gifting. Surely the Holy Spirit cannot be controlled or his gifts disseminated by human beings. Neither can any charismatic ministry of the church be institutionalized. It was the sin of Simon Magus to seek to procure and control the gifts and power of the Holy Spirit. This became subsequently known as "simony," and we do well to remember that Simon was cursed as a result (Acts 8:9–24).

We can never possess our vocations or institutionalize and therefore control them. Rather, we are simply to humbly accept our callings and attempt to live a life in obedience to Jesus and his kingdom. It is because of the Spirit-conceived nature of calling that when we use the word *apostle* throughout this book, we lean strongly on the functional and vocational side and veer sharply away from any notion of institutional offices. Apostolic ministry and leadership originate in the realm of gift and calling, and thus they are the property of the Spirit. Apostles (and the other vocations) are mere stewards of this calling who are called by God, but their calling can be recognized only by the body of Christ.

Paul as Prototype

So how are we to reimagine the function of apostleship beyond that of the original twelve?

Although we elaborate this later in the prototypal work of Peter, at this stage we draw primarily from Paul's ministry because so much of our understanding of the church's ministry stems from him. Clearly there are other apostles, and therefore other models of apostleship, but the quantity of Paul's writings and our focused exposure to his ministry through scripture have made his apostleship stand out as the norm throughout history.

Paul can be used as a legitimate prototype if we extrapolate some generic descriptions from his apostolic vocation. We can do this by looking at the various terms he uses to describe his role; 1 and 2 Corinthians serve us well in this regard (see Figure 5.1). Ironically, it was because some were questioning the legitimacy of Paul's apostleship that he was forced to map out his role through metaphors and analogies. A brief glance at these two letters reveals at least five insightful metaphors for the apostolic role:[4]

- *Planter.* A basic feature of apostolic ministry is seeding the gospel and the genetic codes of ecclesia into unbroken soil. It is catalytic

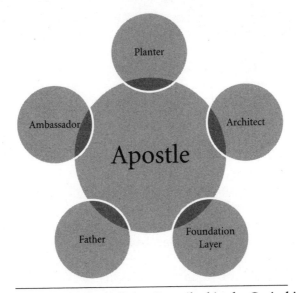

Figure 5.1 Paul's Apostolic Roles as Described in the Corinthian Letters

in this respect, bringing soil and seed together, yet the source of life and growth is contained within the gospel and God's activity. This is perhaps one of Paul's most organic metaphors for apostolic ministry (1 Corinthians 3:6–8). All contemporary apostolic ministry shares in this planting function.

- *Architect.* Our translations use the word "master builder," but the exact wording in Greek is *archetekton—arche* meaning origin or first, and *tekton* meaning craftsman or planner, which offer the idea of primary designer or blueprint crafter. The word is loaded with notions of design, innovation, and strategic craftsmanship. Yet unlike modern architects who rarely visit job sites, the cultural understanding of the architect in Paul's day was of one who not only designed the building but directed the building process (1 Corinthians 3:10). Apostolic ministry is on-site work, not just ivory tower ideation.

- *Foundation layer.* Paul qualifies the constructive metaphor of architect by limiting it to the initial phases of building. Architects may envision the entire project from start to finish and sketch plans accordingly, but the apostle's primary work includes laying solid foundations as well. Paul makes it clear that the community must build on these foundations as well. If the foundations are weak, the community will not stand (1 Corinthians 3:10–15).

- *Father.* Paul sees himself as a father to his churches because he was the catalyst who brought them into existence by the gospel. As such, Paul occupies a unique role within those communities. As their spiritual father, he retains the right to step in and intervene in communal affairs when he perceives they have deviated from the essential truths of the gospel (1 Corinthians 4:14–21). Paul also uses this father metaphor in 2 Corinthians to explain his interests in guarding his daughter's virginity in order to present her as a chaste, pure bride to her bridegroom; here the notion of purity and integrity comes to the fore.[5]
- *Ambassador.* As in our day, the decisions that the ambassador makes legally bind the person or country that they represent. There is real representative authority in the role. The apostle is one who is fully empowered to represent the missional interests of the *missio Dei.* He is an emissary of the King. This kingdom agency infuses all the functions of the apostolic ministry (2 Corinthians 5:16–21).[6]

There are undoubtedly more metaphors beyond the Corinthian letters that delineate the contours of apostolic ministry. Words like *custodian, partner, slave, coworker with God, last in the procession,* and *aroma of Christ* all provide further valuable insights into the nature of apostolic ministry. But to get to the heart of what apostolic ministry is responsible for, we have to allow the word itself to direct us. The apostolic task will always have a missionary function. And given that mission, arising as it does from the *missio Dei,* the organizing principle of the church, this gives a clue to the critical role that the apostle plays in keeping the church true to its calling.[7]

The Apostle and the Gospel

The vital importance and irreplaceability of the apostolic ministry is best understood by the apostolic role as being custodian of the genetic codes of God's people or as a custodian of the gospel, the genetic code of the church.[8]

Paul refers to himself as a steward of the gospel in 1 Corinthians 4:1–2. When using this term (*oikonomia*), he draws directly from a well-known and distinctive role in Greco-Roman society and therefore gives it definitive content. The steward, usually a servant or slave, was empowered to take care of something on his master's behalf; the task was to make sure the object kept its value and viability. Paul alludes to this same principle in Ephesians when he says that God has given him the administration, *oikonomia,* of God's grace (Ephesians 3:2).[9]

So when Paul uses this term, he is claiming that he is commissioned as a guardian, a custodian, of the gospel. To talk of the apostle as custodian clearly does not make the gospel an exclusive apostolic possession. He is not saying that he owns the gospel. Far from it. Stewards do not own the master's property; the gospel owns and authorizes the apostle. But Paul is saying that he has a unique association with the gospel as theological code—not as its originator but as its custodian and therefore its guardian. Paul is setting forth a distinct relationship between Jesus, the apostle/steward, and the gospel itself.

John Schutz, arguably the foremost New Testament scholar on this topic, notes this indissoluble link between gospel and apostle: "Nothing is more closely associated with the 'apostle' than the 'gospel.' No apostle can separate his or her calling as apostle from their core purpose—to serve the gospel. . . . *The terms apostle and gospel are more than just intimately connected; they are functionally related* [italics added]."[10] Because the apostle is always a steward, a slave of Jesus Christ, and a servant of the gospel, Schutz continues, "There is no possibility that he or she will ever usurp the proper, determinant role of the Gospel. The Gospel is itself the norm and source of apostolic behavior."[11] To its stringent demands, the apostle is completely subordinate. The whole of apostolic life and work is a reflection of the forces made manifest in the preaching of the gospel, and this is possible only because the gospel itself continues to make manifest the power of God.[12]

When we say that apostles are the custodians of the DNA of the gospel, we are not just pointing to issues of doctrinal integrity. The gospel also has a functional quality of the extension and renewal of the Faith. The apostle's calling to open up new territories for the gospel aligns them with the explicitly groundbreaking nature of the gospel itself. As the sent ones, apostles are custodians of the genetic codes of the gospel and are aligned with the missionary significance of the gospel. David Bosch, the great South African missiologist, agrees when he says that the terms *gospel* and *apostle* are actually correlates and that both are inexorably missionary in nature.[13]

Of all the ministries, the apostolic is the one that is most keenly aware that the gospel belongs to all people and to feel that their calling is to ensure its spread and extension, as well as its authenticity, among the nations. It is the apostle (and in a very different way, the evangelist as well) who ensures that the gospel moves out of the confines of the host community and is transmitted faithfully into a new cultural context. Once the gospel is embedded into that culture or group, it is once again the role of the apostolic to ensure that this process of transmission is repeated and maintained throughout the movement. As far as we can tell, this process should continue until all the nations are reached by the gospel of Jesus, something that has not yet been achieved. To fully grasp what is being said here, imagine the gospel as a force that is able to accomplish something, having a purpose toward which it proceeds. It is meant for the redemption of the world and therefore is strongly linked to the missional ministry itself.[14]

Although all Christians participate directly in the gospel and are called to extend it, without the uniquely missional contribution of the apostolic person, it is not likely to reach far beyond the narrow confines of ethnicity or escape the cloying self-interest and search for security evident in all people when in the name of some supposed safety, they close ranks and insulate themselves from outside influences. The gospel must be taught, explained, and engaged with by all within the community of faith. But until it breaks out of the enclosed system and comes into direct encounter with new groups, it remains one-dimensional, church bound, captive to a people's collective fears and insecurities, and therefore unable to achieve what it was designed to achieve in the first place: the redemption of the nations.

With this association between apostle and the genetic codes of the church firmly entrenched, we explore more fully the practical implications, as well as the core functions that apostles are responsible for. We specifically highlight how this relates to the church in every time and context.

An Apostolic Job Description

It is hard to find a list of functions from the various writings on the subject that comprehensively provide an adequate job description of the apostle. For instance, in *The Apostle's Notebook*, Mike Breen identifies four apostolic functions that can take their cue from the apostleship of Jesus as prototypical apostle: pioneer, planter, bridger (by which he means cross-cultural aspects), and builder.[15] David Cannistraci suggests eight responsibilities of apostolic ministry: planting churches, overseeing, strengthening churches, developing leaders (imparting), ordaining ministries, supervising and coordinating ministries, managing crisis, and networking with other ministries.[16] To these descriptors we add interpreter of gospel, agent of doctrinal integrity, designer, innovator, change agent, networker, and founder.

Still, we have described only what apostolic people do, not who they are or how these functions dynamically interrelate as a whole in their identity and calling. In order to truly comprehend the meaning of apostolic ministry in all Christian movements, we need a three-dimensional picture of what occurs when these disparate functions come together in a single, distinctive ministry vocation. If we are to comprehend its systemic nature and impact, we must probe what can be called a phenomenology of apostolic ministry.

Taking the aspect of custodianship of the genetic codes of God's people as our cue, we suggest four interrelated functions or dimensions that together delineate apostolic ministry, create a system that incorporates all the functions listed by Breen, Cannistraci, and others, and come together to create a singular field or atmosphere of apostolic ministry.[17] The four functions and their impact are illustrated in Figure 5.2.

Apostolic things happen in apostolic fields: anyone coming into this field will enter into the ambit of a distinctive type of influence called apostolic influence. The following sections describe the four functions and together explore the impact they create.

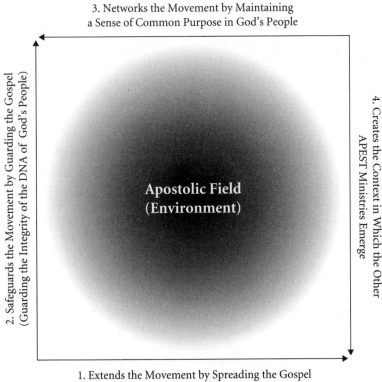

3. Networks the Movement by Maintaining
a Sense of Common Purpose in God's People

2. Safeguards the Movement by Guarding the Gospel
(Guarding the Integrity of the DNA of God's People)

**Apostolic Field
(Environment)**

4. Creates the Context in Which the Other
APEST Ministries Emerge

1. Extends the Movement by Spreading the Gospel
(Seeding the DNA of God's People)

Figure 5.2 Atmosphere of Apostolic Ministry

Seeding the DNA of the Gospel and the Church by Pioneering New Ground

At heart the apostle is a pioneer, and it is this pioneering, generative spirit that makes it unique in relation to the other ministries. But as custodian (steward) of the DNA of Jesus's people, the apostle is also the messenger and the carrier of the DNA of Christianity. So as the one who is sent, he or she advances the gospel into new missional contexts and cultures and plants the gospel there, subsequently cultivating new expressions of ecclesia.

If you were to observe the movement of the gospel, it would look something like this. It begins in Jesus's encounter with the disciples and the people around about him and is then carried by the apostles and the early disciples into the Jewish context (Jerusalem and Judea, for example). From there it moves into the semi-Jewish world of Samaria, and then, using the Jewish communities scattered throughout the empire as bases for launching the messianic movement, the apostles, especially Paul working on his Romans 1:16 formula, plant the gospel in and among the Gentile nations (for example, Galatia, Colossae, Corinth, and Rome).

With the benefit of time and space, we can observe this from a phenomenological point of view. The mission to the Roman Empire looks something like the pattern of an epidemic as it spreads across populations. As each community (different shape) is seeded with the ever-infectious good news of the kingdom of God, it begins to infect people who come into and leave its orbit. All disciples in effect become missionaries carrying the message into every sphere of life, and the community itself also sends missionaries and planters to other groups and across cultural boundaries.

This pattern, based squarely on the scriptures, can be observed in all dynamic apostolic movements in history. It demonstrates the trademark features of apostolic ministry, especially in the Pauline mode:

- Apostolic ministry usually concentrates at the spearhead of all Christian movements where the gospel is extended and received across cultural and spatial spheres (see Figure 5.3 to illustrate the gospel moving from one cultural group to the next).
- Apostles maintain outward momentum as they oversee the contextual embedding of the gospel (the DNA of ecclesia) in the culture. Once the gospel is embedded, they endeavor to keep the communities aligned with the call to maintain participation in the broader mission of Jesus.

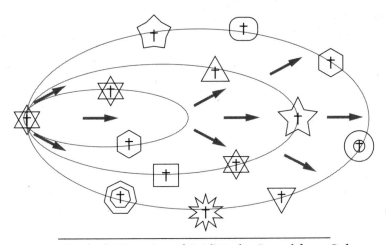

Figure 5.3 Apostolic Function of Seeding the Gospel from Culture to Culture, Place to Place

Note: *The figure shows the gospel planted across cultures in a multiplication pattern and organized as a movement. Each shape in the figure represents a different culture, tribe, or people group. The cross at the heart is the gospel planted in that culture. The arrows indicate the outward-bound forces inherent in the mission of the church.*

If we represent different churches in the movement as different cultural shapes, diagrammatically it might look something like Figure 5.3, which shows the gospel planted across cultures in a multiplication pattern and organized as a movement.

Paul's missionary journeys can be viewed as following this pattern. He moves in four ever-increasing sweeps, planting culturally embedded churches as he goes. The churches he plants take up the missionary mandate and plant more churches, and so the movement takes root in the Gentile world. Wesley and the Methodist circuit riders followed the same pattern, as did Patrick and countless other apostles through history.

It is worth being more specific at this point. The seeding involves more than just communicating the good news of Jesus and then relinquishing all responsibility once the person or group has accepted Jesus as Lord and Savior. If the gospel really is the basis of the salvation of the world and the root of all possible future movement (ecclesia), then seeding that DNA requires much more than simply the evangelistic task of sharing the gospel verbally with others. Viewed apostolically the task requires actually embedding the very genetic codes of the church so that it views itself correctly, engages the world in a certain way, and remains true to its missional (that is, apostolic) calling.[18]

Guarding the DNA of the Gospel and Ecclesia Through the Integration of Apostolic Theology

If we take the cue that apostle is what apostle does, then we can say that they first engage in missionary work, ensuring that new communities are initiated and founded, and once these communities are established, they tend to move off to new frontiers. But much more is evident as well. They are very aware that the movement's theological integrity can be compromised by some mutation in the primary codes—modifications that left uncorrected would destroy the ecclesia, render it unsustainable, or damage its role as a viable, witnessing Jesus community. And because of this, they are quick to weed out what they perceive as heresy and error. For instance, Paul addresses such core issues in each of his letters: the gospel itself (Romans), ecclesiology (Ephesians), Christology

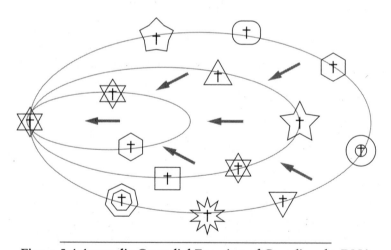

Figure 5.4 Apostolic Custodial Function of Guarding the DNA

Note: Here the apostles act to maintain the movement's connection to the gospel, maintain unity of the movement, and guard against mutation in the core DNA of the church. Each shape in the figure represents a different culture, tribe, or people group. The cross at the heart is the gospel planted in that culture. The arrows are now pointing backward into the movement itself, maintaining integrity and health.

(Colossians), and eschatology (Thessalonians), for example. By doing so, he is eliminating potentially serious mutations in the genetic codes (Figure 5.4).

As the person called to be the custodian of the genetic codes of the church, the apostle ought to be the person most concerned about issues of primary scripting, paradigms, and templates of ecclesia and ensuring that they do not mutate into something other than what God intended them to be. This impulse to ensure theological integrity is therefore another key characteristic of apostolic ministry that forms the basis of the Christian faith; without it, the church would not exist today.

Cultivating Translocal, Fully Networked Movements Through Vision, Purpose, and the Management of Meaning

The functions of seeding and guarding the genetic codes of ecclesia in effect produce a burgeoning multicultural, multidimensional movement networked across a wide cultural landscape. But how does leadership maintain a sense of meaningful unity in a movement that is spreading rapidly into so many different realms? Apart from the necessary work of the Holy Spirit in maintaining identity and cohesion, the answer reaches back into the nature of the gospel codes themselves, as well as the management of the meaning inherent in the gospel itself.

This is where theological identity, meaning, and purpose blend to create a common identity with a unique sense of destiny and calling. Much apostolic work, both then and now, has been focused on these very issues.[19] We belong together; we have a common root and destiny and a mission that only we can fulfill because of what Jesus has done in and for us. This forms the basis of our fellowship and provides the very fabric of movement. The apostle both mediates this knowledge and draws on it to keep the movement going.

A sense of common meaning and purpose both initiates movements and keeps burgeoning networks together. This is especially the case in relation to Jesus movements in history and is clearly evident in the movement we can observe in the New Testament itself. In the early church, there was no central body issuing orders and delegating responsibilities. Ecclesia in the scriptures is clearly a more liquid, more movemental phenomenon, one that is more like a distributed network. Networked movements have the advantage of being able to reproduce easily and can spread very fast, but leading them requires significantly different gifts and skills from the centralized bishop or CEO type of leadership that we have become so accustomed to.

The most authentic forms of apostolic ministry forgo the hierarchical, top-down, transactional forms of leadership and power and draw mostly on what can be called inspirational, or moral, authority.[20] Built on vision, meaning, and purpose, inspirational authority is able to motivate and sustain networks without the promise of remuneration that the transactional forms of leadership are built on. In effect, apostolic ministry therefore creates the web of meaning that holds the networked movement together. It does this by reawakening the people to the gospel and embedding it into the organizational framework in ways that are meaningful. It is because of this apostolic meaning web that the movement maintains itself over the long haul.

This distinctly apostolic, decentralized, networked approach, where order and chaos are held together in dynamic tension, is critical to all people movements because it is the only way a translocal movement can hold together. Each individual, church, or agency relates to the apostolic leader only because it is meaningful for them to do so (by virtue of the gospel itself) and not because they have to. It is because the gospel is implanted, and the Holy Spirit is present in every Christian community, that apostolic leadership can maintain the network and develop the movement network. So it might look something like Figure 5.5.

So to sum up to this point, we can say that the apostolic ministry is basically a stewarding function that is responsible for the extension of the gospel's cause. It does this by seeding the DNA of the gospel through mission and church planting and guarding it against mutation by addressing any theological issues that threaten the integrity of the gospel. The

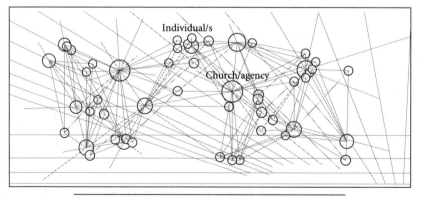

Figure 5.5 Apostolic Web of Meaning
*Note: The smaller circles represent individuals and the larger ones
groups of various sizes within the burgeoning network.*

combination of these two initial functions creates an environment in which ecclesia as movement can hold together as well as expand. If we combine these first three functions and represent the various churches throughout the movements as representing different cultural shapes, it can be represented as in Figure 5.6.

Creating the Environment in Which the Other Ministries Emerge

All leaders and organizations have a certain effect over the people they lead and create different environments. For example, McDonald's creates a different atmosphere from the Cheesecake Factory, and Ross Dress for Less has a different atmosphere than Nordstrom does. People at these different places behave accordingly depending on context. So too leaders have a distinct effect on people. Nelson Mandela exudes joy and invites it in those who follow. Hitler emitted fear and loathing and invoked it in those who came under his sway. And this is so with APEST ministries.

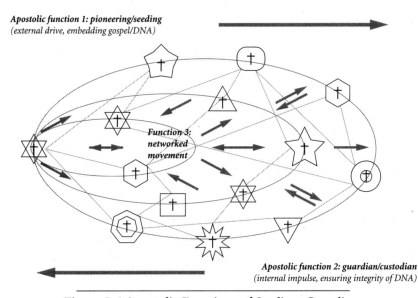

Figure 5.6 Apostolic Functions of Seeding, Guarding, Catalyzing, and Networking

Note: Each shape in the figure represents a different culture, tribe, or people group. The cross at the heart is the gospel planted in that culture. Now there are backward and forward dimensions, as well as a functioning network.

A shepherd creates an entirely different field from that of a prophet: social cohesion and love are the effect of shepherds, and spiritual intensity results from prophets. In the same way, by fulfilling these four critical functions, apostolic leaders create an apostolic field in which distinctly apostolic things will happen.

This issue of apostolic environment partly explains why the apostle is always listed first in all the various lists of ministries in the New Testament (1 Corinthians 12:28; Ephesians 4:11), as well as in Ephesians 2:20, where Paul says that the church is built on the foundation of the apostles and prophets. We do not believe that this is because of some hierarchical conception of leadership, but rather because it is foundational and provides both the springboard and catalyst for the other ministries mentioned in scripture.[21] That is why in seeking to affirm apostolic ministry in this book, we put it in the context of the APEST system in Ephesians 4: the apostolic ministry and APEST are inextricably bound together.

Alan Roxburgh also recognizes that apostolic ministry is "foundational to all the other functions."[22] That is, it lays a base for the other ones and provides them with their appropriate point of departure, their context. Once again this can be seen as part of the custodial function in that the apostolic function maintains the base codes of the church and its ministry. The founding and development of APEST is therefore a natural extension of the custodial nature of apostolic ministry. The apostolic ministry creates the environment for the prophetic ministry, the prophetic ministry creates the environment for the evangelistic ministry, and so on. Using the most comprehensive statement of this ministry structure, that of Ephesians 4:71–11, it would look something like Figure 5.7.

Although we firmly believe that all five ministries of Ephesians 4 are needed to engender, call forth, and sustain a Jesus movement, the apostolic function is the catalytic one needed for it to be a fully fledged missional one. As far as we can tell, there has never been a highly transformative, exponential people movement in the history of the church that has not been catalyzed by apostolic ministry. There have been prophetic movements (Martin Luther King Jr. and the civil rights movement, and the 24–7 prayer movement come to mind), evangelistic movements (such as Billy Graham's crusades and the church growth movement), shepherding movements (those associated with charismatic renewal in the 1970s, for example), and teaching movements (Calvinism and the New Reformed movements), but in themselves they have not, indeed cannot, produce the kind of multiplicative movement rightly categorized by the term *apostolic movement*. The apostolic creates the proper context for the

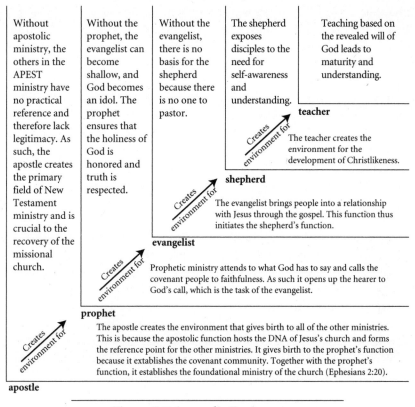

Figure 5.7 Apostolic Environment

other ministries to emerge and produce the fruit that they are intended to produce.

The presence of the apostle is highlighted in situations where there has been leadership that catalyzes the other ministries. For instance, Neil Cole and the associated organic church movement starts two to four new churches every day, and this is not counting second- and third-generation churches—those produced from the new churches themselves. Such results are inconceivable without a fivefold APEST form operating in an apostolic environment. Another contemporary example of the many movements around the world that operate with an apostolic environment is New Covenant Ministries International (NCMI).[23] Adherents of NCMI, started by apostolic founder Dudley Daniel in the early 1980s, state that they are not a denomination of churches but simply a movement of God's people committed to advancing the kingdom of God through mission and networking. They do this through developing an apostolic network led by apostolic-prophetic teams and are held together by a common purpose and friendships. They have planted thousands of churches worldwide, they network with hundreds more, and they are currently working in about fifty countries.

The same is true for the early Vineyard movement under John Wimber, as it is of early Methodism, the Campbell-Stone movement of the 1800s, the Celtic missions, and others. The apostolic role has had an immense influence on every Jesus movement in history. And conversely, its omission from the ministry mix has been detrimental to the health and mission of the church.

Conclusion

We have suggested that recruiting apostles is strategic to the renewal of the organization, and at the very least, it gives equal legitimacy and access to reverse the exile of distinctly missional forms of leadership. To exclude apostolic influences from any position (as the church has typically done up to this point) is to effectively lock out the distinctly missional leadership that churches so desperately need to recover. We need to level the playing field, give equal access, widen the gates, and expand our vision of what biblical ministry is. Consider the following deficits that emerge when apostolic ministry is left out of the equation:[24]

- *Without apostolic multiplication, we stop at evangelistic addition.* Salvation is seen as individualistic as we fail to see how God wants to start a gospel pay-it-forward movement though the life of every believer.
- *Without apostolic action, we fail to experience the promised presence of Christ.* Spiritual authority comes when we operate as an apostolic people sent to disciple the nations (Matthew 28:18–20).
- *Without apostolic clarity, our identity and purpose become murky.* We fail to think strategically about the underlying value systems and core ideologies that define a community.
- *Without apostolic modeling, we miss out on a culture of releasing and empowering.* Instead we contend with a culture of management and control.
- *Without apostolic parenting and releasing, multigenerational mentoring and leadership development are replaced by a dependence on the ministry of professionally training clergy.*[25]
- *Without apostolic accountability, we fail to ask the obvious questions of strategy and sustainability behind our best practices.*

Consider these examples: "Do we really need to have million-dollar budgets, seminary-educated leaders, and fifty to one hundred Christians to start a church?" "Do we need to have land and a building to be the church?" Because apostolic ecclesiology is more movemental in nature, it can go beyond thinking of the church in concrete ways.

- *Without apostolic imagination, we fail to ask questions of scalability.* Instead of reproducibility and scalability, we opt for "go big" and "launch large," forgetting that big movements grow out of small ones done well. The New Testament is our best and most basic example of this.
- *Without apostolic vision, we fail to ask the questions of reproducibility and transferability.* We so complicate the message and training process that few know it and are able to pass it on to others.
- *Without apostolic passion, we fail to embrace our role in the big picture of kingdom mission.* Rather we busy ourselves with the smaller vision and goals of our organizations instead of embracing our calling to actively participate in the global movement of the kingdom.

We believe the idea of custodianship establishes the correct relationship that apostolic people have in relation to their Lord, the gospel, and the ecclesia—namely, that of a slave or a servant. A great deal is contained in this idea: the custodian both seeds and guards the theo-genetic codes of the church, and this helps generate and sustain movements as well as catalyze the incredible potential locked up in the ministry of Jesus's church. Exclude the apostolic, and it becomes hard to see how a fully formed, mature, and expansive ecclesia can possibly take place. Most likely the church would be limited to good preaching, groovy contemporary worship, and Bible studies. We suspect that Jesus intended much more for the movement that he started.

6

come Back, Peter; come Back, Paul

THE RELATION BETWEEN NUANCE AND IMPACT

*After a time of decay comes the turning point. The powerful
light that has been banished returns. There is movement, but it is
not brought about by force. . . . The movement is natural, arising
spontaneously. The old is discarded and the new is introduced.
Both measures accord with the time; therefore no harm results.*
I Ching

My mission is to introduce Christianity into Christendom.
Søren Kierkegaard

*In the coming world, God will not ask me: "Why were you not
Moses?" Instead he will ask me: "Why were you not Zusya?"*
Rabbi Zusya

*Two little blackbirds sitting on a wall,
One named Peter, one named Paul.
Fly away Peter, fly away Paul,
Come back Peter, come back Paul!*
Nursery rhyme

IT IS FASCINATING TO PONDER HOW THE VARIABLES OF AN INDIVIDUAL'S
history and personality play themselves out in the worlds he or she
inhabits. For instance, consider how Winston Churchill's story—his
upbringing, his education, his experience as a war correspondent—came
together to make him the person who led Britain through its darkest hour
in World War II. The little things that come together to make us who we
are also determine to a large degree the kind of impact we will make on

those around us, for good or for ill (Hitler also had a history). Personal history and individual nuance in terms of personality and vocation certainly shape the impact we have.

In this and the balance of the chapters in Part Two, we will be analyzing the nuances of apostolic ministry, reserving the bulk of our reflections on apostolic leadership for Part Three and moving on to issues of organization in Part Four. Given the complexities of human nature and the unique particularities related to our individual callings, we should not be surprised that there are nuances within the broader category of the apostolic.

Using scripture, we can construct significant biographical portraits of the two major apostles, Paul and Peter, that offer insight into the range of possible nuances for expressing apostolic ministry. We are indebted to Dick Scoggins for first calling attention to the functional difference between these two models of apostleship.[1] Scoggins, who now works at the U.S. Center for World Missions, spent many years as a missionary among Muslim peoples in North Africa and seriously engaged in pioneering church planting and contextual evangelism. When he left Africa for Europe, he began engaging with already existing groups of God's people. This meant a move from a radically resistant missionary context to a profoundly churched (or perhaps dechurched) one. With that transition, he sensed a significant shift in his apostolic function and approach. He went back to scripture in search of possible insights and found it in Galatians 2:8–10, which proposes two distinct types of apostles that if taken as paradigmatic and archetypal, would have important implications for how apostolic types might conceive of themselves and pursue their callings.

In this passage in Galatians, Paul states that the apostolic council had recognized his and Barnabas's calling as apostles to the Gentiles while at the same time acknowledging that Peter's calling (along with that of James and John) was to Israel and the Jews of the diaspora. Scoggins notes, "So we see that there is an apostolic ministry to the unreached (the Pauline), but there is also an apostolic ministry to the existing people of God (the Petrine). For me the clincher was that Jesus is . . . the forerunner of both (Hebrews 3:1), but the bulk of His apostleship was to Israel." Scoggins concludes that while most forms of apostleship are modeled on the Pauline, much of the New Testament writing is actually seeking to achieve Petrine outcomes.

This is an intriguing distinction because it allows us to broaden our view from a one-dimensional, predominantly Pauline conception of apostle as pioneer-founder to include that of the apostle as organizational architect. This is particularly important when we consider that a good portion of the work that is needed in Western contexts is corrective and relates to internal, more distinctly reformational issues that are likely to be more the jurisdiction of the Petrine apostle. Although the Pauline apostle is likely to extend Christianity and start new movements on new frontiers of the church, the Petrine apostle is likely to be the one to remissionalize the church as we now experience it.

Pauline and Petrine Apostolic Ministries

Ministry is never a one-dimensional affair. It is always nuanced by an individual's distinctive calling, personality, APEST profile, culture, context, and relationship to the other influencers in his or her orbit. The distinction between Pauline and Petrine adds one more variable into that mix, and it might well prove to be one well worthy of deeper reflection.

This distinction should be seen primarily as a differentiation within the broader function of apostolic ministry. Although there will be differences, there are also great overlaps in function between the two. Much like being right-handed or left-handed, the function of a hand remains the same, but almost everyone has greater dexterity and capacity in one or the other. Both the Pauline and Petrine forms of apostolic ministry share in the core functions of apostolic ministry as custodian, guardian, networker, and translocal activity. But the dissimilarities make all the difference. We illustrate the overlapping yet distinct features of Pauline and Petrine apostolic ministry in Figure 6.1.

In modern equivalents of apostolic ministry in Western contexts, the Pauline is called to extend and establish Christianity onto new ground in the West, while the Petrine is called to help reframe the nature of Western Christianity itself. The one form is thus primarily pioneering and cross-cultural and the other innovative and intracultural.

The Pauline Model: Cross-Cultural Pioneer Founder

The Pauline model represents those who are called to pioneer and explore unreached peoples (the Gentiles). The apostle is the one who is the most translocal, and its function requires a more itinerant lifestyle. Paul, for instance, never seems to stay very long in a single place and feels compelled by a spiritual urge to move on to something new and adventurous (Romans 15:20–22). Following this model, Pauline apostles are natural

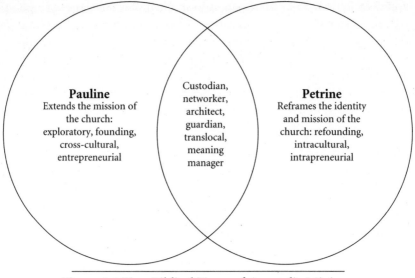

Figure 6.1 Two Biblical Types of Apostolic Ministry

entrepreneurs, constantly scanning their context for new opportunities. They likely thrive in wide-open frontiers and have both a vision and a passion to reach the nations with the message of Jesus. And they will likely resist the tighter, more bureaucratic constraints that are imposed by more institutional contexts and centralized organizations.

It undoubtedly takes high levels of sustained commitment to engage in apostolic ministry on any frontier. It must be deeply rooted in the intrinsic forces contained within the gospel itself; in the redemptive purposes of the *missio Dei*, its outward drive to the nations; in the salvific message of Cross and Resurrection; and, perhaps most important, in sustaining union with Christ. It is not surprising that some of our most profound theology (mystical, philosophical, and forensic) comes from Paul.[2] And although he produced the unique works that were to become a vital part of our canon, all apostolically inclined people should be bonded to the message they carry.

Patrick's missions to the Irish well demonstrates this aspect. It was also subsequently embodied in the missions of Columbanus and Aidan to what is now known as mainland Britain. The Celts, and what became the Celtic movement, had many classic Pauline apostles and reached far beyond Ireland's shores.

The Petrine Model: The Intracultural Visionary Architect

Petrine apostles tend to have a somewhat more internal ecclesiocentric focus, are less missionary in the truly cross-cultural sense of the Word, and are called primarily to serve the already existing people of God. So while they might go into new geographical territories, their initial destination is not to unreached groups of that area (the markets and the philosopher's forums) but to existing churches in a select region. We clearly see this pattern in Peter's ministry throughout the book of Acts.

Furthermore, we seldom see Peter directly engaging marketplaces, philosophical discussion forums, and the like as Paul seems to do (Acts 2 is the exception; but even there he is speaking to Israel).[3] Rather, in Acts 9:32–42, while traveling the country, a sure application of the translocal implications of his ministry, Peter visits the two predominantly Jewish cities of Joppa and Lydda, where he spends the majority of his time.[4] As a result of his impact on them, many people were converted to Christ (verse 42). His primary work was in and through the ecclesia itself. He does much the same thing in Antioch with Paul (Galatians 2:11–14) and, to a lesser extent, with the converted God fearer Cornelius (Acts 10).[5]

This more inwardly focused dynamic of Petrine apostleship comes to the fore at the end of John's gospel, where Peter's calling is renewed by Jesus's threefold challenge to feed his sheep. It seems that although Peter retains his apostolic vocation as a sent one, his ministry takes a decidedly more pastoral aspect. His letters clearly bear this out.

Petrine spirituality is rooted in a call to missional discipleship, one that does not forget obligations to the Lord and to the world. In his letters and speeches, Peter recalls God's mighty works in human history, his redemptive purposes in and through every believer, and the vital agency of the church as exile in diaspora, and he reminds his hearers of the indicatives and imperatives implied in the gospel and in Christ's work for the benefit of humanity. He is vocationally wired to see the entire body of Christ mobilized to fulfill its missional vocation. As custodian of the church's genetic codes, the key Petrine tools are the internal scripts, core ideas, and other elements of organizational culture that serve to fund ongoing sustainability and mission. By applying these tools to how the church conceives itself, Petrine apostles remove barriers to authentic ecclesia, in effect mobilizing the church to fulfill its mission and calling in the world.

It seems the Petrine types exhibit a greater tolerance for more traditional contexts and flourish in reframing and reinterpreting an existing institution and its organization. In this sense, they are more akin to what

D. Myerson calls the "tempered radical"—someone who works toward positive change, often taking radical action that falls just short of getting the person fired. Tempered radicals are quiet leaders who act as catalysts for new ideas, alternative perspectives, and organizational learning and change; they balance organizational conformity with revolution.[6] In this way, they work consistently toward sustaining the permanent revolution that is the church.

Whereas Pauline apostles tend to cross cultures to pioneer new missional communities, Petrine apostles tend to mobilize existing communities to become and remain missional.[7] Therefore, if Pauline apostles are classic entrepreneurs, Petrine apostles can be described as intrapreneurs—those within organizations who take direct responsibility for turning an idea into a viable outcome through assertive risk-taking and innovation.[8] For example, Alan is more Petrine in his expression, whereas Tim leans more toward the Pauline type. Mike Breen is a good mixture of both, with strong Petrine leanings in his current phase of ministry. And although the three of us have significant crossover in aptitude and sensibilities, each of us is more comfortable in his primary type. Tim is most comfortable on some frontier; Alan works primarily within and through the church as a remissionalizer; Mike does both.

One might even go as far to speculate that the difference between the types might have a lot to do with personality and character traits; for instance, for those familiar with the Myers-Briggs Personality Profile, Alan is an INTP and Mike is an ENTJ, while Tim is an ENTP. J's are often more at home in organizational contexts, and I's are less drawn to engage with outsiders, making Alan's profile more accommodating to the Petrine type of apostleship. Tim, an extravert and perceiver, is more prone to engage outsiders and has a greater degree of tolerance for a lack of order and structure, a staple feature in the initial phases of entrepreneurial ventures. So these distinctions could be seen as a classic differentiation between an intrapreneur (idea shaper and mobilizer) and entrepreneur (pioneer) model.

Currently Reggie McNeal (Leadership Network), Tim Keller (Redeemer Presbyterian), Felicity Dale (House-2-House), and Alan Roxburgh are high-profile examples of people functioning within a predominantly Petrine model of apostleship in the West. Neil Cole (Church Multiplication Associates), Dave Ferguson (New Thing Network), Ralph Moore (Hope Chapel), and perhaps Erwin McManus of Mosaic are examples of the more Pauline variety in the same context. (Table 6.1 summarizes Petrine and Pauline apostolic ministry types.)

Table 6.1 Petrine and Pauline Apostolic Ministry Characteristics

	Pauline	Petrine
People skill set	Culturally savvy	Politically savvy
Primary metaphor	Pioneer	Mobilizer
Specialization	Founding	Refounding
Task	Mission	Remissionalize, revitalize
People orientation	Outsiders	Insiders
Response to status quo	High dissonance	Medium to low dissonance
Missional focus	To the nations	To the people of God among the nations
Leadership type	Entrepreneurial	Intrapreneurial
Assignment duration	Shorter term	Medium to long term
Level of risk involved	High risk	Moderate to low risk
How they are viewed by the institution	As a dissenter (a change agent)	As an agitator (a change manager)

Pioneers, Miners, Networkers, and Mobilizers

We think it is possible to cultivate a more thorough categorization of apostolic types based on these two archetypes to bring about a deeper appreciation of what this might mean for the church in our time. In order to do this, we extend the insights garnered from the previous material into more suggestive categories. The material in this section constructs a limited morphology of apostolic ministry based on the Pauline-Petrine distinctions.[9]

To gain further insight into the Pauline-Petrine distinction, we have developed a way of categorizing some of the distinctive orientations by cross-referencing the distinction with that of outwardly pioneering mission (what we call explorer) and that of an innovative organizational development (the catalyst).[10] We suggest the following matrix of metaphors: pioneers, miners, networkers, and mobilizers (Figure 6.2). First, we give some definition to the left axis of explorer and catalyst and then unpack each of the types within the matrix.

Explorers

A common and easily identifiable vocational descriptor associated with both types of apostolic gifting is that of the explorer because in many

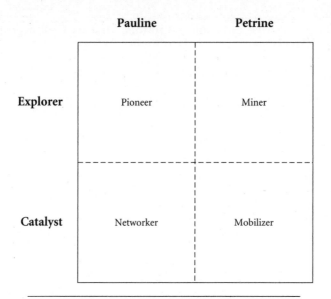

Figure 6.2 Pauline-Petrine Matrix

ways, that is precisely what apostles are: trailblazers, scouts, and founders. The word *explorer* captures the expansive seeding function identified in Chapter Five. It evokes ideas of surveying the land, assessing possibilities, open-ended journeying, and odysseys of discovery. Yet this explorative feature will manifest itself differently within Pauline and Petrine apostles.

THE PAULINE EXPLORER: THE PIONEER. A Pauline type of explorer takes an active role in advancing the gospel into new territories. These explorers' capacity for risk, along with a deeply internalized passion for the lost, combine with their distinct vocational imperative (their sentness) to drive them to plant the gospel among previously unreached people groups. Pauline explorers are therefore the quintessential missionaries; as boundary crossers, they embody the most radical and undomesticated form of pioneering missional leadership in our scriptures and our history. Hudson Taylor, pioneer of the Inland China Mission, and Roland Allen of the Church Missionary Society are good examples from the nineteenth and early twentieth centuries.

Following the hard-driving (some might even say reckless) example of Paul, these explorers will risk their life in order to fulfill their compelling sense of sentness to the nations (1 Corinthians 9:16; 2 Corinthians 11).

Where others might withdraw, and in fact often do (Mark and Barnabas are examples), Pauline explorers seem to be able to thrive on the edge and find their most satisfying environment in the wide-open frontiers of untouched territories. As might be expected, these hard-edged explorers tend to have the strongest critiques of institutionalism, especially where and when it obstructs missional extension. Constantly scanning the horizon, they are not likely to be satisfied with a status quo of any sort. Balking at organizational constraints, they will likely push the boundaries, and for the same reason, they will spark innovation along the way in their search for alternatives.

We devote a fair amount of the material in Part Three on apostolic leadership to articulating the innovation and entrepreneurship side of this form of apostolic ministry, but for now, we simply note that risk, adventure, entrepreneurialism, and renewal all come together in the pioneer.

THE PETRINE EXPLORER: THE MINER. Petrine explorers are more concerned with the home base. They are less boundary-crossing missionary-pioneers and tend to be missional mobilizers or engineers. That is, they tend to focus their energies around issues intrinsic to the faith community. Playing a role much more akin to internal meaning maker, they focus on issues relating to rootedness in the faith, intrinsic motivation, and the identification of unused sources of human capital and identifying and removing internal barriers to the mission of Jesus's people.

This is still is a form of exploration, but instead of the wide-ranging, culture-crossing ministry of the Pauline explorer, the miner explores and unearths the deep structures that either impede or assist an organization in developing responsiveness and agility for mission.[11] The label of miner conjures up images of going down into the depths, of excavation, and the drawing out theological, systemic, and ecclesial treasures that are buried deep within the people of God and their context.

Peter's very naming and commissioning by Jesus in Matthew 16:13–20 hints at the miner's excavatory, (re)founding, and (un)locking aspect of his apostolic vocation. After Peter confesses Jesus as Messiah and Lord, Jesus says to him:

Blessed are you, Simon son of Jonah, for this was not revealed to you by man, but by my Father in heaven. And I tell you that you are Peter, and on this rock I will build my church, and the gates of Hades will not overcome it. I will give you the keys of the kingdom of heaven; whatever you bind on earth will be bound in heaven, and whatever you loose on earth will be loosed in heaven.

And although Peter clearly had a unique role in the founding of the church, there does seem to be something implicit in the type of apostolic ministry itself that works on this level.[12] Petrine apostleship seems to have a supervisory role in relation to the keys, or foundational codes, of the church. That binding and loosing might have to do with the primal thought world of the church. In other words, it is a further application of custodianship.[13]

EXPLORERS AND MOVEMENT MOMENTUM. In many ways, the apostolic exploring of both Pauline pioneers and Petrine miners is about maintaining and sustaining movement. More specifically, it involves cultivating a movemental ethos (a high-energy, decentralized network where all adherents, or most of them, are active agents) and developing an increasing momentum. This combination of movement and momentum is what Dave Ferguson and I (Alan) call "movementum" in our book *On the Verge: A Journey into the Apostolic Future of the Church*.[14]

This issue of gaining and maintaining movementum is a no small task. Edgar Schein, the eminent organizational theorist, is right to note it is difficult because most communities quickly develop an organizational culture with an internal resistance to change before the mature mobilization process begins.[15]

Movements are started by exemplary spiritual events and people; they tend to be somewhat spontaneous in nature as an idea takes root to capture the heart and mind. But maintaining this kind of outward energy is another matter entirely and requires distinctive, and deliberate, skills: the capacity to appreciate what motivates or demotivates people and to debunk the inevitable rationalizations arising from fear and laziness that undermine human agency. And along with an almost instinctive awareness of the dynamics of institutionalization, a mobilizer needs to be able to develop the often naive idealism of early movements into sustainable visionary realism that maintains outward impetus over the long haul.

We will look into the dynamics of both apostolic leadership and organization in Parts Three and Four, but for now, it is worth noting that according to Schein, three levels of organizational culture have to be deciphered before getting to the basic assumptions, stories, metaphors, and paradigms that constitute the primal thought world that gives rise to an organization's culture. Almost identical to the shift process proposed in *On the Verge*, Shein suggests these three levels:[16]

- *The tangible.* The first level is the tangible—the things most easily observed by an outsider when looking at an organization, that is, the way it organizes itself, its language, its style, and other elements that can be heard, seen, or felt. This first level can give clues about the culture of an organization, but it cannot answer the question, "Why?" To understand why an organizational culture is the way it is requires going deeper.

- *The theory.* This is what the organization officially claims about its values, mission, goals, and beliefs. This level of culture does help shape the organization, but it has more to do with what people say about the organization than about what people actually do.

- *The thought world.* The primal source of an organization's culture comes from the third level associated with the "brain" of the organization—the source of consciousness and its thinking. At this level, the basic assumptions operating behind the scenes that powerfully shape the way an organization sees itself, other people, God, and their place in the world can be discerned. These basic assumptions are captured in the controlling stories, metaphors, and paradigms that the organization lives and interprets its world by. The thought world is the ideological fountain out of which organizational culture flows.

Those who are looking to mobilize an existing community for mission may be tempted to look at the tangible and theoretical aspects of a community's culture and think that the barriers to mobilization for mission are to be found in those more visible areas. Current ministry programs, language, and organizational structure can offer clues as to why a church is being missional or not, but they are only visible indicators of the hidden theological and ideological foundations of that community. Changing vision and mission statements, programs, and staff titles engage only the theoretical level of culture. Truly mobilizing a community for mission requires engaging that community's deepest paradigms—its ideological scripts and foundations.

Petrine miners go deep down into the organizational culture to unearth the controlling scripts, myths, paradigms, language, and dominant metaphors that make up their collective thought world—its basic assumptions that powerfully shape the way an organization sees itself, other people, God, and their place in the world. This is often a difficult process because it inevitably involves bringing the hidden assumptions or ignored problems in a community to the surface so that they can be dealt with. In current parlance, it means naming the elephants in the room.

But apostolic custodianship is not just about protective guardianship (see Chapter Five). All apostolic ministry also involves maintaining the outward-looking missional function. True to their calling, miners not only excavate the organizational culture; they also identify the dormant and unused potential within the ecclesia. Sometimes this potential is being suppressed by organizational systems and needs to be unlocked and drawn out. But there is also the possibility that the people of God have overlooked their own nature, resources, and giftedness or have forgotten how to activate them.

This role of remembering who we really are is writ large throughout the Bible. It lies at the root of various liturgies and is a vital part of the apostolic function. Perhaps this is part of what is meant by the "keys of the Kingdom." The very title of *The Forgotten Ways* implies that it is part of apostolic function to help the church remember the sheer potential inherent in the apostolic movement. Furthermore, I (Alan) argue that apostolic movements themselves are always infused with what I called apostolic genius, which is largely dormant in most churches but latent within all authentic expressions of God's people; it needs to be reactivated. We do not need to import these ideas or methods from outside the church; they are already there, and we need to live into them.[17]

This task of reawakening or remembering who we really are lies at the heart of apostolic custodianship, and perhaps it is especially the focus of the Petrine explorer, the miner.[18] Handling resources deeply embedded in the Israel story and tradition and reinterpreting them in the light of Jesus and the new covenant (for example, Acts 2), Petrine explorers work to fund the apostolic vision and mission of the church from within the codes themselves. Miners are able to investigate the roots of Christian community, discover innate resources and skills, and bring them out into the open.

Catalysts

In the world of chemistry, a catalyst is defined as a substance, usually used in small amounts, that initiates, modifies, or accelerates the rate of reaction without being consumed in the process. This is a useful metaphor to describe some aspects of apostolic ministry. Clearly both Pauline and Petrine types act as initiators—people who fuel passion and accelerate certain processes.

THE PAULINE CATALYST: THE NETWORKER. In a way, catalytic ministry is also about movementum, only this time the emphasis falls on the movemental side of the equation rather than the momentum side. If Petrine catalysts mobilize existing communities for mission, Pauline catalysts accelerate movement by establishing the pathways by which the gospel travels from person to person, from group to group, and from one culture to another. This is why we have opted to call the Pauline catalyst the *networker*.

Pauline networkers make the connections and subsequently move on to broaden the network; they do not seem to stay long in a single place. Their influence and leadership are therefore very much translocal. Their home, as well as the locus of their ministry, is the movement at large (not the local church)—the church as a translocal social force—and they thrive at this level of ecclesia. They are classic cross-pollinators and are indispensable weavers of the organizational fabric of movement—the network. Without them, any translocal movement is unsustainable, but also unlikely. The networker is essential to movement generation and health.

The networking function is also vital in maintaining the social fabric of a people movement. By connecting people, developing hubs (Troas), nodes (Ephesus), and hot spots (Galatia, Jerusalem, Rome), and then by relating them to one another, the networker creates a web of relationships (see Chapter Five).

Much has been written about the science of networking recently. In fact, entire new categories of science (appropriately called "the new sciences") are building on it; chaos theory, emergence, and innovation come to mind. And contrary to what it seems at first, networking is more than just connecting people and the flow of information. It is actually the source or, more accurately, it is the means by which most human innovation takes place.[19] Networking creates the pathway for ideas to generate and flow. Malcolm Gladwell famously highlighted this aspect of networking in his seminal book, *The Tipping Point*. He notes that movement happens (tips) when mavens (information junkies) connect with salesmen and networkers, allowing ideas to move through social networks.[20]

We are not suggesting that Paul knew that he was deliberately modeling the creative dimensions of the science of chaos theory when he traversed the Roman Empire as he did; doubtless he was just doing what he felt was part of his apostolic calling. Nonetheless, as he crisscrossed the empire, planting the gospel, establishing communities, knitting them together, developing and sending leaders, and resourcing and catalyzing the movement, he was cross-fertilizing the Israel story with that of the various Gentile nations. The result was the creative generation of new forms of ecclesia unbound from the distinctly Jewish template and culture and allowing them to follow the indigenizing cultural logic of the incarnation.

In order to advance the gospel onto new ground, Paul's cross-cultural interpretation revealed ever deeper understandings of the person and work of Jesus. By rubbing the Jewish religious concepts up against those in Greco-Roman culture, he formed an understanding of gospel that was truly universal in scope. In network theory, this is referred to as crossing weak links and joining previously disparate ideas.[21] Paul was demonstrating best practices in innovation dynamics without even being conscious of it. But in profound ways, the networking itself was doing the work for him. If he had not been involved in apostolic networking, it is doubtful whether Paul would have been able to articulate his key doctrines the way he did; justification by faith is a case in point. It could not have been done in Jerusalem alone. It was through the extension of the gospel into new cultural contexts (the Gentiles) that Paul was forced to work out the fuller meaning of the death of Christ in relation to the Gentiles. It appears that not only is mission the mother of good theology, as German theologian Martin Kahler noted, but mission, along with the networking of the apostolic catalyst, is the mother of adaptive ecclesiology.[22]

THE PETRINE CATALYST: THE MOBILIZER. Although they retain an entrepreneurial orientation, the Petrine catalysts, true to their gifts, will not likely pursue specific opportunities far beyond the established organization. Instead, they are likely to develop an approach designed to address the community's inherent capacities for mission. To generate an urgent reaction in God's people, mobilizers have to generate motivation internally by connecting believers to the church's core theological truths. That is why their contribution to the organization can be described as catalytic. As Steve Reicher, Alex Haslam, and Nick Hopkins point out, "The transformative potential of leaders lies in their ability to define shared social identities. It is through redefining identity that they are able to shape the perceptions, values and goals of group members. The agency of leaders consists in their ability to mobilize people to transform society on the basis of these perceptions and goals."[23] That is, the fundamental task of a leader is to define reality.

If Petrine explorers mine the community to reveal both its dysfunctions and its potentials, Petrine catalysts accelerate the process of mobilization for mission by helping a community become inherently more creative and entrepreneurial. Effectively they are optimizers; they help mainly established communities become more focused on purpose and geared toward their missional calling. The mobilizers are helpful in remissionalizing established organizations and operationalizing movements. In other words, the Petrine catalyst cultivates an internally generated pressure for movement and after achieving that works to maintain motivation and momentum.

As custodians of the gospel, all apostolic people work with the elemental theological forces contained within our primary scripts: they can legitimately fund mission and ministry only by making the necessary connections with the gospel itself. Understandably the Petrine catalyst as apostolic type is likely to develop movementum by emphasizing these ways:

- *The outward (centrifugal), profoundly movemental impulses of the missio Dei.* Moblizers call the church to remember that God is a redeemer and that the church is the uniquely called people who exist to extend that mission (Acts 2:39; 1 Peter 2:5, 9). Apostolic movements align with the sentness of the church as a redemptive movement into the world.
- *The deepening, contextualizing drives of incarnational mission that follows in the way of the Incarnation of Jesus.* Apostolic movements are inspired by the Incarnation of God in Jesus Christ and therefore always engage, redeem, and create culture. Mobilizers help the church to engage mission in incarnational ways.
- *Remembrance of the universal significance of the person and work of Jesus.* Mobilizers help people remember that the church is the principal recipient and carrier of Jesus's message and is responsible to deliver that message. Receiving a message, one intended for us and others beyond ourselves, makes us messengers. Apostolically guided movements call the church to be faithful to the evangelistic significance of our calling.
- *The holy, eschatologically loaded urgency of the Lord's return.* Eschatology is important because it is the context in which the church plays out its role as the key agent of the kingdom. It also creates the conditions of holy urgency that are essential to apostolic movements everywhere. In the same way, urgency plays an energizing role in any organization, just as complacency is likely to sicken it (see 1 Peter 2:11, 16, 3:15, 4:7).[24] It is interesting to see how eschatology plays itself out in Peter's writings. One can even say that he works teleologically, beginning with the end in mind, leading the church from (and into) its own future. Mobilizers understand the importance of urgency. Apostolically led movements operate in the unremitting tension of the now and not yet and allow this tension to infuse all that they do with holy urgency.[25]
- *The local, translocal, and movemental significance of the church.* While Petrine ecclesiology seems to be more conservative and not as culturally generative as the Pauline counterpart, Petrine apostles

nonetheless work with a view to the universal significance of the
Jesus movement (see Acts 2:14–41; 1 Peter 1:1–3; 2 Peter 1:1).
Similarly all mobilizers recognize the worldwide significance of the
church and constantly generate missions. Apostolic movements
know that ecclesia is not just a local phenomenon; it is profoundly
movemental in nature and scope.

- *The positive, always creative, redemptive, dimensions of the gospel.*
  It is interesting to view Peter as permission giver and legitimizer.
  Wherever Peter goes, he seems to try to see and discern what God is
  doing with a view to legitimizing it (examples are the conversion of
  the Samaritans in Acts 8 and the Cornelius episode in Acts 10 and
  15 and in Galatia). This we take to be an aspect of apostolic ministry everywhere and therefore suggest that the apostolic ministry,
  and especially that of the mobilizer, rather than being a ministry of
  naysaying, is by nature sensitive to God's prevenient grace outside
  the church, and is (like Peter) characteristically upbeat and culturally constructive.

The mobilizer, being a Petrine type and operating with a distinct sense
of what is strategic within a given community, will tend to focus efforts
on developing the home base. Any home base leadership will understand
the dynamics of change and how to manage it over time.

It is not hard to see the significance of this particular type of apostolic leadership in the church. Working with existing faith communities
of churches requires relational, political, and organizational intelligence,
as well as a fair bit of patience. In this sense, the Petrine approach is
very Jewish in many respects. Not only does Peter work primarily with
Israel (his home base of deeply formed, faith communities), but he is
also steeped in Jewish perspectives, and therefore organization, on life.
The Jewish biblical worldview, well formed by the time of the New
Testament, had a highly developed sense of the meaning and workings
of history. Through their experience, the Jewish people had learned to
recognize that God is always mysteriously at work in all the rough-and-
tumble we call history, made up of nations, individuals, institutions, the
forces of good and evil, human possibility, and tragedy.

As a well-formed Jew, Peter has a theology imbued with a sense of the
sovereignty of God and the inevitability of his will in and through Israel,
the church, and the nations. He also understands the destiny-shaping
power of ideas and tradition, as in his reapplication of the meaning of the
Messiah and the priesthood of all believers (1 Peter 2:4–11).

We suggest that all subsequent apostolic ministry in the Petrine mold will tend to operate with the same sensibilities. It involves working through the community memory, reframing inherited ideas in light of the messianic ministry and mission, trusting God to achieve his will through his people, and a capacity to wait on God.

CATALYSTS, MOVEMENTS, AND MOMENTUM. Institutions create their own needs and have a mysterious way of becoming obsessed with self-preservation. Resistance to change is a notorious characteristic of institutions. It takes a certain skill set and capacity to navigate the institutional dynamics that resist change. If Pauline apostles are generally culturally savvy, then Petrine apostles are politically savvy.[26] They have the capacity to manage competing interests within the community and redirect them into an alignment with missional values and practices.

Now consider the matrix in Figure 6.2 once again. We do not suggest that these four aspects are watertight compartments to squeeze people into. In reality, humans can never be grouped into a set number of categories. There are always going to be nuances, and each type bleeds over into each other. As far as we can tell, apostolic people have more in common than not, and therefore most can function in all four roles. So, for example, a pioneer type can function as a networker and a miner, but they will function in those roles at different levels of intensity and effectiveness.

Functional Profiling

Might we be able to assess to what degree any single apostolic person might manifest any of these types in some sort of mix? We think so. Figure 6.3 shows how we might profile Mike Breen, the ebullient British apostle, using the Pauline-Petrine matrix.

We hazard a guess that the APEST combinations of the four types might tend to be this:

- Pioneer = Apostle, prophet, and evangelist
- Networker = Apostle, evangelist, and shepherd
- Miner = Apostle, teacher, and prophet
- Mobilizer = Apostle, shepherd, and evangelist

From the matrix in Figure 6.3, Mike is predominantly a mobilizer and therefore would likely have a vocational profile of ASETP or some

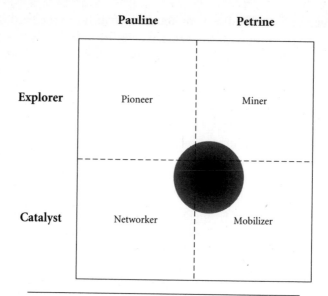

Figure 6.3 Profile of Mike Breen According to the Pauline-Petrine Matrix

Note: The diffused dot indicates Mike's likely profile in relation to this matrix.

variation (the first three are the ones that matter most). Alan, veering more toward the miner, is similar to Mike here, and Tim is more of a pioneer. We suggest that readers (with feedback from some people who know their ministry) try to locate themselves on the profile and see if it fits.

We need to reiterate that because of the almost complete lack of material and research in this regard, we are making educated guesses. Nevertheless, we believe that these guesses, weighted with long and hard reflection, indicate something of the richness of the apostolic function when it is activated in any system, local or translocal. It also indicates something of the impoverishment of the ministry when these ministry types are excluded from the mix.

7

Living from the center
APOSTOLIC MINISTRY AND THE RENEWAL OF CHRISTIANITY

To encounter God is to change.
Dietrich Bonhoeffer

The Church must be forever building, and always decaying,
and always being restored.
T. S. Eliot

Learning to observe the whole system is difficult.
Our traditional analytic skills can't help us. Analysis
narrows our field of awareness and actually prevents us
from seeing the total system.
Margaret J. Wheatley

THE SCRIPTURES ARE REPLETE WITH EXAMPLES OF RENEWAL IN AND AMONG God's people. From the so-called deuteronomic cycles (Judges through Chronicles and Kings) to the eschatological promises of God through the prophets (for example, Isaiah 40–66) and from Jesus's radical renewal of Israel to the call to repentance in the churches (Revelations 1–3), a consistent cycle of renewal is present. Renewal takes place both corporately and individually. Without regular cycles of renewal and revitalization, what were once dynamic movements will degrade to the point of closure (see the Appendix).

Apostolic influences can almost always be detected in and around all the major cultural shifts in church history. The Celtic missions that followed the fall of Roman civilization are a case in point: these missions saved Western civilization. It is not surprising that the influence of the apostles (as well as that of prophets, again highlighting the relationship) should manifest at times of great shifts. They are effective game changers for both the church and broader society. It is precisely at this time that we have to return to our fundamental scripts in order to find new direction. The apostolic custodian comes to the fore; reform and renewal are generally the result for those who successfully negotiate the shift. Those who do not perish.

Thus, the issue of systemic renewal highlights the ongoing role of the apostle in the life of the church, the topic that this chapter addresses. To do this, we must look into the reasons for reform and renewal in the first place.

Along the Life Cycle

Much study has gone into how movements begin, grow, experience moments of renewal, and, for some, end. Life cycle models hold true for all kinds of social movements, but in many ways they are exemplars of how Christianity has tended to advance, have its impacts, and decline. Because these models also provide direct clues as to how groups, organizations, and societies are renewed and revitalized, they can be seen as mirrors to our current situation and experience.

Organizational life cycle diagrams for dynamic movements follow a bell curve that starts with birth and moves through growth, maturity, decline, and eventually death. Along the way a group embraces certain beliefs and develops compatible goals and structures; at its peak, the organization fulfills its sense of calling. Business strategist Ichak Adizes identifies ten organizational stages of the organization:[1]

1. *Courtship:* The events that lead to the initial development or creation of the organization.
2. *Infancy:* The time after launch.
3. *Go-go:* The time of frantic and energetic early growth and, sometimes, chaos.
4. *Adolescence:* The organization is still developing but is more established and defined.
5. *Prime:* The organization is at its fittest, healthiest, and most competitive, popular, and profitable.
6. *Stability:* The organization is still effective and popular, and it can still be profitable, but it is beginning to lose its leading edge.
7. *Aristocracy:* The organization is strong by virtue of market presence and consolidated accumulated successes, but it is slow and unexciting and losing market share to competitors and new technologies and trends.
8. *Recrimination:* Doubts, problems, threats, and internal issues overshadow the original purposes.

9. *Bureaucracy:* The organization becomes inwardly focused on administration, seeks exit or divestment, and faces many operating and marketing challenges.

10. *Death:* The organization is closed or bought for asset value or customer base only.

Putting aside the decidedly corporate nature of this categorization, it is not hard to identify examples of churches and organizations that follow this kind of bell curve. Think of a local group that had a dream to plant a church in a new suburban area of a large, growing city. At the peak of the curve, the church was dynamic and growing, full of young families with their children and offering a variety of ministries and activities. But as the demographics of the suburb shifted, with young people moving out and young families unable to afford to buy houses in the community, the curve began to fall. Members questioned structures and the original message. Before long, a sense of nostalgia about the earlier days of the church set in that led eventually to polarization and eventual closure. This is not an unusual scenario, especially for many churches and mainline denominations that are now on the wrong side of this curve.

The importance of the life cycle concept for churches and Christian organizations is clear: assuming the renewing role of the Holy Spirit in the life of his people, we can say that there are critical stages that must be negotiated if a movement is to have a lasting impact. Certain decisions must be made under the guidance of the missional Spirit to maintain growth and learning or else decline will invariably set in. Leadership, in both nature and quality, is one of the critical factors that keeps decline from being inevitable. Growth can be maintained for a long time if leadership maintains the right overall perspective and the right leadership mix, and makes the right choices at the right time.

Clearly there is a correlation among the life cycle, the ethos, and the type of leadership that predominates at certain points. In fact, ample research in the sociology of leadership makes a direct link in this regard, although as far as we are aware, this has never been applied to the life of the church in an accessible way.[2]

Lawrence Miller's typology of leadership is especially useful in pointing to the correlation of life cycles and leadership roles:[3]

- *The prophet.* The visionary who creates the breakthrough and the energy to propel the organization forward
- *The barbarian.* The leader of crisis and conquest who commands the organization on the march of rapid growth

- *The builder/explorer.* The developer of specialized skills and structures required for growth who can shift from command to collaboration
- *The synergist.* The leader who maintains the balance and continues the forward motion of a large and complex structure by unifying and appreciating the diverse contribution of the other types
- *The administrator.* The creator of the integrating system and structure who shifts the focus from expansion to security
- *The bureaucrat.* The one who imposes control, crucifying or exiling new prophets and barbarians, thereby ensuring the loss of creativity and expansion
- *The aristocrat.*[4] The inheritor of wealth, alienated from those who do the productive work, and therefore the cause of rebellion and disintegration

Miller maintains that every organization begins with the compelling new vision of a prophet and the aggressive leadership of an iron-willed barbarian who implements the prophet's ideas. New techniques and expansions are pushed through by the builder and the explorer, but the growth spawned by these managers can easily stagnate when the administrator sacrifices innovation to order and the bureaucrat imposes tight control. And just as in civilizations, the rule of the aristocrat, out of touch with those who do the real work, invites rebellion—from staff, adherents, and other stakeholders. He suggests that when this happens, it will take the synergist, a leader who balances creativity with order, to restore vitality and ensure future growth. Without the synergist, organizational death is inevitable.

Miller seeks to present an intelligent solution to a stubborn old problem: how to halt a organization's descent into wasteful, stifling bureaucracy. He argues that corporations, like civilizations, have a natural life cycle, and that by identifying the stage of the organization, and the leaders associated with it, leaders can either enshrine decline or avert it, thus allowing the organization to continue to thrive. The impact of these leadership roles can be observed when we insert them into the organizational life cycle (Figure 7.1).

At the very least, the direct correlation between leadership type and growth, maintenance, and decline is clear. We believe that this point has great relevance to our formulas for a permanent revolution. If the implications are not obvious yet, let us be explicit: much of the success of the permanent revolution depends on the nature and scope of our leadership.

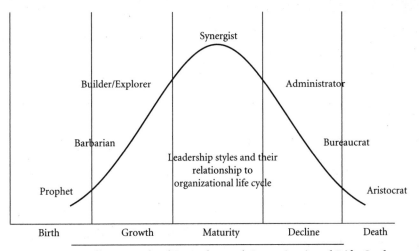

Figure 7.1 Miller's Leadership Styles and Organizational Life Cycles

We have already argued that APEST provides the right leadership mix to generate and sustain movements, but we have not yet articulated how they fit into the life cycle itself. We suggest that APEST correlates well with the best thinking in current organizational theory on the role of certain types of leaders at different stages of the organization life cycle.

APEST Leadership and Movement Ethos

If instead of using Miller's leadership typology and its relation to the life cycle, we simply apply the APEST typology from Ephesians 4, we can say with some confidence that APE types will dominate in the early phases of movements. They will soon have to integrate with shepherd and teacher types in order to achieve sustainable growth, develop the organization, and pass the founding ideals on to others—significant skills that shepherds and teachers have. The movement will be at its peak when it is operating in a fully fledged fivefold form.

It is also clear from all the studies that the more equilibrium-seeking types (shepherds and teachers) will tend to eventually take over and proceed to exile the more disequilibrium-seeking types (apostles, evangelists, and prophets). It is interesting that Miller uses the term *crucifies* in this regard.[5] We are not sure if he is being deliberate here, but it is not too hard to see that the same impulses for self-preservation and control stimulated the Crucifixion of Jesus, the archetypal apostle-prophet.

Ministry as Jesus intended it is always a dynamic complex of multiple vocations and gifts and should never be simply onefold, twofold,

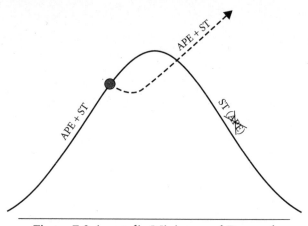

Figure 7.2 Apostolic Ministry and Renewal

or anything less than fivefold. Healthy churches need to be fully aware of the factors that can revitalize them. In fact, simply reinstating a fully functioning Ephesians 4 ministry can bring about what is called *sigmoid growth* in business circles and simply *renewal* in ours. As we said in Part One, it is almost a silver bullet.

Recognizing the role of leadership in organizational life cycles highlights the role of the more generative impact of the apostolic, prophetic, and evangelistic ministries in the ongoing growth and renewal of the church. If the APEs are allowed to occupy a strategic place in the organization along with the STs (the dotted line in Figure 7.2, which is sigmoid growth), they will do more than exert a generative influence at the onset of the organization; they will also help revitalize and hold at bay the forces of decline that set in at the peak of the organization's development.

The presence and function of the apostle creates the conditions for the other types to emerge and operate properly. In other words, the apostolic function is critical to the renewal process. Furthermore, although all apostolic work stimulates progress in some way along the life cycle, it is the Petrine form that comes into its own in the context of the renewal of the church. In other words, to apply our model to Miller's, Pauline forms are the natural prophet-barbarians (initiators of movements), while Petrine apostles are the natural synergists—those who maintain the integrity and continue the forward motion of the Jesus movement.

A good example of the renewing power of apostolic ministry is useful here. John E. Johnson, professor and director of the doctor of ministry program at Western Theological Seminary, is also the team leader at Village Baptist Church in Portland, Oregon. Recently he told us that after reading *Shaping of Things to Come* several years ago, he began to ask, "How is it that the church tends to miss the apostles?" He says, "I realized we were giving little honor to those catalytic, visionary, entrepreneurial types—and it was little wonder they were finding a home in parachurch ministries that thrive on their giftedness. About that same time, I was in Syria with a missional leader, and as we sat up in the mountains, all he could think about was the next mountain. Again, I realized we needed to tap into this missional impulse at Village [Baptist]." Some time ago, John invited every apostolic type of person he could think of to join a group. He subsequently reported, "Our best ideas for doing ministry are generated in this context . . . they helped us see things that the leadership was missing up till that time." It also helped his church work out what he calls a "go to them" (missional) strategy based on Matthew 10. Currently this group is restructuring its eldership on the APEST model.

A Journey to the Center of the Church

Understanding the life cycle and the role of APEST in general and the apostolic in particular helps us see the processes of renewal from a macro perspective. They provide a conceptual map to understand how leadership types affect the way the organization functions and, in the end, whether it can be sustained. In this sense, they map an external process. But what then about the internal processes within the spirituality of the ecclesia itself? How does the apostolic function play a role by reframing and shaping the spiritual life of the church or organization?

Renewal, be it organizational or personal, involves something of a dialectical algebra—a dynamic, oft-repeated interaction between two interrelated poles of existence; the life and truth found in union with God and the life that seeks to live for God in the context of everyday life. This interaction must never be conceived as static or linear, but rather as a constant back-and-forth between our direct experience of God and the subsequent attempt to live consistently with that encounter in the arena of life. Indeed this dynamic lies at the heart of spirituality, and therefore it is not surprising that it should provide a model of renewal in the church. We want to know God and be known by him, and to live a life pleasing with him.

This two-poled dynamic could be conceived as a constant journeying between two dynamic locations: our life center (our home) and the borderlands. Our center represents the cache of core truths and defining experiences we find in a personal encounter with God himself. Our primary sense of who God is, a theology of salvation, the central themes of covenant and kingdom, our sense of identity in Christ, and other themes form the core of these ideas. It is here where our deepest sense of identity abides. When we truly engage the God of the Bible, we corporately and individually will find ourselves deeply loved, embraced, and indeed saved.

But that is only part of the experience. To know God is to change, and to be saved by him implies a commitment to live a life consistent with who he is. This is why such a way of life is called *ethical monotheism*— monotheism is as much an ethos as it is theology or worldview. Our Savior is also our Lord, and because God demands to be taken seriously in all aspects of life, we will find ourselves deeply compelled to maintain the truth of that encounter in everyday life—in other words, through our discipleship.

Furthermore, because it is an encounter with the sending God (*missio Dei*), we will also find ourselves deeply obligated to extend the message contained in and transferred to us in the God encounter. We must retain a living connection with our Savior-Lord while we also live and carry this message into all aspects of life. It is out of, or from, this center or living core that we are called to live.

We cannot stay at the center; true spirituality necessitates that we fulfill our calling to be disciples in a fallen world by traveling to the borderlands, sometimes far from home. Even if it were possible, we are certainly not called to live life in the ecstatic moment—to live in the temple, so to speak. That is why the Bible has so much to say about ethics and life in the world. All of life is the arena for the sacred; we are commissioned agents of the King, and we must take responsibility to understand, integrate, and extend the central truths into all spheres of life. This is the other aspect of the dialectical journey—the necessary border work that all disciples and churches are called to. What religious philosopher Maurice Friedman says of all cultures is certainly true for the church: "Each of the cultures of history originated in an original relation event, and each must return to such an event before it can find renewal. Similarly, religious forms and symbols arise out of elemental religious experience and must be renewed and transformed by such experience if they are to retain their living reality."[6]

It is one of the remarkable features of human existence that wondrous and awesome things become familiar and banal, that we live in the world completely and self-satisfyingly blind to its marvels. In the words of scripture, we forget what the Lord has done for us. And so border work, while necessary, is arduous and can make us lose touch with the defining truths of our spiritual center. That is why we need to constantly return from the fringe. By returning again and again to the living center, we gain fresh conviction, perspective, and courage to face the adventure that comes with the border work.

With this metaphor of center and borderlands, we can perhaps appreciate the apostolic function and its importance, not just in terms of external missionary impact (implications for the border) but also in relation to the ongoing missional renewal of the church.

As we indicated in Part Two, the key role of the apostles' ministry is not as originators of Christianity but as custodians, stewards, guardians, and communicators of the core ideas of Christianity, that is, the gospel. As a custodian, the apostolic person seeks to retain the living connection that we must have with God and gospel, with the *missio Dei* and the mission he has conferred on us. But they are also people who inhabit the borderlands of the faith—the edges where the mission of the church is extended to new territory. Because of this dual role, they can act as catalysts for renewal.

Home Is Where the Heart Is

The original purpose of a touchstone was to test the authenticity and the relative value of metals; the metal was scraped across the surface, and if it was the right type, it would leave a certain mark. When we now use the term, it refers to a measure by which the validity or merit of a concept can be tested. The church, being a community founded on a distinct ethos and set on a unique calling, clearly has its own touchstones. And because it is lived out in a fallen world and subject to all forms of decay and degeneration, every now and again, the church needs to be tested as to its authenticity to its founding purposes. Here lies the need for the ongoing renewal of the church, a recalibration of sorts through which we rediscover its original meaning and purpose.

Figure 7.3, another example of sigmoid growth, shows the founding as well as the refounding process and its close association with apostolic ministry. But in delineating the Pauline and Petrine forms, we have said that although there is some crossover in function, there are also clear differences. We explored how the more pioneering Pauline type of apostleship deals mainly with issues of planting the right DNA and laying the right foundations. It is easy to see this in terms of a founding ministry—the ability to start new ventures from the ground up.

The Petrine form, in contrast, is more about refounding, the process by which a community rediscovers the role and ethos of its founder (what we call *reJesus* in the book by that name), connects with its originating purpose, and thus recovers the potency of its primary message. Given

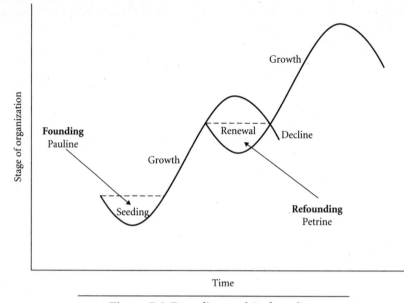

Figure 7.3 Founding and Refounding

that the Petrine is more a home base ministry (to the church), it has more to do with the renewing, revitalizing aspect of the Christian experience. Rather than starting from scratch, it is likely to involve a more evolutionary process of refounding a community around the *missio Dei* revealed in and through Jesus the Messiah (Figure 7.4). So there is a certain dialect between the two: reform, renewal, and revitalization are the natural focal points of the Petrine forms of apostolic ministry, yet these same focal points inevitably relegitimize, empower, and release Pauline forms of apostolic ministry from those churches, creating a synergistic impact of apostolic ministry across the board.

Apostolic ministry is not just about founding new churches and movements; it is as much about the renewal of existing organizations, that is, helping the church retain its primal movemental nature and stay vibrant. And so it has ongoing relevance for established churches as well.

Without explicitly using the term *Petrine,* movement theorist Steve Addison says:

The apostolic role within established churches and denominations requires reinterpreting the denomination's foundational values in the light of the demands of its mission today. The ultimate goal of these apostolic leaders is to call the denomination away from

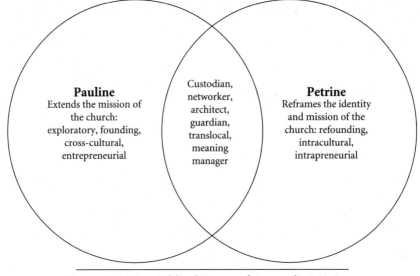

Pauline
Extends the mission of
the church:
exploratory, founding,
cross-cultural,
entrepreneurial

Custodian,
networker,
architect,
guardian,
translocal,
meaning
manager

Petrine
Reframes the identity
and mission of the
church: refounding,
intracultural,
intrapreneurial

Figure 7.4 Two Biblical Types of Apostolic Ministry

maintenance, back to mission. The apostolic denominational leader needs to be a visionary, who can outlast significant opposition from within the denominational structures and can build alliances with those who desire change. Furthermore, the strategy of the apostolic leader could involve casting vision and winning approval for a shift from maintenance to mission. In addition the leader has to encourage signs of life within the existing structures and raise up a new generation of leaders and churches from the old. The apostolic denominational leader needs to ensure the new generation is not "frozen out" by those who resist change. Finally, such a leader must restructure the denomination's institutions so that they serve mission purposes.[7]

An example of deliberate unfreezing of the apostolic vocation is taking place through the Pastoral Leadership Institute (PLi), a key think tank and network of senior leaders in the Lutheran Church (Missouri Synod). The PLi has fully recognized the need for apostolic leadership and is going about relegitimizing the term and actively empowering people to their apostolic callings. The institute is experiencing some new energies as a result. One of the outcomes was a summit-like conference in June 2011 run by a vibrant new network in Texas, FiveTwo Wiki, itself a new movement for church planting and leadership development within the Lutheran Missouri Synod. Similar Petrine responses are being activated at the top level of other denominations, including, for example, the Christian and Missionary Alliance (in the United States and parts of Canada), Pentecostal Assemblies of Canada, and Nazarene. Something big is happening.

The Mission Has a Church

All the talk about missional church might lead us to believe that it is simply that we have to determine a mission and get on with it. But this would not be theologically accurate and misunderstands the nature of mission as rooted in the being and purposes of God. Our task as his people is to discern what God is doing and join with him. It is not so much that the church has a mission but that the mission has a church.

Being the church that Jesus intended means that we must participate in God's eternal purposes for his world. Renewal means more than reinventing ourselves; it means rediscovering the primal power of the Spirit and the gospel already present in the life of the church—reconnecting with this purpose and recovering the forgotten ways. This purpose and potential have always been there, but individuals and communities have largely lost touch with them. They have been displaced by subsequent overlays of border work, involving tradition, rituals, dogmas, and worldliness.[8]

Robert Quinn calls the rediscovery of our primal founding scripts "discerning the inner voice of the organization" and argues that every organization has an inner voice that constitutes its moral center.[9] Quinn is right when he says that the "articulation of the inner voice of an organization is often the first step toward revitalizing [an organization] and uncovering a vision filled with resonance."[10] So rather than simply concocting a mission from scratch, we need to listen again to the inner voice of the church—to touch base with our defining scripts and our compass, as well as engage with our deepest sense of meaning.

This is where Petrine apostleship comes in. Petrine approaches to renewal (refounding) are not so much to impose a purpose on an organization's members as to help them rediscover it and train them to listen for the inner voice within the church or organization. Although such attempts to realign the institution with its inner voice will threaten its status quo, built as it is on self-preservation, it must be done to renew the ongoing vitality and legitimacy of the Christian movement.

In his study of religious orders, Lawrence Cada refers to the "founding charism" of an order to describe its unique vision of the world transformed by the gospel.[11] The use of the term *charism* (grace) implies that the purpose of an organization is a gift that lies at the heart of the organization—a divine bequest, unique to that particular organization. And the recovery of that gift means a "return to the sources."[12]

If apostolic refounding is about anything, it is about a return to the sources. Organizational renewal therefore involves the discovery of an organization's true identity and mission. The authority to bring transformation to the church does not rest in the person of the leader or group but in God's calling. Therefore, the key to the revitalization of religious organizations is to reappropriate, or recover, their founding charism. When Dallas Willard, an influential theologian and thinker, urges younger leaders to "stir the primal coals of your movement, do what they did, say what they said," he is wisely encouraging them to be radical traditionalists.[13]

This radical traditionalism must not be construed as a blind return to a lazy, moribund conventionality. Rather, it involves an innovative insight, a reinterpretation as to how the founding charism can be expressed in the contemporary world.[14]

Consider Volkswagen's innovative reinterpretation of the Beetle to illustrate this process. This iconic car ceased production in the late 1970s and then was resurrected for the new millennium. The new Beetle that emerged has continuity with the original one but in some sense is radically new. The same is true of the Mini and the PT Cruiser. These cars have been great successes and are powerful illustrations of the kind of radical traditionalism involved in refounding organizations. The same impulse can be discerned in religious organizations and denominations. For instance, renewal in Methodism at large has always in some ways been a return to the more primitive forms associated with the original ministry of Wesley; the early Wesleyan denomination is a case in point. In the same way, the charismatic renewal of the 1980s was a radical reinterpretation of the Pentecostal movement within mainline denominations.

All apostolic ministry in some sense involves this return to the founding message as well as purpose. The missional task that follows is to reinterpret it radically into various contexts. To use the words of leadership gurus Jim Collins and Jerry Porras, the key to dynamic entrepreneurialism is to "preserve the core *and* stimulate progress."[15] Thus, there is both a continuity and a discontinuity in the revitalization process, involving both a conservative dimension and a radical one. Radical traditionalism involves a rediscovery of the founder's vision, but it must be matched with spectacular innovations that are as yet undreamed of.[16] As such, it is the apostolic intrapreneur's (the Petrine apostle) basic method of renewal.

Renewal with a Long Tail

Both Pauline founding and Petrine refounding require the crafting of, and living into, new organizational rhythms and practices required to operate out of that foundational framework. Both require the reseeding of key ideas related to being apostolic movements—for example, recentering the church on its Christological roots, developing discipleship processes and quality, creating leadership development pathways, forging new approaches to mission, shaping organizational structure to fit, and getting over risk aversion. Both founding and refounding take time, and results might not be immediately evident. When seeds are planted and there is no apparent fruit when the seed is germinating, this does not mean that God is not at work or that seminal ideas that are correctly planted and fertilized will not have massive consequences. And because the apostolic task is foundational in nature, the most important work happens below the surface and can remain somewhat unnoticeable for long periods of time.

Both ecclesia planters and established leaders understand this. Simply having a lot of charisma or ample financial resources will not mean that practitioners can avoid times of apparent fruitlessness that goes with these phases. It is built into the nature of all entrepreneurial ventures. Many start-up ventures fail during the founding and refounding phases because they lack the perseverance and courage to press forward based on strong commitment to the core ideas. Business strategist Jim Collins, in his book *Good to Great*, speaks of the "flywheel effect": consistent, repetitive, meaningful action will eventually generate a revolutionary breakthrough but you have got to keep at it in the initial phases. This is how Collins put it:

> In building a great organization, there is no single defining action, no grand program, no one killer innovation, no solitary lucky break, no miracle moment. Rather our research showed that it feels like turning a giant, heavy flywheel. Pushing with great effort—days, weeks and months of work, with almost imperceptible progress—you finally get the flywheel to inch forward. . . . You keep pushing, and with persistent effort, you eventually get the flywheel to complete one entire turn. . . . You keep pushing, in an intelligent and consistent direction, and the flywheel moves a bit faster. It builds more momentum. . . . Then, at some point—breakthrough! Each turn builds upon previous work, compounding your investment of effort. The flywheel flies forward with almost unstoppable momentum. This is how you build greatness.[17]

This idea of laying foundations for growth has also been called "the long tail." This means that apparent successes almost always have a long, unspectacular prehistory. Successful enterprise seldom, if ever, just pops up from out of nowhere. For instance, the massive adaptive challenge that obliterated the Chinese institutional church also produced the largest and fastest-growing Christian movement in the history of the church (from 2 million to an estimated 120 million in sixty-five years). Although it is tempting to see this phenomenal movement as arising somewhat ex nihilo, in fact it drew on some of the seminal, ground-laying work of people within the Chinese church itself that was pointing to the idea of apostolic movement long before the Maoist revolution decimated the established church.

Many readers will be aware of the almost prescient, profoundly apostolic work of Roland Allen that helped the Chinese church reorganize itself after 1950, but he was not entirely original and alone in his thinking.[18] In many ways in his writing—*The Spontaneous Expansion of the Church* and *Missionary Methods*, being the main ones—he was building on the work that others (including Henry Venn and Rufus Anderson) had been doing before and around him. For instance, the three principles of self-governance, self-support (that is, financial independence from foreigners), and self-propagation (that is, indigenous missionary work) were first articulated by Henry Venn, general secretary of the Church Missionary Society from 1841 to 1873, and further developed by Rufus Anderson, foreign secretary of the American Board of Commissioners for Foreign Missions (1832–1880).

Their work is an exceptional example of apostolic imagination and practice. But they were really drawing on ideas inherent in the DNA of the New Testament church. The profoundly apostolic seeds laid by these remarkable apostolic practitioners bore fruit in the adaptive challenge presented in the Communist revolution. All these, and many other early missionary entrepreneurs, anticipated, and in some ways prepared, the Chinese church for what was to come. The underground Chinese church had a long, long, tail.[19]

In many ways, the idea of the long tail reflects Jesus's teachings on the subversive nature and growth of kingdom—seeds grow slowly into big trees, yeast invisibly leavens the dough, wheat and tares are mixed together, and so on. It also mirrors the pattern of the gospel itself. It is the self-emptying of the son of God and his pouring out of himself in obedience to the father. Jesus, the trailblazing apostle, laid the foundations for the redemption of humanity through the Incarnation, Crucifixion, and Resurrection (Philippians 2:5–12). At least initially, his efforts seemed insignificant, but they proved to be massively effective in the long run. In laying foundations, or in re-laying them, we must be patient and trust the power of the ideas themselves: DNA will do its work if it is given the right conditions for healthy emergence.

Adventures in the Borderlands

We believe there is a dialogical process by which renewal occurs. On the one hand, renewal will require some sort of reconnection with the central, founding ideas of the faith. On the other hand, renewal involves being stimulated by events and experiences at the outer edges of the organization. Remember that it is the dynamic oscillation between the two that brings about spiritual and organizational renewal. Having considered the importance of touching base with the central home truths, we now turn to the other end of the dialectical process: our venture to the borderlands.[20]

As important as the life center is in defining us and for maintaining our connections with our originating impulses (and therefore our integrity), we will never be faithful in the biblical sense if we never move from home base. The redemptive move outward into life itself is vital to the revitalization process. In fact it seems that renewal is largely precipitated by engaging the fringes or, to use a phrase from living systems theory, "surfing the edge of chaos."[21] It is through our engagement with the world around us that we are forced to interpret and translate our message meaningfully. And so learning occurs when information and experiences from the edge force us to make sense of them with our fundamental message. Mission, engagement, and active discipleship catalyze theological and spiritual renewal. They provide us with that distinct edge intelligence that comes through taking risks and innovating new forms, which we need to keep invigorated.

Religious historian W. C. Roof is right in noting that "the main stimulus for the renewal of Christianity will come from the bottom and from the edge, from sectors of the Christian world that are on the margins."[22] This is partly because movements of mission outside the church usually generate movements of renewal inside the church. New insights are gained and old ideas renovated as the church engages in mission, and this has a positive impact on the church as a whole (examples are the Celts, Wesley, the restorationist movement, and the missional movement of the late twentieth century).

For this reason, and as far as we can determine, it is movements of mission that fuel movements of spiritual and theological renewal, and usually not the other way around. Systemic renewal seldom comes from disengagement from the world or some dualistic detachment from life. This is why fundamentalism is so inherently moribund: it has no internal (or external for that matter) dialectic for being renewed. Mission forces us to understand our core ideas in an attempt to translate them. And as disciples, we must transmit these ideas through the very medium of our lives and into a watching world in ways that are accessible and comprehensible.

Once again, it is by recovering and reengaging our mission as God defines and embodies it that we rediscover God as well as who we ourselves are intended to be in the world. So we might say that in many ways renewal comes directly from the distinctly missionary nature of apostolic work. Apostolic ministry brings the much-needed edge intelligence into the equation.

As strange as this might seem to those inclined to more conventional, well-worn paths, pioneers are invigorated by the tensions created by the demands of the frontier. And some people are uniquely gifted to be able to cope with the uncertainty and risk inherent in frontier work. They have to be, for what is considered routine and normal in the settlement does not necessarily relate to what is experienced on the frontier, away from the relative safety of the settlement. The situation requires an open-endedness, even a playfulness, whereby new possibilities can be discerned and a new kind of learning takes place.

Left to their own devices, most organizations tend toward a sort of sociological conservatism that will increasingly forgo engagement with their context in favor of preserving what they see as their repository of inherited ideas. In other words, they turn away from missional engagement and toward an increasingly traditionalist, sentimental interpretation of reality. Instead of looking forward to a possible future of which they are called to be a part, they look back to an idealized past. Without engagement at the borderlands of the church, where the gospel is extending its reach into previously unreached peoples and cultures, whatever wisdom we retain in our many organizations becomes a trap for our mind instead of a guide to possible action. We are captured by past successes.

It is not hard to see how we look to our past successes, formularize them, and then expect that they will apply to every situation. Yet most denominations are built on that very assumption; they are well-used algorithms or templates. But as far as organizations go, it is axiomatic to say that we are perfectly designed to achieve what we are currently achieving. The leaders who inhabit the system are inevitably the ones who have drunk its Kool Aid and are therefore deeply vested in it. And it stands to reason that the existing leaders in these organizations will tend to operate as maintainers and legitimizers of the inherited paradigm. The problem is that it becomes a profoundly self-reinforcing system, highly resistant to change because of all the vested interests.

These are classic insiders—the fussy traditionalists who operate close to the center and seldom break with convention. In such traditionalistic organizations, intelligence and decision making tend to be drawn out from the reservoir of inherited wisdom. These inherited ideas are seen to be inviolable, even sacrosanct. Furthermore any decisions, such as they are, will be mediated by the conservative elite installed by that very system to guard and maintain it in the first place. There will be no dialectic here, only a one-way, top-down traditionalist approach.

In such situations, knowledge is outdated (or irrelevant) even before it reaches the edges of the organization because it tends to comprise the algorithms formulated at a different time and for a distinctive situation. This is not radical traditionalism; it is plain old traditionalism, and it amounts to *acedia*, a slothful reliance on other people's spirituality and hard work. It is not hard to see this reactionary dynamic at work in the more highly institutionalized high churches, but it is no less real in low church, so-called nonconformist denominations, where decline has certainly begun to set in, the Southern Baptists being a case in point.

Real learning or renewal requires a dialectic with what is known and what is not known, which produces the kind of intelligence that comes only from direct wrestling with the challenges inherent in pioneering new ventures. Donald Schön noted in *The Reflective Practitioner* that "there are those who choose the swampy lowlands. They deliberately involve themselves in messy but crucially important problems and, when asked to describe their methods of inquiry, they speak of experience, trial and error, intuition and muddling through."[23] These pioneering practitioners take the risk, often at great cost, to open up new and unexplored territory or fields of inquiry. But what they learn can be hard to pass along because the knowledge is bound up in the particular practitioner's acquired skills, habits, and intuitions. Being largely experiential in nature, they are hard to conceptualize and therefore often remain unarticulated. However, every now and then, someone comes along who is able to articulate knowledge and compress it into principles and concepts accessible to others. In doing so, they bring much-needed edge intelligence into the equation. Such reflective practitioners are very important in any organization because they are able to translate their learning in terms of ideas useful and meaningful throughout the rest of the organization.

And so although there is much to learn from inherited wisdom and genuine appreciation of tradition, the center should never be the only place where knowledge and intelligence can emerge. The edge is the sweet spot for knowledge and innovation because it is where the organization must intelligently engage its environment. If it fails to do this, it will eventually fail and die. To stop learning, adapting, and responding to stimuli leads to death in any living system, including human organizations.

From a missional standpoint, then, the edge is where the church has to do the hard work of translating its message. Furthermore, because it is a manifestation of the kingdom of God, the church must often do this in an environment fundamentally hostile to it, at times violently so. This is no mean feat, and it makes survival, let alone progress, difficult. But the threat to the organization's survival serves as the much-needed jolt to bring the dying organization to life. The sad fact of Protestant history is that new movements have generally been ejected from the host organization (Francis of Assisi, John Wesley, William Booth, and Pentecostalism were all initially rejected and persecuted). The mission that takes place at the edges is the main catalyst for learning and innovation in the church. Such learning seldom, if ever, comes from the center.

A missional church is one that lives in the tension of being the commissioned recipient (and carrier) of a distinct message and having to deliver that message to its hearers in a way that is credible and comprehensible. To do this, it must remain faithful to its founding truths and impulses, but it also has to develop serious levels of savvy in being able to pass the message on in ways that are meaningful. It needs to be in regular touch with its home truths, but at the same time it must be willing to adventure again to the borderlands. Faithfulness does not exist in one or the other. A missional church is a church that must live the dialectic. It must stay in the journey.

Drawing Near to God, Taking It to the Streets

Perhaps we are now in a better position to assess the nature of renewal and how apostolic ministry facilitates it. Drawing on what we have already stated about the nature of apostolic ministry, we can simply point out that the apostolic type is the one best suited to mediate this dialectic.

As classic edge people, apostles are at the forefront of extending Christianity into new situations. As seeders of the DNA of God's people, they are directly associated with the mission of the church and are keen to ensure that the message is transmitted from one culture to another. They have to be innovators and entrepreneurs because what works in one context might not necessarily work in another. As the ministry functioning furthest from an institutional center, apostolic ministry is most likely to bring what we call edge intelligence into the movement at large. This will facilitate a new kind of learning that brings new perspectives to the old truths contained at the center.

As guardians of the DNA, apostles are concerned that God's people preserve and live true to their core. The letters of the apostles give evidence to this concern. Get it wrong at the level of DNA, and everything that follows will somehow be mutant. When Collins and Porras say, "Preserve the core *and* stimulate progress," they are reflecting an deeply held apostolic concern in secular terms.[24]

And finally, because of the translocal concern and sphere of operations, of all the APEST ministries apostles are best placed to understand the implications of mutations in the DNA on the movement as a whole. As foundations are important in any construction, so foundational truths must be guarded and sustained lest the whole project fail. As people tasked with keeping the movement healthy and growing, apostles can fully understand that without adherence to the core DNA of the gospel, the movement will become toxic and eventually disband.

It turns out that the missional ministry of the apostolic person is vital not only for the extension of Christianity to new ground but also with maintaining the health of the home base as well. Founding any movement in a fallen world will eventually necessitate refounding as the movement recedes ever further from the revelatory moment that gave it birth. Maintaining the core ideas and interpreting them again and again into ever-changing situations requires the enduring ministry of the apostle. A permanent revolution requires a permanent revolutionary. Given the massively changed conditions of this century, we can no longer rely on the formulas and algorithms inherited from our Christendom storehouse. We must return to our deepest home, the movemental ecclesiology of the New Testament, and so rediscover the power of apostolic movement.

•

PART THREE

Apostolic Leadership

8

The Enterprise of Movement and the Movement of Enterprise

The reward of the search is to go on searching. The soul's desire is fulfilled by the very fact of its remaining unsatisfied, for really to see God is never to have had one's fill of desiring Him.
Gregory of Nyassa

In a revolutionary era of surprise and innovation, you need to learn to think and act like a revolutionary. People in revolutions who don't act that way have a particular name: victims.
Joshua Cooper Ramo

He who rejects change is the architect of decay. The only human institution which rejects progress is the cemetery.
Harold Wilson

IN THE EARLIEST DAYS OF EUROPEAN SETTLEMENT IN NORTH AMERICA, there was a vast territory that was essentially unexplored by those who landed on the east coast of the continent. The New World was considered to be a frontier in the truest sense of the word. They had already traveled so far, and some could not imagine venturing much beyond the settlements. For them, settling down was of utmost importance. Others were not so easily satisfied. For these somewhat more curious souls, even watching the sunset served as a reminder that new discoveries lay just beyond the horizon. The westward territory was a constant invitation to adventure, new experiences, even mystery. Looking westward meant peering into risk, danger, and adventure.

Lewis and Clark were two such adventurers who thrust themselves into this frontier and became known as the pioneers who blazed the trail for future pioneers by opening up the Northwest Passage. The arduousness of the journey itself—they trekked twelve thousand miles over mountains and through rivers, across the plains, with a team of thirty-three—required tenacity and courage. It was a near unbelievable feat of vision and well deserves its place in the annals of American heroism and history.

After Lewis and Clark returned from their expedition in early 1806, Thomas Jefferson predicted it would take over one hundred generations to populate and settle the frontier so bravely explored by the group known as the Corps of Discovery. But Jefferson seriously miscalculated the pioneering spirit that Lewis and Clark's journey would evoke in the broader population. In 1890, the American West had reached a point that the line between settlement and frontier was significantly blurred. The U.S. Census formally declared that the frontier was no longer a meaningful designation.[1] In just a little over eighty years, for all practical purposes, the frontier was closed.

For influential historian Frederick Jackson Turner, this closing had monumental implications. He saw the forging of the national identity as occurring precisely at the juncture between the settlement and the wilderness. He considered the dynamic of these oppositional conditions as engendering a process by which citizens were literally made—citizens with the capacity to tame the wild and on whom the wild had cultivated strength and adaptability. He eventually wrote his controversial and hotly debated frontier thesis as a warning to the nation. In his mind, the absence of a meaningful frontier meant the loss of the fundamental driving force that helped move the nation forward into what it had become. He concluded his paper, "The Significance of the Frontier in American History," delivered before the American Historical Association in 1893, by saying: "What the Mediterranean Sea was to the Greeks, breaking the bond of custom, offering new experiences, calling out new institutions and activities, that and more, the ever retreating frontier has been to the United States directly, and to the nations of Europe more remotely."[2]

Being a pioneer is no easy task. It requires a certain kind of person willing and able to move from the known to the unknown, from the familiar into what is essentially uncharted territory. A certain kind of character and resilience is formed in such conditions. Things are experienced on the journey that cannot be manufactured in the comforts of any settlement. And so while Turner turned a blind eye to sometimes atrocious violations of the human rights of the Native American peoples, he nonetheless made an important connection about the relationship between the frontier and national character that emerged from that arduous migration across the land. Turner's notion that the frontier itself, and even the very concept of the frontier, indelibly shaped the character and trajectory of the American people is equally a word of caution to us here in the West.

Challenges of Pioneers

This reflection on American history suggests something significant about leadership in general and apostolic leadership in particular. This should not be surprising, given the nature of Christianity and the role and model of our pioneer and founder, Jesus. However, what is surprising is that not much reflection has been devoted to fully exploring the implications of the pioneering spirit in Christian leadership. This not only indicates deficiencies in our understanding of leadership; it shows deficiencies in our understanding of faith itself. We are inheritors of a faith that is meant to remain a pioneering one because it is always to be an apostolic, or missional, one.

Christianity is about living out an ethos that is embodied in our founders and pioneers; this is called discipleship because it follows in the way of those who opened up the passage for us in the first place. Jesus's apostolic ministry sets the primary agenda for the entire Christian movement, then and now. In Hebrews, the biblical book that dedicates itself to the idea of ongoing pilgrimage and journey, Jesus is called the "pioneer and perfecter" of our faith, and disciples everywhere are encouraged to take cues from him as they seek to faithfully fulfill their own respective callings wherever they find themselves (Hebrews 1–3). Furthermore, Paul's missionary journeys are textbook descriptions of the adventures of a truly remarkable pioneer. It was through his brave, groundbreaking work that the gospel took root in the Gentile cultures and has been passed down to us. Something of this heroic, pioneering spirit is embodied in the faith itself.

The same pioneering character can be discerned in the greatest apostolic practitioners throughout history. Anyone reading about Patrick and the founding of Celtic Christianity cannot but marvel at the courage, resolve, and love of the man as he evangelized pagan Ireland and, beyond that, Western Europe through the many missionaries who, inspired by Patrick and other founders, undertook brave feats in order to reach Europe with the gospel. There is something inherently frontiersman-like about the apostolic. This is something important for us to rediscover at this time in history.

The Anatomy of a Pioneer

Those who feel called to function apostolically will either mobilize the community to voyage toward the edge and explore the frontier or will themselves move out from the center of the organization and venture toward the edge. Those who would pioneer a journey that moves from the center to the edge face unique challenges. Pioneering is not for those who prefer the comfortable life, and it certainly does not always pay good rewards. Many pioneers die on their journeys of exploration—literally and metaphorically. And so it comes with its own unique set of challenges and adversities.

Pioneers have a number of essential characteristics.[3]

An Ability to Invent the Future While Dealing with the Past

Clearly we are living in an in-between time; indeed it has been called "a parenthesis."[4] We are living at the end of Christendom (the settlement) and peering into the rest of this century, a frontier filled with challenges, dangers, and opportunities. We are just beginning to recognize that the maps that got us to this point are not necessarily going to make sense of the new territories ahead. Pioneers often experience the realities of inefficient methods and outdated strategies. The pioneers of the American West sometimes took maps with them, but they were often inaccurate and outdated. Perhaps another way to look at this is to say that a map of Los Angeles might well be accurate, but it is not going to be any use in making your way around New York.

One of the most challenging parts of pioneering work is having to create new maps from scratch. This means charting new paradigms and creating strategies to move forward in a new direction. Pioneers often have to describe, explain, and develop innovative ways of being on a mission without the same resources and legitimacy that are available today. Because of this, they create new maps that challenge our existing ways of seeing.

A Willingness to Break with Traditional Ideas and Methods

The frontier has its own set of rules. What works in domesticated spaces may not work in undeveloped territory. When we are confronted with new challenges, we instinctively fall back on the familiar. Certainly tradition may be helpful back at the settlement, but the challenge of moving forward in uncharted territory forces them into innovative forms of living. Pioneers often have to develop their own language and methods. If pioneers are often seen as iconoclasts, it is because the frontier forces them to break with traditional ways.

An Ability to Play Multiple Roles at the Same Time

Pioneers not only have to cook their own food; they have to find and kill it as well, that is, they have to be both chefs and hunters. They not only have to navigate unknown landscapes, they have to be map makers as well. There is a certain degree of complexity that comes with the role. Robert Hoojberg calls this capacity to thrive in the midst of complexity "leaderplex." Some people have the ability to not only engage but excel in environments that require cognitive, relational, and behavioral adaptation. The leaderplex model implies that there is a certain category of people who can process and reorganize new and existing information, recognize and adopt new social patterns and roles, and ultimately translate these new elements into innovative practices and behaviors.[5]

For instance, leaderplex is well demonstrated in the way Paul describes his relationship with his communities. He can see his role or function through multiple metaphors that define him and change the equation of his relationship to the churches he serves—for example, as planter, architect, foundation layer, ambassador, and partner. He can also approach problems differently when in Jerusalem or in Athens, Corinth, or somewhere else. He is methodologically open-ended and culturally versatile and is well able to use Greek categories of thought in Hellenistic environments and Jewish ones in more Jewish contexts (1 Corinthians 9:20). Because apostolic ministry is by nature a pioneering, translocal activity, the apostolic agent is plunged into multiple roles in different cultures. People in such situations are exposed to a level of complexity that catalyzes a more adaptive approach and an innovative spirit.

A High Tolerance for Risk

Pioneering takes great sacrifice, time, and risk. Investing in this work is loaded with unforeseen challenges. Yet those who stay at home often have little understanding of the nature of pioneering work and its inherent risks and challenges. Thom Kelley, founder of IDEO, a global design firm, is known for saying, "Fail early, fail often." Failure is almost a certain reality at some point in any new venture. There are two kinds of pioneers: those who have already experienced failure and those who will. The challenge is not failure; it is how we deal with it when it happens that presents the most potent challenge.

A Need to Be Different While Supporters
Want the Pioneer to Be the Same

Those who want to support pioneers often expect them to use familiar and conventional processes. Sometimes there is great pressure for a pioneer to abandon something that is working to appease a traditional support system that wants to measure success through traditional metrics. Those who support pioneers need to develop a high tolerance for ambiguity and delayed results. This is especially true when it comes to incarnational approaches to ministry.

Pioneers have to be a particularly hardy bunch. New social and religious movements inevitably arise as a protest against the status quo, which arouses sometimes stern opposition from the system from which they emerge (examples are the Celts and the Roman Catholics, St. Francis and the popes, John Wesley, and William and Catharine Booth and the Anglicans, and Martin Luther King Jr. and the civil rights movement). Machiavelli was not far wrong when he said, "Nothing is more difficult to carry out, nor more doubtful of success, nor more dangerous to handle, than achieving a new order of things."[6] Would-be innovator-reformers will have adversaries who directly benefit from the old order, and halfhearted defenders (halfhearted largely because of fear of adversaries real and perceived) who would benefit from the new. It is the reason that prophets and apostles are almost always persecuted and tend to stand alone.

An Understanding That Many Want the Pioneer to Fail

Pioneers come back from their ventures with stories. Their new maps challenge our old assumptions, and their novel methods force settlers to reexamine their own. People may even like it when a pioneer fails. Their failure subtly reinforces our conventional wisdom, but it also forces those back home to think, "There is something beyond us, beyond our current understanding and ways of doing things." Whether the pioneer fails or succeeds, those in the community have to evaluate their posture toward the frontier, and this is most clearly demonstrated in their posture toward pioneers themselves.

Apostolic leaders need to be category makers, but in order to do that, they need to be category breakers first. They must break away from the certainty provided by institutional domains and live with the uncertainty that comes from engaging possibility. At all turning points in history, when the older forms are dying, new possibilities are created by a few people who are not afraid to stand out and risk their sense of security. Susan B. Anthony, the remarkable civil rights activist and pioneer of the woman's suffrage movement in the United States, said, "Cautious, careful people, always looking about to preserve their reputation and social standing, never can bring about a reform. Those who are really in earnest must be willing to be anything or nothing in the world's estimation, and publicly and privately, in season and out, avow their sympathy with despised and persecuted ideas and their advocates, and bear the consequences."[7] This sounds as if she took her script from Paul in 2 Corinthians and the book of Acts. But Anthony could have been talking here about any archetypal apostles: Peter, St. Patrick, John Wesley, or Jesus, for that matter. Our greatest pioneers are in a very real sense our "holy rebels" who are contrarian enough (for all the right reasons) to break from the herd mentality, innovate, and pave the way for others to follow.

Entrepreneurial Intensity

Those who feel called to function apostolically are essentially being called into a vocation with unique challenges. However, with these unique challenges come unique opportunities to excel in the process of innovation. New and unfamiliar problems require new and unfamiliar solutions. It is in the frontier, at the edge, that we are forced to encounter another reality, which throws us into a process of reflection, learning, and experimentation. Since entrepreneurship is an essential feature of apostolic ministry, we should have an inkling of how it happens and what stimulates it.

Realizing the limitations of formulaic approaches does not mean forsaking them. There needs to be a both-and strategy that allows the exploitation of proven models within select environments while simultaneously exploring innovative strategies within new contexts.[8] Negotiating the limitations of our existing formulas means creating the necessary white space in the organization that not only allows innovative effort but places a commitment to missional entrepreneurialism at the heart of the organization. That is best done through apostolic ministry because it can negotiate new territory and develop and try out the new ecclesial algorithms necessary for the church to fulfill its mission.

Entrepreneurship is by no means the only characteristic of the apostolic vocation, but it is a very important one, especially in times of radical disruption like that we are currently experiencing. For this reason, we explore the nature of entrepreneurialism in general and a distinctively apostolic entrepreneurialism in particular in this chapter; in the next chapter, we explore innovation dynamics.

Every entrepreneurial endeavor is risky. Even when proven models and strategies are used, the risk remains that not all will not go as planned. As a start-up, pioneering form of ministry, apostolic ministry is no different. This ministry is opened up perhaps to even greater levels of risk by its emphasis on seeding the gospel cross-culturally because incarnational mission requires a deviation from preexisting models.

Characteristics of Entrepreneurial People

Risk taking and innovation are not preferred courses of action for the vast majority of people, who would prefer to travel well-worn paths. Perhaps this is especially so in churches because they are generally socially conservative and backward looking. It takes a courageous act of visionary leadership in churches to refocus the organization, give it the needed sense of urgency, and then reallocate the resources necessary to create a more enterprising ecclesiology.

We wholeheartedly believe that God has provided the types of leadership that can best produce entrepreneurial effort. And while it is likely to arise from somewhere within the generative types of apostle, prophet, and evangelist, entrepreneurialism will probably to be most concentrated in the apostolic function. So in many ways, the first step in developing an entrepreneurial approach to church and mission is to identify and empower people who are not bonded to the status quo, have the intellectual freedom to explore new possibilities, are not risk averse, and are able to recombine ideas in a creative and innovative way. We suggest that seven elements are present to varying degrees in genuinely entrepreneurial people.

An Internal Freedom to Explore

While anchored to the core ideas of the faith (the gospel), apostolic entrepreneurialism must have an innate sense of freedom to explore how different expressions might manifest in different contexts and conditions.

In search of better alternatives, we must learn to explore, try new options, and experiment. One lesson we all learn early in life is that if what we are doing is not working, we consider another method. This does not mean giving up at the first sign of negative feedback; it means that if, over time, what we are doing is not producing the desired results, we change strategy. Does the square peg not fit in the round hole? If this is the case, we may have to think outside our immediate task (like cramming the recalcitrant square peg so that it does eventually fit in the round hole) to the larger task at hand (which pegs go into which holes). This sounds basic and fundamental, yet most of us often forget it. The answer is waiting for us if we cultivate holy curiosity.

A Sense of Holy Dissatisfaction

Apostolic entrepreneurs often feel deeply that the church has not reached a state of perfection and that it can do a whole lot better than what we are doing now. All missional enterprise will be predicated on the fact that some people feel a holy need to advance the mission of God by developing new and appropriate ways of being and doing church.

Capacity for Ideation

The various elements of ideation—the ability to put together concepts arising from different disciplines, an imaginative ability to originate new ideas, a capacity to theorize, intuitive right-brain possibility thinking, and others—are all vital to the entrepreneurial process. And contrary to what we might think, these are not simply the product of intuitive geniuses but rather involve the skill of combining ideas from different sources in pursuit of solving certain problems.[9] It is worth noting here that all true apostolic ideation is theological in nature; it gains authority from its relation to the gospel and to biblical worldview.

An Ability to Take On Risk

A common mistake is to equate innovative thinking with being entrepreneurial. Although ideation is a necessary prerequisite to entrepreneurship, simply generating new ideas will not guarantee that entrepreneurial ventures will take place. Innovative thinking needs to move beyond theories and mental models. An apostolic entrepreneur, being a revolutionary, will take the risk to apply those ideas, even at great personal and social cost. William and Katharine Booth, the founders of the Salvation Army, are examples of people who put their radical ideas into action. Thinkers not willing to take such risks are basically just dreamers. Theory and dreaming are good, but in and of themselves they will not change the world or advance the cause of Christ. It is ideation plus implementation that will shape the future.

A willingness to take risks does not equate to being reckless. People who take risks for no other reason than to experience a rush of adrenaline or to get accolades from overly bored audiences are rightly called gamblers and thrill seekers. It is hard to see how this can do anything but harm our cause. However, innovativeness and risk taking find their greatest potential for entrepreneurial impact when they intersect and fuse together (Figure 8.1).[10]

Permission and the Space to Experiment

It is an act of enterprising, apostolic leadership to give social permission to people to experiment and subsequently to protect them from others in the system who are threatened by such innovation. If leadership does not create a culture of experimentation, along with the willingness to learn from failure—variously termed *research and development, skunk works, white space*, or something else—it is hard to see how any progress can be made. Investing in such activities is critical.[11] Apostolically inclined leaders, who have great stakeholding in what they believe, need to be proactive in setting up whatever is needed to open up new options.

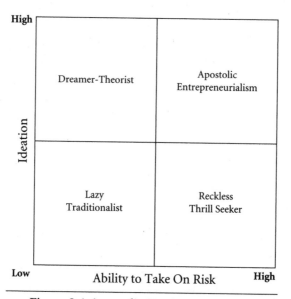

Figure 8.1 Apostolic Entrepreneurialism
Source: Adapted from M. H. Morris, Entrepreneurial Intensity: Sustainable Advantages for Individuals, Organizations, and Societies *(Westport, Conn.: Quorum Books, 1998), p. 44.*

Entrepreneurial Intensity

This idea refers to the degree of risk-taking inventiveness, as well as the frequency with which a person or an organization engages in entrepreneurial activity. For instance, if an organization only randomly engages in risky initiatives, it hardly qualifies to be called entrepreneurial in the true sense of the word.

The concept of entrepreneurial intensity is designed to capture the combined effects of both the degree and frequency of entrepreneurial activity. Being clearly entrepreneurial, apostolic ministry will likely be somewhere at the higher end of the continuum because such people demonstrate higher levels of risk, innovativeness, implementation, and frequency (Figure 8.2).[12] The vertical axis in Figure 8.2 is the extent to which endeavors can be characterized as risky and innovative. The horizontal axis represents the frequency in which those endeavors occur.

The apostolic ministry required to address the situation that Western Christianity finds itself in is going to have to possess a certain level of entrepreneurial intensity in its nature and scope. It will need to take place more frequently than it is now and demonstrate an increased capacity for risk and innovation. There will need to be intentional, strategic

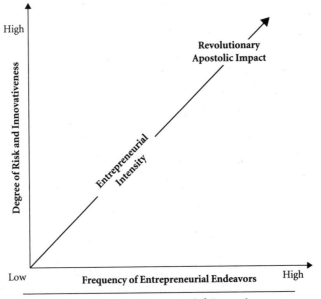

Figure 8.2 Entrepreneurial Intensity

Source: Adapted from Morris, Entrepreneurial Intensity, *p. 19.*

forethought as to the trajectory that apostolic leadership needs to take if it is going to respond adequately to our adaptive challenge.

Dogged Resiliency

Ideation, risk taking, permission, and space to experiment certainly are required, but a more personal quality is also needed for those who are engaged in risky experiments in which outcomes are unknown: a dogged determinism to see one's dream come true. Before Thomas Edison invented the light bulb, he discovered eighteen hundred ways not to make it. It is hard for many to imagine the kind of determination to succeed that is required to be truly entrepreneurial. One has to really believe in one's cause, especially in the face of the inevitable naysayers and other hindrances to develop groundbreaking models and ideas. It was the same kind of determined action that drove Paul relentlessly across the empire and through all kinds of hazards, not a few of them death defying.

A Typology of Entrepreneurship

Based on Morris's model of entrepreneurial intensity, we have identified four basic types of entrepreneurship (Figure 8.3):

- *Nominal:* There may be some commitment to the idea of enterprising activity, but it has the lowest levels of entrepreneurial frequency. In a church, there might be a recognition that new forms are needed, but it has no sustained commitment to any form of entrepreneurial effort and innovates, if at all, within the constraints of the prevailing ecclesial paradigm or algorithm.
- *Sporadic:* This type engages in bouts of serious innovation and risk taking but tends to lack a cohesive vision to enact a regular and strategic activity at the heart of the organization or church. There is some level of ability to take risk, along with some commitment to ideation, but not enough to alter the host organization fundamentally. The more progressive wing of evangelicalism likely fits this type. Knowing that structure and wineskins need to change is held in tension with an innate conservatism.
- *Franchised:* This type, which is popular in the United States, takes its cue from the massively franchised chain store economy. Developing a franchise might not require seriously innovative work, but it does mean finding a successful formula, standardizing it, and making it an algorithm that can be used in various

settings. Entrepreneurialism is taken seriously, but it is seldom of a genuinely innovative, groundbreaking variety. Risk is minimized by limiting variation and requiring conformity to the brand or franchise.

- *Dynamic:* In its most intense forms, dynamic entrepreneurialism can involve highly disruptive types of innovation that have the potential to create new industries overnight, while outdating others at the same time.[13] Less intense (and more common) types retain the heartfelt commitment to entrepreneurialism that puts the organization in a state of constant learning, adaptation, and pursuit of better alternatives. This kind of entrepreneurship sustains a commitment to innovation and risk taking in a sustainable manner.

Although all of these types are appropriate to a particular context and situation, given the situation of the church in the West, we advocate a more intense, dynamic form of entrepreneurial engagement.

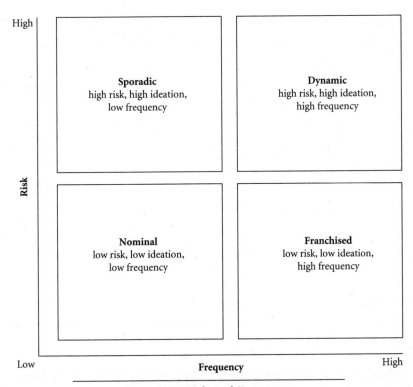

Figure 8.3 Risk and Frequency

The State of the (Entrepreneurial) Union

It seems to us that the church as it now stands seems to be fluctuating among the nominal, sporadic, and franchising models; only on rare occasion do we encounter churches and organizations that operate at the dynamic level. For instance, many mainline evangelical denominations now recognize that the inherited formulas from the church growth era are no longer effective, and they are beginning to look to more creative and experimental forms. These churches are interested in the so-called emerging church (the renewal movement associated with Brian McLaren and Tony Jones, among others) and, beyond it, the missional church, but they lack a tradition of risk taking and innovation to engage in a way that makes a difference, so their interest remains nominal for the most part. They not only need to legitimize and incorporate the generative forms of ministry—risky given their historical suppression of them—but also to learn to embrace entrepreneurialism as vital to their future. We suggest that more than lip-service to entrepreneurial mission is required. We suggest a fifty-fifty split in the budget between mission and ministry, which will surely have an impact in weighting the system in favor of radical change.

Furthermore, the potential for making a lasting impact on the landscape of Western Christianity is being seriously undermined by the refusal to legitimize apostolic ministry in mainline denominations. They do not generally recognize that to be missional is to be apostolic—they are in fact the same words and convey the same meaning and potentials. They are, as we have said many times, achieving what they are designed to achieve. We worry that if this does not change, the current trend of decline will accelerate, and at an exponential rate.

There are more sporadic types of entrepreneurial activity within the evangelical wings of mainline churches. They are beginning to take risks and think creatively, but they tend to lack the policy framework to keep the levels of frequency up or locate entrepreneurialism at the heart of the organization. Perhaps one such endeavor is the trailblazing Fresh Expressions initiative coming out of the United Kingdom.[14] This is a deliberate effort of mainline British denominations (predominantly Anglican and Methodist) to develop new expressions of church—a kind of skunk works created to operate far from the epicenter of the organization of the church. It has generated some wonderfully creative new forms (for example, Sanctus 1, Bolton Network Church, and Sports Village Church), but it seems to have had only a marginal impact on its host organizations.[15] Wholesale renewal has not come about through its efforts precisely because it is a skunk works project—operating far from the center of the organization. In many ways, this was a similar problem experienced by the Australian wing of Forge Mission Training Network, the organization I (Alan) founded to develop missional leaders and experiment with new forms. Unless these experimental forums are heartily owned by the broader system, their paradigmatic change remains a pipedream.

If entrepreneurial effort is only sporadic, then serious systemic missional change is unlikely. Innovation and risk have to become a regular, integral part of what it means to function apostolically, and it will have to take on an iterative quality. Engaging in more regular, consistent apostolic ventures will largely depend on whether the church continues to awaken to its missional vocation as well as empowers those in the community who can produce innovative forms of missional engagement.

For the more franchised forms of church, the successful megachurch model is an effective example. This is particularly the case in the so-called multisite movement. Having intuited that a successful (and somewhat innovative) formula that has appeal to upward of 40 percent of the general population, leaders codified the model and rolled out across a system. Examples are Seacoast Church, New Thing Network, Mars Hill (Seattle), and, perhaps especially, Craig Groeschel's Lifechurch.tv.[16]

The alluring aspect of franchising is the level of efficiency it can deliver. Mass-producing a successful model means efficiency and a higher degree of reliability—and therefore success. Yet an overwhelming desire for efficiency can also mask a covert aversion to ongoing risk taking and innovation. We are all drawn to keep perfecting and honing what we already know, to develop mastery over our current way of operating. A purely algorithmic franchising approach can pose a deceptive threat to becoming genuinely missional. Although it holds out the alluring quality of efficiency and frequency, it lacks the levels of entrepreneurial intensity that stand to create impact on the culture beyond its current reach. To reach untapped groups in our society will require cross-cultural, more consistently apostolic engagement with our context.[17] It also means that we need more than one model or solution to our problems. This problem of limited reach and relatively high expense is now being faced by many of its best practitioners, and many are exploring the idea of moving toward being fully fledged apostolic movements.[18]

Dynamic entrepreneurialism does not occur often in churches. Perhaps it is mostly brought about by massive disruptive change that forces the church to find a radically adaptive solution. A perfect example is the

Chinese Church undergoing the fires of the communist revolution. In such a situation (a massive black swan event), the church had to find a totally new form or fail. Perhaps the vision of the organic church movement, that movement seeking to simplify the ecclesiology to be closer to the house church movement of the Bible, led by apostolic leader Neil Cole, among others, represents such a wholesale recalibration of the church in our context.[19] However, at this stage, complete wholesale change in the West is unlikely. Although we must learn from movements like the organic church, we are unlikely to engender the revolutionary type of innovation that occurs in other contexts. Interestingly, movements like these are almost inevitably led by apostolic people.

It seems that the degree to which a system is willing to acknowledge and legitimize apostolic ministry is directly proportional to its ability to be entrepreneurial and have higher levels of entrepreneurial intensity.

Dynamic Apostolicity

We in the church need to learn what it means to engage in dynamic apostolicity along with a high but sustainable degree of entrepreneurial intensity.

In the words of entrepreneurial expert James March, apostolic ministry needs to be characterized by both exploitation and exploration.[20] We need to draw on existing models that have proven successful and leverage their potential for missional impact. But we also need an equally rigorous commitment to exploring innovative strategies to seed the gospel beyond current adherents. March insightfully explains the inherent tension but necessary interplay between these two factors:

> Exploration includes things captured by terms such as search, variation, risk taking, experimentation, play, flexibility, discovery, innovation. Exploitation includes such things as refinement, choice, production, efficiency, selection, implementation, execution. Adaptive systems that engage in exploration to the exclusion of exploitation are likely to find that they suffer the costs of experimentation without gaining many of its benefits. They exhibit too many undeveloped new ideas and too little distinctive competence. Conversely, systems that engage in exploitation, to the exclusion of exploration, are likely to find themselves trapped in suboptimal stable equilibriums. As a result, maintaining the appropriate balance between exploration and exploitation is a primary factor in system survival and prosperity.[21]

Hilary Austen, in her book *Artistry Unleashed*, reframes the language of exploitation and exploration in the more comfortable language of mastery and originality. Fusing the conservative, more predictable features of mastery with the disruptive, more innovative features of originality will create what Austen calls "dynamic disequilibrium," which she compares to "traveling on the surface of a continuous helix. As the spiral circles, it passes through mastery on one side and originality on the other."[22] Rather than mastery or originality being destinations, they are phases every adaptive system passes through, only to return when each has run their course.

Allowing a system to oscillate between mastery and originality may make for a turbulent and sometimes disruptive experience, but it is precisely this dynamic experience of disequilibrium that propels every living system toward adaptive responses and a thriving existence. Getting stuck in either phase could spell death to any enterprise.

Using Austen's ideas, we can see how the biblical apostles went about their work. They had to learn to live in the dynamic disequilibrium of mastering a situation and constantly venturing outward in order to plant the gospel in different cultures and contexts. Allowing the dynamic interplay of mastery and originality to characterize apostolic ventures is clearly a critical issue for the church to wrestle with. It is one thing to awaken the church to its apostolic vocation and quite another to allow the apostolic vocation to function within the full range of its capacity for exploration and innovation. But when it is legitimized and accessed, we should expect ecclesial innovation to be front and center. For example, the apostolic ministry of John Wesley led to proliferating new ecclesial forms and innovations.

Organizations, and perhaps especially churches, resist disequilibrium and opt for mastery of the prevailing algorithm or paradigm. Speaking about the forces of equilibrium in organizations, leadership guru Seth Godin says cogently: "When you fall in love with the system you lose the ability to grow."[23] The desire for conservation and mastery will exercise a gravitational pull that is hard to break out of. He is right. Any move toward change is difficult and will likely be resisted, but without it, the organization cannot progress and will inevitably decline. We need to be realistic; embracing the apostolic paradigm will at first mean that inputs will initially exceed outputs. And it is going to take effort and will to make it happen. It will almost certainly not feel very comfortable. Godin says: "At first, the new thing is rarely as good as the old thing was. If you need the alternative to be better than the status quo from the very start, you'll never begin."[24]

Choosing to stay our current course, with our current algorithms of mastery, has consequences for the vitality of Christianity in the Western context. We either innovate or continue to experience decline. Moving toward a more dynamic pattern of apostolic ministry can align us with a new trajectory that can position us for revolutionary impact.

The Permanent Revolutionary

In high-risk activities, the outcomes are uncertain. If people avoid risk and seldom actively engage in ideation (unless prompted by black swan events and the like), they almost always lack the resolve needed to do something new and see it through without being forced to do so. Innovativeness, risk taking, and implementation have to operate together if entrepreneurial ventures are to take place. This explains why genuine entrepreneurialism is so rare in Christian circles. We suggest that churches or other organizations that want to become more missional need to be intentional in determining policy and deliberate in making budgetary commitments in a missional direction.

Some may write this all off as idealistic. And while we certainly have an apostolic vision for the church, we are also completely convinced about the capacity of the apostolic vocation, given to the church by our Lord himself, to both catalyze and maintain movements. This is not just wishful thinking: it is historical and theological thinking. As we have seen, both scriptures and church history clearly link the presence and function of the apostolic in exponential movements and in church growth and health.

Some will question whether it is truly possible to experience a permanent revolution. The routinization of charisma, the process of institutionalization, reification, and a host of other factors all conspire to work against such durability. Entropy and dissipation are part of the physical and social fabric of reality, yet the very nature of the church's mission calls for continuous movement; it requires the ever-expanding saturation of cultural and geographical spheres with the gospel until the task is done or our Master returns. We suggest that the concept of perpetual advance and renewal is directly linked to the presence and activity of the apostolic ministry; they are the permanent revolutionaries who maintain the permanent revolution. As long as Wesley was alive and active, the movement continued to grow. The same is true for people as diverse as Aimee Semple McPherson and John Wimber. The loss of the apostolic influence opens the door to encroaching decline.

It is not that the apostolic ministry is all that is needed. We have already noted its interdependent relationship with the other four giftings in the APEST ministry matrix. But each of these giftings is designed to make a unique contribution to the church being fit for its missional task. The apostolic gifting is specifically given to the church to generate and sustain missional movement.

The Pauline Entrepreneur

Entrepreneurial energy, although not exclusively associated with Pauline forms of apostleship, is nonetheless the mark of it. Paul embodies both the pioneer and the entrepreneur. He was also a top-rate innovator who was able to translate the gospel and plant it in new cultural contexts without imposing Jewish cultural forms—no mean feat.

Because Pauline work involves breaking new ground when seeding the gospel into new territories, it takes time for seeds to germinate, grow healthily into plants, and begin to produce fruit. Neil Cole is instructive here. He dedicates three chapters of his seminal book *Organic Church* to exploring the slow, unobserved, even subversive nature of seedlike growth. All plants begin with underground, invisible-to-the-eye, seemingly unfruitful work of seed growing.[25] In all these cases, the quality and nature of the initial DNA is of extreme importance.

Skipping the stage of laying foundations of church life and then expecting good results is like tilling and watering the ground without planting the seeds and expecting fruit; all you will get is a field of mud. Cole also reminds us that if we are deceived into thinking that simply getting people to sit in an auditorium one morning a week for an hour is what it takes to start a church, we have completely missed the significance of many of Jesus's teachings about seeds and trees and the like.[26] Seed sowing involves the patient work of the farmers, somewhat all too aware of their reliance on elements outside their control. Planting the gospel properly will produce healthy growth, fruit, and ultimately a harvest, but it all depends on whether we work the basics correctly. And here again we come back to the DNA work, which implants original meaning and purpose of ecclesia. And although this in a sense belongs to all ministry, it is particularly bound to the function and calling of the apostle as the custodian of the DNA of God's people.[27]

The implications of attention to the apostolic work of seed sowing are worked out in Cole's subsequent book on organic movements, *Church 3.0*.[28] Here he compiles a list that he and colleague Paul Kaak created of what they call "the ten essential principles of spontaneous multiplication movement":[29]

- Decentralized without a central control center that must approve all decisions.
- Self-contained and self-replicating units of people at every level of development.
- Minimally structured; it is dictated by the life of the church, not the other way around.
- Not financially crippled and not dependent on outside resources. All resources for the harvest are found in the harvest.
- Driven by ordinary Christians who have been transformed by God and feel an urge to share the good news.
- Relationally linked rather than corporately or organizationally bound.
- Reproducing at all levels simultaneously (developing from micro to macro).
- Driven by a momentum that must be first and always spiritual and then strategic. Personal transformation precedes community transformation.
- Characterized by evangelism that must move from individual conversions to group conversions.
- Aware that kingdom life must begin to touch the domains of society and culture, not just individual lives.

We list them here not just because they are a brilliant example of apostolic imagination and practice, but also because they demonstrate that movements are in fact a direct fruit of what is sown in and through the initial seed planted. In other words, if we must begin with the end in mind, we must also end with the beginning in mind. If what you want is apostolic movement, you must begin with an apostolic seed—the foundation. Each seed contains the whole potential for the forest, but it is all contained in the initial seed. Each element in the system has the full capacity for the whole.[30] Founding the church in the way of the archetypal entrepreneur Paul requires keen attention to the nature and quality of gospel seeds and church foundations.

Navigating Risk

Facing the issues raised in the founding phase raises questions of the relationship between risk and responsibility. How do we know if our efforts will be productive? How much time and energy do we invest before we decide to move on? Risk taking is one thing, but being irresponsible and reckless is another story. The entrepreneurial feature of apostolic ministry clearly involves risk taking, but how do we navigate and manage these risks?

The startling fact is that 80 percent of all starts-ups fail. This alone causes many people to avoid starting anything at all; there is a very high chance of failure and no one wants to fail. But understanding why failure rates are so high can help us maximize our chances of success. Most start-ups fail because they lack in one or more of the following aspects: a thorough grasp of the key ideas that inform the project, the right people to lead and operate it, or adequate resources (financial or otherwise) to get them over the initial high-investment phase. This was some of the hard-earned learning from some of my (Alan) biggest failures—closure of a major missional project called Elevation, which involved a business that experienced some hard times.[31] I soon discovered that surviving a start-up requires at least three essential components:

- *The right idea.* Having the right idea basically goes back to the issue of the DNA of the missional enterprise. Not only is this an issue of theology (who), ecclesiology (what), and the like, it is also a matter of strategy (how). In business circles, this is the business plan, and it requires a thorough grasp of every aspect of the business: market research, product placement, budgeting, customer relations, and the unique selling proposition (what makes this project different in relation to that of the competition). For apostolic practitioners, this will involve helping the key stakeholders see and understand the nature of God and the gospel, but it must also move beyond that into helping them conceptualize how the community will go about its core tasks.
- *The right people.* There is no doubt that having the wrong people in the right places is disastrous for any project—even more so when the stakes are high, as in entrepreneurial start-ups. Choosing wisely here is critical in high-risk ventures. This is clearly a principle in the New Testament church. People of the right calling, character, and commitment are to be placed in leadership of the church (for example, Romans 12:1–8; 1 Timothy; 2 Timothy). People without these characteristics should never be put in a start-up. One of the key lessons I learned from the Elevation experience was what I call the stakeholder principle: all members of the core team must have significant skin in the game in order to participate fully in the decision-making process. People who are not stakeholders should not be allowed to make key decisions because they do not have to live with those decisions. The greater the degree of

stakeholding, the greater the right to make determinative decisions. A metaphor may help. Two animals, the chicken and the pig, contribute to a breakfast of bacon and eggs. One contributes something that can be reproduced and the other gives its life. Both are stakeholders in the breakfast, but only one gives everything. The principle here is that in entrepreneurial start-ups, the pigs must rule![32]

- *The right resources.* This one is obvious to some degree. Although it relates to the issue of funding, it should not just be thought of narrowly as buildings and budgets. It should include personal resources as well. At core this means assessing whether you have the wherewithal to go the whole distance, financially and otherwise. Jesus's warnings about counting the costs in constructing a tower or going to war, while referring to discipleship in particular, is appropriate advice here as well (Luke 14:28–32). You do not want to start something you are not willing to finish. Entrepreneurs should plan for the worst-case scenario in relation to uptake.

All entrepreneurial start-ups should try their best to have all three aspects figured out if they want to maximize sustainability beyond the early phases and want to become part of the 20 percent that survive. While some with two bases covered might survive, it is highly improbable that any enterprise, business or missional, will survive long with just one. In retrospect, Elevation probably had one and a half (wrong people, half-baked business plan, enough money), and it cost us dearly in both financial and leadership capital as a result.

Before this is dismissed as mere business-speak and inappropriate to the issue of apostolic ministry, it is not hard to find a very similar approach in Paul's practices. As the archetypal apostolic entrepreneur in the church, clearly he dedicated much of his life to articulating the DNA of the emerging movement and ensuring it kept on track with the right ideas. Also, he was clearly very interested in making sure the right people were in the right places. Remember his refusal to include John Mark in what most people categorize as his second missionary journey (Acts 15:36–40). In fact, at times he sounds like a line manager issuing orders about who should and should not be leading (see 1 Timothy 3:1–13; 2 Timothy 4:14; Titus 1:6). Paul also spent significant time on the issue of resourcing. For instance, he arranged for offerings to be taken up and distributed throughout the budding movement, and he himself was a tent maker.

All three of these aspects of entrepreneurialism can be demonstrated in the ministries of the great missional entrepreneurs like St. Patrick (and the Celts) and John Wesley (and the Methodists) and in more contemporary ones like Mike Breen, the McManus brothers, and Neil Cole. The American evangelist George Whitfield famously called his revival a "rope of sand" (unsustainable) because it lacked the strategic capacities and long-term impact that the strongly apostolic Wesley seeded into the movement he founded. These included classes (discipleship), training and equipping laity, church planting, accountability to DNA, and decentralized organization. Whitfield had little or no idea of how to create movement that went beyond the salvation response. He did not have a comprehensive plan and did not mentor leaders (did not recruit the right people) even though he probably had significant support (resources). Apostolic movements clearly have strategy, good theology, method, and the right personnel. That is partly why they change the world.[33]

Apostolic leadership is entrepreneurial in nature. To the degree to which we can value it and embed high-intensity entrepreneurialism into the culture of the organization itself, we create the kind of missional movement that can advance the cause of Jesus in our day. To value something is to give it the weight of your commitments, live into it, and see whatever project arises from these commitments through. It is time to get entrepreneurial in the church; in other words, it is time to become apostolic again.

9

The spirit of innovation

CREATING NEW FUTURES FOR
THE JESUS MOVEMENT

*We are better at (involuntary) doing out of the box than
(voluntary) thinking out of the box.*
Nassim Taleb

*The society that abolishes every adventure makes its own
abolition the only possible adventure.*
J. Jordan

*When the forms of an old culture are dying, the new culture is
created by a few people who are not afraid to be insecure.*
Rudolph Bahro

GEORGE BERNARD SHAW ONCE FAMOUSLY SAID, "The reasonable man adapts himself to the world while the unreasonable one persists in trying to adapt the world to himself. Therefore all progress depends on the unreasonable man." Although that may seem foolish, actually Shaw grasped what many social science writers are now only beginning to explore: the supposed lack of apparent rationality in many of the choices we make.[1] Not only are we all far less rational in our decision making than has been assumed, but what often is called ridiculous and contrarian can turn out to be the source of much creativity.

Consider the following statements that arose squarely from the predictable thinking of their day:

"The telephone has too many shortcomings to be seriously considered a means of communication."—Western Union internal memo, 1876

"The problem with television is that the people must sit and keep their eyes glued on a screen; the average American family hasn't time for

183

it."—*New York Times,* after a prototype demonstration at the 1939 World's Fair

"The horse is here to stay, but the automobile is only a novelty—a fad."—Advice from a president of the Michigan Savings Bank to Henry Ford's lawyer, Horace Rackham, who ignored the advice and invested $5,000 in Ford stock, selling it later for $12.5 million

Now consider that Albert Einstein failed the most basic measure of conventional rationality: matriculation in college. Add to this that Apple's Steve Jobs and Mark Zuckerberg of Facebook fame were both college dropouts, not to mention that our Lord was crucified for being a radical maverick. Clearly an unconventional, contrarian mind is often a characteristic of innovators and category breakers.

While all this hints at the almost perennial issues of pragmatism versus idealism and conventional versus contrarian thinking, it also relates to the ability to take risks, break out of tradition, and face derision. These so-called unreasonable people are responsible for the vast majority of innovations and entrepreneurial ventures. History, it seems, does favor the brave fools who are willing to break from conventional wisdom to explore new options.

Apostles are, in the end, our "unreasonable people," the pioneers and "holy fools" (2 Corinthians 11:16–21) who adapt the world to suit their vision of it as defined in Christ. They are responsible for the real spiritual progress across the ages.

The Age of the Unthinkable

When Plato said that "the problem with the future is that more things might happen than will happen," he was alluding to the general annoyance we feel when confronted by uncertainty and ambiguity.[2] It would be much safer to move into the future knowing exactly how it will look. But we do not get to experience the future in that way. In fact, as we know all too well, life itself is not risk free, certain, or predictable. There will always be a degree of uncertainty and open-endedness to life and the human experience.

Stanley Gryskiewicz, in his book *Positive Turbulence,* addresses the importance of ambiguity in the creative process:

Ambiguity is a state in which many possibilities exist. To make an analogy, when an artist faces a completely blank canvas, there are literally millions of pictures that could be created. It has been said that the first stroke of the artist's brush destroys countless numbers of possible paintings, and each successive dab of paint limits the number of paintings that are possible on that canvas even more.[3]

But as history amply shows, we prefer regularity and predictability and want to forgo the perils of adventure in exchange for a more manageable experience of life, especially in institutions. Here, at least in part, lies the psychology behind institutionalism: all institutions, religious or otherwise, are designed to provide the safety of predictability achieved through ritual, dogma, and control through regulations, policies, the promise of reward, or the threat of discipline. That is not necessarily a bad thing. In many ways, this is the boon that institutions confer on us: by providing regularity, recognizability, and ritual, they relieve us of having to incessantly develop new ways of doing things.

But when risk averseness becomes obsessive or a core aspect of the ethos of any organization, it is destructive. This is particularly true for the church. Christian spirituality requires that we find ourselves by giving ourselves away, that we risk loving until it hurts us, and that we engage in the risky enterprise of mission. We are to be the kind of people whom Jesus himself modeled.[4]

Oddly, mission, the very thing that births the church in the first place and remains its abiding call, sets the preconditions for perpetual movement. Mission implies that we have a preferred future, a definite and desired outcome. Furthermore, being based on God's particular, and as yet a partly fulfilled vision for the world, its adherents cannot accept the status quo. Mission is dicey because of the real possibility that things will not go as planned. And it is precisely this uncertainty, the contingency of it all, that makes investing in a mission risky business. Yet there can be no avoiding it: God's people are called to be a missional movement. This means we must act even when it seems to violate our penchant for safety and security—and perhaps especially then.

The most common way people deal with risk and uncertainty is by analyzing past events and circumstances to discover consistent patterns and predictable outcomes. We believe we can significantly minimize risk by embracing strategies and models that have already been tried and tested. Roger Martin calls these proven models or strategies algorithms—a predefined formula that, when applied, produces reliable outcomes.[5] Yet when algorithms are applied to new situations that require a new approach, they can prove disastrous.

When strategy and environment become radically incongruent, as they are in our day, we need to explore innovative strategies in order to effectively reengage that environment. This is true for existing churches that are trying to engage their own contexts, but it also has a wider, more systemic application for Christianity as a whole.

As we alluded to in Chapter Four, in order for any system to survive, the complexity within it has to be equal to or greater than the complexity of its environment. Putting aside all the other factors at play in our increasingly globalized world, the cultural landscape in the West has become increasingly complex and diverse, which has created a black swan event for the church. We need to move beyond our overreliance on the church growth algorithm and explore different approaches to missional engagement, as well as innovate new expressions of church.[6] We need to develop entrepreneurial skills and strategies.

The Strange New World of Innovation

In this and the previous chapter, we categorize apostolic leadership as being the archetypal pioneer/entrepreneurial form of leadership. Entrepreneurship is composed of a number of key ingredients, including the capacity to take risks, develop ongoing and sustainable practices, and innovate. In this chapter, we focus on innovation.

Negotiating the Intersection

Contrary to what is generally thought, innovation is not the sole province of rare imaginative geniuses. To be sure, there are such people, but there are more universal dynamics at work, ones that most of us can learn if we are willing to do so. Something more generic than pure genius is at play in breakthrough creativity, and that something provides a clue to why apostolic people seem to be inherently innovative. It is all about bringing what Richard Ogle calls different "idea spaces" together and managing the outcomes.[7]

So, for instance, in *The Medici Effect*, Frans Johansson credits the birth of the Renaissance to a wealthy dynasty that managed to bring a diverse range of artists, philosophers, musicians, financiers, poets, architects, and even scientists together in one place—Florence, Italy. According to Johansson, it was the intersection of these fields and disciplines that provided the context, as well as the catalyst, for the cultural revolution that was the Renaissance and literally changed the course of history. Johansson is absolutely right here: when existing ideas and concepts collide to form new and unusual combinations, they create a spark for innovative thinking to take place. He observes that when you step into an intersection of fields, disciplines, or cultures, you can combine existing concepts into a large number of extraordinary new ideas. For instance, a person who immerses himself in a different culture experiences an extreme disorientation and is geared up for learning new things. But he also brings new ideas into the host culture. So for instance, "The mere fact that an individual is different from most people around him promotes more open and divergent, perhaps even rebellious, thinking in that person. Such a person is more prone to question traditions, rules, and boundaries—and to search for answers where others may not think to."[8] This is an important clue for understanding the potential for innovation in apostolic ministry. To be sure, apostolic people are partly wired for innovation, but the potential goes beyond innate capacity. The translocal, cross-cultural feature of apostolic ministry arranges a collision of information to take place in both the apostle and the host culture. It is this collision of gospel ideas and diverse human culture and experience that provides the essential spark for ecclesial innovation to take place. We have already observed these dynamics in Paul: his theology, his methodology, and his creative ecclesiology.

Information technology guru Clay Shirky rightly notes that all good ideas have social origins. He notes how people who cross over from one social group to another are more likely to think innovatively:

> People whose networks span structural holes have early access to diverse, often contradictory, information and interpretations which gives them a good competitive advantage in delivering good ideas. People connected to groups beyond their own can expect to find themselves delivering valuable ideas, seeming to be gifted with creativity. This is not creativity born of deep intellectual ability. It is creativity as an import-export business. An idea mundane in one group can be a valuable insight in another.[9]

I (Alan) can discern within my own life disparate experiences that have brought further insight into my task. For one, I am Jewish and nurtured into a Jewish worldview. This has meant that I bring a somewhat different perspective to the tasks than others tend to have due to the blind spots in their own worldview. I was not churched. In fact, far from it. I was converted to Christ as a young adult. Add to this that I have changed countries three times in my life (I was born and raised in South Africa, lived most of my life in Australia, and am now living in the United States), and mix with some pretty weird people at times (I go to Burning Man art festivals and the like), have a highly intuitive personality and lots of world travel: all that crossed together has produced an intersection in my own life that seems to be a seedbed of new possibilities. No less is true for missionaries planting the gospel in other countries, as well as reaching out to people very different from themselves.

However, a mere collision of new and old thinking does not automatically produce innovation. Someone must observe, interpret, and apply this collision. Innovation rises when these new interpretations find a voice and are experimented with. Innovators have the capacity to combine new parts with existing parts and rearrange those parts into new patterns. As management guru Rosabeth Moss Kanter says, "It is as though they are looking at the world through a kaleidoscope, which creates endless variations on the same set of fragments."[10] Innovative breakthroughs largely come from seeing new possibilities in the relationships between seemingly disconnected things.

It does take imagination to be innovative, but such imagination is catalyzed by exposure to such conditions, and we all can do it. To illustrate, I (Alan) was in a recent conversation about innovation with some senior church leaders. We were talking about missional strategy, and the issue of innovation came up. One of them stated adamantly that not everyone could be an innovator. I replied, "Unless their lives depended on it." The point was taken. Given the right conditions and contexts, everyone can be an innovator because every human has the gift of imagination.[11]

The intersection gives us our best chance to innovate. The gift of imagination and intuition has a direct correlation to our ability to engage new ideas seriously, be exposed to out-of-the-ordinary experiences, and encounter different cultures and contexts.[12] For instance, engaging a culture different from one's own involves seeing how others process things differently, how they use different tools and technologies to solve problems, how and why they behave differently, and so on. In fact, research indicates that people who have lived in multiple cultures are more likely to be innovators, which accounts in part for the massive increase in innovation in the past few decades.[13]

That Paul was raised Jewish but lived in non-Jewish settings and practiced his ministry across many cultures has everything to do with his capacity for innovation. For one, he did not have a racially stereotypical view of Gentile culture. And being fluent in Greek also meant that he was exposed to a different worldview from his native Jewish one. Having studied Greek philosophy and observed Greek arts and poetry meant that he understood something of the existential issues faced in the culture (Acts 17:16–32). N. T. Wright uses the metaphor of Greek and Jewish ideas meeting like two tectonic plates throwing up the craggy mountain range we call New Testament theology. His thinking was the direct result of an interplay between of two world views and cultures.[14] Add to this his deep sense of calling to the nations, which he could translate in ways that his hearers could understand and respond to, and we can understand why Paul was so innovative. He was a living intersection.

Beyond cultural experiences, recombinations of technologies alone are fertile ground for ideation. For instance, Johannes Gutenberg combined the existing but unconnected technologies of the coin punch and the wine press (along with movable type) to create the printing press. Facebook is simply a combination of the concept behind the college yearbook and the massive connectivity provided by the Internet. We venture to suggest that in many ways, the megachurch movement arose in part from a willingness to combine the concept of the shopping mall with the local church and was driven by the newly rediscovered evangelistic impulse and fueled by the insights of marketing and the social sciences. We all take it for granted now, but it was an innovation in its time.

All it takes is for people to be willing to allow the possibility of these recombinations to take place, to be playful, to allow the imagination to be stimulated, and not to be held by conformity to one way of doing things. Social theorist Daniel Pink calls the kind of people who can do this "boundary crossers" because they often "reject either/or choices and seek multiple options and blended solutions." They are open-ended and "lead hyphenated lives filled with hyphenated jobs and are enlivened by hyphenated identities."[15] Innovation is not genius; it comes from a willingness to learn and explore possibility without recourse to the prevailing repertoire of solutions.

To be sure, novelty, change, and unfamiliar environments can stress some of us, but they stimulate others, including apostolic types. Because the apostle's key task is to translate and embed the gospel faithfully into new cultural contexts, they have to be productive and cannot rely on old solutions. They need to have the innate or learned capacity to capture the innovative possibilities that come about when two entirely different and previously unrelated idea spaces intersect.

In other words, as the church's natural pioneers, apostles have instinctive leaderplex—the capacity to process and reorganize new and existing information, recognize and adopt new social patterns and roles, and ultimately translate these new elements into innovative practices and behaviors. This apostolic open-endedness and the highly stimulating and missional context that the intersection provides create the conditions for ecclesial novelty to emerge. And this holds promise for the extension of Christianity as well as its renewal.

Living with Ambiguity

Human life as a whole is one vast ambiguity lived out in an equally immense unknown. For instance, who can predict the outcomes of a single day? This ambiguity makes us insecure. We do not like the fact that we are not in control, so we take refuge in past successes and formulas rather than search for new ones, even though we know that better options can be found should we be committed enough to search for them.

Perhaps one of the greatest characteristics of apostolic pioneer-innovators is their seemingly innate capacity to live, even thrive, in the face of ambiguity. Even as they learn from the past, they tend to be more future oriented, and that makes them better able to cope with the ambiguities of the human condition. In fact with the right mind-set, ambiguity itself is fertile ground for new discoveries because it means being less set in our ways and thinking. Columbus set out looking for India; instead he discovered the New World. And like Columbus, true pioneer-innovators have the ability to live with the various unknowns that make up their world. Paul in 2 Corinthians amply demonstrates this capacity to live in an almost constant ambiguous state. In fact, 2 Corinthians 1 alone is exhausting to most of us who struggle with similar conditions. Faith is nurtured in such conditions.

Innovation, especially in the beginning stages, or what some call the fuzzy front end, is saturated in ambiguity (Figure 9.1). At this phase of innovation, nothing has totally taken shape, and there are more questions than answers and fuzzy outlines but not fully defined shapes. With

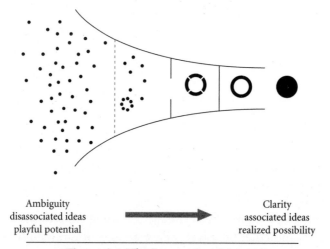

Ambiguity		Clarity
disassociated ideas	⟶	associated ideas
playful potential		realized possibility

Figure 9.1 The Innovation Process

brainstorming and refinement, this ambiguous phase eventually gives way to a clearly defined prototype that is ready for experimentation. Granger Community Church, an American United Methodist megachurch in Granger, Indiana, has an open-ended experimental program that is spearheading efforts to reinvent itself beyond the home base church. So does Community Christian Church in Chicago. Although people are encouraged to experiment, they are not entirely sure of what will emerge.

The ambiguous, fuzzy front end is the necessary, and perhaps even annoying, phase of the innovation process, yet no innovation is possible without it. At this stage, the innovator has to take a counterintuitive approach of deferring judgment, embracing uncertainty, and exploring all options. Ambiguity calls for listening and waiting, not immediate action—hence, the concept of ambiguity tolerance. New possibilities bubble up when we resist the urge to define and categorize problems and their solutions too quickly. Innovation and creativity need ambiguity to flourish. We have to starve our cravings to impose order, close boundaries, and map out every detail before we begin the journey. We have to delay closure so that new possibilities have a chance to emerge.[16]

Thinking Like a Beginner, Not an Expert

Innovation usually arises out of a sense of need, sometimes bordering on desperation. So, for instance, living systems theory consistently maintains that the sweet spot of innovation takes place at the edge of chaos or on what has also been called the burning platform—situations where the organization is threatened with possible dissolution.

Donald Kuratko, a scholar of entrepreneurship, notes that certain environmental factors force people to be creative. One major factor is displacement: political, cultural, economic, or geographical.[17] Being placed into radically new contexts requires an almost total relearning of everything we thought we knew. As we have seen, we might have been experts in our own culture, but when we are in a completely alien one, we have to start again. This can trigger the innovative spirit, because such displacement puts a person or an organization in the cultural intersection of an environment that creates the possibility of opportunity recognition, as well as in a place to go on a learning journey. We therefore suggest that one of the key rules of innovation is to place yourself in situations where you have to learn to think like a beginner, not an expert.

At Forge Mission Training Network, we take this principle seriously. To train new leaders to think and act missionally, we require them to step out of their comfort zone. If they are not out of their comfort zone, all they will learn is what they already know—in other words, they are experts in what they already know. However by placing themselves at risk (that is, a situation that is largely unfamiliar), thereby increasing the possibility of failure, the intern has to learn to think like a beginner or fail.

Getting Over the "F" Word

Groundbreaking innovators always experience more failure than their more conventional counterparts do because they experiment more often. Wayne Gretzky, the great Canadian hockey player, said: "You miss 100% of the shots you don't take." Anyone pursuing innovative forms of mission has to embrace the reality that not all experiments succeed. If we are not willing to face the possibility of failure and keep moving, we will never enter into innovative forms of mission or new forms of ecclesia.

What we really need is a new way of defining success and failure. When innovation becomes an essential ingredient in what it means to be missional, then a refusal to innovate and experiment becomes the most potent definition of failure. Success means embracing risk and launching into the frontiers of mission. We need to begin celebrating the people who are willing to say, "Let's try it!" as well as the people who come out on the other end saying, "We did it!"

Improvisation: Innovating as You Go

Improvisation involves learning to build the plane as you are flying it, managing in a makeshift way when things do not go according to plan, learning to make do with whatever is at hand. This is a key part of innovative apostolic leadership.

All of us know of churches that started with a commitment to reach unchurched people but ended up simply attracting other Christians. Because of financial pressures, it becomes more feasible to cater to already churched people. But the result is a loss of mission, and the associated innovation, as the church veers toward what is known and therefore to the conventional. Many times real innovation is short-circuited because of a loss of vision, nerve, and an inability to improvise. To be innovative in such situations requires staying true to the original missional focus and seeing it through.

The word *improvisation* has its roots in the word *provisio*, which means to supply something in advance, before it is needed, or to do something premeditated. Putting the prefix *im* before the word means that you are describing the opposite of *provisio*. Improvisation is tied in with the unseen, the unexpected. Being able to improvise means being able to adjust plans in response to unforeseen circumstances and conditions.

Innovator Paul Berliner defines it this way: "Improvisation involves reworking pre-composed material and designs in relation to unanticipated ideas, conceived, shaped and transformed, under the special conditions of performance, thereby adding unique features to every creation."[18] Think of jazz, which involves making music as it unravels. It is music on demand. Although it does follow certain guidelines that provide the superstructure, the musical content itself is largely unplanned and happens in the moment.

Formulating strategies in the context of performing them is one of the most fertile ways to arrive at success. But it requires leadership, flexibility, a tolerance for ambiguity, and a willingness to fail. There is truth in the idea that form follows failure only if improvisation is part of the equation. Revising a strategy halfway through is not only a sign of good learning; it is essential to being adaptable, which in apostolic ministry is the short-term means to the ends of long-term effectiveness.

Another way of describing improvisation is as continuous (or incremental) design. Rather than specifying the system completely before development starts, this involves creating or modifying a system as it is being developed, in iterative bursts along the way. Organizational strategist Karl Weick explains it well: "Design, viewed from the perspective of improvisation, is more emergent, more continuous, more filled with surprise, more difficult to control, more tied to the content of action. . . . Emergent, continuous designing is sensitive to small changes in local conditions, which means the design continuously updates as people and conditions change."[19]

This squares well with both the nature and practice of apostolic leadership and incarnational mission. Because apostolic ministry is design focused (that is, architectural) and is also highly sensitive to context and locality, it is likely to be incremental and iterative. Apostolic leaders need to be what Donald Schön called "reflective practitioners": "The practitioner allows himself to experience surprise, puzzlement, or confusion in a situation which he finds uncertain or unique. He reflects on the phenomenon before him, and on the prior understandings which have been implicit in his behavior. He carries out an experiment which serves to generate both a new understanding of the phenomenon and a change in the situation."[20]

Front-loading missional projects with detailed blueprints for action may well bolster confidence in the beginning, but this kind of planning assumes too much about the intricate cultural nuances of the target context and will be unlikely to generate innovation. Church planting and leading an apostolic movement have got to be more improvisatory. No one can know all the variables until they immerse themselves in that context and begin to act intentionally within it. It does not mean starting without a plan; it just means those plans need to be somewhat more open-ended and nimble. When Jesus sends out his disciples with nothing other than what they have in their hands (Luke 9:1–10), he sets them up to experience their ministries as an open-ended improvisation. They are not given a model, they are given a mission, and they will have to make it up as they go.

Missionary and Missional Innovation

Leaders can be innovative in many ways, but this does not necessarily mean that they are apostolic. So what does a distinctly apostolic form of innovation look like, and how can it be encouraged and developed?

Once again, the clue to this answer is found in the distinctive role of the apostolic person as custodian of the DNA of God's people. This is manifested through the apostolic focus on extending the impact of the Christian movement through mission, maintaining the integrity of the movement in relation to its core DNA, and providing the overall context for the other ministries to emerge in a healthy manner. We mention these here because the apostolic person has absolutely no mandate to tamper with the DNA itself—apostles are mere custodians, not generators, of that DNA—but they do have to be thoroughly innovative in two major ways. The two basic forms of, and contexts for, apostolic innovation are in the mission field as the gospel is extended into new contexts and cultures (what we call missionary innovation) and in search of new forms of ecclesia and methods for existing churches (what we call missional innovation).

MISSIONARY INNOVATION. What works in one context might not necessarily work in another. In fact, an application of a previous ecclesial algorithm might even have the opposite effect to what was intended. Besides being plainly culturally imperialistic, ill-fitting approaches violate the central New Testament teaching of the Incarnation of God in Jesus Christ, one of the most important doctrines that should inform every aspect of the way we conceive of and do mission.

If to incarnate (to en-flesh) is the way that God has chosen to engage the world (and it plainly is) and if we as his people are called to follow in the ways of Jesus, then we too must adopt an incarnational approach to mission: "As the Father sent me, so I send you" (John 20:21). The Father sent Jesus into the world as a complete human being, who lived incognito as a Jew among the Jewish people, spoke their language, ate their food, sang their songs, and participated as a Jew in Jewish blood and history. He was of the line of David and from the tribe of Judah, born in Bethlehem at a distinct time. From within this particular humanity, God chose to redeem the world, and this must forever change the way we think of God. This informs the meaning of the *as* in the verse just quoted. We are to do what we do in the way that Jesus did what he did: incarnationally.

If we allow the Incarnation in Jesus to shape our understanding of and approach to sharing the good news, as it must, then we must step outside our predetermined patterns and algorithms and learn how to transmit the gospel from within a given culture. All Pauline apostles have to be innovators because they are tasked with transmitting the gospel meaningfully into a given culture and ensuring that a genuinely indigenous church emerges from it. This requires innovation.

The role of innovation in mission strategy and methodology ensures that the gospel is embedded in ways that can reproduce virally within that culture. This is precisely the dilemma we are facing here in the West. Our old forms are no longer working. We need new forms that have reproducibility (or scalability) built into their basic core. This requires an apostolically inclined leadership.

Once again, Paul shows us the way. We can observe such incarnational methodology and innovation from the way he goes about fulfilling his apostolic calling. For instance, in Athens, he starts by exegeting the culture through an analysis of their current idols, a sure way to identify their yearnings and aspirations, as well as the Resulting gaps in their attempts to connect with and experience something outside and above themselves. He ends with a proclamation of the Resurrection of Jesus. He takes local culture seriously enough to study their religion (their idolatrous forms), philosophy, art, and poetry. He uses a totally different method when preaching in Jerusalem or in the synagogues; there, he exegetes the scriptures and their messianic threads and ends up with contemporary culture, with the messianic fulfillment in Jesus (Acts 13:13–42). By thus communicating from within either culture, Paul establishes a natural beachhead for the gospel in different contexts. So from context to context, Paul developed new ways of speaking about Jesus that translated the core meanings of the gospel into existing cultural frameworks.

The challenge is to bring the two "texts" of (biblical) text and (cultural) context into dynamic relationship so that the gospel can be transferred meaningfully into the culture. Apostles, in whatever context, must be specialists in culture and gospel, anthropology and atonement. New

Testament scholars Joel Green and Mark Baker describe how Paul contextualized the gospel in various locales:

> As he moves from community to community, Paul weaves a theological language that moves between the story of Israel as this is reflected in and interpreted by the advent of Christ, on the one hand, and the exigencies and settings of his audiences on the other. In this way, language takes shape within an ongoing conversation, as language is adopted and adapted that both fits the particular circumstances to which Paul addresses himself and toils to reconfigure experienced reality so that it accounts more fully for what God has done in Christ. This means that Paul can use one set of metaphors with the Colossians, another with the Galatians, while remaining true to the gospel and bearing witness to the same actuality . . . he throws himself into the difficult but crucial task of serving as a midwife to a conversion of worldview.[21]

Missiologist Dean Flemming also asserts that contextualization goes beyond crafting a culturally relevant message. It involves "the dynamic and comprehensive process by which the gospel is incarnated within a concrete, historical or cultural situation."[22]

Incarnational mission, by its very nature, sparks missional innovation. In Figure 9.2, which shows the dual process of incarnational contextualization and missional innovation, innovation (the internal circle) follows a similar pathway as the process of contextualizing the gospel and church into a given context (the outer square) and in fact takes place within the broader context of the process of incarnating and contextualizing the gospel. Certainly both involve learning, conceptualizing, doing, and embodying. It can be seen how the two different but profoundly interrelated are parts of the same movement.

For instance, IDEO, arguably America's best design firm, maintains that all innovation starts with a serious commitment to observe without recourse to solving the problem; it therefore requires a primary posture of learning and listening. Innovation then moves into a phase of interpreting the data, gleaning insights, discerning opportunities, synthesizing the information, and deciphering the culture codes to find doorways and keys to the culture (or market, depending on context.) These in turn lead directly to the dynamic process of ideation, prototyping a model, formally researching, and deciding on an approach. The final phase involves testing and applying the idea or product: refining, optimizing, and readjusting until it is optimized.[23]

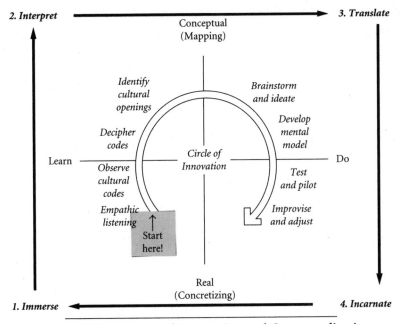

Figure 9.2 The Process of Incarnation and Contextualization

It is not hard to see the correlation between best practice in innovation and the missionary process by which the gospel is planted and the ecclesia allowed to develop. Although it does not use the same language, Church Multiplication Associates trains people to follow the same basic pathways.[24] All best practice missionary work does the same thing. All this highlights how the new missional situation we face in the West means that we have to learn the skills of innovation. In fact, the greater the contrast is between the culture of the (missionary) messenger and the (cultural) receivers, the greater will be the need for missional innovation to take place. Apostolic strategist David Watson honors the incarnational-innovational approach when he says, "*Their* culture and structure should determine *our* strategy and approach."[25]

Approaches that forgo this process of contextualization and innovation will end up either simply imposing previous (traditional) algorithms on a group or opt for some form of ecclesial franchising. Although these might be effective in contexts where people are within the church's cultural orbit (for example, highly churched settings like the American Midwest and South) in a genuinely unchurched setting, it actually works directly against the goals and methods of incarnational mission. Think of

European liturgies and ecclesiology, developed over centuries in Europe, formulaically applied in the middle of Africa. They are imposed on a people, not grown from among the people, and end up violating a people's natural faith posture toward God. The same applies to a Southern Baptist missionary to San Francisco trying to use what works in South Carolina or street preaching, which might have worked in the revivals in Old West but today likely produces the opposite effect intended, offending people rather than bringing them closer to Jesus.

There is something deeply wrong about all forms of ecclesial imperialism that so easily violate the very meaning of the Incarnation and its significance for how we should live in the world. Apostolic leadership must first ensure that the gospel is properly communicated and contextualized. Only once the gospel is truly transmitted, received, and embedded do they seek to encourage new, indigenous forms of Christian community that naturally emerge from an authentic encounter between Jesus and the people. This is at the core of the apostolic task in the missionary environment: to plant the gospel with the understanding that if we do our part, Jesus will build his church (Matthew 16:18, 28:16–20).

MISSIONAL INNOVATION. The kind of innovation needed to keep the established church relevant and actively engaged in its current context and situation is most suited for the Petrine forms of apostleship, which work primarily with and through the established people of God. It has been said that the best way to preserve tradition is to have children, not to wear your father's old hat, but it seems that we have tended to believe that the old hat is what we are called to wear. Nothing could be further from the truth. Certainly we are called to remember the covenants God made with his people, but we are called to do this in dynamic tension with what it means to participate in the ever-urgent not yet of the kingdom of God. Because the church is a sign, symbol, and foretaste of the kingdom of God, it is ever the agent of the kingdom that operates in and through it. Until such time as the kingdom is fulfilled, the movement that Jesus started will always need to be looking for ways in which to be more faithful and true to its calling.

We are not called to remember the covenants simply as tradition but rather as the basis of a living relationship between God and his people, then and now. This is a relationship that we testify to every day with our lives and our witness. How did we ever get to believe that faithfulness involved simply retaining past forms and thinking? With the Creator God as our Father, how did we ever become the socially conservative stiflers of innovation that we are so notoriously perceived to be?

It goes without saying that in a fallen world everything tends to wind down, and what resonates strongly in one generation might likely miss the next one by a mile; generation gaps are classic examples of serious missiological problems. One culture can completely miss another. Symbols and ideas that were once vibrant become bankrupt when they no longer convey the right meanings as a result of the changing environment and changing conditions.

The same is true of the cultural forms of ecclesia. As we have already noted, failure to regularly innovate inevitably results in cloying traditionalism, theological stagnation, cultural isolation, and, inevitably, organizational decline. The church and its peoples need ongoing theological and spiritual renewal, which necessitates a near-constant search for new and better ways to be the church that Jesus intended. Truly *ecclesia reformata, semper reformanda*; the church reformed ought always to be reforming.

Innovation is deeply rooted in our theology. In fact, we can basically acknowledge that simply to encounter God is to change; it will always require change in us, as Dietrich Bonhoeffer wrote. Erwin McManus, leader of the creative church movement called Mosaic, rightly sees God as both the originator of change and the one who demands it from us. He points out that many of the most important words in the scriptures (*repentance, justification, conversion, discipleship, new life, sanctification*) involve movement and change. He then goes on to encourage leaders to keep up with the leadership of God in this matter by promoting innovation and embracing a culture of change:

> Everywhere God moves, there is change. Everywhere God moves, he creates the future. Everywhere God moves, hope is alive and well. The church must be grounded in a proper theology of change, not simply to address the radically changing world in which we live, but to advance the cause of Christ in a world that cannot produce the real change that has to take place.
>
> Remember that momentum is related to the distance covered in a certain period of time. For the church, momentum is more about time than distance. When we do not change, we actually distance ourselves from the world around us. When we cling to the past, we create distance between ourselves and what God is doing in the present.[26]

While all the APEST ministries need to be active and engaged to keep the church on track, spiritually and missionally, much of the pressure for change and innovation will likely come from the combination of the prophet as the provocateur who reminds us of our need to change and the apostle who in all likelihood will act as the key entrepreneur, change agent, and manager. However, we believe that innovation itself will most likely come from apostolic leadership for at least three reasons:

- *Their role as re/founders.* Genuine apostolic people are radical traditionalists; they operate from the central core of ideas and radically but consistently reapply these ideas in different contexts. They are the ones charged with the primary custody of our defining concepts that keep us being the church that Jesus intended and thus maintaining theological validity. This is the all-important DNA checkup that we need to keep us from becoming pragmatic faddists and novelty seekers, both of which distort the truth of the church rather than extend it. Whatever we do must have a deep congruency with our core beliefs and founding ideas. Furthermore, as the resident radical traditionalist, the apostolic leader is also the mediator of the systemic renewal process that we called refounding the church (see Chapter Seven), a process that takes our deepest ideas and reinterprets them in new ways and forms. The former requires theological intelligence, while the latter requires explicit innovative skills.
- *The systemic scope of their function.* The combination of the architectural nature of their ministry and their missional commitment to advance Christianity as a fully integrated religious system onto new ground aids apostles in their primary responsibility for ensuring the ongoing development and extension of the system as a whole. They are best able to evaluate and jettison decaying forms as well as cultivate the development of new ones.
- *Their oversight of the missional cause.* They are the sent ones who keep up the pressure for missional advancement by virtue of their calling. It is not claiming too much to say that mission is not only the mother of theology; it is also the mother of ecclesial innovation. Mission by its nature exerts a constant pressure for innovation, and so most breakthroughs in thinking and methodology come from missionary innovation.

Because Pauline apostles are likely to engage directly in missionary situations, they can mediate the learning from the edge of the frontier to the rest of the movement—an element critical for learning, renewal, and development. But Petrine apostles also generate innovation by constantly (re)aligning the movement around its missional theology and cause. Authentic missional pressure from within will also generate ideation throughout as the church seeks to find new and better ways to be who Jesus intended we should be in the first place.

Conclusion

Innovation thrives from an apostolic vision of the church that encompasses holy discontent, constant change, adaptability, and development. If the church is simply a place where believers are cared for (a kind of pastoral hospital) and taught the basics of the faith (an extension of the seminary), then it will likely lack the energy needed to generate new ideas and forms and the courage required to implement them. Every advancement of the church is predicated on having a transformative vision of the world. This in turn has a transforming effect on the church itself: we become a movement.

•

PART FOUR

Apostolic organization

movements R US

THINKING AND ACTING LIKE
A MOVEMENT

Our nature lies in movement, complete calm is death.
Pascal

Of course a movement must be embodied in some organized form, but once Christians had begun to think of the Church as a structure to be compared with and related to other structures in society, it became one of the very principalities and powers that the Gospel was supposed to withstand.
.J. V. Taylor

The life I touch for good or ill will touch another life, and that in turn another, until who knows where the trembling stops or in what far place my touch will be felt.
Frederick Beuchner

THE COMMONWEALTH OF OCEANA BY JAMES HARRINGTON was published in England in 1656. Despite its controversial story line, it managed to escape full-blown censorship by the order of Oliver Cromwell. Harrington's fortunate connection with one of Cromwell's daughters somehow created space for the novel to pass through the printing press and into the hands of the common people. What made his novel so controversial is not just that was a thinly veiled carica-ture of England's government but that it proposed an alternate way of organizing the state that gave power back to the people. After describing the governments of ancient Israel, Rome, Sparta, and Venice, Harrington painted a picture of an imaginary island, called Oceana, that had an alternative way of organizing. His work may have been fiction, but it spoke directly to the swelling tensions of the day.

We think the apostolic organizations—movements—speak in much the same way to the issues of our day.

Mobilizing Bias

God is always on the move, and he intends to take us on the journey with him. One gets the feeling from reading church historian Kenneth Scott Latourette that the history of the church is the history of God's relentless mission to redeem the world and that apostolic movements arise when God, impatient and inexorable in his love, extends the reach of his kingdom through people willing to follow the *missio Dei* to wherever he leads.[1] Movements happen when the church manages to shake off its collective fears and plunges into the mission of God in the world, where, while experiencing risk and disorientation, they also get to encounter God and each other in a new way.

We recently came across a cartoon that represented a peasant, cap in hand, appealing for help before a king sitting on a throne. The king is depicted as saying, "I can't solve your problem. I am your problem." This seems to convey pretty well the nature of the issue faced when dealing with the existing situation.

Such a view of the church will invariably reframe the way we normally conceive of and subsequently structure the various organizations we inhabit. If we think that the primary purpose of the church is to sustain a common liturgical life, offer pastoral care, and deliver teaching and that the mission of the church is secondary to these purposes (as is the commonly held view), then these functions set the agenda for how we organize ourselves. The net result is that we end up with an organization that deliberately prioritizes these more internally focused, service-oriented agendas and outcomes.

The reality is that all organization involves the mobilization of bias; organizations embed a predisposition, a certain bent, into the social life of the community. It is because of this that in some deeply inexorable sense, we get in the end what we wanted even though it might not be all that God intended. The disturbing problem is that organizational bias is often at direct odds with the implicit motivations, as well as explicit purposes, of the God revealed in our Lord, Jesus Christ. By extension, the church that takes God's mission as its organizing principle will be biased, that is, structurally predisposed, in favor of achieving that mission. The result is that it will inevitably look and feel different from the way we have historically tended to see the church in the West.[2]

Mission as Organizing Principle

Political scientist Elmer Schattschneider first defined organization as the mobilization of bias.[3] What he meant is that we humans tend to organize ourselves in ways that help us actualize our latent or expressed values, interests, and aspirations. If this is true, then whether mission is at the forefront of our organization will be most clearly demonstrated in the way in which we organize ourselves. If mission is patently lacking in terms of outcome, then clearly we do not value it enough for it to inform our organizational bias. There is no way to evade this reality.

As should be amply clear by now, when we talk about an apostolic church we are in effect calling the church to be a missional church, that is, a church that allows its missiology to determine and guide in the formation and understanding of its ecclesiology. In saying this, we are also implying that the church's purpose and context will guide the cultural forms and expressions of the church in any given setting. In *The Forgotten Ways,* I (Alan) say it this way: "When the church is in mission, it is the true church. The church itself is not only a product of that mission but is obligated and destined to extend it by whatever means possible. The mission of God flows directly through every believer and every community of faith that adheres to Jesus. To obstruct this is to block God's purposes in and through his people."[4]

If evangelizing and discipling the nations lie at the heart of the church's purpose in the world, then it is mission, and not ministry (to one another), that constitutes the true organizing principle of the church. In other words, the various functions of the church are best catalyzed by the missional one: "Experience tells us that a church that aims at ministry seldom gets to mission even if it sincerely intends to do so. But the church that aims at mission will have to do ministry, *because ministry is the means to do mission.*"[5]

When mission becomes the organizing principle of the church, it necessarily calls into question the prevailing forms and structures of our organizations. If we are honest, most of our organizations, while they may have initially started out as movements or support structures for mission, over time drift into a more ministry-oriented mode of existence. In pursuing an apostolic mode of organization, we are simply trying to put mission back into the basic equation of the church.

If organization is the mobilization of bias, then apostolic organization is the mobilization of apostolic, or missional, bias. And the net result will be apostolic movement. This chapter explores the nature of movements and how to organize and lead them.

Power to the People Again

Movements are the quintessentially apostolic, missionally biased form of the church. Given that most movements start with grassroots missional engagement in a context generally far from the cultural epicenter of the established church, this statement ought not to be surprising. In fact, just about every Christian organization today started as a people movement of sorts. For instance, most of the orders, renewal movements, parachurch agencies, overseas mission organizations, and church planting movements started as movements. Even the origins of all the Protestant denominations (except perhaps the Anglican, unless one considers the demands of King Henry VIII for a divorce as starting a movement) fit this category.

But the idea of organizing around movement need not simply apply to the beginning phases, as if it were some kind of preliminary scaffolding that ought to be dismantled as the church matures naturally into more institutional forms. Rather, if we believe that the church is in essence apostolic, then it ought always to retain and engender organizational forms that align with its missional purpose. Ecclesia ought always to be movemental to some degree, or it ceases to be the church that Jesus intended it to be.[6]

For more established institutional churches, becoming more movemental provides them with a way forward—a kind of back-to-the future approach to organizational development. It will mean recovering that which they have lost, like finding lost treasures in the church's historical basement (or attic) where it has laid hidden, misplaced, or forgotten. Movement, and the possibility of it, is written into the genetic codes of the church.

We have already observed that inserting apostolic bias into a plateauing or declining organization brings with it the possibility of sigmoid growth and renewal. If leaders continue following the logic implied in the apostolic approach, wholesale renewal will take place. Where apostolic imagination and influence are maintained throughout the life of an organization, they bring with them the kind of self-understanding that allows an organization to retain fluid and adaptive forms that allow movement to take place. For instance, a major Pentecostal denomination in Australia has maintained sigmoid growth over the long term, whereas the original denomination in the United States has been experiencing significant decline. They are the same in almost every way; the only significant difference between them is that the Australian wing has managed to maintain a sustained commitment to apostolic (and, by extension,

APEST) ministry. In the U.S. expression, the language of fivefold has largely fallen into disuse because of a history of various disputes about power and roles.

An apostolic approach to organization will ensure that churches and organizations are inherently adaptive, flexible, self-renewing, resilient, learning, and intelligent. An apostolic movement takes its cue from the biblical teachings about the church as the body of Christ (1 Corinthians 12; Ephesians 4:12–16), the living temple (1 Peter 2:4–5), the ecclesia as movement, as well as Jesus's teachings about the organic nature of the kingdom of God. We must allow these metaphors and ideas to reframe the way we see God's people as a movement. Taken together, they provide powerful, theologically substantial pathways to reimagine organization from an apostolic perspective. Our hope in the West lies in the recovery of a more fluid and dynamic apostolic imagination and practice.

We have to be vigorous in recovering this understanding because the prevailing forms of organization dominate the way we think about church and organization. Apostolic movements require that we see church beyond its more institutional forms—as a movement of the whole people of God active in every sphere and domain of society. Seen through the lens of institution, the church will be conceived of as being primarily made up of its external forms and not its inner nature—as being made up of the combination of theological preferences, professional clergy, elaborate rituals, denominational templates, distinctive buildings, and the like. Clearly this is not what the New Testament itself means by ecclesia, and although it can be included within more movemental understandings, it is not what we mean by apostolic movement.

We need a new influx of apostolic imagination to dislodge the hierarchical, machine-like metaphor that imbues our more inherited ecclesiologies and that has so captured our imagination. We have to think differently about how we conceive of ourselves if we are to see different results. The conventional way of thinking views the church as solid and static, the other as more fluid and dynamic.

When we allow the apostolic, movemental way of thinking to reshape our idea of church, we begin to see the sheer transformational power of the church that Jesus designed—a church where each part in the system, be it individual disciple or community, has the full potential of the whole and therefore is intrinsically empowered to achieve what Jesus has set out for us to achieve. We begin to realize that, at least potentially, every believer ought to be considered a church planter and every church should be thought of as a church-planting church. Just as there is the full potential of a forest in every seed, so too is the task of leadership to help every disciple to be a movement in the making.

In Jesus's kingdom, everyone gets to play—even hookers, dodgy businessmen, and political insurgents—hardly what we would normally consider to be the A-Team, the cream of the leadership crop. Therefore, anything blocking the God-given agency of each disciple must ultimately derive from the Evil One.

When we think this way, then we are thinking movementally, that is, apostolically. Conversely, if we are not thinking about ecclesia in this way, we are not seeing the church as the New Testament itself intends us to see it.

In light of this, apostolic leadership recognizes that every member or group in a movement already has everything it needs to get the job done. They just need permission and empowerment to live into that truth. Rather than attributing more and more power to an increasingly centralized (centripetal) organization, movement dynamics require that power and function flow away from the center to the outermost limits, giving the whole movement a profoundly centrifugal feel. As Darin Land observes in his book *The Diffusion of Ecclesiastical Authority,* the leaders in the book of Acts took this very approach: "By consistently sharing their authority with others, these leaders allowed the diffusion of authority to new individuals rather than the concentration of authority in the hands of the few. . . . They were able to do this because their authority was based on deference and mutual honor, not only on legal rights. Thus, the diffusion of ecclesiastical authority resulted in a net increase of authority, which in turn propelled the growth of the church."[7] This is the very stuff of movements, and it is also underscored in current best-thinking books on organizations, including Peter Senge's *The Fifth Discipline,* Dee Hock's *Birth of the Chaordic Age,* Steve Addison's *Movements That Change the World,* Bob Roberts's *Glocalization,* Ori Brafman and Rod Beckstrom's *The Starfish and the Spider,* Clay Shirky's *Here Comes Everybody,* and Don Tapscott and Anthony Williams's *Wikinomics: How Mass Collaboration Changes Everything.*[8] So let's delve a bit further into movements, the most primal form of ecclesia.

Organizing Movements

Andrew Jones, who blogs under the name of Tall Skinny Kiwi, did research to assess whether the current missional movement fits the characteristics of being a genuine movement. He asked a veteran Fuller church history professor, Paul Pierson, who provided those characteristics:[9]

- They always begin on the periphery of the institutional church.
- They are motivated by a transforming experience (grace) of God by an individual or group.
- The result is the desire for a more authentic Christian life that often leads to concern for the church and world.
- Face-to-face groups for prayer, Bible study, and mutual encouragement are important.
- New methods of selecting and training leaders become important. These are less institutional and more grassroots and lay oriented.
- There are theological breakthroughs, that is, rediscovery of aspects of the biblical message that have been forgotten or overlooked by the church; usually they focus on the gifts of every believer. Biblical concepts ignored by the traditional church but relevant to the hearers are often discovered.
- There is a leveling effect as distance decreases between clergy and laity, social classes, races, men and women, and denominations.
- The movement is countercultural in some ways, often because it reaches out to those who have not been valued by their society.
- Consequently there will be opposition by many in the dominant culture and church.
- There will often be manifestations of spiritual warfare. Such movements sense the reality of evil and the need to recognize the victory of Christ in the Cross and Resurrection.
- At times there will be unusual manifestations of the power of the Holy Spirit: healings, visions, speaking in tongues, miracles, and so on.
- More flexible structures of church and mission will be needed and often emerge, different from traditional structures.
- The movement will be led to significant recontextualization of the Christian message, which will be communicated more widely by laypersons to those outside the church.
- New cultural forms and art are often a characteristic.
- There will be a growing concern for those who are marginalized, often expressed in ministries of compassion.
- At a later stage, this often leads to concern for broader social transformation.
- As the movement matures, there will be concern for the renewal of the broader church.
- As the movement continues to mature, many will see themselves not only as part of the movement but as citizens of the kingdom of God, transcending their own movement.

- Every movement is less than perfect and often messy at the edges and sometimes the center. This is inevitable as long as sinful humans are involved.

We might add more characteristics like clear thought leaders, differentiated culture and self-understanding, a strategy for leader training, and others. And although not all movements display all of these characteristics, they ought to be present to some degree.[10]

In pulling all these together in a cohesive model, we suggest that distinctly apostolic forms of movements have the following traits:[11]

- *Apostolic movements thrive in the atmosphere of belief.* All movements breathe an atmosphere of "can do" or, perhaps even better, "will do." Apostolic movements believe their message, see themselves as conduits of that message, and are willing to put their lives on the line to deliver it. They have a transformational vision for society, and a sense that they have a role to play in its transformation. They are believers.

- *Apostolic movements exhibit the structure of networks.* The favored structure of dynamic apostolic movements is that of the more fluid, decentralized, adaptive network where power and function are dispersed throughout the organization, even at its outer edges.[12] To use a rather unfortunate comparison, the apostolic form will tend to look like the structure of an al Qaeda, where operatives, cells, and organizations are highly adaptive, easily reproduced, and hard to eliminate. More positive examples of dynamic networking in movements are the Apaches in the wars against the conquistadors, Alcoholics Anonymous, the women's movement, and environmentalists. Clearly this was the form of the early church as well as that of early Methodism and the Chinese underground church, and, of course, the early church.

- *Apostolic movements spread like viruses.* All powerful ideas spread like viruses. They are in a real sense caught and passed on, and they do so in a viral, epidemical way. Apostolic movements that reach the power curve of exponential impact are in a real sense, pay-it-forward movements. They transfer ideas exponentially, and these ideas are profound enough to lodge themselves in people's minds and change the way they think and act. For an idea to be spreadable, it needs to be simple enough for the audience to understand it. But to take root and transform the audience, it needs to be complex enough to carry a load of meaning. The rallying cry, "Jesus is Lord," and the gospel itself carry both of these aspects within it.

• *Apostolic movements are reproducing and reproducible.* Such movements are precommitted to multiplication formulas of growth and not simply addition. But the commitment to reproducing everything easily and rapidly implies a commitment to keeping things reproducible. For instance, evangelism, discipleship, leadership formation, ecclesiology itself, and church planting need to be relatively easily reproduced by any serious and committed agent (churches and individuals) in the system. (Because this is a major issue in organization, we explore this more fully in the discussion of four-self principles in the next chapter.)

Further explorations can be found in *On the Verge*, Neil Cole's *Church 3.0,* and Dwight Friesen's *Thy Kingdom Connected.*[13]

We simply state these here because if leaders wish to move to a more apostolic approach to organization, it stands to reason that they need to (re)learn how they function and operate. To be a movement, we need to learn how to think like a movement, and then to act like a movement.

The Starfish and the Spider

A further aspect of highly transformative movements worth more exploration is the idea of decentralization and networking. Based on numerous examples of decentralized networks, ranging from Alcoholics Anonymous to Skype and Wikipedia, the authors of *The Starfish and the Spider*, Ori Brafman and Rod Beckstrom, present a model of decentralized organization and the new rules it implies.[14]

Perhaps the best way to describe the power of decentralized movements is to elaborate on the metaphor in the title of the book. In terms of organizations, a spider and a starfish might look the same (at least each has eight legs), but their organization are worlds apart. A spider that loses a leg might well be able to function. It might even be able to operate minus three legs, although its survival would be endangered if it lost four. However, it will die if it loses its head, because its central nervous system is located there. The starfish is a different animal altogether. Cut a leg off a starfish, and it grows back, and the leg that was cut off will actually grow into another starfish. Cut the starfish into ten pieces, and you end up with ten starfish. In other words, every element in its system has the full capacity to reproduce itself. If one observes what is going on in the book of Acts, one can easily discern that New Testament ecclesiology is more like the starfish than the spider. The same is true for the grassroots church in India, Church Multiplication Associates, and many other apostolic movements.

Furthermore, on closer examination, movements are composed of many circles, or a fractal-like network of networks.[15] Each circle is an independently functioning decentralized network consisting of autonomous and interdependent units. And these tend to lack the hierarchy or structure normally associated with centralized command-and-control organizations.

Instead of normal hierarchy, people movements depend on ideas and beliefs to hold the system together and reach their objectives; they are built on a foundation of shared ideology. These beliefs are self-enforced by the various members of the movement. Knowledge and intelligence are deliberately spread throughout the organization. And because everyone is a stakeholder in the outcomes, there is a sense of reliance and trust throughout the community. Furthermore, because the organization is decentralized and intelligent, individual units in the movement adapt quickly to changes in their various environments and can advance and grow under the radar.

In Brafman and Beckstrom's view, leadership comes initially in the form of the catalyst, who either initiates a new circle or enhances an existing one.[16] However, once the circle is up and running, the catalyst moves on, transferring active leadership to the members and the more socially cohesive leadership of the champion. Leadership does not exist to create dependencies in the members but rather for the full empowerment of the other members in pursuit of the movement's goals. Think of Alcoholics Anonymous and Greenpeace here. If we relate this to APEST typologies, it is most likely the Pauline apostle who will initiate new movement, lay the foundations for its ongoing sustainability, and then move on to other frontiers. This makes space for the ministries of the Petrine apostles, prophets, and evangelists to step up to the fore and propel the movement forward, the evangelist in our view being the one most likely to fulfill the role of the champion. We see this taking place in Paul's ministry when he leaves a church that he has planted and nurtured or sends Timothy to Ephesus and tells him to do the work of an evangelist.

Although these characteristics are true for all kinds of people movements, they certainly describe the dynamics of apostolic movements as we find them in the Bible and in history. It is not hard to discern, for instance, that this is how the massively expanding movements of the contemporary developing world operate. Interestingly Paul explicitly considers himself to be an apostle, an evangelist, and a teacher (1 Timothy 2:7; 2 Timothy 1:11); in terms of starfish dynamics, this equals a combination of catalyst, champion, and original thinker in one person. Paul's contribution to the Christian movement signals precisely this form of catalytic influence, and it is still felt as powerfully today as it ever was.

In the New Testament, though, we move beyond the somewhat two-dimensional idea of leadership in *The Starfish and the Spider* to the fivefold APEST form, which easily incorporates the typology of catalyst and champion and integrates the more operative forms of shepherd and teacher as well. It is much more sustainable as a result. Truly New Testament ecclesiology is biased toward movements.

Ending with the Beginning in Mind

It is now common to hear the phrase that we must begin with the end in mind, and it is perfectly true for leadership as well as organizations. If you want apostolic movement, you must begin with a clear understanding of what this means or miss the mark entirely. This is exactly why builders need blueprints in order to build a skyscraper, or even a large house for that matter.

But if we must begin with the end in mind, it is also true that we must end with the beginning in mind. To be genuinely apostolic, the basic organizational formulas factored into the initial movement should be sustainable over time and throughout the life of the organization. An apostolic algorithm should be consistent at front and back. The following are applications of this principle.

Learn from the Fractal

Apostolic organization is very similar to that of the fractal, "a rough or fragmented geometric shape that can be split into parts, each of which is (at least approximately) a reduced-size copy of the whole."[17] When the basic unit is paired with the same shape, it grows accordingly but retains the characteristics of the original shape. The smallest part therefore is reflected in every part and throughout the whole. When a simple triangle multiplies on itself, a pattern emerges (Figure 10.1). This design can develop into infinite complexity and still be based on the initial formula.[18] This fractal, one of the simplest, demonstrates the principle that is true to all fractals: the whole is made up of the recursion of the smallest part. What is remarkable is that the iterative and recursive design found in fractals is integral to many aspects of life itself.

Neil Cole elaborates on this in his seminal book *Organic Church.*[19] He rightly notes that fractals can, indeed must, apply to discipleship, leadership development, church planting and reproduction, and eventually into

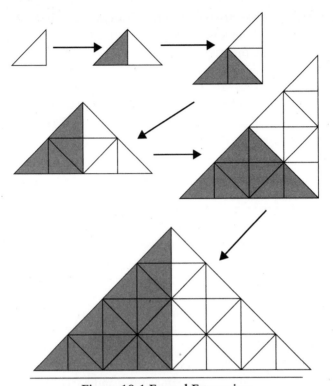

Figure 10.1 Fractal Expansion

Source: From Organic Church: Growing Faith Where Life Happens
*by Neil Cole. (San Francisco: Jossey-Bass, 2005). Reprinted with
permission of John Wiley & Sons, Inc.*

movement extension itself: "The pattern remains the same no matter how
many times it is multiplied. To have a leadership structure that grows
with the body, we need to have a similar design that maintains its own
integrity no matter how many times it is multiplied. Likewise, a global
movement can be divided into smaller units that all maintain the same
core formation."[20]

The triangle in Figure 10.1 shows that no matter how far down you
divide the shape, the original fractal design remains true. This can provide a pattern and direction for units exploding in a chain reaction,
whereas the traditional organizational model cannot. That last phrase
rings true for apostolic approaches to organization. Movements thrive on
simplicity, reproducibility, and scalability.

If you believe that discipleship is basic to what it means to be a church,
put a clear pathway to discipleship in the process at the start. If you try

to factor this in later, it is very difficult and is unlikely to succeed. The same is true for leadership, multiplication, reproducibility, and so on. Again, if the initial model is not readily reproducible by the "nonprofessional" regular Christian, then it will not be magically reproducible by them later on. If it is built on a professional model of ministry and leadership (clergy), then that is what you will have to deal with all along the way, and at a great price. Get the base formula or algorithm right, pray like mad, and the rest will flow well.

Plant Movements, Not Churches

If you want to end with a movement, you need to start with a movemental idea and approach. This seems obvious, but all denominations started as dynamic movement, but because they were not attentive to the shifting issues of organization, they likely ended up in another place altogether. So plant movements, not churches.

This is a big part of why it is important to begin with the end in mind: if you want a movement, you must think of ecclesia beyond the idea of a single local church before you begin. Once again, as every seed has the full potential for a tree and the tree the full potential of the forest, so too every church (indeed every believer) has the full potential of a movement in it. This is implied in the powerful slogan of an underground Chinese church movement: "Every believer is a church planter, and every church is a church-planting church." Every believer has ecclesia (church) in him or her, and every ecclesia is responsible for the reproduction of others; in other words, they all make a movement.

This approach is also useful in getting beyond distorted, highly institutionalized ideas of the church in order to focus on planting movements instead of planting churches. The distinctly apostolic form of thinking behind this is to think movements and not churches.

Plant the Gospel, Not Churches

Yet another way of beginning with the end in mind and ending with the beginning in mind is to plant the gospel, not churches. This does not cancel out what we said above; it simply changes the equation in a way that helps us think differently about the same task.

One of the core tasks of apostolic ministry is to plant churches, but we are increasingly convinced that the term *church planting* itself is problematic. That is partly because we are never actually commanded to plant churches. In the Bible, that is always considered to be Jesus's job; for our part, we are called to evangelize the world by making disciples (Matthew 28:18–20). But the phrase is also problematic because of associations with the word *church* in the cultural memory of the West. For Christians and non-Christians alike, the word *church* almost always conjures up the profoundly stylized images of buildings, clergy, rituals, and denominational templates. We have a very well-formed, or rather often misinformed, idea of what the church is and what it is all about.

To get to the real heart of the Great Commission, we suggest that it might be useful to drop the phrase "church planting"; instead we should begin to focus on the approach of "gospel planting." This is actually very useful because it takes us to the core of what missionary work is about in the first place: planting the message of Jesus and cultivating contextualized communities of faith that shape themselves around it. It involves a process that is Jesus focused and strong on incarnational forms of mission. As such it squares with the approach that it is Christology (the kingdom of God as it expresses itself in Jesus) that must directly shape our missiology (our purpose and mission in God's world), which in turn must shape our ecclesiology (the cultural form and function of the church).[21]

Chaordic Ecclesiology

Some years ago, Dee Hock, the brilliant founder of Visa Corporation, coined the word *chaordic* to indicate the kind of organization that manages to balance some kind of enduring structure at its center, which develops the strategic direction and maintains and enforces the movement's core ideas and yet allows the kind of regional extension, scalability, and rapid-fire adaptability required to advance its cause. The word is a combination of *chaos* and *order*.

This type of organization is what Hock calls chaordic—one that has a deeply held purpose and set of principles at the very center (these provide the order, the intellectual center, and the basis of decision making and operations) and yet also has high creativity at the edges (normally associated with chaos). See how this chaordic approach works its way out in these following statements: "Purpose and principle, clearly understood and articulated, and commonly shared, are the genetic code of any healthy organization. To the degree you hold purpose and principles in common among you, you can dispense with command and control. People will know how to behave in accordance with them, and they'll do it in thousands of unimaginable, creative ways. The organization will become a vital, living set of beliefs."[22] And he says elsewhere, "An organization's success has enormously more to do with clarity of a shared purpose, common principles, and strength of belief in them than to assets, expertise, operating ability, or management competence, important as they may be."[23] Order and chaos, structure and creativity, find a perfect and productive balance in organizations of this kind.

The Internet and many Internet-based organizations, Alcoholics Anonymous, Semco (Ricardo Semler's companies), and Hock's own Visa International are examples of organizations built squarely on chaordic principles.[24] Hock's ideas deserve serious attention: he has developed and led one of the biggest businesses in the world—one that has an annual turnover of $1.2 trillion, no headquarters, and only five hundred employees. Visa is truly a globally recognized brand that is organizationally invisible at the same time. This is no mean feat and well worthy of our study.

As an advocate of living systems approaches to organization, Hock is describing something built into the rhythms and design of life itself as it applies to human organizations. This kind of chaordic organization is close to what we can see in the early church and other apostolic movements. Early Methodism, for instance, grew rapidly in spite of a lack of centralized organization and telephonic communications. Similarly, if one were to ask how the early church held together and expanded in a cohesive way in spite of having little that we take for granted as basic, one can answer only that the Holy Spirit chose to use something like what Hock calls chaordic principles. It had no central organization to speak of, no payroll, no denominational headquarters, and no executives. It held together based on adherence to the grand idea of Jesus as Lord, a call to live and extend his mission, and organized differently in different places.

Chaordic principles, with their roots in living systems theory (with links to cosmology and how the Creator has designed things), their way of connecting community and an individual sense of purpose, their respect for human dignity, and their being deeply principled in nature offer us a nearly perfect approach to developing apostolic movements. They also capture well the concept of apostolic leadership and architecture that holds fast to the core DNA of the church while at the same time giving massive permission for ongoing cultural innovation, organizational adaptability, and missional extension. The original Jesus movement was chaordic, and that is exactly what is needed now.

Verge Church Process

Whether one is working with an established church or starting a new one, chaordic approaches are relevant throughout the life cycle of the organization. So as far as the concept of a chaordic organization is concerned, apostolic movements tend to have the following characteristics:

- Are based on clarity of a theologically substantial sense of purpose, methodology, and principles
- Are self-organizing and self-governing in whole and in part
- Exist primarily to enable their constituent parts
- Are consistent with the kingdom of God
- Are powered from the periphery and unified from the core
- Are durable in purpose and principle and malleable in form and function
- Learn, adapt, and innovate in ever-expanding cycles
- Liberate and amplify ingenuity, initiative, and judgment
- Equitably distribute power, rights, responsibility, and rewards ("to each is given"; Ephesians 4:7)
- Harmoniously combine cooperation and competition
- Are compatible with human dignity and spirit in that the organization gives more than it takes
- Compatible with and foster diversity, complexity, and change
- Constructively use and harmonize conflict and paradox

Changing the organizational self-understanding and culture needs time and a good process. Following similar principles, I (Alan) have sought to develop a thoroughly chaordic approach to developing apostolic movements in *On the Verge,* my book with Dave Ferguson.[25] Here, we give a brief summary of the process laid out in significant detail there.

To initiate and maintain movemental organizations requires a definite apostolic leadership vision as well as a keen sense of process. We suggest the following main parts of that process.

IMAGINE. To be and become an apostolic movement, we have to have the right image and imagination of the organization. Apostolic imagination guides how we think about ecclesia and move on to imagining new possibilities. Imagination allows us to see the mission as Jesus sees it. Failure to capture the mind and heart of leadership at this point will mean frustration and failure in anything that follows. This highlights the importance of apostolic vision and leadership in helping people think differently about the church.

SHIFT. Shift has three aspects:
  1. *The process of embedding a core DNA at the very heart of the organization,* one that is entirely consistent with apostolic movement paradigm. This means re/setting the organizational brain (or DNA, scripts, codes, or the like) to think apostolically about the church.

Recall the discussion of this earlier in this book and also in *The Forgotten Ways:* when the apostolic genius system (comprising the dynamic interplay between Jesus's lordship, discipleship, incarnational mission, APEST, organic systems, and communitas) becomes the interpretive paradigm at the core of the organization, it will guide all subsequent thinking and acting throughout the organization.[26]

2. *Developing an ethos and culture that are consistent with the paradigm and do not hinder its progress.* It involves developing language and core values, identifying the heroes who embody the vision and values, along with coherent branding and communication, rituals and symbols, and missional metrics. Together this apostolic ethos creates the platform with which to develop the next stage.

3. *Developing sets of practices that shape and guide the members' actions and rhythms.* Most people, particularly nonleaders in the community, do not have to grasp all the conceptual ideas to be able to do it. In fact, simply doing certain well-constructed and rhythmic practices, woven into the fabric of the community and over long periods of time, changes people.

INNOVATE. The need for genuine innovation arises as a natural outflow of the embedding of apostolic identity, ethos, and practices contained in the shift process. People need permission and skills to help the church or the movement generate new cultural forms and expressions of the kingdom of God. Everybody needs to innovate.

MOVEMENTUM. *Movementum* can be defined as the process of gaining missional momentum until we birth an apostolic movement. It occurs when we are continuously taking our church through the preceding three stages: imagine, shift, and innovate.

Driving It Home

Developing a self-organizing, self-governing, trustworthy organization usually requires intensive effort. Taking the necessary time and not rushing it is important. During this time, a representative group of individuals (we call them the drafting team) is drawn from leadership in all parts and levels of the organization. Led by an apostolic person, they should meet regularly and work through the initial framing and implementation of the process. Then it is vital to identify all key stakeholders—people who are directly affected by changes and have much to lose or gain in the process. Invite the sharing of the concerns as well as their ideas. Do not limit this to top-level leadership. One of the best applications of this aspect of the process has been done at Granger Community Church in Indiana, where even its technical team is well informed about missional movement and how the leaders intend to get there. Everyone feels informed and in some way involved.[27]

Covering the Bases

One of the gifts of thinking movementally about the church is that it gives us an idea of the church that encompasses and embraces the contributions of every part. Nothing is left out in the kingdom economy of church as Jesus designed it. For too long, the church has left the vast majority of players off the field. In a movement, as many as possible are activated. Every person, collective, church, and organization plays a part in the destiny of the whole. Seen in this way, the church contains incredible potential and latent capacity. Apostolic organization seeks to capture this intelligence and focus on the task set before it. To get this idea across, recently Dave Ferguson had members of Community Christian in Chicago who were willing to be missional in all of life to stand up, and he subsequently ordained them. They certainly got the message that they were all valuable and equal players in God's kingdom.

Movements tend to start with individuals, who together form into groups around a common cause and eventually mobilize for continuous movement by using ever more expansive levels of organization. In the words of living systems theory, ecclesia is a nested hierarchy consisting of an increasingly complex organization, much like Russian nesting dolls where each doll is encompassed by another doll, all the way to the outermost doll.[28]

In a nested hierarchy, each layer builds on the next, incorporating what precedes into what follows and never leaving anything behind. Even the smallest, apparently inconspicuous part of the system is an irreplaceable part of the whole. For instance, in New Testament ecclesiology, Paul insists we are all the body of Christ, and each one of us is a vital part of it (see 1 Corinthians 12:12–27; Ephesians 4:7–16). There is a deep and profound interdependence of each part—all of God's people are chosen and have destiny and significance. This is exactly why the church damages its own capacity to function as Jesus intended when we marginalize any member of the body of Christ.

When we apply the idea of nested hierarchy to apostolic organization, we need to be attentive to the basic unit of ecclesia as much as we need to attend to the larger issues of movement and multiplication. All aspects are vital. There are at least four layers of nested hierarchy in the ecclesia: the individual/human, the social/communal, the organizational/system, and the movement/exponential multiplication (Figure 10.2).

Apostolic movements will always require varying levels of organization—the individual, community, organization, and movement. But each level requires a different leader's response, skill set, and focus. What is required at the base level of the individual will not produce movement, but if the base level is not attended to, no movement will be possible. Trying to achieve significant movement without paying attention to each successive layer and what is required there is like pressing harder on the gas pedal while remaining in first gear: RPM will increase, but without shifting gears, it will not accelerate movement.

The same is true in an apostolic movement. In order for motion to translate into movement, there need to be strategic shifts along the way that

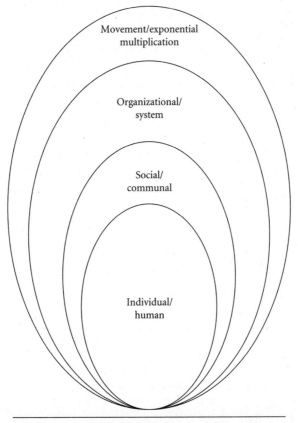

Figure 10.2 Nested Hierarchy of Ecclesia

release different potentials and capacities throughout the organization. Anticipating, and hence preparing for, these consecutive transition points will help prevent a movement from recoiling in on itself.

This does not minimize the importance of the individual elements at the base level. In fact, it only highlights their determinative nature. Without a good basis in each preceding level, the ecclesia cannot develop into a fully fledged movement, even though it contains all the potential to do so.

In Figure 10.3, you can see some of the essential functions of foundational apostolic ministry: discipling, networking, architecting, and resourcing. These are foundational but are also reflected throughout the whole. As foundations, they form a platform for all subsequent layers in the nested hierarchy. Although they are always present at every level, the focus shifts as the level of organization moves to the next stage. At all stages, leadership should have these four functions in mind, but emphasis will shift as the organization develops toward movement.

So while strategic emphasis will shift depending on the level of organization, development at every level should still be attentive to building individual, social, systemic, and exponential capacities. Discipling the individual should begin with the end in mind and end with the beginning in mind.

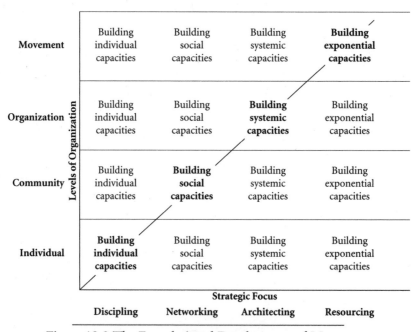

Figure 10.3 The Foundational Development of Movement

Remember, in every believer is the possibility of a movement. As the forest is contained within the potential of a seed, so in every individual Christ follower is the possibility of community, and in a community the real possibility of a translocal, transformative movement. Seeing people in this way (we believe it is the way Jesus sees us) changes the way we perceive and do "church" forever. It is this dynamically apostolic, profoundly movemental quality that the institutional view of ecclesia conceals from our view.

An example of this movemental approach can be seen in Trinity Grace Church in New York City, led by movement starter Jon Tyson, from Australia. As an apostolic leader, he is attentive to basic algorithms, reproducibility, discipleship, scalability, and core theology. As a result he has developed a flourishing, fully reproducible movement in the making in one of the hardest contexts for the gospel in the United States. 3DM adopted a similar approach with its lifeshapes model, which embeds key practices at every level of organization. It has eight distinct shapes, each representing a different aspect of discipleship and church life. All members are apprenticed into using the shapes as a way of forming their lives and formatting their ministries.[29]

In this chapter we have suggested that the archetypal organizational form for apostolic ministry and impact is that of the people movement. No one would doubt that the New Testament church, as well as the subsequent early church, was a formidable, highly transformative people movement. Whenever that movement form was explicitly adopted since then, either because of circumstance (for example, persecution) or because of new apostolic work among new groups, the church has grown exponentially. Whether it was the Celtic church that evangelized Western Europe, the early Methodists who had a profound impact on the world, the Moravians, early Pentecostals, the Chinese underground church, and the others, movements are the forms of the church that change the world. We are now seeing the early adoption (or maybe readoption) of these forms among more established churches. The movement that emerged from St. Thomas Crookes in Sheffield is a good case in point. But churches as diverse as Southside (in British Columbia), the Austin Stone, the Tampa Underground, Granger Community Church, New Thing Network, and Missio, all are heading in this direction.

Organization matters. It involves the mobilization of bias in one form or another. If we hope to be a missional movement in our age, we must set about designing and biasing the church to be the high-impact missional agency it was intended to be in the first place. The effectiveness of the church and the healthy spread of the gospel are inextricably connected with our capacity to organize rightly. The medium must become the message and strive for more consistency with it. We have no doubt that the apostolic movement is the form that gives the church its best opportunity to extend Christianity far into this century. Far from being alien to who we are, movements are our most primal form, and we are at our best behavior and have the greatest impact when we are moving along with the Holy Spirit. Movements R Us!

Apostolic Architecture
THE ANATOMY OF MISSIONAL ORGANIZATION

Much of what we face can't be deterred, prevented or even predicted. Thus we need to become resilient.
Joshua Cooper Ramo

There is nothing neutral about the way we organize.
Gareth Morgan

The most important ideas of all are meta-ideas, that is, ideas about how to support the production and transmission of other ideas.
Paul Romer

DEE HOCK, THE FOUNDER OF VISA WHOM WE MET IN CHAPTER TEN, was called in by the banking system in the 1960s to find a solution to the increasing complexities presented by the introduction of the credit card system. It was widely agreed that credit cards themselves were a major innovation for the finance and banking sector, but at that point, each bank and corporation had its own credit card. This meant that consumers had to carry up to twenty different credit cards. The bankers knew that this was unsustainable, so they called Hock in to help sort out the crisis.

Hock knew that if a solution was left to the bankers, their focus would be on order, which would result in massive bureaucracy—an unproductive no-win situation. He reasoned that if the problem was left to the more creative types, there would likely be a lot of new ideas but a lot of unsustainable chaos, and the credit card would not survive. That is when Hock designed the chaordic system.

How we structure organization has a direct impact on outcomes—for good or for ill—and leadership must be aware of the implications and face the consequences.

Church Resource Ministries founder and international director Sam Metcalf maintains that apostolic impact comes about when the apostolic mission is providing the appropriate structures. His basic formula is that apostolic ministry plus apostolic structure equals apostolic effectiveness. We agree. Forms and structures can either inhibit or promote a cause, and they need constant revitalization to ensure that they do not become ends in themselves. Organizations exist to maintain and deliver the function for which they were made. It is no good trying to build a revived apostolic ministry and structure it around forms and organizations that are built to deliver something fundamentally different. The wineskin won't hold, and the wine will be wasted (Luke 5:37–39). That is why we need to explore new ways of organizing that are more consistent with the function. The forms we suggest here are those consistent with apostolic and missional bias for movement.

We have already mentioned that over time and under the influence of an increasingly institutionalized view of the church, the apostolic ministry so evident throughout the biblical and postbiblical period was eventually sidelined and delegitimized. The apostolic imagination was lost and the view of the church and its mission narrowed. Increasingly, the ecclesia of Christ was identified exclusively as the local church, with a nod toward the overarching concept contained in the idea of the church's catholicity—the belief in the church universal. The more translocal, distinctly movemental understandings of ecclesia were lost. The significantly diminished view of New Testament ecclesiology was disastrous to the mission and effectiveness of the kind of church that Jesus intended. The church came to be viewed as a hospital for ailing souls or a bastion of theological truth, or some combination of both. Gone was the grand vision for a transformed world. The church had given birth to the so-called Christian civilization, only to become its subservient chaplain. The movement originally made up of pioneers and settlers became increasingly dominated by the settlers to the exclusion of the pioneers.

It is not our goal here to write extensively about every possible aspect of apostolic organization, but rather to outline ways in which we believe it is likely to take shape. Here we apply apostolic imagination on the way organization ought to be both conceived and designed. Based on what we know from history and from best practices in organizational theory, we advocate some specific characteristics that are more suited to the missional challenges we face and will foster the much-needed adaptation demanded of Christian organizations now.

Design Matters

Leadership is unlikely to achieve X objective when the organization is biased to achieving a Y objective. Apple trees are, to put it metaphorically, unlikely to produce oranges. So too, organizations produce according to their kind. Design matters. We think that the church of Jesus Christ is designed for missional impact, and if it is not achieving that, then something has gone wrong in the design department. Linda Bergquist and Allan Karr's book, *Church Turned Inside Out,* takes issues of design seriously: the approach they suggest of design, redesign, and alignment is very useful at this point.[1]

Organizational imagineer Gareth Morgan rightly maintains that "organizations are rarely established as ends in themselves. They are instruments created to achieve other ends."[2] Organizations are designed with a distinct purpose in mind. This is also true for our understanding of ecclesia, particularly insofar as the distinctly organizational aspects are concerned. The church, in confessing that it is a sign, symbol, and instrument of the kingdom, recognizes that it is a tool, an instrument, in the hands of her Lord.

Problems in organizational design arise when the context changes and the organization itself does not, when the organization itself becomes the mission, or when the organization veers from the path of its original designers. If leaders choose to ignore the issue of design (and the question of constant redesign) and how it directly determines outcomes, then they will inadvertently hand the organization over to latent forces that can be directly at odds with the purposes that members want to achieve. The inevitable result is frustration, even lots of it, at every level of the organization.

Such situations are natural seedbeds for dissension, dissatisfaction, and even revolution. As Clay Shirky, the author of the best-selling *Here Comes Everybody*, observes, "The hallmark of revolution is that the goals of the revolutionaries cannot be contained by the institutional structure of the existing society. As a result, either the revolutionaries are put down, or some of those institutions are altered, replaced or destroyed."[3] This again echoes Jesus's clear warnings about the problem of wineskins (Matthew 9:14–17).

Because we are perfectly designed to achieve what we are currently achieving, if the church is in decline, then at least in part it reflects the fact that we are not operating according to its original apostolic design. The church that Jesus intended and designed is made for impact—and massive, highly transformative impact at that. Jesus said, "I will build My church, and the gates of Hades shall not prevail against it" (Matthew 16:18). Note here that Jesus says that the gates of hell do not prevail against us. It is we as God's people who are on the advance here, not the forces of hell. Contrary to many of the images of church as a defensive fortress suffering the relentless onslaughts of the enemy, the movement that Jesus set in motion is designed to be an advancing, untamed, and untamable revolutionary force created to transform the world. And make no mistake: there is in Jesus's words a sense of inevitability about the eventual triumph of the gospel and the ecclesia, his chief instrument. If we are not somehow part of this grand movement, then we have to question, among other things, if there is something wrong in the prevailing ways we have designed and organized ourselves.[4]

Four-Self Dynamics

Some serious movemental thinking can be observed in the seminal missiology of Henry Venn and others who developed the concept of generating indigenous churches based on what became known as the three-self principle: self-governance, self-support, and self-propagation.

While recognizing that in fact Jesus is Lord and that the reference to "self" here is not meant to be interpreted in the sense of the autonomous self so prevalent in our Western culture, the principles here are intended to capture the God-given right of all peoples to have their own distinct cultural identity. Following their missionary instincts, along with the methodological clues contained in the scriptures themselves, movement starters must encourage local, indigenous forms of ecclesia and discourage the adoption of foreign cultural forms. Missionaries must actively discourage any childlike dependency by the new churches that would hinder their growth and maturity. This kind of dependency can be observed in many missionary contexts (Africa and Papua New Guinea, for example), where new churches were made dependent on external missionary support and failed not to flourish as a result. They became known as "rice Christians"—people who converted for the benefits such as rice that the foreign missionaries brought. The same principle is true for many denominational church plants in the West. New "parachute" church plants that are fully funded by denominational headquarters and lack a grassroots mission approach to evangelism and mission have less independence and are less likely to flourish.

An ardent disciple of the three-self principles, seminal thinker Roland Allen taught that the church's missionary activity derives not from organizational control but from "the expression of the spontaneous individual activity of its members; for every member was potentially a missionary."[5] Out of his mission experience around the turn of the nineteenth century in China, he reflected on the factors that encouraged and inhibited the spontaneous expansion of the gospel. These were his conclusions:

Factors That Encourage Spontaneous Expansion

- When people whose lives have been affected profoundly by the gospel tell their story to those who know them.
- When from the beginning, evangelism is the work of those within the culture.
- When new Christians are immediately given the opportunity to learn by ministering to non-Christians rather than sitting in a classroom.
- When the church is self-supporting and provides for its own leaders and facilities.
- When true doctrine results from the true experience of the power of Christ rather than mere intellectual instruction.[6]
- When new churches are given the freedom to learn by experience.[7]

Factors That Inhibit Spontaneous Expansion

- When paid (foreign) professionals are primarily responsible to spread the gospel, which is then perceived as an alien intrusion.
- When the church becomes dependent on external funds and leadership.[8]
- When spread of the gospel is controlled out of fear, and both error and godly zeal are suppressed. Allen believed the great things of God are beyond our control. He observed that control produces sterility. Thinking of the Western missions he experienced in China, he noted, "Our converts have not gone astray, but neither they have produced anything."[9]
- When it is believed that the church is to be founded, educated, and equipped, established in the doctrine and ethics and organization first; then it is to expand.[10]
- When emerging leaders are restricted from ministering until they are fully trained. In this way, they learn the lesson of inactivity and dependency.[11]

- When we attempt to convert by clever argument rather than the power of Christ.
- When a professional class controls the ministry and discourages the spontaneous zeal of those who are not members of their profession.[12]

There is a lot of apostolic movement power in the principles of spontaneous expansion (and a lot of stopping power in the inhibiting factors). For instance, in 1899, John Livingston Nevius, an apostle to China and a devotee of the three-self principles, trained a groups of missionaries who were going into groups of previously unreached people in Korea in the use of the three-self principles.[13] The missionaries sent to establish the Korean church adopted them, and the mission was wildly successful.

The historical irony is significant. The ideas themselves were originally formulated in China, prior to the communist revolution, but the Chinese church never took the three-self principles seriously, and therefore the growth in China was painstakingly slow. The mission in Korea adopted them wholeheartedly, and the movement grew exponentially and continues to do so to this day.[14]

The lessons are stark: the way we organize has a direct impact on the church's capacity to be the transformative people movement it was originally designed to be. To underscore this point, we need only recognize that the exponentially expanding Chinese underground movement was not born until after the purging of foreign missionaries from China in the early 1950s. In the wake of this and after waves of serious persecution, the church was forced to discover the power of indigenous, organic growth. It seems that God had to remove the professional Christians, along with the institutional forms of church that they maintained, so that the people of God could become the people of God. This perhaps was the real revolution going on in the Chinese Revolution.

We suggest that the original three-self principles could be updated and expanded to four: all apostolic movements ought to strive to be self-organizing, self-generating, self-sustaining, and self-reflecting (Figure 11.1).[15] Using this framework will undoubtedly steer us away from many problems related to institutionalization, not to mention the avoidance of unhealthy dependencies down the track.

Self-Organizing

Essentially any organization is an effort to contain, channel, or mobilize resources. The idea of self-organization is no different. All living

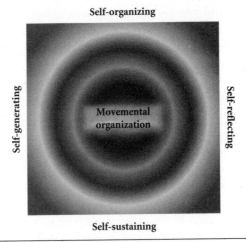

Self-organizing

Self-generating

Movemental
organization

Self-reflecting

Self-sustaining

Figure 11.1 Four-Self Principles

systems have the seemingly natural capacity to organize themselves in order to achieve the desired outcomes. This is perhaps especially true for the ecclesia, which not only has the guiding presence of the Holy Spirit (1 Corinthians 3:16), and a direct relationship with the Lord, but has built-in spiritual intelligence by which it can operate (Ephesians 4:7–16; 1 Corinthians:12–14; Romans 12:1–7).

This is entirely consistent with the concept of self-organization in living systems theory, which both recognizes and seeks to enhance the innate potential within groups of people to self-organize through an evolving process that draws on existing resources within and around the group. Thought leaders Margaret Wheatley and Myron Kellner-Rogers rightly note:

> All living systems have the capacity to *self-organize*, to sustain themselves and move toward greater complexity and order as needed. They can respond intelligently to the need for change. They organize (and then reorganize) themselves into adaptive patterns and structures without any externally imposed plan or direction. . . . In these systems, change is the organizing force, not a problematic intrusion. Structures and solutions are temporary. Resources and people come together to create new initiatives, to respond to new regulations, to shift the organization's processes. Leaders emerge from the needs of the moment. There are far fewer levels of management. Experimentation is the norm.[16]

Although they did not use the term itself, self-organizing is exactly what the original apostles sought to develop in the life of the local communities they helped establish.[17] Clearly they took people and place, with the associated cultural forms, seriously. For instance, what worked culturally and theologically in Jerusalem would not necessarily work in Corinth, and they did not assume it would. Because their particular sense of calling, together with their desire to faithfully witness (and sometimes their very survival), were at stake, local disciples and communities became real stakeholders, experts at processing the problems they faced.

In this way, they allowed group involvement and participation to constantly deepen. Learning was shared not as a formula or model for others to copy, but as an application of missiological thinking and approaches to problem solving. Steve Addison is right when he says that "centralization and standardization are the enemies of innovation."[18] We have already seen that the truly great organizations do not make their best moves by brilliant and complex strategic planning. What they do is "try a lot of stuff and see what works" and then freely share their learnings with others.[19]

The concept of local leadership (elders and deacons) itself supports the idea of local disciples being ultimately responsible for witness and health as a Jesus community in their area. When Paul sends members of his apostolic team to help establish elders in the local churches, he is doing precisely this (Titus 1:5). All efforts at helping the local churches get established and grow to maturity involve an increasing transfer of power from the founder to the community that he or she has founded. To do otherwise would be to create dependencies that undermine the idea of the church as the body of Christ, and therefore as an expansive people movement. Although Paul certainly takes a parental interest in the congregations around the empire, he does not (even cannot) dominate or disempower them. Although he does exercise spiritual authority and leadership when it matters, over time he seeks to wean them from his direct influence.[20]

Self-Generating

Each community was responsible for not only its own survival but also for extending the message by evangelizing, discipling, and planting the gospel. A message exists to be passed on, and the church of Jesus is at core a message tribe. This is what the original framers of the three-self principles called self-propagation; the Bible calls it fruitfulness. Both point at the reproductive capacities of the ecclesia. As Neil Cole rather wryly notes, "If you can't reproduce disciples, you can't reproduce

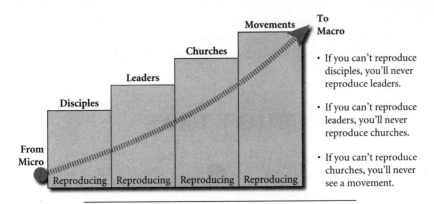

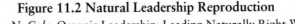

Figure 11.2 Natural Leadership Reproduction

Source: N. Cole, *Organic Leadership: Leading Naturally Right Where You Are (Grand Rapids, Mich.: Baker, 2009). Used with permission.*

leaders. If you can't reproduce leaders, you can't reproduce churches. If you can't reproduce churches, you can't reproduce movements."[21] This is illustrated in Figure 11.2, which shows that reproduction should occur naturally at every succeeding level of complexity, beginning at the smallest, simplest level.

It is hard to get around the sheer truth of this. Generativity, involving the commitment to reproduction and reproducibility, must be factored into the base equation of the apostolic movement. The commitment is at the DNA level—as inviolable as genetics is in forming and perpetuating life itself. To leave this out in principle means to end up with an organization or system that, like an infertile mule, not only will not reproduce itself but in fact cannot do so. Most prevailing forms of church cannot be easily reproduced except by professionals, and even then, it is done well only by very few of them. Of the 400,000 churches in the United States, only a few can be considered reproductive and fruitful. For instance, Neil Cole, reflecting on research done by the Southern Baptist research and resource center called Lifeway, notes that only 4 percent of Southern Baptist churches in the United States will plant a daughter church. Extrapolated across the denominations, that means that 96 percent of the conventional churches in the United States will never give birth. Cole goes on to show the missionally perilous misconceptions inherent in this thinking:

> Many think this is fine. I have heard people say, "We have plenty of churches. There are churches all over the place that sit empty, why

start new ones? We don't need more churches but better ones." Can you imagine making such a statement about people? "We have plenty of people. We don't need more people, just better ones. Why have more babies?" This is short-range thinking. No matter how inflated you think the world population is, we are only one genera-tion away from extinction if we do not have babies. Imagine the headlines if suddenly it was discovered that 96% of the women in America were no longer fertile and could not have babies. We would instantly know two things: this is not natural so there is something wrong with their health. We would also know that our future is in serious jeopardy.[22]

This failure to think about and organize for the ability of ecclesia to reproduce lies at the root of much of our frustration with the persistent failure of so many church planting projects. There are precious few third- or fourth-generation church planting movements to be found. And even when some churches manage to plant one or two new churches, they seldom last to the third generation, which is considered the beginning of real movement.[23] This is partly because reproduction feels unnatural and the system is way too clunky to be able to easily reproduce.

Movements require commitment from the start in order to be self-generating. All apostolic movements demonstrate this principle to vary-ing degrees.

Self-Sustaining

Anyone who has been in leadership very long realizes that finances have a massive impact on how we conceive of and carry out a church, a plant, or a mission project. What few realize, though, is that the reasons are actually counterintuitive to what we normally think. We generally think that the more money we give to a particular mission effort, the more chance it has of succeeding. Actually the opposite is true. Our assump-tions once again come from the institutional paradigm of the church, which is building bound and expensive. But that thinking marginalizes the real power of the church—the ministry of all of God's people in every sphere and domain. Church growth movement founder Donald McGavran warned in 1990:

The congregation should be of such structure and pattern that com-mon people can operate it and multiply it indefinitely among the masses. In North America, the indefinitely reproducible pattern is not the highly successful church, led by a very exceptional preacher, which erects a set of buildings covering a city block and counts its members in the thousands. That is one good pattern in certain situations, but it is impossible in most places.[24]

It is not possible to reproduce movementally, let alone sustain a movement, if churches require exorbitant amounts of money to start and operate. Our friend and movement expert Steve Addison has long maintained that Christianity flourishes when it is no longer dependent on external organization, funding, and control. He quotes missiologist Wayne Allen, who discovered that the impact of foreign subsidies for national church workers generally has an inverse relationship to the decline or plateau of the national churches.[25] There are three reasons for this:

1. *Loss of lay involvement.* Subsidies resulted in a move away from lay leadership to a reliance on paid professional clergy.
2. *Loss of focus.* Paid workers subsequently gave less attention to evangelism in unreached villages and more attention to meeting the needs of existing congregations in line with the expectation of the foreign mission agency providing the funds.
3. *Loss of devotion.* As the people realized that the mission became funding their pastor, they lost a sense of ownership and came to see the pastor as the parent organization's hired hand. In turn, the hired pastor tended to give greater attention to pleasing the mission organization and seeking salary increases.[26]

The implications are profound for churches everywhere—not just the developing world. If we hope to activate movements, we have to ensure that we do not lay the seeds of professionalism in the base models we use. We need to keep an eye out for long-term sustainability and ongoing momentum. Remember that every believer is an agent of the King, every son and daughter of the King is a missionary, and our Lord provides for each one in his own way. This is not to say that monies should not be raised and some people paid through centralized sources, but serious care must be taken to avoid the perils that Wayne Allen outlined. Movements must not be dependent on the availability or otherwise of clergy salaries; it is a sure way to stop a viable movement in its tracks.

Beyond the issue of money and support, sustainability needs to be able to be carried out by the whole church and not outsourced to experts or a priestly or pastoral caste that almost inevitably replaces and thus marginalizes the priesthood of all believers. Furthermore, methods must be simple enough so they can be reproduced easily, rapidly, and sustainably. Table 11.1 lists some examples of sustainable and unsustainable practices.

Self-Reflective

Local disciples and communities need to have the internal tools to analyze, reflect, learn, and adapt without having recourse to some central system that regulates what is, and is not, permitted. Guided by a love for God, the presence of the in-dwelling Spirit, and a deep commitment to the scriptures, God's people are able to make the right choices and grow to maturity on their own.

Table 11.1 Church Planting Practices

Unsustainable Practices	Sustainable Practices
Fully fund every church plant.	Train church planters to raise funds or become tent makers, or both.
Require seminary training for every church planter.	Multiply trainers in the field.
Provide a coach for every church planter.	Equip established church planters to coach the next wave of church planters.
Provide long-term subsidies for struggling church plants.	Allow churches to take responsibility.
Parent churches take responsibility for the budgeting and administration of church plants.	Empower church plants to set up their own systems.
Centrally plan and coordinate where and when churches are to be planted.	Expect churches and church planters to seek God, do the research, and multiply churches wherever there is a need.
Start a church.	Multiply churches.
A denomination that is solely responsible to identify and recruit church planters.	Every church planter trains apprentices for future church plants.
Satellite congregations that are dependent forever on the sending church.	Satellite congregations graduate quickly to interdependence and become multiplying hubs.
A movement that is held together by tight organizational systems of control.	A movement held together by a common cause and relationships.

Source: Movements That Change the World *by Steve Addison (Smyrna, Del.: Missional Press, 2010), pp. 112–113. Reprinted by permission of the author.*

How else can we account for the stunning growth in movements like the contemporary Chinese and Indian churches? Besides, as we have seen in Ephesians 4, Jesus provided each church with APEST to ensure that they can stay true to their calling and can grow to maturity: "From him the whole body, joined and held together by every supporting ligament, grows and builds itself up in love, as each part does its work" (Ephesians 4:16).

Missiologists have called this self-reflective ability "self-theologizing," and it provides a basis of the fourth principle for framing movement organization: God's people need to think contextually and interpret the gospel into their own particular context. If they fail in being able to do this, they will fail to be a fully incarnated church—fully faithful to the gospel while at the same time being profoundly relevant to their culture.

When others do all the thinking for them, then people will never learn to think (and act) for themselves, and they will remain immature and dependent. In movement thinking, each unit of the church has everything it needs to do its job, like the starfish. Outsourcing basic functions, ones intrinsic to the viability of the church to be church, are usually well intended but prove to be utterly disastrous in the long run. For instance, we believe that making a church dependent on external institutions to do its theologizing lies at the root of many of the organizational as well as the missional problems we face. The denominational seminary is a classic case in point. If one organization is set apart to handle all the ideas and leadership training, then the local church no longer believes it has to do the hard work of these itself. As a result, it becomes lazy and dependent on the external organization. If we are not careful, creating external training and licensing bodies can be a death knell to a movement and cultivate a propensity toward institutionalism.

If you doubt this rather controversial statement, consider this: prominent sociologists Rodney Stark and Roger Finke, widely considered to be the premier sociologists of religion alive today, undertook a detailed study to track the remarkable growth and subsequent decline of the early Methodist movement. Within decades of arriving in the United States in the 1760s, Methodism could claim to be discipling over 30 percent of the population throughout the nation. All the elements of apostolic movement were evident in early Methodism; classes, small groups, apostolic organization, church planting, people movement, and so on.

The so-called circuit riders were a key factor in this success.[27] These profoundly apostolic laypeople were passionate disciples who, with some rudimentary training, rode from town to town, planting churches as they went. They would then circle back to ensure that the churches were growing and healthy. Stark and Finke discovered that around 1850, the stunning growth turned into trended decline. They discovered that during this period, the more institutionally inclined Episcopalians and Presbyterians had relentlessly mocked the Methodists as being uncouth and not knowing Latin, Greek, and Hebrew. Under this barrage of insults, the Methodist leadership decided that the circuit riders should do rigorous seminary training at least equal to that of their antagonists. The circuit riders were then required to do four years of seminary training as a prerequisite for licensing to the ministry. Methodism in America has never regained a positive growth pattern lost in that fateful decision.[28]

This is by no means the only example. An aspect worth considering is that the current training system was started and is still operated by the teacher and shepherd of the APEST typology. One has to wonder what a system designed by and for a fully fledged APEST ministry would look like.[29] What would change? What would be the likely outcomes? To produce something fundamentally different is going to require a thorough audit and recalibration of prevailing practices.

We should not be surprised, in constructing a theological training system (a tool) based squarely on variations of the Oxford-Cambridge model of theoretical academy-based learning, and subsequently requiring that all pastors should attend full time for at least three years to be ordained, that it should utterly change the most fundamental movemental algorithms that lie at the heart of biblical ecclesiology.[30] We are not saying that education and learning are bad—far from it. But requiring a formal, classroom-based degree as a necessary basis for ordination, a concept itself completely alien to the New Testament, violates the calling and ministry that Jesus has clearly given to every disciple and lends itself to a professionalized elitism that Jesus himself detested. In addition, over the course of these programs, divinity students are socialized out of the context of leadership, ministry, and mission, anathema to movement dynamics because of the loss of needed momentum.

This outsourcing of learning to institutions and professionals has a double impact: the impact on the so-called laity is that it discourages use of their own capacities to think and theologize for themselves. Serious theologizing (that is, reflecting on God), intrinsic to discipleship itself, is thus outsourced to professionals. It creates a needy dependence on the clergy, which produces intellectual apathy in the so-called laity. (Ironically, this is something the clergy complain about all the time.) Stated more bluntly, the system itself, the one they steward, perpetuate, and defend, nurtures the very thing that they bemoan.

In all these reflections, we do well to remember the profound words of Roland Allen when he reflected on the apostolic movements—what he rather poetically called "the spontaneous expansion of the church":

> The spontaneous expansion of the Church reduced to its element is a very simple thing. It asks for no elaborate organization, no large finances, no great numbers of paid missionaries. In its beginning it may be the work of one man, and that a man neither learned in the things of this world, nor rich in the wealth of this world. . . . The organization of a little church on the apostolic model is also extremely simple, and the most illiterate converts can use it, and the poorest are sufficiently wealthy to maintain it. . . . No one, then, who feels within himself the call of Christ to embark on such a path as this need say, I am too ignorant, I am too inexperienced, I have too little influence, or I have not sufficient resources. The first apostles of Christ were in the eyes of the world "unlearned and ignorant" men: it was not until the Church had endured a persecution and had grown largely in numbers that Christ called a learned man to be His apostle.[31]

On a more disturbing and personal note, and one that has serious implications for the whole Christian information system from publishing to seminaries, I (Alan) remember Chinese underground church researcher Curtis Sergeant once challenging me about this. In the West, he told me, we seek to become experts in order to "sell" our knowledge for mainly economic reasons—we thereby try to make ourselves indispensable—linchpins who intentionally create dependency. We do not give our knowledge away freely because that is our means of income and the source of our value proposition to churches and Christian organizations. In many ways, this is a legitimate form of income, but it becomes problematic precisely at the point where it impedes the capacity of Jesus's ecclesia to grow and mature. Sergeant noted, and I believe rightly, that apostolic movements give knowledge away and would never think of attaching a dollar value to it. The original apostles were not consultants and did not seek to create dependencies based on their specialized knowledge.

From an apostolic point of view, biblical truth belongs to the people of God, and we, if anything, are simply its stewards. This sounds a clear warning to all those (including the two of us) who consider ourselves educators, knowledge workers, consultants, and authors who try to make ourselves indispensable to the transfer of essential information. We must ask ourselves if we are creating unnatural dependencies or are empowering God's people to live into their own truths.

There are existing models of education and training that are more consistent with discipleship approaches and apostolic bias than the ones we now have. We must find a way to make them more the norm in leadership and spiritual formation. Placing theological reflection back in the local ecclesia itself is a good step in the right direction. And if we do not have models that suit, leadership should seek to produce them. We can, and must, design and innovate our way out of the current training morass if we are committed to being more movemental.

A Balance in the Force

Planting the gospel and thinking in terms of movements as opposed to planting churches are good ways of conceiving the processes, or foundations, involved in architecting movements. But the process needs to be bolstered by frameworks if they are to find expression. Frameworks imply structure, and indeed some form of structure and organization is needed.

We suggest that one of the useful ways of structuring for movements is to develop what has been called *sodalic*, or sometimes apostolic, groupings or bands. Movements attempt to harness the energies of all their members, but they also discover ways to release the potential of their most committed workers for the benefit of the wider movement. The role of this more select group of people is to act as the pioneers of the movement going into previously unreached fields, as well as the consolidators who strengthen existing gains.

Jesus mobilized the masses, but the driving heart of his movement consisted of the twelve apostles and the seventy-two disciples sent out by the Lord (Luke 10:1). Patrick intuitively understood this principle as did the later Catholic religious orders, the Moravians, the Methodists with their circuit riders, the Protestant missionary societies, and the Salvation Army.[32]

Ralph Winter has argued that God's redemptive mission has been advanced by two complementary but distinct structures. He describes these redemptive structures as *modalities* and *sodalities:* "A modality is a structured fellowship in which there is no distinction of sex or age, while a sodality is a structured fellowship in which membership involves an adult second decision beyond modality membership and is limited by either age or sex or marital status" (Table 11.2).[33]

Most local churches fit into the modality definition. They are structured to be home grown, evangelistic, and discipling agencies. Commitment to Christ is the basic requirement for membership, and only the most serious of offenses result in expulsion. In the New Testament, most of the churches that received letters fit this description. In contrast, Paul's missionary band (comprising up to thirty people, including Titus, Timothy, and Barnabas) could be described as a sodality or task-oriented mission structure. Inclusion was not automatic; a second adult decision was required to join the band. Not only commitment to Christ but continued commitment to the purpose and standards of the group was required of members.

It is tempting to see Paul (as well as the other apostles) as doing it all alone, but clearly this is wrong. Like all the other ministries, apostles saw themselves as extensions of the ministry of Christ and his body, the ecclesia. Furthermore, they seldom, if ever, operated without others around them. Although Paul is often placed in the spotlight when it comes to the gospel spreading throughout the Mediterranean, a close reading of the text indicates that he did not work alone: he had anywhere from thirty-five to ninety-five coworkers who, with different levels of regularity, were involved in his apostolic ministry.[34] He most definitely had an organization with various levels of involvement and stakeholding. Whether you call them coworkers, fellow-soldiers, or just plain teammates, Paul had a mosaic of partnerships with people who aided him in his apostolic

Table 11.2 Modalities and Sodalities: A Comparison

Modalities	Sodalities
The church local	The church in mission form
Diocesan, parish form	Task oriented, selective focus
Structured primarily for nurture and care	Mobile, flexible, lean
Conserves new ground	Breaks new ground, crosses barriers
First decision people[a]	Second decision people[a]
Pastoral leaders	Apostolic leaders
Resources for sodalities	Creates modalities and sodalities
Occasionally multiples	Inherently expansionistic
Five-generation life cycle	Extended generational life cycle
Connectional ecclesiology	Can be transdenominational
Near-neighbor missionality	Cross-culturally capable
Builds and establishes	Inherently entrepreneurial

[a]*All believers make a decisive first choice to become followers. But only some are converted again to surrendering their lives to serve Jesus in a concentrated and intentional way.*

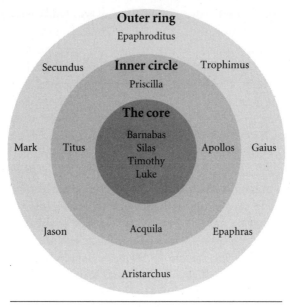

Figure 11.3 The Pauline Sodalic Team

ministry.[35] From what we can discern, Paul's apostolic band might look like that in Figure 11.3.

The demanding, translocal, cross-cultural nature of Paul's ministry necessitated a structure different from that of a local church. Paul's ministry involved evangelism and gospel planting in a hostile environment spread out over a wide geographical area. It could be carried out only by a team of individuals called together for that specific purpose. It would not have been realistic to expect such work from every member of the church at Antioch. Paul did expect the local expression of the church to participate in his mission through prayer and financial support. But he called only a few individuals out of their local church to join his apostolic band who all added to the strength of a highly focused team to Paul's missionary endeavors.[36]

Ralph Winter argued that the expansion of the church has always been carried on most effectively when these modalities and sodalities accepted each other's legitimacy and worked together.[37] The New Testament church existed in both forms—the translocal and the local—and each had elements of one in the other. Neither is inferior. When each accepts and receives the other's role, the church is wired for movement (Figure 11.4).

Reframing church structure around modality and sodality helps us understand one of the roles that the local church is to play in relation to

Figure 11.4 Modalic Function and Sodalic Function Together

apostolic ministry: to empower what is already taking shape in apostolic people. This implies a higher level of sensitivity and flexibility than is usually found in the local church. It takes a real commitment to the extension of Christianity for a local community to release its apostolic leaders to pursue their callings. In our experience, when the local community does not release them, they likely end up leaving anyway, but without the network or resources to best fulfill their calling.

Church Resource Ministries' Sam Metcalf, a keen advocate of Winter's typology, gives a good summary in his lecture notes that shows the issue of commitment is a critical factor that distinguishes these two basic structures:[38]

- Sodalities are primarily task oriented and focus around a shared sense of mission that is often narrowly defined (examples are most parachurch agencies like Navigators and Campus Crusade for Christ).
- Part of their function is to help modalities be healthy and to create new modalities (examples are Church Resource Ministries, Exponential, Future Travelers, Forge, Missio, 3DM, and other parachurch agencies created to support the church).
- Sodalities frequently multiply modalities as well as more sodalities, as church planting agencies do.
- They are apostolic structures in that they facilitate and extend the apostolic ministry.
- The life span and life cycle of a sodality are typically longer than those of a modality because the sodality can enforce discipline.

People can be fired from a sodality for not doing their job. That is a standard that the church in its local form rarely attempts.

- Although sodalities can form within denominations in the Protestant movement, they are frequently transdenominational in reach and focus.
- The stimulus for ongoing renewal and spiritual vitality most commonly flows from sodalities into the modalities.

In the urban church planting movement in Melbourne that I (Alan) used to lead, we took the modality-sodality dimension with great seriousness. So when we planted a church in our red-light district, we first set up a sodalic group, St. Kilda Gatehouse. Gatehouse performed all the functions of a sodality (missional functions, outreach, church planting, training) in the local area and in effect planted, and subsequently supported, the church plant called Matthew's Party, which did the discipling, ran local services, conducted counseling, and so on. Matthew's Party in turn supported Gatehouse in any way it could, such as financially and by releasing possible new leaders into the wider ministry. We did the same when planting congregations in the Jewish community of Melbourne: we set up Celebrate Messiah (led by my brother, Lawrence), an agency that has planted three congregations and has led international work among Jews in Israel and Russia. This proved to be an effective strategy, but the key is to be sure that the sense of mutuality and relationship is maintained in both structures, even if it means writing such a relationship into the constitution or by-laws. They must be deliberately designed for interdependence. Hugh Halter and Matt Smay also recommend and illustrate a similar approach in their book *And,* based on the experience of working for Missio, a training agency, and planting a local movement with many congregations (called Addulum).[39]

There have been, and continue to be, some remarkable sodalities in the history of the church: the monastic movement in the early period (Cistercian, Benedictine), the missional orders (Franciscans, Sisters of Charity), the Protestant missionary organizations (China Inland Missions, Overseas Missionary Fellowship), and the parachurches (Campus Crusade, Youth for Christ) are all classic examples of sodalities that have advanced the cause of Christ and brought renewal to the church. Some of the more notable examples of new sodalic missional orders in our day is associated with the so-called New Monasticism, a movement deliberately committed to taking the gospel to the poor. Examples include, among others, Rutba House Fellowship in North Carolina; Urban Neighbors of Hope in Melbourne and Bangkok; Innerchange in San Francisco,

London, Cambodia, Romania, and Venezuela; and The Simple Way in Philadelphia.

To Organize or Not to Organize?

Putting aside the Christendom heritage and how that still biases our organizations, most denominational templates were formed following the model of the centralized management systems of the industrial era, models that are now rightly considered defunct by most corporations. We believe that it is well past time for us to return to our most primal and effective form: the apostolic movement. There can be no doubt that we are at our very best when we have little of the paraphernalia that we now consider vital to the church. The U.S. church spends over $70 billion every decade on plant and resources, and we are experiencing decline in adherence and membership at an unprecedented rate. This is unacceptable. Leadership needs to look beyond the expediencies of the status quo and make choices to design for advance and health.

We do not think it is possible to improve on the blueprint that is written in the New Testament. In reembracing the permanent revolution, we will be well on our way to the recovery of a church inherently designed for advance.

CONCLUSION

IT WAS DESIGN EXPERT BRUCE MAU who said that we typically do not pay any attention to design until something goes wrong. Design seemingly comes out from hiding at these moments, and we suddenly begin to pay attention to the deeper, often unseen world of design that so radically shapes, informs, influences, and directs our imagination and practice.

We stand at a pivotal moment in history where the issues of design are calling out for us to pay attention and reimagine our vocation from within a context where Christianity is increasingly finding itself at the edge of the cultural landscape. It is from within this place of marginality that we are poised to rediscover and reactivate our most generative forms of ministry and leadership. And while the prophetic and evangelistic ministries invite a more thorough exploration, it is the apostles, and their distinctly missional vocation, who present themselves to us at this hour. They are, like the other four APEST ministries, a gift of grace to the church in all ages, and a particular grace for this time and place.

As with all of God's other gifts and graces, they beckon a response. To the degree that we allow ourselves to stand under the ascended Christ and allow his wisdom and authority to shape our imagination and practice, we will experience revolution. We are designed for continuous movement, and apostles are the permanent revolutionaries given to the church to catalyze the permanent revolution. If we can receive them yet again, we not only open ourselves up to a permanent revolution, we also open ourselves up more fully to the One who has given them to us. It is not too much to say that in the vocation and person of Jesus, apostles stand at the door and knock. If we let them in, we will, once again, God willing, experience the permanent revolution that we were intended to be in the first place.

AFTERWORD

I CAN remember coming out of theological college in England in the early 1980s and moving into my first parish job where I was to be the local vicar. I had an endless number of ideas and aspirations of how this local expression of the body of Christ could, with God's Spirit, push the kingdom forward. There were places of great darkness, and we would bring the light of Jesus. The kingdom would advance and heaven would be brought to earth.

We would do things that were beyond out of the box, that were beyond the hallowed halls of the Sunday worship service. We would continue worshiping on Sunday, of course, but we would innovate vehicles of mission and discipleship to push forward the destiny of God's sent people. Much to my surprise, this was met by a less-than-tepid response by my parishioners: "That's not your job. Your job is to care for us [as a pastor would] and teach and preach from the Bible on Sunday and Wednesday nights [as a teacher would]. We give our tithe to pay missionaries in other countries [and your salary]. You're the pastor. Don't forget that."

Now I had not grown up in the church. At sixteen I picked up the Bible, read it cover to cover, and became a Christian. I was under the impression that what I had read in the Gospels and in the book of Acts was how the church actually functioned. It was a bit jarring to walk into the local church for the first time and see that it was only a shadow of what I'd read in scripture.

As you can imagine, that's always a tough pill to swallow and let's just say the pill only went halfway down. I continued with the pastoral care and brought strong preaching from the Word, but on the side (and then slowly into church life) we brought these more entrepreneurial kingdom endeavors. Some of them worked, some of them didn't. But asking me to stop trying new things to advance the kingdom was like asking a fish not to swim in the water: *It's how I was created. It's how I function.* I recognized the importance of pastoral care and teaching, and I certainly wasn't suggesting the removal of them in our church. But intuitively I was asking for the addition and the proper place of the Apostolic voice. And at that time I didn't even know that's what I was asking for. All I knew was that I was called to lead this particular church, and I couldn't help but start new things.

So I continued in the local church, serving faithfully in the traditional senses, but constantly experimenting and responding to fresh vision and revelation from the Lord, pushing into places where there was no gospel presence. After several years of doing this, serving in the poorest place in all of Britain, a few years in the United States, and then back to the United Kingdom, something happened: All of that pioneering led to the creation of a spectacular missional vehicle that would not only transform our church into the largest church in England, but also spawned a missional movement in Europe and now onto the shores of American soil. Today, these midsized groups of twenty to fifty people on mission together are called *Missional Communities* and they have, in many places, started to change the way the Western church functions.

Now this book you are holding is not about Missional Communities, and it is certainly not about my story. But it is about how my story doesn't need to be a rare one or even the exception to the rule. The truth of the matter is that most apostles, after years of being misunderstood or cast out, simply give up, either by leaving the church or by slowly conforming to the more accepted and traditional roles of teacher/pastor. I struggled for years and years, never realizing there was another way of understanding my vocation, and when I finally understood how I was created, God used our church and my leadership for his purposes. *But that only happened when I fully embraced my place as an apostle.* My story can be the common story.

This book is about the searching for that common story, about how the releasing of the apostolic genius in the local church will bring about other missional and discipling vehicles that will lead the body of Christ to its destiny. It's about understanding the place of the apostle within the whole of the five-fold ministry gifts, how it functions uniquely within the church, and how it can be released to take the church into the future. To watch the kingdom unfold before us as the Spirit leads. Like the Paul or Columbo or Aidan or John Wesley before us, the Western church desperately needs to re-legitimize the apostolic voice. Not only understand it. Release it.

Why the urgency? I come from a place where less than 1 percent of the population is in a church on any given Sunday. I look around in the states, in this place I now call home, and I see that Gen Y (the oldest of whom have already turned 30, had kids, bought homes) are only attending church on any given Sunday at a 4 percent clip. The Western church, yes, even the North American church, are staring over the precipice of complete irrelevance and stagnation and the apostolic voice needs to step up into its God-given place and be the catalyst of a new missional and discipling movement. I am not a "doom-and-gloom" futurist about the church in the West, but I am a realist. We need all five ministries from Ephesians 4 in their proper place, functioning together for this movement to happen. That means now is time for the restoration of the apostolic voice.

For that to happen, what we must see is that every "vocation" develops its own scriptural templates, practices, and paradigms. But for quite some time the apostolic *vocatio*, long in exile, has lacked these basic necessities that have been so readily available to the shepherds and teachers. One of the signs of a particular vocation—churchwise or secular—is the acceptance and development of these tools, which confirms its own legitimate standing in relation to other vocations. I see this book as a significant step forward in that legitimization process. It develops a vocational language and practice, intertwining features and paradigms from other overlapping disciplines and thought constructs, and combines them to formulate a unique platform. It allows those in other vocations, like the shepherd for example, to look in on the apostolic and say "Ahh! That's what the apostolic does! That's what they are good at! That's where they fit in the big picture!" It isn't to say that the apostolic is more important. It's to say that without it, the Body of Christ is incomplete as it serves a key function in leading the church toward its destiny in the same way that we are incomplete if we lack compassion for hurting and broken people.

When I started in ministry more than thirty years ago, no such strain of thinking or book existed. I was looked at with dis-ease and a certain amount of paranoia. It was generally accepted that I was called to the local church, but no one quite knew what to do with me. My hope and prayer is that if you find yourself in a similar situation, if you have been created with that apostolic gifting and voice, that you will find hope and fresh vision within the pages of this book. If you are not, my prayer is that God will give you revelation as to why apostles are so necessary and how he might be intertwining your life and ministry with that of this specific ministry gift. The truth of the matter is that they are inexorably linked.

Above all, know that this book is truly a gift, one that many before you hoped for long ago, and one that has finally been written.

MIKE BREEN
senior pastor of St. Thomas Church
Sheffield, England

APPENDIX

A QUESTION OF LEGITIMACY: THE
RESTORATION OF THE APOSTOLIC MINISTRY

*You can no longer remain unconscious where you slept before;
one way or another, you are creating your future. Wake up
before you find that the devils within you have done the creating.*
Stephen L. Talbot

*It isn't that they can't see the solution. It's that they can't
see the problem.*
G. K. Chesterton

WHEN SHE DIED ON JANUARY 5, 1172, Donna Berta di Bernardo, a wealthy widow of stature, left sixty coins to her church. This money was to be used toward the purchase of a few stones that would start the construction of a community bell tower. This building project was initiated by the local church leaders who decided they needed several new buildings in what they called the Field of Miracles. A year later, after digging a hole approximately five feet deep in soil composed of clay, sand, and shells, they laid the foundation and began what regrettably became a two-hundred-year building project beset by significant foundational issues. The tower began to lean just after the third story was completed and continued to lean incrementally, yet sporadically, toward the south over the next seven hundred years. Recent efforts to straighten the tower and keep it from falling over have varied from placing 960 tons of lead on the north side of the tower to removing earth beneath the north side of the foundation. In June 2001, the tower had been straightened up approximately 16 inches, returning its position to what it was in 1838, about 13 feet off center.

Foundations for Authentic Ministry

We think the Leaning Tower of Pisa is an appropriate metaphor for foundational aspects of the church's function and ministry. Foundations are just as vital to organizations (including churches) as they are to all other

255

buildings and structures. Shoddy work at the foundational level inevitably results in serious, and often disastrous, problems later. Attention to the underpinnings of the church's ministry and biblical foundations therefore is imperative. And we believe that negligent inattentiveness to biblical foundations accounts for a number of the problems we face in being the church that Jesus intended us to be.[1]

We want to make clear that while we affirm the foundational ministries of Ephesians 2:20, we wholeheartedly acknowledge that Jesus is the one true foundation of the church and any attempt to build on any other foundation is rightly labeled heresy.[2] There is a category difference between the Founder's unique ministry and the subsequent work constructed on that foundation. The work of the foundational ministries (apostle and prophet) is not to replace the role of the Founder, but to build on and so extend his ministry. This is exactly how we should understand Paul's passionate labors in Jesus's cause and why he outright rejects any attempts by others to put him in Jesus's place (1 Corinthians 1:11–24, 3:1–12; Colossians 1:24–25).

The fact that we have all but eliminated the possibility of an active, ongoing apostolic function from our consciousness and vocabulary, let alone from our practices, indicates that we have somehow messed with the foundations of leadership and ministry, at least in the way the New Testament church itself experienced these. As we have seen, New Testament ministry clearly included the ministry of apostles and, beyond that, of APEST. The words *apostle* and its derivatives are used over ninety-five times in the New Testament, whereas now *apostle* has been all but edited out of our vocabulary. Whereas it is used only once to describe a function in the church, we use the word *pastor* as a catch-all title for just about every aspect of ministry. And while the biblical understanding of teacher is circumscribed in the Bible itself (James 2), we refer to theologians as the sole dependable source of authority. How can we account for such a massive discrepancy? While accepting the ongoing role of the shepherds and teachers, we have to ask how it is we can claim to have a truly biblical understanding of ministry devoid of the active presence and participation of those who occupy the overwhelmingly prominent place in the biblical material itself.

This radical mismatch between New Testament APEST ministry and contemporary Western understandings serves only to highlight the issue that what we call ministry today is a substantively different from the original forms. Either this delimitation of ministry to shepherd and teacher functions is what God intended, or it is not. And if it is not what he intended, then we have made a terrible error along the way and must do all that we can to correct it.

Retrofitting the Church for Movement

If the role of apostolic ministry is as we have suggested in this book—the apostolic person is the legitimate custodian of the genetic coding of the church—then it is easy to see that apostolic ministry is of vital importance for the life, ministry, and health of the whole movement. And in fact we are unlikely to be able to fulfill our calling and mission as ecclesia without it. Surely to miss this is to make a serious mistake. We think that radical repentance is now needed to reestablish the church on its intended foundations.

The truth is that much of the traditional interpretation, undergirding the prevailing ecclesiology that pastors and theologians have scripted over the centuries, has seldom, if ever, been subjected to critical review and challenge. In fact, in researching this book, we could not find much evidence of any real debate at all. The fact that we have disputed issues as trivial as to how many angels can dance on the head of a pin, but have managed to avoid this issue for so many centuries, ought to make one seriously wonder about our sanity. The inherited position, undisputed as it is, is now assumed to be true; that is why one looks in vain for any significant exposition of the alternative in the standard commentaries and ecclesiologies that fill our shelves.[3]

Most suggestions that there is more to ministry than the standard forms meets with duration and rejection. This is a clear case of the so-called Semmelweis reflex—where the work of Ignaz Semmelweis, in discovering that mortality rates in patients with infections could be reduced tenfold if doctors would wash their hands with a chlorine solution, was rejected by his contemporaries. Here, the reflex-like denunciation of apostolic ministry and APEST is rejected because it contradicts entrenched norms.

Author and politician Upton Sinclair once said, "It is difficult to get a man to understand something, when his salary depends upon his not understanding it!"[4] There is something disturbingly insightful in this statement. The fact that most of the teaching determining apostolic legitimacy, or rather denying it, is generally produced by the very people who are most vested in the traditional arrangement should concern us. We are not exactly getting an unbiased picture here. Our academies are hardly intellectual centers for thinkers with distinctly apostolic leanings. Quite the contrary, seminaries are the very bastions of the shepherd-teacher type of ministry. And even if seminaries do not consciously intend it, their very purpose, their organizational bias, together with the self-selecting nature of the curriculum, tends to exclude the more generative (APE) types.

Consider the content of the standard courses for a master of divinity degree. Comprising biblical studies, systematics, ethics, church history, pastoral studies, and perhaps spirituality, these hardly contribute to a study in apostolic ministry—or prophetic and evangelistic ministry, for that matter. Besides, even if one were inclined to question this, it would be naive in the extreme to think that spiritual temperament, ecclesial politics, and an inveterate tendency toward organizational equilibrium do not play a major factor in upholding the inherited interpretations on the issue. People dynamics are people dynamics, in the church and out of it.

Whatever historical factors have conspired to get us to this point, at the very least our current mission-critical situation in the West necessitates a serious reevaluation of the foundations as well as restoration of the kind of ministry that can effectively meet those challenges. We believe that God has already provided for the church in the form of apostolic ministry. And while Parts Two through Four positively describe the various aspects of this remarkable form of ministry, the rest of this Appendix will show some of the reasons how, and perhaps why, we ended up delegitimizing the apostolic gift in the first place.

From Movement to Monument: The Process of Institutionalization

Paul could point to the foundational nature of apostolic ministry without the need for further explanation only because the role itself was patently self-evident in the Christian movement of his day. Although at times he had to argue for the validity of his own particular apostolic calling, he never had to make an argument for the concept of apostolic ministry itself; it was universally accepted as being a vital part of what it meant to be church. The very existence of Christianity throughout the Mediterranean was the direct result of apostolic ministry in the first place; it could not be denied.[5]

However, in spite of this clearly identifiable role in the founding and establishing of the early church, the apostolic function was increasingly marginalized as the movement grew and established itself over the next few centuries. We believe that the reasons for this shift are not theological but rather arose from changing social conditions. Contrary to what some would suggest, there are absolutely no textual grounds for the elimination of apostolic ministry from the church. There is nothing in the New Testament itself to suggest that the APE ministries would, or should, be abrogated once the canon of scripture and the institution of the church were fully formed. Whatever exegesis was used to justify this idea had to have imposed an extrinsic meaning on one or two selected texts (for example, Ephesians 2:20) and is a theologically anachronistic, politically motivated, procrustean reading to make the text suit the sensibilities of the later institution.[6] We are saying that no case can be made from scripture itself; it came from elsewhere.

The process involving the restrictive narrowing of the fivefold ministry (and the apostolic) can be better explained by reference to social realities that eventually confront every religious (and human for that matter) movement over time: namely, institutionalization itself along with the battle to define what is to be considered orthodox and conventional. Both of these key aspects are captured in what sociologists call the routinization of charisma—the process whereby the initial unique insight or experience (*charism*) of the founder is embedded or routinized into the very structures of the organization in the attempt to ensure that the organization itself survives the passing of its founder.[7] The church followed the classic pattern that can be discerned in all organizations as they move from early stages to later development. And all this in turn is part of the broader process of institutionalization.

While analyzing these sociological phenomena might seem somewhat abstract, and to the ears of pragmatic church leaders overly technical, it is no mere theory. This self-same process is going on in your organization as we speak and has been doing so since it started. We are wise to be alert to what is actually going on. Furthermore, grasping these will help us appreciate how spiritual and organization renewal takes place. Also, understanding these dynamics helps us to see how and why the more generative forms of ministry were marginalized from the movement and will continue to be so unless something intentional is done to guide the process in a more sustainable direction.

From Routine to Routinization

The New Testament church was undoubtedly what we would call an organic, grassroots people movement with direct concerns relating to issues of community, organization, discipleship, and leadership. And like all other human organizations, it was inevitable that they would seek to define social roles (elders and deacons, for example), proclaim what is valued and normative (ethics), create rites and liturgies, encode core beliefs, develop standards for discipleship, and build structures, all in the attempt to ensure the transmission of the message to generations that would follow. In so doing, they were developing various institutions and traditions that were intended to help preserve the faith beyond the first generation.[8] But as New Testament scholar James D. G. Dunn notes, the result was creeping institutionalism, where ecclesia is increasingly identified with the external forms of the institution itself:

> Increasing institutionalism is the clearest mark of early Catholicism—when church becomes increasingly identified with institution, when authority becomes increasingly coterminous with office, when a basic distinction between clergy and laity becomes increasingly self-evident, when grace becomes increasingly narrowed to well-defined ritual acts . . . such features were absent from first generation Christianity, though in [later] generations the picture was beginning to change.[9]

In these ways, the first movement sought to store and transmit the initiating energies of the movement and the charism of the Founder. But they did not realize that the very process itself is fraught with such tragic consequences. Ironically, it is Thomas O'Dea, a Catholic sociologist, who has best understood the nature of catalyzing encounters that kick-start movements that fade with the passing of time.

In his seminal work, he notes, "Worship is the fundamental religious response [to such encounters] but in order to survive its charismatic moment worship must become stabilized in established forms and procedures."[10] But he goes on to show that this desire to capture the sacred creates an unavoidable paradox for religious movements because the ultimate and the sacred cannot be contained in institutional structures without those structures taking on a life of their own and, in the end, corrupting what they were intended to preserve in the first place. And so the tragic dilemma arises: without some form of institutionalization, remarkable religious experiences by themselves will not sustain long-term movement, but too much codification kills the movement as well.[11] It is not hard to see how the apostolic ministry, with its strong association with founding impulses and, ironically, a participant in routinization, became one of the victims of the process itself.

While institutionalization as described can to varying degrees be seen as a normal process in any group, it had some hazardous effects on the ecclesia that Jesus intended in the first place—to be both agent and expression of the kingdom of God. Like the Israelite attempt to store the manna in the desert, routinization of charisma is in the end an attempt to grasp the fading splendor of the God encounter and an effort to preserve it in priestly codes, ritual, and process. As such, institutionalization easily slips into institutionalism. And when it does, it inevitably creates problems because the institution will in the end tend to insert itself into the God relationship.[12]

Unchecked, institutionalization (along with routinization) easily regresses into a sinful endeavor to retain, control, and direct the initiating energy of the Christian movement. In a word, it becomes an attempt to domesticate and mediate God. But God, kingdom, Spirit, and gospel are much larger than any possible human codification can contain. While these create the church, they cannot be contained within or simply identified with the church. The church can simply be witness to these greater realities. To claim otherwise is to make the church an idol.

Unregulated routinization also results in the institutionalization of grace that so characterizes the Christendom doctrine of the sacraments, where grace is captured in the sacrament, mediated only by ordained priests and restricted to the confines of the church's internal organization. In these conditions, the church will tend to take on an authority and importance that it was never intended to have. This certainly proved true in later Catholic theology, where the church is viewed as the mediating institution between people and God and takes on a divine status.[13]

It is in this centuries-long process of encoding the initial charism into institution that somehow the dynamic energies of the apostolic ministry were apparently extracted from the apostolic persons themselves, routinized into the institution, and passed on ritually through the generations.

From Vocation to Manuscript

Another (sub)routine in the overall process of routinization is the encoding of key ideas and values into the writings that emerge from dynamic movements. Here too we can discern the supplanting of the apostolic vocation itself.

As movements encounter the problem of how they might preserve and propagate their unique message, they begin to generate manuscripts. New writing and the new ideas associated with them are a sure sign that a movement is taking place. Witness, for instance, the burgeoning literature sparked by the missional movement over the past few years or the social media phenomenon in the broader culture. But the dilemma we face in the production of literature comes about because although we clearly need manuscripts, their production adds to the processes of institutionalization that become so problematic later.

The reason is that the writings, especially when divorced from the original context and abstracted from the called person, will tend to displace the people who started the movement in the first place.[14] In other words, grand, universal ideas, divorced from particular life and biography, easily degrade into mere ideology. And ideology in turn easily produces ideologues (partisan people who seek to impose ideas, or control others through ideas), who can become ruthless and controlling people; witness the Inquisition, Nazism, Islamic extremism, Christian fundamentalisms (to the left and right), or the Stalinist purges for good examples of the drive for ideological and institutional purity.[15]

Ideas are thus separated from the charisma and calling of the original generator of those ideas. Rather than pointing beyond themselves to greater realities, they become important in and of themselves, and eventually take on a life of their own. It would be like saying that in writing this book, we (the writers) become less important than the material we write. We thus depersonalize the ideas, so they easily become an "it," an object for our manipulation. And here we have, albeit in embryonic form, the seed for the later concept of apostolic doctrine that, mediated through the religious institution and its doctrine, would eventually supplant the active role and presence of the apostolic person.[16]

The sad irony is that the production of official, defining manuscripts, combined with the other paraphernalia of institutionalization (apostolic succession, bureaucracy, and official cultus), comes at significant cost.

From Apostolic Calling to Apostolic Succession

Routinization also explains how we arrived at the idea of apostolic succession in the first place. This doctrine, held by some Christian denominations, asserts that properly ordained bishops were the chosen successors of the twelve apostles (particularly Peter) and that these bishops exist in direct continuity from the first-century bishops to the present day. Hence, like some ecclesiastical nobility, those ordained by the bishops inherit spiritual, ecclesiastical and sacramental grace, authority, power, and responsibility, and they pass it on to others. Thus is the line of succession secured from the first pope (understood to be Peter) to the current bishops and through them the clergy. Although all but the most catholic of Protestant churches rightly reject this doctrine as highly erroneous, it does explain the very mind-set that gave rise to, as well as maintains, the marginalization of the apostolic function. Apostolic succession was a direct way to try to supplant apostolic ministry, and in many ways it succeeded.

From Pneumatocracy to Bureaucracy

When we track the work of the Holy Spirit in the book of Acts from Pentecost onward, we see that in almost every instance, it is seen to be energizing, legitimizing, or catalyzing the outward-bound mission of the church. Here we see the disciples entrusted with the mission of Jesus moving beyond the narrow nationalistic confines of their temple theology and ethnocentric understandings of the gospel.[17] And so the movement that flowed out from the epicenter of Jerusalem into global mission was inspired and empowered by the sending (apostolic) Spirit.

This leads us to conclude that the early church is what we might call a pneumatocracy—a people under the empowerment, rule, and guidance of the Spirit of God. It is this uncontrollable pneumatic aspect of New Testament ministry that seems to fly in the face of the human urge to control. And yet it is precisely this all-too-human attempt to determine our own destinies that lies at the root of organizations that so easily become ends in themselves. This human struggle with pneumatocracy highlights the often vexing relationship between organizations and the people who lead them. The general rule is that over time, vision and mission are increasingly downgraded in the name of management and administration. In other words, increasing bureaucratization seems to be the rule.

As we have seen, this arises because as organizations grow through their life cycle, unless they are very intentional about it, they will almost always tend toward a state of equilibrium. Following the ordinary course of events, organizations become increasingly internally focused and progressively more risk averse. The felt needs of safety and security that subsequently dominate the community's concern ultimately shape the kind of leadership the community seeks and validates. And so the organization generates the type of leaders it thinks will best cater to the felt needs of the community in its devolving state. Religious sociologist Peter Berger describes this phenomenon of bureaucratization: "Bureaucracies demand specific types of personnel. This personnel is specific not only in terms of its functions and requisite skills, but also in terms of its psychological characteristics. Institutions both *select* and *form* the personnel they require for their operation. This means that similar [bureaucratic] types of leadership emerge in the various religious institutions, irrespective of the traditional patterns in this matter."[18] In other words movements, which are created by more generative types, increasingly become bureaucracies, which increasingly become self-selecting and self-reinforcing systems. As a result, unless the leadership of the organization is intentional about resisting this deterioration with significant resolve, leadership will inevitably become increasingly bureaucratic in nature.

This trend is well documented and accepted in the field of social studies. For instance, leadership consultant Lawrence M. Miller has identified certain critical stages of the lives of organizations, businesses, and movements and the seven leadership styles that dominate during each stage.[19] He notes that as the organization moves from being founded and led by the generative types (he calls them prophet, barbarian, builder/explorer, and synergist), power subsequently shifts to the more operative/maintenance type of leader (what he calls the administrator, bureaucrat, and the aristocrat).[20]

This squares well with our understanding of the exiling of the generative (APE) functions in favor of the more operative (ST) types.[21] But as Berger indicates, when organizations become increasingly security oriented and more bureaucratic, they tend to suppress the more disturbing original message and mission that generated the organization in the first place.

SUMMING UP. Perhaps we can sum up institutionalization processes this way: although to some degree inevitable, it was not theologically scripted in the New Testament itself but rather has more to do with sociopolitical dynamics. The eventual winners in this process of institutionalization rewrote the ministry codes as to what was considered acceptable or not. The apostolic functions (along with the prophetic and evangelistic ones) were edited out of the codes. The resultant Christendom system seldom demonstrated the motivation or the will (political, theological, or otherwise) to adjust it back to fit the biblical categories.

Not only was this exiling unnecessary and detrimental to the health of the movement, it lent itself to religious institutionalism that became the entrenched form of the church. We illustrate the process of institutionalization in Figure A.1.

Our point in outlining this "movement-to-museum" aspect of church history is to show how the foundational, pioneering, translocal, and custodial leadership of the apostolic ministry was eventually eclipsed by the more local, increasingly maintenance-oriented leadership roles of bishops, elders, and deacons. There irony is painful and costly: the local Christian communities (modalities) that owed their existence to apostolic pioneers (sodality) in the first place effectively rejected their apostolic heritage and thereby undermined their own capacity to generate and maintain authentic apostolic movements. The chaordic dynamics of the early Jesus

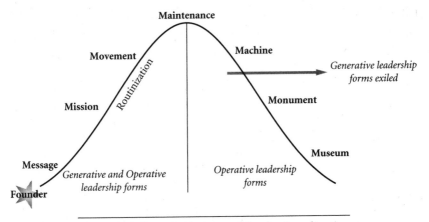

Figure A.1 Generic Process of Institutionalization

movements were replaced by an often oppressive ecclesial system that was to become known as Roman Catholicism.

The Reformation, while rescripting our theology of salvation, failed to deconstruct the embedded Christendom paradigm of the church, and so it still rules the thinking of the vast majority of Protestant churches today. Missiologist Ed Stetzer rightly points out, "When the Reformers (and later evangelicals) deemphasized the apostolic nature of the church, they inadvertently lessened the sending nature of that apostolic church. The church that 'reformed' lost touch with the God who sends, and the mission of the church suffered."[22]

And while we fully recognize that history is always more complex than what a diagram can convey, nonetheless this pretty much tracks the trajectory of the church from the more organic early forms to the much more institutionalized forms of Christianity associated with the Christendom paradigm.[23] And sadly, this categorization fits all too well with the current decline of the European church. In previous eras, Christendom retained complete dominance through its direct association with the state. However, once the processes of secularization were introduced by the French Revolution and increasingly adopted throughout Europe, the church's hegemony was broken, and it has been in decline ever since.

Apart from the basic fact that the church belongs to the Lord Jesus and that he will achieve his purposes in spite of us, the fact that Christianity in the West has at times grown at all can be traced to the all-too-brief emergence of generative forms of ministry and leadership that usher in new missional movements and the associated movements of renewal.

In spite of the marginalization from the centers of ecclesial power in the church, APE types have been largely responsible for any real kingdom advance through the church: witness the work of St. Francis, Count Zinzendorff, Ignatius Loyola, John Wesley, William and Catharine Booth, R. A. Torrey, Alexander Campbell, Aimee Semple McPherson, and others). God is still at work in his church, and the most fruitful aspects in terms of missional impact have most often come from so-called upstarts: people and movements that have been pushed to the margins of the church but have nonetheless been used by God to extend the kingdom and to bless the broader church.

Orthodoxy Versus Orthopraxy: How Apostolic Doctrine Supplanted Apostolic Practice

Another distinctive feature that accelerated the institutionalization of the church, and the marginalization of the apostolic function along with it, was the effective substitution of impersonal apostolic doctrine for the active and living ministry of the apostolic person. This process was grounded in distinct historical experiences as the burgeoning church engaged with nonbiblical worldviews.

As the Jesus movement began moving into the maintenance phase, the relative stability, along with the dominant needs of the day, initiated a shift in leadership type that favored a more distinctly theological-philosophical response to the threats of heresy together with a pastoral one to deal with the dissension that threatened to damage the integrity of the church.

The message of a crucified and risen messiah exploded onto the scene immediately after Jesus rose from the dead, and for approximately seven years, it managed to avoid any significant controversy related to the content of the message itself. It was not until the conversion of the Gentiles that we see any substantial conflict about the gospel itself, along with its implications for missional expansion.[24] This was to be the beginning of the many theological controversies for the Jesus movement in the first century. The apostles subsequently dealt with issues of legalism, Jewish nationalism, asceticism, occultism, early Gnosticism, and various other ideologies and influences that found their way from the pagan religious and ideological context into the nascent communities.

Furthermore, as the Jesus movement expanded in the second and third centuries, churches were now almost exclusively non-Jewish in ethnicity and context. As a result, the essentially Israel-shaped basis of Christianity was now confronted with a host of alien, extrabiblical ideas and doctrines all competing for dominance in the Christian mind. Perhaps the major threat came from the Gnostic interpretations of Christ, but other issues relating to canon, authority, the nature of God, Trinity, and so forth also presented the fledgling underground movement with challenges. Except for some bloodletting and name-calling, by and large the theologians handled the issues well, and the pastors kept the church pretty much intact.

But for obvious reasons, orthodoxy, understood here sociologically in terms of the codification and standardization of belief and behavior, became the driving concern for the church. In order to survive these heretical threats, church leaders looked for a fixed, legitimate, and authoritative source of teaching. Being rightfully viewed as the authoritative sources of the church, the writings of some of the original apostles (including Paul), became the cornerstone on which the New Testament canon would be built. In this process of establishing the much-needed canon, we can also discern the roots of the later idea that was to become known as apostolic doctrine.

It was this understanding of the nature of doctrine itself that was later used to justify the eventual abrogation of the apostolic function itself. By overlooking the critical functional role that apostles (as people) play in generating and sustaining movements, and believing that they had somehow successfully extracted the essence of their teachings, the church leaders at the time questioned whether apostolic ministry itself was still needed. Clearly they concluded that it was not.

Like a caravan of intrepid explorers pioneering across the wilderness, the church did what might be expected when under attack: they circled their wagons and focused their energies on repelling the impending threats and keeping unity in the ranks. But defensiveness, although necessary at times, ought not to be the church's primary stance, at least not in the advancing church of Jesus Christ. Jesus never intended that we be primarily a defensive agency but rather one on the offensive (Matthew 16:18).

As a pioneering voyage, it is a strategic mistake to allow a temporary interruption to undermine the fact that it is a journey after all, and that a journey is not over until the voyagers reach their destination. The turning point was not so much that they had to circle their wagons—this is to be expected on occasions in all journeys of exploration. The pivotal moment came when the kind of leadership needed for that crisis became the permanent definition of what legitimate leadership in the church looked like. The expansive pioneers were exchanged for the more defensive home builders, and a different form of leadership began to dominate the consciousness of the church.

The die was thus cast. But the shift in emphasis toward purely doctrinal issues and church conformity altered the trajectory of Christianity from being primarily conceived as a missionary movement with a trans-formative vision for society toward being a more defensive and self-referential community of believers.

And so although the development of orthodoxy was clearly the right thing to do, the mistake was to throw the apostolic baby out with the bathwater as if the two could not coexist. Certainly they had to this point—and to great effect. Furthermore, we suggest that not only could they exist together, they actually *should* exist together. That much is clear in the New Testament model itself. The demise of the apostolic function tilted the leadership balance in favor of the operative (maintenance) types. This also meant that the driving missional emphasis (embodied in apos-tolic ministry) was effectively displaced, with an ever-increasing emphasis placed on the role of doctrine. Another result was the move away from the chaordic, decentralized networking associated with the movemental forms. What we ended up with is all the increasingly centralized authority of bishops, who favored more bureaucratic, hierarchical, high-conformity forms characteristic of the Roman culture then and Christianity now.

None of this is indicated in the teachings of the New Testament itself. On the contrary, the scriptures suggest an organically integrated ministry made up of at least fivefold forms, without which, we are warned, we cannot pos-sibly mature. And there is nothing to indicate that certain elements of the church's ministry were to pass away while the others would abide forever. Only a highly deductive and prejudiced reading of the New Testament can come to that understanding. It was purely human choice, historical circum-stance, and sociopolitical forces that determined this outcome.

We can no longer afford to delude ourselves into thinking that simply believing apostolic doctrine is going to be enough. If theological ideas were enough to create a mature church and usher in the kingdom, it would surely have happened by now. We have literally hundreds of mil-lions of words of theology stored up in our libraries. For too long, we have allowed ourselves to be deceived into thinking that because we advo-cate apostolic doctrine that we are somehow going to automatically be an apostolic church. History has proven this to be patently false: having mil-lions of theological books has not kept us from being profoundly heretical at times. God save us from thinking that another volume of systematic theology is going to fix things up.

It is not that we do not believe in the power and necessity of good doctrine: we have already fully recognized the central importance of theology for the health of the church. But doctrinal integrity is more than adequately provided for within the holistic fivefold ministry itself. Apostolic custodianship over the genetic codes, the prophetic concern for covenantal faithfulness to God, the teacher's rigorous commitment to understanding what has been revealed, the evangelist's commitment to truth telling, and the pastor's commitment to personal development and cohesion all collaborate to ensure that the Jesus movement stays on track.

Furthermore, if pastoral approaches alone could resolve the issue of the church, we should have gotten it after thousands of years of pastoral ministry. Patently it is not enough: people are still hurting, we lack discipleship, the church is in long-term decline, many are bored, and most churchgoers complain that they do not get enough "feeding." There is not a preaching series or counseling program in existence that will fix these. Surely if that was the case, we would have had the solution by now. Perhaps even improving pastoral and didactic programming adds to the problem by disguising the real dysfunctions in the system. We do not suggest removing these ST influences, but simply complementing and supplementing them with more generative forms.

However we configure it, the situation of contemporary Christianity has utterly changed from that of the Christendom era, when the church completely dominated the religious and cultural landscape. Not only are we experiencing what is legitimately called a post-Christendom, post-Christian culture, but we are in a situation where people are increasingly antagonistic to Christianity. In other words, we are now back in a distinctly missionary situation, and although we still have some heresies to fight, the overwhelmingly strategic issue is the survival, let alone the advance, of Christianity in the West. This requires a recovery of apostolic imagination and practice—nothing less.

Out from the Cold: The Return of the Apostolic

If at an early stage and for various sociopolitical reasons, the church opted to expel the apostolic ministry (and the APE ministries with it), did it entirely disappear? Did the vocation itself, as a calling by God, cease? Clearly not. Institutions, although they can delegitimize, cannot snuff out callings because they are ultimately derived from God, and God exists beyond any restrictions imposed by human will. As a result, the influence of apostolically gifted people is clearly evident in every missional movement in the history of the church. Along with the examples already given, here are some other more easily recognizable examples from all over the world:[25]

- Columbanus, one of the key Celtic monastics, planted more than one hundred monasteries across Europe, which then sent thousands of church planters out across Europe.

- St. Martin of Tours, known as the founder of Western monasticism, inspired the Celts to found missions and monasteries. He is sometimes called the patron saint of Europe because of his passionate missional vision and work.
- Saints Cyril and Methodius pioneered the mission to convert the Slavic peoples.
- Saint Hilda, the abbess who hosted the synod of Whitby, played a major role in the extension of the Celtic movement. Her apostolic influence extended to leaders, nobles, and kings.
- Ignatius Loyola, founder of the Jesuits, in his own lifetime had missionaries going to India, Japan, and South America, in addition to various parts of Europe. His writings are thought to have partly influenced Wesley.
- Henry Venn invented the now famous and profoundly apostolic three-self principles and influenced the development of indigenous missions just about everywhere.
- Hudson Taylor's work with the China Inland Mission is credited with laying the foundations for the growth of the Chinese church today.
- Bishop Crowther is the first African bishop; he has indelibly shaped West African Christianity.
- Joan of Arc was credited with bringing modern France into being. A very influential teen!
- Mary Slessor was a remarkable missionary who deeply influenced the course of West African missions.
- John Lake and P. Le Roux are thought to have shaped most of African Independent Church development in southern Africa.
- Nicholas Bhengu, referred to as the South African Billy Graham, personally planted more than one thousand churches and is thought to have inspired and fathered those who planted tens of thousands of churches.
- Enoch Adeboya is the father of the fastest-growing denomination in the world today: the Redeemed Christian Church of God.
- Aimee Semple McPherson was an outstanding female apostolic influence in early Pentecostalism. She founded the FourSquare movement.
- Gladys Aylward was a missionary in China whose exploits were made into a Hollywood blockbuster, *The Inn of the Sixth Happiness,* starring Ingrid Bergman.

So much for the founders of massively influential movements. But where apostles have managed to operate within the confines of the established churches, they have done so with minimal recognition and legitimacy, operating surreptitiously under the radar.

Other than that, they have been dormant within the community and have tended to express their gifting outside explicit ecclesial settings: in commerce, aid and development work, and other secular contexts where ideation, design, and entrepreneurialism are valued.

And so the official exile from the church is very real. Those who do not fit the standard ministry profile are made to feel that there is something wrong with them or that they are of no value to the church. When they assert themselves, they are easily labeled as recalcitrant or immature. It is largely because of their impatience with the status quo that they are so labeled, but ironically (as we shall see) it is precisely this holy unrest that constitutes their distinctive gift to the church—contemporary or otherwise.

Evangelical Covenant Church missiologist Kyle J. A. Small prophetically challenges the status quo of his denomination:

> Apostolic has a rich identity, offering both the commitment to God's history, and a vision for participation in God's future. It is an action-oriented image rooted and centered in God's larger story. On the one hand, apostolic keeps to the inherited faith of the church. On the other hand, apostolic means commitment to the edges. Apostles refuse to leave any stone unturned and are willing to explore new ideas and territory. Apostles yearn to see where God is acting in the world: even more, they invite the People of God to join them in these spaces. Ordination becomes a living into addressing the leadership deficit that was first perceived in the Book of Acts. . . . The office of the apostle needs to continue today in the leadership of the church. Ordained leadership needs to be recruited and formed with a disposition for apostolic imagination.[26]

And so the challenge stands. We have huddled and cuddled, taught and preached, the church to near death. It's time to grow up! It's time to allow some holy chaos to enter so we can break loose from the iron cages of oligarchy and engage the missional challenge to extend the gospel in this century. Inviting disequilibrium will help us deepen and broaden our understanding and practice of ministry in Jesus's church. A recovery of apostolic gifting means that the church of Jesus Christ, in all its expressions, will begin to open itself up to a more missional, definitely more movemental, and, we hope, a more faithful future.

NOTES

Foreword

1. D. Guder (ed.), *Missional Church: A Vision for the Sending of the Church in North America* (Grand Rapids, Mich.: Eerdmans, 1998).
2. A. Hirsch, *The Forgotten Ways: Reactivating the Missional Church* (Grand Rapids, Mich.: Brazos, 2007), p. 238.
3. Ibid.

Preface: A Briefing for the Journey

1. H. Van Campenhausen, *Ecclesiastical Authority and Spiritual Power in the Church of the First Three Centuries* (Stanford, Calif.: Stanford University Press, 1969).
2. We fully affirm the Evangelical Manifesto as well as the Lausanne Covenants as statements of identity and theology. http://www.anevangelicalmanifesto .com/ and http://www.lausanne.org/covenant.
3. Our friends and colleagues Neil Cole and J. R. Woodward are also producing material around the Ephesians 4:11 typology, and we highly recommend that readers look for practical application there. Neil's book will be out spring 2012 and J.R.'s in fall 2012. Mike Breen is also considering updating his previous, somewhat more personal, reflections on this subject: *The Apostle's Notebook* (London: Kingsway, 2002). These will provide excellent corroboration with our book.
4. This prevailing paradigm is largely a by-product of the two-fold ministry structure of the shepherd and teacher. We address this in the chapters in Part One, but for now we merely allude to the fact that the other three roles— apostle, prophet, and evangelist—have been effectively exiled from the ministry matrix of the church and therefore significantly alter our conception of what the church is and can be.

Introduction: The Crisis of Infertility and What to Do About It

1. All the major research agencies report declining attendance and conversion. The Pew Report, Barna Research Group, Ed Stetzer, and others are

in general agreement about the overall characteristics of this trend. *USA Today* ran an article in March 2009 that highlighted the research of the American Religious Identification Survey (ARIS) that gives a graphic interpretation of this trend: "The percentage of people who call themselves in some way Christian has dropped more than 11% in a generation." To put this decline in perspective, the article said that "despite growth and immigration that has added nearly 50 million adults to the U.S. population, almost all religious denominations have lost ground since the first ARIS survey in 1990." "Most Religious Groups in USA Have Lost Ground, Survey Finds," *USA Today,* Mar. 17, 2009, http://www.usatoday.com/news/religion/2009-03-09-american-religion-ARIS_N.htm.

2. Quoted in T. Ahrend, *In This Generation: Looking to the Past to Reach the Present* (Colorado Springs: Dawson Media, 2010), p. 172.

3. The sobering truth is that this decline, along with the full potential of the future decay, set in when the church failed to reform itself in accordance with its greater mission. Those who cannot deliver the transformational message of the gospel eventually will be forced to doubt the veracity of the message itself. Theological and ethical doubt generally follows after operational doubt. See D. Kelly, *Why Conservative Churches Are Growing: A Study in Sociology of Religion* (Macon, Ga.: Mercer University Press, 1996).

4. R. Martin, *The Design of Business: Why Design Thinking Is the Next Competitive Advantage* (Boston: Harvard Business School Press, 2009).

5. Martin, *The Design of Business,* p. 43. See also A. Hirsch and D. Ferguson, *The Faith of Leap: A Journey into the Apostolic Future of the Church* (Grand Rapids. Mich.: Zondervan, 2011), which explores paradigms and paradigm blindness and their relationship to how we conceive of church in a significant way.

6. See A. Hirsch and M. Frost, *The Faith of Leap: Embracing a Theology of Risk, Adventure, and Courage* (Grand Rapids, Mich.: Baker, 2011), chap. 6.

7. N. N. Taleb, *The Black Swan: The Impact of the Highly Improbable* (New York: Random House, 2010).

8. J. C. Ramo, *The Age of the Unthinkable: Why the New World Disorder Constantly Surprises Us and What We Can Do About It* (New York: Little, Brown, 2010).

9. See a review of this book: G. Rosen, "Global Imperative," *New York Times Sunday Book Review,* June 19, 2009, http://www.nytimes.com/2009/06/21/books/review/Rosen-t.html.

10. M. Gladwell, *Outliers: The Story of Success* (New York: Hachette Book Group, 2008).

11. Acts 1:8. Not only is this missional trajectory inherently movemental, it is also exponential in nature. The movement starts locally and mushrooms into a global phenomenon.

12. We recognize that Leon Trotsky also used the "permanent revolutionaries" phrase to describe the ongoing need for renewal in the communist

revolution. In many ways, he was trying to incite the same capacity for ongoing development and renewal of the communist order.

Chapter One: Activating the Theo-Genetic Codes of APEST Ministry

1. This is the clear-cut claim of one of my (Alan) books: *The Forgotten Ways: Reactivating the Missional Church* (Grand Rapids, Mich.: Brazos, 2007). It proposes six elements that together create apostolic movements. All six will be present in every movement that hits the power band of exponential growth patterns (such as that of the early church and China). One of these relates to APEST, or fivefold, ministry. If APEST is removed, a fully fledged apostolic movement is impossible.

2. There are nevertheless some excellent pieces of reflection in articles, books, and commentaries: Markus Barth's commentary on Ephesians is one of them, as are an excellent piece by Darrell Guder, the short articles by Robert Clinton (they can be found on his Web site: http://jrclintoninstitute.com/), and some reflections by former Princeton seminary president John A. Mackay in his book *God's Order* (New York: Macmillan, 1957). Doubtless there are more, but they are largely incidental pieces written as part of larger works on other topics.

3. Dowsett's reflections on the missio Dei, kingdom of God, and Creation (on which he did his doctoral dissertation) helped him see that God was always preveniently involved in the world even before his church joins him in that mission. Gleaned from discussions and e-mail correspondence with Andrew Dowsett. Used with permission. A. Dowsett, "Recovering the Five-Fold Ministry of the Local Church," unpublished doctoral dissertation, St. John's College, Nottingham.

4. Ephesians 1:22, 3:10, 21, 5:23–25, 27, 29. Also, some distinct textual clues in Ephesians support this notion that it is a generic letter, intended to be circulated and read by multiple churches. For example, elements that typically characterize many of Paul's other letters are not included in the text. Things like personal greetings, an axe to grind about a particular false teaching, and the addressing of specific problems uniquely related to a particular community, are all staple features of Paul's letters, and yet they are curiously absent from Ephesians.

5. M. Barth, *Ephesians: Translation and Commentary on Chapters 4–6 (The Anchor Bible)* (New York: Doubleday, 1974).

6. W. Ocasio, "The Opacity of Risk: Language and the Culture of Safety in NASA's Space Shuttle Program," in W. H. Starbuck and M. Farjoun (eds.), *Organization at the Limit: Lessons from the Columbia Disaster* (Cambridge, Mass.: Blackwell, 2005), p. 103

7. C. Wright Mills made the same observation about vocabularies: "A vocabulary is not merely a string of words; immanent within it are social

textures—institutional and political coordinates. Back of a vocabulary lie sets of collective action." C. W. Mills, "Language, Logic, Culture," in J. Beck, C. Jenks, N. Keddie, and M.F.D. Young (eds.), *Toward a Sociology of Education* (New Brunswick, N.J.: Transaction, 1978), p. 520.

8. Ocasio, "The Opacity of Risk," p. 109.

9. In relation to our use of the term *vocation* or *callings,* theologian Jack Deere states that apostleship is a calling, not a gift or an especially gifted or powerful person. See his *Surprised by the Spirit* (Grand Rapids, Mich.: Zondervan, 1993), pp. 242–243.

10. Many have argued that APEST actually constitutes a fourfold ministry because the conjunction between the shepherd and the teacher might indicate that this is the case. We are not convinced from the text itself or from experience. There are many teachers who are not pastors, and vice versa. But, in fact, for our purposes, it does not matter at all. Some readers may prefer to join the role of the shepherd to that of teacher, and that is fine with us

11. It is interesting to note that Paul uses the verb form for the word *truth* in this verse. It literally should read *truthing.*

12. The implications of the text lead us to believe that without the fivefold, we will access only a limited perspective on the faith. Each of the APEST ministries offers a unique perspective on Jesus, thus enriching our overall understanding of Jesus and the gospel.

13. Paul addresses ethics and morals in the rest of Ephesians 4 and in Ephesians 5.

14. The word *kataptismo* has nuanced meanings because it is used to describe several activities that essentially achieve the same result. The word is also used to describe the mending of fishing nets. We will draw insight from this particular contextual use of the word later in the chapter, but the overarching meaning of the word has to do with adding aptitude or capacity to something. See G. Kittel (ed.) and G. W. Bromiley (trans.), *Theological Dictionary of the New Testament* (Grand Rapids, Mich.: Eerdmans, 1964), p. 475.

15. A. G. Patzia, "Ephesians, Colossians, Philemon," in *The New International Bible Commentary* (version, commentary verse 4:11). CD.

16. J. Calvin, *Institutes of the Christian Religion* (J. T. McNeill, ed., and F. L. Battles, trans.) (Philadelphia: Westminster Press, 1960), 1057. Quoted in D. Guder, "Walking Worthily: Missional Leadership After Christendom," *Princeton Seminary Bulletin,* n.s., 2007, 28(3), 276.

17. A. Roxburgh, *The Missionary Congregation: Leadership and Liminality* (Harrisburg, Pa.: Trinity Press, 1997), and his "Missional Leadership: Equipping God's People for Mission," in D. L. Guder, *Missional Church: A Vision for the Sending of the Church in North America* (Grand Rapids, Mich.: Eerdmans, 1998).

18. Paul suddenly includes himself in the discussion here. He moves from, "I urge *you,*" in 4:1 to, "But to each one of *us,*" in 4:7. Paul is likely doing a play on words here. He just listed the seven "one's" and is now saying that each "one" of us has received something from the "one" Lord.

19. *Grace, given*, and *gift* are the same words that Paul uses to describe how God "graced" him with his apostolic ministry in Ephesians 3:7–8. Notice the comparison between the texts:

Ephesians 3:7–8	Ephesians 4:7, 11
. . . of which I became a minister according to the gift (*dorea*) of the grace (*charis*) of God, given (*didomi*) to me by the effective working of his power.	But to each one of us grace (*charis*) was given (*didomi*) according to the measure of Christ's gift (*dorea*)
To me who am least of all the saints this grace (*charis*) was given (*didomi*), that I should preach among the gentiles the unsearchable riches of Christ.	And he gave (*didomi*) some to be apostles, some prophets, some evangelists, some shepherds and teachers.

Once Paul gets to Ephesians 4, it is almost as if he is saying, "Yes, I received grace and a gifting from God, but I am not the only one. Each one of us has received grace according to the measure of Christ's gift. Each one of us has received a ministry from Christ." Paul then uses the same language of "each one" in verse 16 where he explicitly says "From him the whole body, joined and held together by every supporting ligament, grows and builds itself up in love, as *each part* does its work." Paul brackets his entire discussion of APEST with distinctively inclusive language. For a random sampling of the word in the New Testament, see Matthew 16:27, 18:35; Luke 16:5; Acts 2:8; Romans 14:12; and Hebrews 6:11.

20. M. Frost and A. Hirsch, *The Shaping of Things to Come: Innovation and Mission for the 21st Century Church* (Peabody, Mass.: Hendrickson, 2003), pp. 170–172; Hirsch, *Forgotten Ways,* pp. 171–172.

21. E. Peterson, *Practice Resurrection: A Conversation on Growing Up in Christ* (Grand Rapids, Mich.: Eerdmans, 2010), p. 47.

22. These roles typically evolve into an official position within the movement and contribute to the process of institutionalization through the creation of offices and a centralized leadership structure.

23. We discuss how APEST does this in Chapters Two through Four. For now, we only want to draw attention to the fact that the text makes this claim about APEST.

24. Some scholars believe that the gift of prophesy mentioned in Romans 12 has more to do with preaching, or proclaiming the word, rather than miraculous revelations or prophetic utterances.

Chapter Two: An Elegant Solution

1. As we shall see in Part Two, the apostle is the most translocal of all the ministries. Apostles have the most responsibility for the regional cohesion of the

movement. But they also have to keep strong relational connections to the local churches—hence, our use of the term *glocal.*

2. See M. Breen, *Covenant and Kingdom: The DNA of the Bible* (Pawleys Island, S.C.: 3DM, 2010).

3. A. Heschel, *The Prophets* (New York: HarperCollins, 1969).

4. For this analogy of the canary, we are indebted to P. D. Patton and R. H. Woods Jr., *Prophetically Incorrect: A Christian Introduction to Media Criticism* (Grand Rapids, Mich.: Brazos Press, 2010).

5. Heschel, *The Prophets,* p. 21.

6. For an insightful look into how institutions shape discourse, and hence imagination, see M. Douglas, *How Institutions Think* (Syracuse, N.Y.: Syracuse University Press, 1986).

7. For instance, church historian David Aune, in his comprehensive study of the nature of the prophetic, notes the complex relationship between the prophetic ministry and the increasing institutionalization of the church: "In the absence of the more complex bureaucratic organization which accompanied the institutionalization of early Christianity, prophets appear to have played a more visible and active role in guiding Christian communities in decision making by reiterating the norms and values which were an integral part of Christian tradition and by providing the communities with visible evidence of the presence and activity of God and Jesus. The growth of local bureaucracies, often in the form of the triad of offices consisting of bishop, presbyters and deacons, resulted in the increasing exclusion of prophets from active roles in the guidance of the communities." D. E. Aune, *Prophecy in Early Christianity and the Ancient Mediterranean World* (Grand Rapids, Mich.: Eerdmans, 1983), p. 211.

8. M. Marquardt, *Leading with Questions: How Leaders Find the Right Solutions by Knowing What to Ask* (San Francisco: Jossey-Bass, 2005). S. Finkelstein, "Zombie Businesses: How to Learn from Their Mistakes," *Leader to Leader,* 2004, *32,* 25–31.

9. M. S. Malone, *The Future Arrived Yesterday: The Rise of the Protean Corporation and What It Means for You* (New York: Crown, 2009), p. 207.

10. W. Brueggemann, *The Prophetic Imagination* (Minneapolis: Fortress Press, 2001), p. 3.

11. See R. Rohr, "Life on the Edge: Understanding the Prophetic Position," *Huffington Post,* Mar. 22, 2011, http://huff.to/fVm9ET.

12. Patton and Woods are helpful here: "The impulse of some artistic, passionate, and outspoken members of a church—those, perhaps, with heightened prophetic sensibilities—is to withdraw from the community of believers who might not faithfully support their art or adequately appreciate their outcries over injustice. They may feel free in their isolation, but only for a while. Why? In their seclusion, they end up surrounding themselves only with others who agree with them. As such, they abandon the more complex, demanding, and often frustrating environment of the larger community. Yet sometimes the frustration within the community is the very

thing that energizes and refines the prophetic sensibility." P. D. Patton and R. H. Woods Jr., *Prophetically Incorrect: A Christian Introduction to Media Criticism* (Grand Rapids, Mich.: Brazos, 2010).

13. For instance, Kim says, "Would we have embraced the church growth movement as readily as we have otherwise with its goal of 'bigger = better'? Would we have as uncritically let business world practices, language and 'job descriptions' encroach into church life and administration (e.g., 'executive pastor')? Budgets, baptisms and butts in the seats—is that the best we can do metric-wise?"

14. M. Kim, "Our Journey into Rediscovering Apostolic and Prophetic Foundations Part 2," *House to House Ezine,* Jan. 22, 2010, http://bit.ly/8pbTHz.

15. M. Gladwell, *Tipping Point: How Little Things Can Make a Big Difference* (New York: Little, Brown, 2002).

16. Ibid.

17. D. Goleman, *Social Intelligence: The New Science of Human Relationships* (New York: Bantam Dell, 2006), and *Emotional Intelligence: Why It Can Matter More Than IQ* (New York: Bantam Dell, 1995).

18. R. Peace, *Conversion in the New Testament: Paul and the Twelve* (Grand Rapids, Mich.: Eerdmans, 1999), p. 286.

19. Ibid. Peace outlines the sequence of the apostles' discovery as follows: (1) teacher, (2) prophet, (3) Messiah, (4) Son of man, (5), Son of David, and (6) Son of God.

20. J. Finney, *Recovering the Past: Celtic and Roman Mission* (London: Dartman, Longman & Todd, 1998), p. 40.

21. See Mark 4:1–20; 1 Peter 1:22–25.

22. Apollos spent a significant amount of time in Ephesus, the very name of the letter that advocates evangelism as a vocational expression of the ministry of Jesus.

23. A. Crouch, "From Four Laws to Four Circles," *Christianity Today,* June 27, 2008, http://www.christianitytoday.com/ct/2008/july/11.31.html.

24. The only downside to this is that not everyone is a convincer. This kind of evangelistic training resonates only with the proclamation folks, leaving the others wondering if they are truly evangelistic.

25. Gleaned from many conversations between me (Alan) and Neil Cole on the topic. Also see N. Cole, *Church 3.0: Upgrades for the Future of the Church* (San Francisco: Jossey-Bass, 2009).

26. N. Cole, "The Gifted Teacher," CMAResources.org, Oct. 4, 2010, http://www.cmaresources.org/article/the-gifted-teacher_n-cole.

27. See, for instance, G. D. Stratten, "Saint Patrick and the Liberal Arts: The Missional Future of Christian Higher Education?" *Two Handed Warriors,* Mar. 17, 2011, http://bit.ly/h4BRu8. See especially T. Cahill, *How the Irish Saved Civilization* (New York: Anchor, 1996).

28. For instance, see www.forgeamerica.com.

Chapter Three: Better Together

1. W.C.H. Prentice, "Understanding Leadership," *Harvard Business Review,* Sept.-Oct. 1961, p. 144.

2. Apostolic ministry, when isolated from the other ministries, operates under the same human restraints as the other callings: it does not give us complete access to a panoramic view of the gospel. But it does provide insight into a foundational part of the gospel that is often displaced: extension. Since the gospel is meant for all, then it is quintessentially apostolic in nature. It is meant to travel across social and spatial boundaries, and apostolic ministry best illustrates this facet of the gospel to us. The missional implications of the gospel, and the trajectory of Christianity as a living system, are functional qualities that find their most vivid demonstration in apostolic ministry. For instance, it is a lot easier to understand Paul as apostle if we begin to see that for him, the gospel was not just a set of propositions to believe but a dynamic spiritual force, a revolutionary movement with a distinct vision, a way of operating, and an agenda—in fact, nothing less than the transformation of the world. This is demonstrated in the universal scope of the gospel as mentioned in Romans 5:18 ("all people"), Colossians 1:19 ("all things"), and 1 Corinthians 15:27–28 ("all things)." At the core of the gospel is a message for all ethnicities, and the apostle's job is to make sure that this message is faithfully delivered.

3. The wording of the subhead for this section comes from W. Simson, who in his *Starfish Manifesto* (Oct. 2009), http://en.starfishportal.net, discusses prophetic intelligence for apostolic architecture. For an online copy of the book, go to http://en.starfishportal.net/.

4. We know that the reference to prophets here is not to the Old Testament prophets because apostles did not exist in the Old Testament. The reference here is to the apostles and prophets of the New Testament church, which Paul mentions again in Ephesians 4. Furthermore, we know this text includes apostles outside the twelve and Paul because it alludes to prophets as well. The question is, which prophets? What were their names? If the scope of application for apostles is only the twelve, how do we apply the same metrics of application to the reference of prophets? Surely one foundational category (apostles) cannot be strictly confined to the twelve or Paul, while the other foundational category can be highly ambiguous, with no apparent point of reference. The only conclusion we can come to is that the reference to apostles and prophets as being foundational refers primarily to the ministries that flow out of these functions.

5. The word *entrepreneur* finds its linguistic roots in Latin and comes from the combination of *intrare,* meaning "to enter" or "to penetrate in between," and *prehendere,* meaning "to grasp or seize hold of." These two concepts of entering and seizing lie behind the concept of the entrepreneurial mind-set. Entrepreneurial people have the ability to recognize opportunities and act on them with innovative vision and zeal.

6. In many ways, this conforms to best thinking in terms of organizational learning, as well as the dynamics of innovation. Learning takes place when programming is subjected to questioning. Serious evaluation, feedback, and some discomfort are necessary prerequisites to learning and innovation. But the key remains the same: asking the right questions. And that is clearly a prophetic function. This process, called anything from "surfing the edge of chaos" to "the burning platform," is vital to getting existing organizations moving again and is the sweet spot for innovation. In fact, what we now know from the fields of leadership and organizations existed theologically long before in the organization of the church, where it is embedded in our deepest ecclesiological codes.

7. Acts 21 describes a rather confusing encounter between Paul the apostle and Agabus the prophet. Agabus warns Paul of the imminent danger for him in Jerusalem, advice that Paul disregards. The likely interpretation is that because Paul was determined to carry the collection from the Gentiles into Jerusalem, he did not heed this warning and ended up short-circuiting his apostolic ministry through imprisonment. Agabus was trying to provide some direction to Paul's ministry, but Paul had his own strategy and time line. He was so invested in his personal mission (here, getting to Jerusalem) that it was hard for him to heed the warning of imminent danger.

8. "Who Are These Guys?" *New Covenant Ministries International*, http://www.ncmi.net/WhoAreTheseGuys/tabid/54/language/en-US/Default.aspx.

9. "The Order of Mission," http://www.missionorder.org/.

10. This law, developed by Jane Mansbridge, a sociologist, maintains that "every social movement tends to splinter into sects, unless it wins quickly, in which case it turns into a collections of institutions." Because the very dynamic that binds people to a movement (its ideology and cause) tends to be idealistic, radical, and exclusive, this will work against them if they cannot produce fruit from their efforts. Their radical exclusivity will inevitably turn on itself. The socialist movement in the United States demonstrates this law. The labor movement turned into an institution and the Communist party into a sect. See J. Goodwin and J. Gasper, *The Social Movements Reader: Cases and Concepts* (London: Blackwell, 2009).

11. We explore the inexorable association with innovation and the generative APE types in Chapter Four.

12. This shift to evangelism as a local church function has precipitated a major crisis in the parachurches that were set up to do evangelism on behalf of local churches. In many ways, the parachurches arose out of the unfaithfulness of local church leadership to take responsibility for evangelism.

13. The Reveal study stemming from the Willow Creek Association acknowledges this problem. Evangelistic ministry, taken on its own, can precipitate great growth in the church, but it is unsure of what to do with new members once they are integrated into a group and attend regularly.

14. Much of the theory and story of the Future Travelers' learning journey is found in A. Hirsch and D. Ferguson, *On the Verge: A Journey into the Apostolic Future of the Church* (Grand Rapids, Mich.: Zondervan, 2011).

15. See ibid.

16. Some point to Phillip as functioning cross-culturally through his travels to Samaria and predominantly Gentile cities, but we have to remember that the name *Phillip* is thought by most scholars to be a Greek, or Hellenistic, name. It is possible that Phillip, through his family of origin, was already acculturated into, and even developed an affinity for, a more Hellenized context—hence, his selection by the church in Jerusalem to work with the Grecian widows who were being overlooked in the distribution of food. They also selected a proselyte from Antioch, which reveals their bias in selecting people who could relate to those who were not of Hebrew descent.

17. We see this same pattern of retreating to places of solitude in several of the prophets' ministries in scripture. Moses, Elijah, John the Baptist, and Jesus spent time away from their context of ministry, only to return to that context to speak or act on what they had experienced. Paul Patton and Robert Woods help bring clarity to this issue of critical distance by contrasting the prophet with the traditional understanding of the detached critic: "Prophetic criticism requires critical distance. But how much? In the conventional view, the critic is an unattached spectator, a dispassionate outsider. In contrast, the prophet is a *connected* critic: someone who is connected to the people she criticizes through a shared tradition and group identity. So, 'critical distance is best measured in inches, not miles.'" The prophetic ministry is not designed for isolation. Critical distance plays its most effective role when it prepares the prophet to return to the community with fresh insight and critical engagement of his or her context. See P. D. Patton and R. H. Woods Jr., *Prophetically Incorrect: A Christian Introduction to Media Criticism* (Grand Rapids, Mich.: Brazos Press, 2010), p. 29.

18. R. Rohr, "Life on the Edge: Understanding the Prophetic Position," *Huffington Post,* Mar. 26, 2011, http://huff.to/fVm9ET.

19. The Internet and media have changed the reach of teachers, but we suggest that even so, they prefer the stability and predictability that the more stable local church or organization provides.

20. K. Smith and D. Berg, *Paradoxes of Group Life* (San Francisco: Jossey-Bass, 1987), pp. 82–83.

21. For more thoughts on pioneers and settlers, see M. Breen, *Building a Discipling Culture* (Pawleys Island, S.C.: 3DM Publishing, 2009).

Chapter Four: Missional Ministry for a Missional Church

1. M. C. Higgins and K. E. Kram, "Reconceptualizing Mentoring at Work: A Developmental Network Perspective," *Academy of Management Review,* 200, 26, 264–288.

2. J. Santrock, *A Topical Approach to Life-Span Development* (New York: McGraw-Hill, 2004).

3. For this approach, see A. Hirsch, *The Forgotten Ways: Reactivating the Missional Church* (Grand Rapids, Mich.: Brazos, 2007). It is articulated through the APEST test (www.apest.org), developed by Alan Hirsch and Brian Schubring of Leadership Vision Consulting, which helps you identify your primary and secondary gifting profiles.

4. Another way of saying it is that in any system of interaction (for example, between individual human beings), the part of the system with the greatest flexibility in its behaviors will control the system.

5. To be sure, when a system increases its complexity, it also increases its ability to engage the complexity of its environment and adapt to its unique challenges. Increasing complexity is tricky business because at some point, too much complexity can become a liability. This is the very thing that overly bureaucratic organizations encounter. Conversely, not enough complexity will limit the organization's ability to engage the complexity of its environment. Too much or too little can cause any living system to lose its edge and become vulnerable to environmental challenges.

6. All the churches going through 3DM training apply the model, and many others report application. Brandon Schaefer, Discipleship Pastor Southland Christian Church in Lexington Kentucky, has been the point leader for strategically integrating the APEST typologies into their key ministry teams. From training their staff, volunteer leaders, assigning people according to wiring and giftedness—Southland has thoroughly implemented the APEST ministry matrix into their approach to leadership and ministry development. http://www.southlandchristian.org/.

7. For the Christian Fellowship church, go to http://www.cfellowshipc.com/.

8. For Northwood Church, go to http://northwoodchurch.org/index.php.

9. See R. T. Pascale, *Managing on the Edge: How Successful Companies Use Conflict to Stay Ahead* (New York: Viking Press, 1990).

10. E. de Bono, *Serious Creativity: Using the Power of Lateral Thinking to Create New Ideas* (New York: HarperBusiness, 1993).

Chapter Five: Custody of the Codes

1. C. M. Francis and H. Agnew, "The Origin of the NT Apostle-Concept: A Review of Research," *Journal of Biblical Literature,* 1986, *105,* 75–96.

2. Kung states, "The charisms of leadership in the Pauline Churches did not . . . produce a 'ruling class,' an aristocracy of those endowed with the Spirit who separated themselves from the community and rose above it in order to rule over it." H. Kung, "The Continuing Charismatic Structure" in R. S. Anderson (ed.), *Theological Foundations for Ministry: Selected Reading for a Theology of the Church in Ministry* (Edinburgh: T&T Clark, 2000), p. 485.

3. Ephesians 4:7–16; Romans 12:1–8.

4. There are undoubtedly more metaphors and terms that Paul uses to frame his apostolic role, but these are the most apparent and because of limited space, we limit our observations to these five. Norman R. Petersen provides a stimulating discussion of Paul's apostolic role in relation to the communities he founds. N. R. Petersen, *Rediscovering Paul: Philemon and the Sociology of Paul's Narrative World* (Philadelphia: Fortress Press, 1985).

5. In 1 Corinthians 4:14–21, Paul is not just reminding them of his instrumental role in bringing them into existence as a community through the gospel. This serves only to frame his parental rights to address the sexual immorality in 1 Corinthians 5 that is threatening the purity and overall vitality of the community. Later in the letter, Paul draws further implications from his role as father by drawing from the traditional Jewish marriage customs in which the father of the bride-to-be is charged with safeguarding his daughter's virginity between the time of their betrothal and the time in which he actually leads her into the bridegroom's house. As the father of the Corinthians, Paul has a vested interest in seeing them remain pure and undefiled, fully devoted to their husband, Christ, until they are presented to him at the wedding. 2 Corinthians 11:1–2.

6. Jeffrey Crofton addresses the notorious difficulty of sorting out the "we" statements of Paul in 2 Corinthians. He accurately observes that Paul uses "we" in 2 Corinthians as a rhetorical device to "blur the distinction between himself and his apostolic task. The presence of Paul in this letter is almost never that of a singular person. Personal apostleship is consistently swallowed up by generic apostleship. There is no apostolic *parousia* [presence] form, for Paul desires to reduce rather than promote the actualization of his presence in the letter. The first person singular pronoun is virtually absent; Paul's consistent use of 'we' rather than 'I' focuses attention away from Paul the apostle toward Paul and his colleagues, toward apostles in general." J. A. Crofton, *Agency of the Apostle: A Dramatic Analysis of Paul's Responses to Conflict in 2 Corinthians* (Sheffield, U.K.: Sheffield Press, 1991), pp. 66–67.

7. On the catalytic role of mission for all the other functions of the church, see A. Hirsch and M. Frost, *The Faith of Leap: Embracing a Theology of Risk, Adventure, and Courage* (Grand Rapids, Mich.: Baker, 2011), and A. Hirsch, *The Forgotten Ways: Reactivating the Missional Church* (Grand Rapids, Mich.: Brazos Press, 2006).

8. Hirsch, *The Forgotten Ways.*

9. Ephesians 3:1–8. Economics is not only about value; it is also about the exchange of value. If we can elaborate on Paul's metaphor here of *oikonomia*, the gospel is valuable in and of itself in relation to God, but its value is fully realized only when it enters the marketplace and interacts within the economy of human relationships, institutions, society, and culture. Apostles are economists of the gospel because they initiate this exchange and add value through the gospel to our social economies.

10. J. H. Schutz, *Paul and the Anatomy of Apostolic Authority* (Louisville, Ky.: Westminster John Knox Press), pp. 35, 36.

11. Ibid., p. 123. What we must realize is that the real power always resides in the gospel itself and that the apostle is always only an interpreter and integrator of its force in the community or movement. The gospel forever remains the ruling concept; all other agents are subordinated to it, including the apostle and the faith community itself. So in Paul's writings, for instance, not a word is said about the community being directly subordinated to Paul. Rather, because the gospel takes precedence, both Paul and the community can be subordinated to it. Paul can preach only what he has already preached, and the community can receive only what it has already received. The gospel is thus a double-sided standard—both preaching and receiving. It is a standard for authentic faith as well as for authentic apostleship. By virtue of their common dependence on and the need for their obedience to the one gospel, faith and apostleship are brought into the closest possible relationship.

12. Ibid.

13. D. J. Bosch, *Transforming Mission: Paradigm Shifts in Theology of Mission* (Maryknoll, N.Y.: Orbis, 1991).

14. Without the apostolic person (and to a certain extent the evangelist), the gospel tends to move around like a ball in the pinball machine. It may bounce around and reverberate through the system, but it never makes it outside the system itself.

15. M. Breen, *The Apostle's Notebook* (Eastbourne, East Sussex, U.K.: Kingsway, 2002).

16. D. Cannistraci, *Apostles and the Emerging Apostolic Movement* (Ventura, Calif.: Renew Books, 1992).

17. What follows is an elaboration of the material contained in Hirsch, *The Forgotten Ways: Reactivating the Missional Church* (Grand Rapids, Mich.: Brazos Press, 2006).

18. In my (Alan) centerpiece book, *The Forgotten Ways*, I suggest that these codes themselves comprise a sixfold complex of distinctive elements, each called mDNA (missional DNA), that together make up apostolic genius—the life force that pulsates through every transformative Jesus movement in history. The six interrelating elements are (1) *Jesus is Lord*—the heart and soul of Jesus movements, which is the central and organizing element; (2) *disciple making*—ensuring the embodiment and transmission of the message through adherence to Jesus's way; (3) *the missional-incarnational impulse,* describing a way of extending and planting the Jesus movement; (4) *an apostolic environment,* which explores the nature of the at least fivefold ministry that is the subject of this book; (5) *organic systems,* which explore the church's organization as movement and its viral, reproductive tendencies; and (6) *communitas,* which describes the type of community that forms in the context of ordeal, missional challenge, adventure, and risk. Each chapter in Part Two of *The Forgotten Ways* explores each of these elements. See also the glossary in *The Forgotten Ways*, p. 283.

19. For example, it is implied throughout the common use of the indicative and imperatives in the New Testament itself. The indicative creates identity and

gives this a basis in Christ and his work in the world. The imperatives arise directly out of a sense of who we are in Christ.

20. See Hirsch, *The Forgotten Ways*. See also O. Brafman and R. Beckstrom, *The Starfish and the Spider: The Unstoppable Power of Leaderless Organizations* (New York: Penguin, 2006).

21. We acknowledge once again that aspects of this verse refer to the unique role of the twelve apostles. But we, along with others, suggest that something of the foundational aspect of apostolic ministry is inherent in all forms of apostolic ministry. The apostolic function continues to provide something of a catalytic function for the ministry of the people of God. See, for instance, Andrew Lincoln in the Word Biblical Commentary where he notes that the apostles referred to in Ephesians 2:12 encompass the twelve but extend to others who fit the category. "Ephesians," *Word Biblical Commentary,* commentary on 2:12. Compact disk.

22. A. Roxburgh, *The Missionary Congregation, Leadership and Liminality* (Harrisburg, Pa.: Trinity Press, 1997), p. 62. Even the office of the bishop, the institutional replacement of the prior apostolic role, serves as a custodian of apostolicity (viewed here as inherent in the church and in the New Testament scriptures); it is viewed as "having in himself all the other ministries," which are in turn conferred to others by ordination. See J. McQuarrie, *Principles of Christian Theology* (London: SCM, 1966), p. 391. In instituting the bishop, Christendom took the pioneer aspect out of the equation, institutionalized apostolicity in church and office, and reshaped it in a distinctly pastoral image to suit the diocesan context, but it did keep some authentic aspects of the apostolic role that were useful to it. This founding role is one of them, and in it a true function of the apostolic can still be discerned.

23. The information on Cole's associated organic church movement comes from an e-mail dialogue we had with Cole. For information on New Covenant Ministries International, go to http://www.ncmi.net/.

24. Adapted from the insights of Mike Kim in "Our Journey into Rediscovering Apostolic and Prophetic Foundations, Part 3," *House2House Ezine,* Jan. 29, 2010, http://www.story.house2house.com/2010/01/29/our-journey-into-rediscovering-apostolic-and-prophetic-foundations-part-3/.

25. Mike Kim says, "Like scaffolding that sticks around beyond its usefulness, leaders often default on staying longer in their role for the sake of 'ministry quality' that ends up severely limiting the net quality and quantity of workers in the harvest."

Chapter Six: Come Back, Peter; Come Back, Paul

1. D. Scoggins, "Nurturing a Generation of 'Pauline' and 'Petrine' Apostles," *Apostolic Ministry,* Apr. 4, 2009, http://bit.ly/g3xZKf.

2. It was the nineteenth-century German theologian Martin Kahler who is credited with saying, "Mission is the mother of all theology."

3. Even here, Peter is addressing people with large amounts of religious capital, specifically Jews. So although they may be from different countries and provinces, and consequently different cultural spheres, Peter is still within the orbit of the already existing people of God.

4. "Generally, the opening statement of this Peter cycle reports that the apostle 'went here and there among all the believers' or, more literally—'passed through all of them,' that is, through all of the areas in the region where believers resided." F. S. Spencer, *Journeying Through Acts: A Literary-Cultural Reading* (Peabody, Mass.: Hendrickson, 2004), p. 112. The fact that Peter is functioning alone, without any "witnesses" traveling with him (such as the episode in Acts 8 with the Samaritans), shows the generic nature of his ministry in this region. Peter is simply doing what he does best and was commissioned to do by Jesus in John 21. He is feeding the sheep out of an apostolic vision. It is not until Acts 10 that Peter sees the need to take six witnesses with him to Caesarea in order to meet Cornelius, the God-fearing Gentile, and present the gospel to him and his household.

5. It is possible that Peter does the same thing in Corinth in light of the controversies swirling around factional groups claiming "Cephas" as one of their leaders. At any rate, even his interactions with Cornelius reveal that Peter is still interacting within the orbit of people who have significant levels of religious capital, God fearers. This encounter stretched Peter, but it should be noted that Peter is not interacting with Gentile pagans. This kind of cultural distance shows up more visibly in Paul's ministry.

6. D. E. Myerson, *Tempered Radicals: How Everyday Leaders Inspire Change at Work* (Boston: Harvard Business School Press, 2003).

7. Petrine apostles today can take on the form of church consultants. But we need to be clear about this: the impact is not just a more effective operational organization, but rather a more distinctly missional one. And it is not just boosting the church's evangelistic appeal either. Such apostleship should help mobilize the church for missional and incarnational expressions and, as Reggie McNeal says, "change the scorecard" of what growth and health look like. See R. McNeal, *Missional Renaissance: Changing the Scorecard for the Church* (San Francisco: Jossey-Bass, 2009).

8. "Intrapreneurship is now known as the practice of a corporate management style that integrates risk-taking and innovation approaches, as well as the reward and motivational techniques, that are more traditionally thought of as being the province of entrepreneurship." "Intrapreneurship," http://en.wikipedia.org/wiki/Intrapreneurship.

9. The categorizations here are inspired by N. Thornberry, *Lead Like an Entrepreneur: Keeping the Entrepreneurial Spirit Alive Within the Corporation* (New York: McGraw-Hill, 2006).

10. Perhaps the best way to describe what we are attempting to do here is captured by Max Weber's concept of the ideal type. As articulated by Joseph Blenkinsopp, Weber's ideal type is "a construction based on abstraction and

conceptualization that has the purpose of guiding inquiry back into the mass of available data. . . . They are a means of provisional classification, allowing for some preliminary understanding of the phenomenon, creating and testing hypotheses, distinguishing between constants and variables, and identifying deviations." J. Blenkinsopp, *Sage, Priest, Prophet: Religious and Intellectual Leadership in Ancient Israel* (Louisville, Ky.: Westminster John Knox Press, 1995), p. 116. Our effort to classify apostolic people and their ministries should be seen as an attempt to construct an ideal type; as in Weber's understanding, we are not trying to create water-tight compartments with hard-and-fast definitions.

11. The term *deep structure* was first used in R. Drazin and L. E. Sandelands, "Autogenesis: A Perspective on the Process of Organizing," *Organization Science*, 1992, 3, 230–249.

12. It should be abundantly clear by now that we do not believe in apostolic succession as it is formulated by Rome and affirmed to a lesser degree by other variations of sacramental, high church ecclesiology. We see that this was part of the later reappropriation of apostolic authority used to bolster the institution of the church. Furthermore, it is unlikely that Jesus, the archetypal prophet, who reserves his harshest words for religious professionals and religious institutions, would authorize any institution in this way, thereby substituting one for another. Rather, we should read this for what it is: a commissioning of an apostle—in this case, the one who was to lead the others. See the Appendix.

13. For instance, forgiveness of sins is in the gospel itself. It is contrary to the New Testament, and to Protestant, teaching to say that only Peter could forgive sins by binding and loosing.

14. A. Hirsch and D. Ferguson, *On the Verge: A Journey into the Apostolic Future of the Church* (Grand Rapids, Mich.: Zondervan, 2011).

15. E. Schein, *Organizational Culture and Leadership* (San Francisco: Jossey-Bass, 2010). Schein's book is an excellent source for Petrine apostles who want to sharpen their understanding of cultural dynamics within organizations.

16. Ibid., chap. 2.

17. For thorough expositions of this idea, see A. Hirsch, *The Forgotten Ways: Reactivating the Missional Church* (Grand Rapids, Mich.: Brazos, 2007); A. Hirsch and D. Altclass, *The Forgotten Ways Handbook* (Grand Rapids, Mich.: Brazos, 2009); and especially Hirsch and Ferguson, *On the Verge.*

18. There is no evidence, outside of Acts 2 and 10, that Peter founded any churches at all in the Pauline sense. This could be why 1 Peter is addressed to churches in the Asia Minor Province, an area where Paul had developed a church planting movement. Peter seems to be operating in his apostolic vocation by addressing the already existing people of God through these letters.

19. See for instance A.-L. Barabasi, *Linked: The New Science of Networks* (Cambridge, Mass.: Perseus, 2002), and R. Ogle, *Smart World: Breakthrough*

Creativity and the New Science of Ideas (Boston: Harvard Business School Press, 2007).

20. M. Gladwell, *The Tipping Point: How Little Things Can Make a Big Difference* (New York: Back Bay Books, 2002).

21. See Ogle, *Smart World*, for an exploration of network theory and innovation.

22. D. Bosch, *Transforming Mission Paradigm Shifts in Theology of Mission* (Maryknoll, N.Y.: Orbis Books, 1991).

23. S. Reicher, S. A. Haslam, and N. Hopkins, "Social Identity and the Dynamics of Leadership: Leaders and Followers as Collaborative Agents in the Transformation of Social Reality," *Leadership Quarterly,* 2005, *16,* 547–568.

24. A. Hirsch and M. Frost, *The Faith of Leap: Exploring a Theology of Risk, Adventure and Courage* (Grand Rapids, Mich.: Baker, 2011). Also see J. P. Kotter, *A Sense of Urgency* (Cambridge, Mass.: Harvard Business School Press, 2008), and *Leading Change* (Cambridge, Mass.: Harvard Business School Press, 1996).

25. Whatever has been initiated in the *missio Dei*, the Incarnation, and the Cross is not yet complete until Jesus returns, with all that this means for the world and the church. There is also a well-noted relationship between suffering and sanctification in Peter's writings, a suffering that arises from the tension felt between the times. These are distinctly eschatological themes.

26. While Paul is in Jerusalem, he is always stirring up trouble and stepping on toes. He may find himself in politically charged environments, but he does not navigate them well. One has to wonder why he stirs up all kinds of trouble while the other apostles, still ministering in word and in prayer in the Jerusalem church, seem to be getting along fairly well with others in the city. Paul is culturally savvy, but he is not necessarily politically savvy. Peter, in contrast, is quick to accommodate the popular census, evidenced by his actions in Antioch. See Galatians 2.

Chapter Seven: Living from the Center

1. I. Adizes, *Corporate Life Cycles: How and Why Corporations Grow and Die and What to Do About It* (Upper Saddle River, N.J.: Prentice Hall, 1988).

2. See L. Miller, *Barbarians to Bureaucrats: Corporate Life Cycle Strategies* (New York: Crown, 1989), and Adizes, *Corporate Life Cycles,* for examples of this approach.

3. Miller, *Barbarians to Bureaucrats.*

4. Don't confuse this with Adizes's use of *aristocrat;* accept it for what it is used to represent here.

5. Miller, *Barbarians to Bureaucrats.*

6. M. Friedman, *Martin Buber: Life of Dialogue* (New York: Routledge, 2002), p. 48.

7. S. Addison, "A Basis for the Continuing Ministry of the Apostle in the Church's Mission" (unpublished doctoral dissertation, Fuller Theological Seminary, 1995), p. 190.

8. The next six paragraphs draw heavily on A. Hirsch and M. Frost, *ReJesus: A Wild Messiah for a Missional Church* (Grand Rapids, Mich.: Baker, 2009). Also, we reference Steve Addison's exceptional unpublished work on Christian movements. Material used with permission. See also his blog on movements: World Changers at http://www.steveaddison.net/.

9. R. E. Quinn, *Change the World* (San Francisco: Jossey-Bass, 2000), p. 61. We thank Steve Addison for alerting us to the work of Quinn.

10. Ibid., p. 138.

11. Ibid.

12. R. Hostie, *The Life and Death of Religious Orders* (Washington, D.C.: Center for Applied Research in the Apostolate, 1983), p. 277.

13. From a conversation with Dallas Willard in March 2010. All this squares well with the formative thinking of the sociologist Max Weber. Weber maintained that the process of institutionalization and renewal involved a constant return to the charismatic center in order to relegitimize or, in our language, refound the subsequent movement. To remain true, all religious organizations require a form of renewal that encompasses a return to the original ethos and the power of the founder. And whether one applies this to a denomination or to Christianity as a whole, one can refer to this rediscovery of one's original message as radical traditionalism because it goes back to the organization's deepest tradition and reinterpret it for a new context. Quoted in Hirsch and Frost, *ReJesus*, p. 77.

14. Although many people use the term *radical* to mean a departure from the traditional, it in fact refers to a return to the root cause of a thing. Thinkexist .com defines *radical* as "of or pertaining to the root or origin; reaching to the center, to the foundation, to the ultimate sources, to the principles, or the like; original; fundamental; thorough-going; unsparing; extreme; as in radical evils; radical reform; a radical party" (http://thinkexist.com/dictionary/meaning/radical/). We thank Steve Addison for alerting us to the power of the term *radical traditionalism.*

15. J. Collins and J. Porras, *Built to Last: Successful Habits of Visionary Companies* (New York: HarperCollins, 2002), chap. 4.

16. Ibid.

17. J. Collins, *Good to Great: Why Some Companies Make the Leap and Others Don't* (New York: HarperCollins, 2001), p. 165.

18. For instance, R. Allen, *The Spontaneous Expansion of the Church: And the Causes That Hinder It* (Cambridge: Lutterworth Press, 2006). This ingenious work was published in 1927 and was the fruit of years of reflection on how movements arise and how they are hindered. See also Allen's *Missionary Methods: St. Paul's and Ours* (Grand Rapids, Mich.: Eerdmans, 1962). It is also important to note that Chinese nationals like Watchman Nee, the

theologian and writer, also helped develop a church structure that allowed the church in China to go underground.

19. Chris Anderson, the editor in chief of *Wired* magazine, has developed the notion of the long tail for business. The original article he wrote that inspired the book by that name is "The Long Tail," *Wired,* Dec. 14, 2004, http://changethis.com/manifesto/show/10.LongTail. C. Anderson, *Long Tail: Why the Future of Business Is Selling Less of More* (New York: Hyperion, 2008).

20. I (Alan) and Mike Frost have written extensively on the nature of risk, adventure, and courage for mission, discipleship, leadership, and community in our *The Faith of Leap: Embracing a Theology of Risk, Adventure, and Courage* (Grand Rapids, Mich.: Baker, 2011). We highly recommend that readers look into spiritual adventure as a means of wholesale renewal of the church.

21. R. Pascale, M. Milleman, and L. Gioja, *Surfing the Edge of Chaos: The Laws of Nature and the New Laws of Business* (New York: Three Rivers, 2000). Living systems theory is also known also as learning organization theory.

22. W. C. Roof, *Religion in America Today* (Thousand Oaks, Calif.: Sage, 1985), p. 50. This saying is sometimes ascribed to Harvey Cox, but we cannot confirm the source.

23. D. A. Schön, *The Reflective Practitioner: How Professionals Think in Action* (New York: Basic Books, 1983), p. 43.

24. Collins and Porras, *Built to Last.*

Chapter Eight: The Enterprise of Movement and the Movement of Enterprise

1. The key indicator of whether an area was marked on official maps as a frontier or as settled was a population of two or more people per square mile.

2. F. J. Turner, "The Significance of the Frontier in American History," in *The Annual Report of the American Historical Association* (1893), p. 38.

3. The following section is adapted from M. Wheatley, "Supporting Pioneering Leaders as Communities of Practice" (2002), http://www.margaretwheatley .com/articles/supportingpioneerleaders.html.

4. J. Houston, quoted in E. Germer, "What's Your Identity?" *Fastcompany online,* June 30, 2000, http://www.fastcompany.com/magazine/36/futurist .html.

5. R. Hoojberg, "Leadership Complexity and Development of the Leaderplex Model," *Journal of Management,* 1997, *23,* 375–408.

6. A. Hirsch and M. Frost, *The Faith of Leap: Embracing a Theology of Risk, Adventure, and Courage* (Grand Rapids, Mich.: Baker, 2011), p. 93. The quote from Machiavelli is from *The Prince,* trans. Luigi Ricci, (Fort Worth, Tex.: Lulu, 2008), p. 22.

7. Quoted in Hirsch and Frost, *The Faith of Leap,* p. 93.

8. See A. Hirsch and D. Ferguson, *On the Verge: A Journey into the Apostolic Future of the Church* (Grand Rapids, Mich.: Zondervan, 2011), for a thorough exploration of the both-and approach.

9. F. Johansson, *The Medici Effect: What Elephants and Epidemics Can Teach Us About Innovation* (Boston: Harvard Business School Press, 2006).

10. M. H. Morris, *Entrepreneurial Intensity: Sustainable Advantages for Individuals, Organizations, and Societies* (Westport, Conn.: Quorum Books, 1998), p. 44.

11. The designation *skunk works* is widely used in business, engineering, and technical fields to describe a group within an organization given a high degree of autonomy and unhampered by bureaucracy, tasked with working on advanced or secret projects. Although we think the idea is good, what we have in mind is something that is more a part of the actual organization itself rather than being an isolated unit with little or no legitimacy.

12. Morris, *Entrepreneurial Intensity*, p. 19. We are indebted to Morris for the insights set out in this section.

13. An example of this is what is happening to the publishing world today. Digital media are game changers. This has been accelerated by the introduction of the electronic readers and, even more so, Apple's iPad. Also, what is less known about the acute forms of entrepreneurial intensity perhaps is that many of these never make it to the light of day. The problem is that such innovation is so far ahead of the game as not to be able to change it. Such organizations and individuals can find themselves stranded. An example is Macintosh's Newton, its early tablet computer that was way ahead of its time.

14. For more about Fresh Expressions, see http://www.freshexpressions.org.uk/.

15. "The group's purpose is to develop something quickly with minimal management constraints. Skunk works are often used to initially roll out a product or service that thereafter will be developed according to usual business processes." http://bit.ly/dS4Piu. The approach is different from having an in-house research and development function in that it is usually located far from the center of the organization and is somewhat secretive so that it can operate without the normal constraints of the organization. However, because it is thus marginalized from the center, it seldom has an impact on the culture of an organization in a systemic and meaningful way.

16. See Hirsch and Ferguson, *On the Verge,* for the idea of 40:60 appeal.

17. Proven models, or algorithms, can play a significant role in the viability of any enterprise, but that role is inherently limited when we take in the scope of the missional mandate to seed the gospel among every group of people. The entrepreneurial force driving a franchising type of church planting movement will propel it across geographical boundaries, but it will struggle in crossing cultural boundaries. Mass-producing the prevailing models of church may prove to be efficient in the short run, but in the long run, if the nature and scope of apostolic ministry do not begin to expand to include cross-cultural, and therefore incarnational, approaches, then despite our

apparent progress in geographical expansion, we will still be ignoring the more complex dimensions of the adaptive challenge. The nature and scope of apostolic ministry need to experience a sort of disenfranchising in order to reach its full capacity for missional impact.

18. See Hirsch and Ferguson, *On the Verge,* for an exploration of both-and approaches to developing apostolic movements. The main churches involved are part of the Future Travelers group.

19. See, for instance, N. Cole, *Church 3.0: Upgrades for the Future of the Church* (San Francisco: Jossey-Bass, 2010).

20. J. G. March. "Exploration and Exploitation in Organizational Learning," *Organization Science,* 1991, 2(1), 71–87.

21. Ibid., p. 71.

22. H. Austen, *Artistry Unleashed: A Guide to Pursuing Great Performance in Work and Life* (Toronto: Rotman/UTP Publishing, 2010), p. 111.

23. S. Godin, *Tribes: We Need You to Lead Us* (New York: Portfolio, 2008), p. 83.

24. Ibid., p. 93.

25. N. Cole, *Organic Church: Growing Faith Where Life Happens* (San Francisco: Jossey-Bass, 2005).

26. Ibid., p. 65.

27. As we saw in Part Two, custodianship relates to the guardianship of nature and purpose of the gospel and the church. It also involves the work of laying foundations. See Chapter Five on apostolic job description.

28. Cole, *Church 3.0.*

29. Ibid., p. 83.

30. See Hirsch and Ferguson, *On the Verge,* p. 45.

31. I tell a bit of this story in chap. 1 of *The Forgotten Ways: Reactivating the Missional Church* (Grand Rapids, Mich.: Brazos, 2007).

32. In light of this, we suggest that the more standard, and we would suggest secular, approach is to have a board of chickens rule and direct the pigs. This might be fine in big corporations, but in start-ups or, in our case, missional projects, this is not good practice. It is hard to see Paul outsourcing direction and policy to a board.

33. J. Lorenzen, "A Rope of Sand," *On Movements,* Nov. 4, 2008, http://onmovements.com/?p=347.

Chapter Nine: The Spirit of Innovation

1. See O. Brafman and R. Brafman, *Sway: The Irresistible Pull of Irrational Behavior* (New York: Doubleday, 2008), and D. Ariely, *Predictably Irrational* (New York: HarperCollins, 2009), for example.

2. Quoted in R. Murray-Webster and D. Hillson, *Managing Group Risk Attitude Book* (Hampshire, U.K.: Gower Publishing, 2008), p. 3.

3. S. Gryskiewicz, *Positive Turbulence: Developing Climates for Creativity, Innovation, and Renewal* (San Francisco: Jossey-Bass, 1999) p. 36.

4. See A. Hirsch and M. Frost, *The Faith of Leap: Embracing a Theology of Risk, Adventure, and Courage* (Grand Rapids, Mich.: Baker, 2011), for a thorough exploration of the role of adventure and risk in our understanding of God, church, mission, leadership, discipleship, and the formation and development of identity.

5. R. Martin, *The Design of Business: Why Design Thinking Is the Next Competitive Advantage* (Boston: Harvard Business School Press, 2009).

6. Because they have produced a measure of evangelistic success, the purely attractional, seeker-sensitive, church growth models have, until recently, served as our reliable algorithm when it comes to charting our path into the future. Yet these models participate in the same limitations as every other algorithm: although they may have experienced a certain evangelistic success within particular cultural environments, the immensity of the current challenge now requires a different algorithm.

7. See, for instance, R. Ogle, *Smart World: Breakthrough Creativity and the New Science of Ideas* (Boston: Harvard Business School Press, 2007), for a thorough exploration of the inner dynamics of innovation.

8. F. Johansson, *The Medici Effect: What Elephants and Epidemics Can Teach Us About Innovation* (Boston: Harvard Business School Press, 2006), pp. 3, 47.

9. C. Shirky, *Here Comes Everybody: The Power of Organizing Without Organizations* (New York: Penguin, 2008), p. 231.

10. R. M. Kanter, "Creating the Culture for Innovation," in F. Hesselbein, M. Goldsmith, and I. Somerville (eds.), *Leading for Innovation and Organizing for Results* (San Francisco: Jossey-Bass, 2001), p. 73.

11. One of the main theses of Hirsch and Frost, *The Faith of Leap*, is that adventure and risk fundamentally change the way we think and act. By choosing to put ourselves in the risky business of mission, we are more likely to learn new things about God, faith, discipleship, leadership, and church.

12. Kanter, "Creating the Culture for Innovation."

13. Johansson, *The Medici Effect*.

14. N. T. Wright, *Surprised by Hope* (New York: HarperOne, 2008), p. 130.

15. D. Pink, *A Whole New Mind: Why Right-Brainers Will Rule the Future* (New York: Penguin, 2006), p. 136.

16. Tolerance for ambiguity should not be confused with a desire for it. The thing to be desired is the capacity to thrive and navigate in the midst of the initial fuzzy and uncertain phases of the innovative process.

17. D. Kuratko, *Entrepreneurship: Theory, Process, Practice* (Mason, Ohio: Cengage Learning, 2009).

18. P. Berliner, *Thinking in Jazz: The Infinite Art of Improvisation* (Chicago: University of Chicago Press, 1994), p. 241.

19. K. E. Weick, *Making Sense of the Organization* (Malden, Mass.: Blackwell, 2007), p. 61.

20. D. A. Schön, *The Reflective Practitioner: How Professionals Think in Action* (New York: Basic Books, 1983), p. 68.

21. J. B. Green and M. D. Baker, *Recovering the Scandal of the Cross: Atonement in New Testament and Contemporary Contexts* (Madison, Wis.: Inter-Varsity Press, 2000), p. 66.

22. D. E. Flemming, *Contextualization in the New Testament: Patterns for Theology and Mission* (Madison, Wis.: Inter-Varsity Press, 2005), p. 19.

23. This circle of innovation follows the process of innovation prescribed by design firm IDEO. See T. Kelly and J. Littman, *The Art of Innovation: Lessons in Creativity from IDEO, America's Leading Design Firm* (New York: Doubleday, 2001).

24. For more on this process, which it refers to as "Greenhouse," see http://www.cmaresources.org/greenhouse.

25. D. Watson, "Strategy and Structure," *TouchPoint,* Nov. 22, 2007, http://www.davidlwatson.org/2007/11/22/strategy-and-structure/.

26. E. R. McManus, *An Unstoppable Force: Daring to Become the Church God Had in Mind* (Loveland, Colo.: Group Publishing, 1999), p. 90.

Chapter Ten: Movements R Us

1. K. S. Latourette, *A History of the Expansion of Christianity* (New York: HarperCollins, 1945).

2. For an extended discussion on mission as organizing, or catalyzing, principle, see A. Hirsch and M. Frost, *The Faith of Leap: Embracing a Theology of Risk, Adventure, and Courage* (Grand Rapids, Mich.: Baker, 2011).

3. E. Schattschneider, *The Semisovereign People: A Realist View of Democracy in America* (New York: Holt, 1960).

4. A. Hirsch, *The Forgotten Ways: Reactivating the Missional Church* (Grand Rapids, Mich.: Brazos, 2007).

5. Ibid., p. 236.

6. The only way to achieve a global mission is to become a movement. If the great Commission were not enough, Jesus explicitly spells out the move-mental nature of the church by saying in Acts 1:8 that the church is to move from Jerusalem, to Judea, to Samaria, and to the uttermost parts of the earth. Moving from one region to the next requires movement.

7. D. H. Land, *The Diffusion of Ecclesiastical Authority: Sociological Dimensions of Leadership in the Book of Acts* (Eugene, Ore.: Pickwick, 2008), pp. 229–230.

8. P. Senge, *The Fifth Discipline: The Art and Practice of the Learning Organization* (New York: Doubleday, 2006); D. Hock, *Birth of the Chaordic Age* (San Francisco: Berrett-Koehler, 1999); O. Brafman and R. Beckstrom, *The Starfish and the Spider: The Unstoppable Power of Leaderless Organizations* (New York: Group, 2008); D. Tapscott and A. Williams, *Wikinomics: How Mass Collaboration Changes Everything* (New York: Portfolio, 2006);

C. Shirky, *Here Comes Everybody: The Power of Organizing Without Organizations* (New York: Penguin, 2008); S. Addison, *Movements That Change the World* (Downers Grove, Ill.: InterVarsity Press, 2010); and B. Roberts, *Glocalization: How Followers of Jesus Engage in a Flat World* (Grand Rapids, Mich.: Zondervan, 2007).

9. A. Jones, "Are We a Movement?" *Tall Skinny Kiwi*, June 8, 2005, http://bit.ly/fbsyQb.

10. See also Tim Keller's excellent comparison between movements and institutions on the Redeemer Web site. T. Keller, "Ministry Movements," July 27, 2010, http://redeemercitytocity.com/blog/view.jsp?Blog_param=203.

11. Hirsch, *The Forgotten Ways*.

12. In other words, we can say that the centralization of power and function has an inverse relationship to the capacity of a movement to expand and grow.

13. A. Hirsch and D. Ferguson, *On the Verge: A Journey into the Apostolic Future of the Church* (Grand Rapids, Mich.: Zondervan, 2011); N. Cole, *Church 3.0: Upgrades for the Future of the Church* (San Francisco: Jossey-Bass, 2009); and D. Friesen, *Thy Kingdom Connected: What the Church Can Learn from Facebook, the Internet, and Other Networks* (Grand Rapids, Mich.: Baker, 2009).

14. Brafman and Beckstrom, *Starfish*. I (Alan) have become friends with Ori Brafman, and although he is an Israeli Jew and not a follower of Jesus, he is fascinated by the idea of apostolic movements as we articulate them.

15. Hirsch, *The Forgotten Ways*.

16. Brafman and Beckstrom, *Starfish*.

17. B. B. Mandelbrot, *The Fractal Geometry of Nature* (New York: Freeman, 1983), p. 276.

18. Many Web sites allow users to create their own fractals, for example, http://www.shodor.org/interactivate/activities/gasket/.

19. N. Cole, *Organic Church: Growing Faith Where Life Happens* (San Francisco: Jossey-Bass, 2005).

20. Ibid., pp. 128–129.

21. See Hirsch, *The Forgotten Ways*; M. Frost and A. Hirsch, *The Shaping of Things to Come: Innovation and Mission for the 21st Century Church* (Peabody, Mass.: Hendrickson, 2003); and A. Hirsch and M. Frost, *ReJesus: A Wild Messiah for a Missional Church* (Grand Rapids, Mich.: Baker, 2009).

22. D. Hock, quoted in M. Hoffman "Transformation by Design," Jan. 2003, http://www.scribd.com/doc/2534950/Dee-Hock-Transformation-by-Design. See also Hock's *The Birth of the Chaordic Age*.

23. M. M. Waldrop, "Dee Hock on Organizations," *Fast Company*, Oct.–Nov. 1996, p. 84, www.fastcompany.com/online/05/dee3.html.

24. "Ricardo Semler," http://en.wikipedia.org/wiki/Ricardo_semler.

25. Hirsch and Ferguson, *On the Verge.*

26. This means (1) [re]coding the organization around a serious engagement with the Kingdom of God manifested in and through Jesus, (2) the idea of discipleship and the process of disciple making, (3) how and why to engage in incarnational forms of mission, (4) activating a fully fledged APEST form of ministry and leadership, (5) creating organic systems in relation to organization and structure, and (6) engendering a lively sense of dare and the ability to engage and thrive in risky situations (communitas). Hirsch, *The Forgotten Ways*, part 2.

27. For a detailed process of how to implement movemental change in complex organizations, see Hirsch and Ferguson, *On the Verge,* which was written mainly to help larger, more successful megachurches implement movemental ecclesiology.

28. The outer doll holds all of the inner dolls, the next outer doll holds all the remaining inner dolls, and so on. In the world of quantum physics, nested hierarchies form the basis of reality: particles form protons, protons and electrons make up the atom, the atom in turn is the basis of molecules, molecules of compounds, all the way up through the great chain of being.

29. "The Lifeshapes," eLifeShapes.org, http://www.elifeshapes.org/shapes.php.

Chapter Eleven: Apostolic Architecture

1. L. Bergquist and A. Karr, *Church Turned Inside Out: A Guide for Designers, Refiners, and Re-Aligners* (San Francisco: Jossey-Bass, 2009).

2. G. Morgan, *Images of Organization* (Thousand Oaks, Calif.: Sage, 1997), p. 15. The instrumental view of organizations is reflected in the origins of the word *organization*, which derives from the Greek *organon,* meaning tool or instrument.

3. C. Shirky, *Here Comes Everybody: The Power of Organizing Without Organizations* (New York: Penguin Group, 2008), p. 107.

4. A. Hirsch and L. Ford, *Right Here, Right Now: Everyday Mission for Everyday People* (Grand Rapids, Mich.: Baker, 2011).

5. R. Allen, *The Spontaneous Expansion of the Church: And the Causes That Hinder It* (Cambridge: Lutterworth Press, 2006), p. 126. The following comparison is drawn from S. Addison, "A Basis for the Continuing Ministry of the Apostle in the Church's Mission" (unpublished doctoral dissertation, Fuller Theological Seminary, 1995), and used with permission.

6. "This witness of experience brings spiritual enlightenment and spiritual enlightenment quickens the intellectual faculties and prepares the mind for intellectual teaching." Ibid., pp. 67–68.

7. To leave newly born churches to learn by experience is apostolic; to abandon them is not apostolic. To watch over them is apostolic; to be always nursing

them is not apostolic. To guide their education is apostolic; to provide it for them is not apostolic. Ibid.

8. "Nothing is so weakening as the habit of depending upon others for those things which we ought to supply for ourselves. How can a man propagate a religion which he cannot support and which he cannot expect those whom he addresses to be able to support?" Ibid., p. 46.

9. Ibid., p. 60. The great things of God are beyond our control.

10. By inserting this term between the first conversions and their coming into ministry, we teach them to focus on their own progress rather than on outreach. They lose their zeal for the conversion of others. Ibid., pp. 27–28.

11. Heresies are produced not by ignorance but by the speculations of learned men. Allen, *The Spontaneous Expansion of the Church*, p. 62.

12. "Spontaneous zeal is alarming to them. When the faith is spread spontaneously, both the charlatan and the saint find an opportunity for acquiring influence over others. Side by side with Peter is Simon Magus. In the working of an organization, the man who is welcome and at home is the plain, mechanical, orderly man who will keep within the bounds. Not only the swindler but the inspired saint is a difficulty. He appears self-willed, extravagant, eccentric. He is independent and is always on the verge of breaking the orderly methods of the organization." Ibid., p. 148.

13. Nevius wrote his ideas in 1899 in *The Planting and Development of Missionary Churches: His Basic Principles,* where he suggested the following strategic guides to missions. (1) Christians should continue to live in their neighborhoods and pursue their occupations, being self-supporting and witnessing to their coworkers and neighbors. (2) Missions should develop only programs and institutions that the national church desires and supports. (3) The national churches should call out and support their own pastors. (4) Churches should be built in the native style with money and materials given by the church members. (5) Intensive biblical and doctrinal instruction should be provided for church leaders every year. It is amazing that we are still trying to get missionaries to adopt these principles over 110 years later. The "three-self" church strategy states that a church should be self-governing, self-supporting, and self-replicating. These ideas infused Nevius's thinking (they originally were called the Venn-Anderson principles). See the thoughts of missiologist Ted Esler at http://www.esler.org/2010/03/14/ whatsnew/. For Nevius, see "John Livingstone Nevius," http://en.wikipedia .org/wiki/John_Livingstone_Nevius.

14. The further irony is that the state-sponsored church of China today is formally called the "Three Self Church," and although it is growing, it is being seriously outpaced by the underground house church movement, which now intentionally practices the three-self principles.

15. We acknowledge that David Bosch added to the three-self principles the additional concept of self-theologizing. This is a significant addition, but we opt to reformulate these principles for the Western context. D. J. Bosch,

Transforming Mission: Paradigm Shifts in Theology of Mission (Maryknoll, N.Y.: Orbis, 1997), pp. 450–457.

16. M. J. Wheatley and M. Kellner-Rogers, "The Irresistible Future of Organizing," July–Aug. 1996, http://www.margaretwheatley.com/articles/irresistiblefuture.html.

17. Living systems theory, which builds on and develops the idea of self-organization in human organization, is much closer to New Testament ecclesiology than the predominantly mechanistic approach we have relied on for centuries.

18. S. Addison, *Movements That Change the World* (Smyrna, Del.: Missional Press, 2010), p. 113.

19. J. C. Collins and J. I. Porras, *Built to Last: Successful Habits of Visionary Companies* (New York: HarperCollins, 1994).

20. That is why he is so shocked at the Galatians when they fall under the influence of the Judaizer. He expects that they should be mature in Christ and able to discern their own way forward (Galatians 3:1–5).

21. N. Cole, *Organic Leadership: Leading Naturally Right Where You Are* (Grand Rapids, Mich.: Baker, 2009), p. 250.

22. N. Cole, *Organic Church: Growing Faith Where Life Happens* (San Francisco: Jossey-Bass, 2005), p. 119. For research by influential Baptist missiologist Ed Stetzer, go to http://www.edstetzer.com/2010/04/exponential-and-church-plantin.html.

23. N. Cole, *Church 3.0: Upgrades for the Future of the Church* (San Francisco: Jossey-Bass, 2010).

24. D. McGavran, *Understanding Church Growth* (Grand Rapids, Mich.: Eerdmans, 1990), p. 219.

25. From S. Addison, "Movement Dynamics," unpublished document, c. 2004, which Steve Addison shared with Alan. Used with permission.

26. W. Allen, "When the Mission Pays the Pastor," *Mission Frontiers Bulletin*, Jan.–Feb. 1999, pp. 38–41.

27. These circuit riders were modeled and led by Francis Asbury, who traveled around 270,000 miles and preached 16,000 sermons as he made his way throughout early frontier America overseeing the churches.

28. R. Finke and R. Stark, *The Churching of America, 1776–2005: Winners and Losers in Our Religious Economy, Revised and Expanded Edition* (Piscataway, N.J.: Rutgers University Press, 2005), p. 5. The authors compare this to the Baptist growth over the same period and noted that the Baptists insisted on similar educational qualifications only later in the twentieth century, which also initiated the decline of the Southern Baptists at that point.

29. The collegiate university was originally modeled after the inclusion of all the elements of the "universe." As such, it sought to include as part of its repertoire of training and education a sampling of the basic fields and practices found in society. If we reapply this rationale to seminaries and theological universities, it seems logical to include and organize the university around

the universal categories of ministry in Ephesians 4 that no less constitute the very church that those seminaries seek to serve and empower.

30. This is a far cry from the discipleship-based action learning system that the Bible itself maintains is necessary for theological integrity and to transfer faith meaningfully. We typically quote Jesus as saying, "You will know the truth, and the truth will set you free" (John 8:32), but we fail to put this in its immediate context, which changes the equation entirely. To the Jews who had believed him, Jesus said, "If you hold to my teaching, you are really my disciples" (John 8:31). Understanding of truth, and experiencing the freedom found in it, is predicated on first being a disciple. One cannot know truth divorced from the context of discipleship. This insight is gleaned from friend and colleague Caesar Kalinowski.

31. Allen, *The Spontaneous Expansion of the Church*, p. x.

32. Addison, *Movement Dynamics*, p. 73.

33. R. Winter, *Perspectives on the World Christian Movement: A Reader* (Pasadena, Calif.: William Carey Library, 1999).

34. E. E. Ellis, "Paul and His Co-Workers," in *Dictionary of Paul and His Letters* (Downers Grove, Ill.: InterVarsity Press, 1993), p. 183.

35. Paul's network of associates shared one fundamental characteristic inherent to the designation of coworker: their assistance to the apostle during one or more phases of his ministry. Whether the coworkers labored independently on Paul's behalf or served directly at his side, each of them helped him establish and maintain the work of the gospel. This assistance grew out of the special relationships Paul developed with his coworkers. Some of these relationships spanned many years, numerous missions, and various situations. In others, association with Paul was more occasional in nature. For further reflections on this topic, see S. Maness, "Paul and His Fellow-Workers: Determinate Trajectories for the Ministries of Paul's Partners in the Gospel" (unpublished doctoral dissertation, Dallas Theological Seminary, 1992).

36. Taken from the lecture notes of Sam Metcalf and used with permission. The book of Acts provides further insight into the activities of these apostolic bands. In a given city, they preached the gospel and made disciples who were formed into a fellowship of believers. The band then traveled to other centers to strengthen newly formed churches and returned to home base to report on the success of the mission and prepare for the next (for instance, Acts 14:21–28).

37. Winter, *Perspectives on the World Christian Movement*, points to the effectiveness of the monastic orders in the spread of the Christian faith during the postapostolic and medieval eras. He attributes the Reformation's initial missionary impotency to the reformers' suspicion of the Catholic orders. It was not until a later era and the emergence of Protestant missionary societies that Protestants became involved in world missions.

38. S. Metcalf, "Characteristics of Apostolic Structures," *Under the Iceberg*, http://bit.ly/hP0e6Zm.

39. H. Halter and M. Smay, *And: The Gathered and Scattered Church* (Grand Rapids, Mich.: Zondervan, 2010).

Appendix

1. Paul explicitly talks about the apostolic ministry (in this case, along with the prophetic ministry) as being foundational to the whole ecclesial project (Ephesians 2:20). He also says that he sees it as his work to lay foundations (1 Corinthians 3:10–12). Probably reflecting these, elsewhere he says that in relation to the other giftings, God has placed apostles first (*protos*) in the church (1 Corinthians 12:28). However we might envisage this, it must mean that the apostolic has some kind of priority and prominence in the ministry mix. Following the explicit commands and example of Christ in power relations, disciples are not allowed to conceive of their influence in a hierarchical manner (Luke 22:25–27; Philemon 2:1–11), and so when he says "first" in these places, it must mean something more akin to his use of *themelios* in Ephesians 2:20. And so we believe that the apostolic ministry is in fact the grounding, orienting, or simply catalyst, one in relation to the other ministries and has a very important and ongoing place in the church.

2. In fact, Alan has argued that it is precisely this slippage of our moorings from our Founder that lies at the heart of all toxic expressions of Christian religion. See A. Hirsch and M. Frost, *ReJesus: A Wild Messiah for a Missional Church* (Grand Rapids, Mich.: Baker, 2009).

3. Without any consideration for any alternative position, the inherited teachings in this regard have effectively have become the theological justifications of the forces favoring equilibrium, for the spiritual coup d'état, and it has been effectively played out over the centuries.

4. U. Sinclair, *I, Candidate for Governor: And How I Got Licked* (Berkeley: University of California Press, 1935, repr. 1994), p. 109.

5. Prophets also had itinerant ministries, as evidenced in the Didache, a Christian document composed in the later part of the first century of the church, but their ministry was focused on the people of God, not extending the gospel into new territories. Most itinerant prophets ended up settling into a local community.

6. In fact, much of the Cessationist readings of the twentieth century have been shown to be precisely this type of tendentious exegesis—in this case, their personal and preferential distaste for all things charismatic. Any attempt to undermine the fundamentally multidimensional ministry structure of the New Testament church turns out to be a selective, nuanced, and anachronistic reading. Taken at face value and on its own terms, the New Testament itself makes no suggestions of the rescinding of the church's ministry. Quite frankly, any attempt to make it say something else is manipulative and dishonest.

7. See, for instance, L. D. Edles and S. Appelrouth, *Sociological Theory in the Classical Era: Text and Readings* (Thousand Oaks, Calif.: Pine Forge Press,

2010). Every movement goes through phases of evolution and development, and the Jesus movement was no exception. Jesus founds the movement, radically changes and empowers the apostles, and commissions them to disciple the nations (Matthew 28:18–20). The apostles, though not alone in the ministry of Christ to the world, were the effective driving force in the expansion of the church. Their translocal, boundary-crossing, somewhat entrepreneurial form of leadership kept the church on the missional trajectory Jesus envisioned. Their distinctly missional form of leadership was an integral part of the church's life and consciousness and enjoyed a definitive place in the intellectual real estate of the church. It is logical that later generations would seek to try to encode and routinize their dynamic ministry.

8. For instance, this happens in the New Testament itself. Describing the later Pauline communities, historian Harry Maier notes, "The evidence generally suggests that while Paul was still alive the process of institutionalization was in its early stages. The passage of time, the growth of the group, the physical absence of the apostle, the repeated action of certain members—all these factors encouraged the development of organizational patterns, however informal." H. O. Maier, *The Social Setting of the Ministry as Reflected in the Writings of Hermas, Clement and Ignatius* (Canada: Canadian Corporation for Studies in Religion, 1991), p. 39.

9. J.D.G. Dunn, *Unity and Diversity in the New Testament* (Harrisburg, Pa.: Trinity Press, 1977), p. 351.

10. T. F. O'Dea, "Five Dilemmas of the Institutionalization of Religion," *Journal for the Scientific Study of Religion,* 1961, *1,* quoted in Frost and Hirsch, *ReJesus,* p. 77. Chapter Three is in many ways an extensive elaboration of this in relation to the role of the Founder of Christianity in the ongoing movement that claims his name.

11. "Herein lies an irresolvable dilemma for religious organizations: although religious movements are born out of firsthand religious experiences, they cannot survive and prosper without some form of stability and order. The charism (the originating grace or gift) has to be diffused, ritualized, and mediated by the organization so that the initial gift of the founder can be made accessible through the organization itself. While O'Dea saw this process of institutionalization as inevitable and even necessary, he also saw that it was paradoxically the process that would dilute or possibly even obliterate the initial message and ethos of the founder. Yet this routinization of charisma has a tendency to snuff out the life it was meant to protect and enhance. The crisis inevitably dawns when the outward forms of worship no longer match the inward experience and spiritual condition of the participants. Decline becomes inevitable. Authentic Christianity is subverted and constant renewals become necessary . . . hence the need to re-Jesus the movement." Frost and Hirsch, *ReJesus,* p. 77.

12. While institutionalization as structuring the common life is a normal process, institutionalism is another matter entirely. When the institution takes on the

status of an –ism, a belief system, then it invariably begins to lay claims to authority and ultimately becomes idolatrous. Because of this, we think it best to call the level of institutionalizing in the New Testament as "structuring" the organization or "rhythming" the life of the community because it has not yet hardened into the much more rigid institutionalism that would come with the legalization of Christianity with Constantine. In other words, the persecuted underground church of the first few centuries was preinstitutional or simply structural rather than fully institutionalized.

13. The Church in Catholic theology is seen to be the mystical body of Christ, and the priestly system replaces the mediating work of Jesus. The pope becomes the sole representative of Jesus on earth. All this is the result of the transfer of the initial grace/charism of the movement into the institution. The institution is then totemized; it becomes divine in itself. For the tragic struggle between form and function in religious movements, see O'Dea, "Five Dilemmas of the Institutionalization of Religion." Interestingly O'Dea is a Catholic theologian and priest.

14. See J. S. Brown and P. Duguid, *The Social Life of Information* (Boston: Harvard Business School Press, 2000), for a discussion of how social context is important to the development and interpretation of information and ideas.

15. This accounts for one of the reasons that we always have to be deliberate and return continuously to the Founder of the Christian movement in an ongoing loop of renewal and relegitimization. Again this is the core topic of Frost and Hirsch, *ReJesus*. Another aspect worth noting here is that the biblical worldview itself is against such depersonalization of ideas. Theological ideas should always guide and inform the relationship between God and his people. In Hebraic perspective, ideas are never important in and of themselves. They serve a greater reality. This is not to say that we do not believe ideas are not important. We have already asserted that they are. But they must never be depersonalized and abstracted from that which they point to and from where they came from.

16. We are not suggesting that there is not a canon of ideas (rightly contained in scripture) that serves as a authority and standard for the church's thinking and behavior. We are very orthodox (and conservative) in our view of scripture as authoritative for all matters of life and faith. We are simply referring to the distinct idea that infers that we have effectively extracted (and replaced) the essence of apostolic ministry by encoding the doctrine that they taught. This particular doctrine, and it is that, was used as a reason to reject the actual ministry.

17. For an interesting look into the book of Acts from this angle, see M. Sleeman, *Geography and the Ascension Narrative in Acts* (Cambridge: Cambridge University Press, 2009), and F. S. Spencer, *Journeying Through Acts: A Literary-Cultural Reading* (Peabody, Mass.: Hendrickson, 2004).

18. He goes on to note that "the requirements of bureaucracy override such traditional differentiations of religious leadership as 'prophet' versus

'priest,' 'scholar versus saint,' and so forth. Thus it does not matter very much whether a certain bureaucratic functionary comes out of a protestant tradition of 'prophetic' ministry or a Catholic tradition of a 'priestly' one—in either case, he must above all adapt himself to the requirements of his bureaucratic role." P. L. Berger, *The Sacred Canopy: Elements of a Sociological Theory of Religion* (New York: Anchor Books, 1967), pp. 139–140.

19. L. M. Miller, *From Barbarians to Bureaucrats* (New York: Fawcett Columbine, 1989). It seems that certain styles of leadership change as an organization moves through its life cycle. To start something from scratch requires something of the entrepreneurial risk-taking type of leader, something of a visionary (to use Miller's term, the prophet-barbarian). To structure for growth requires a different type of leadership again, one better able to manage the affairs of a growing concern. In fact, when that is necessary, the initiating leader might actually become a hindrance to the organization's health. At the end of the life cycle are people who at best are maintainers of the system and at worst hinder its possible revitalization.

20. See also I. Adizes, *Corporate Lifecycles: How and Why Corporations Grow and Die and What to Do About It,* 4th ed. (Upper Saddle River, N.J.: Prentice Hall, 1998), or I. Adizes, *Managing Corporate Lifecycles* (Upper Saddle River, N.J.: Prentice Hall, 1999).

21. L. Miller, *Barbarians to Bureaucrats: Corporate Life Cycle Strategies* (New York: Crown, 1989).

22. E. Stetzer, *Planting Missional Churches* (Nashville, Tenn.: Broadman & Holman, 2006), p. 29.

23. Applying this to the trajectory of early Christianity, the early experience of ecclesia was drawn from the Greco-Roman household (*oikos*) structure, which naturally supplied the initial organizational template for the church in the beginning. The leadership roles emerged organically, from below, and were a natural development considering the connection the early church had with the household, its primary meeting place. Over time, these roles became formalized and gave birth to models of leadership like those we see in Rome in the writings of Clement with his promotion of the elder-deacon model, or in the writings of Ignatius promoting the threefold bishop-elder-deacon model of leadership. Because these roles ensured the smooth operation of the community along with a higher degree of stability, they formed the templated pattern of organization that later became a formalized, rigid hierarchy consisting of a single bishop ruling over a collection of house churches with a council of elders and administrative deacons. Over time, the clearly biblical roles and functions of apostle (and prophet and evangelist for that matter) are referred to less and less as the more operative, somewhat more bureaucratic approaches to leadership replace them. Here are the roots of the shepherd-teacher hegemony. See Maier, *The Social Setting of the Ministry,* p. 108. See also R. A. Campbell, *The Elders: Seniority Within Earliest Christianity* (London: T&T Clark, 1994).

24. We see a hint of the beginnings of conflict in Acts 8 when Peter and John make a special trip to Samaria to lay hands on the Samarians to receive the Holy Spirit. Mush discussion swirls around this event and why the Holy Spirit was given to them in this way. A plausible explanation was that the gospel was beginning to stretch beyond the ethnic boundaries of Judaism, which would raise questions about the legitimacy of non-Jewish converts. Peter and John go down to Samaria and lay hands on them to legitimize their conversion, communicating the authenticity and acceptance of the Samaritans into the Jesus movement. However, the conversion of Cornelius would stretch their views of who was allowed to enter the kingdom. Instead of the apostles playing a significant role in the legitimization of the conversion of a new people group through the laying on of hands, the Holy Spirit moved separate and apart from them and legitimized the Gentiles' status as having equal rights to enter the kingdom of God.

25. We are deeply indebted to Martin Robinson, the key British missiologist, for many suggestions for this list. The issue of apostolic women is complex because they tend to be more hidden and require more research to uncover. In addition, the limitations placed on women by the wider society means that it is harder to point to them as founding movements and easier to see their moral and practical influence. Nevertheless, some female movement leaders are in this list.

26. K.J.A. Small, "Missional Ordered Ministry in the Evangelical Covenant Church," in C. Van Gelder (ed.), *The Missional Church and Denominations: Helping Congregations Develop a Missional Identity* (Grand Rapids, Mich.: Eerdmans, 2008), p. 231.

THE AUTHORS

ALAN HIRSCH is the founding director of Forge Mission Training Network. Currently he co-leads Future Travelers, an innovative learning program helping megachurches become missional movements. Known for his innovative approach to mission, Alan is considered to be a thought-leader and key mission strategist for churches across the Western world.

Hirsch is the author of *The Forgotten Ways*. He is coauthor of *The Shaping of Things to Come*, *ReJesus*, and *The Faith of Leap* (with Michael Frost); *Untamed* (with Debra Hirsch); *Right Here, Right Now* (with Lance Ford): and *On the Verge* (with Dave Ferguson).

His experience includes leading a local church movement among the marginalized, developing training systems for innovative missional leadership, and heading up the mission and revitalization work of his denomination.

Alan is associate professor for the M.A in Apostolic Movements at Wheaton College (Illinois), as well as adjunct professor at Fuller Seminary, George Fox Seminary, among others, and he lectures frequently throughout Australia, Europe, and the United States. He is series editor for Baker Books' Shapevine series and an associate editor of *Leadership Journal*.

TIM CATCHIM is a grassroots church planter and director of Generate, a coaching and consultancy agency for apostolic ventures. He has wide experience in church planting from the urban context to semiurban people groups. He is currently planting Ikon, a network of missional communities in Clarksville, Tennessee.

INDEX

Other Books of Interest

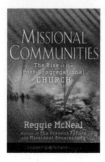

MISSIONAL COMMUNITIES
The Rise of the Post-Congregational Church

Reggie McNeal

Cloth
ISBN: 978-0-470-63345-8

"Every uncharted territory requires a guide that has seen the other side of the mountain. In *Missional Communities*, Reggie serves as that guide who introduces you to the people, practices and scorecard of this fresh growth plate of the kingdom."
—Eric Swanson, coauthor, *The Externally Focused Quest* and *To Transform a City*

"Once again, Reggie McNeal has been reading my mind! He has given voice to those of us who dream of a church that is not just a conspiracy of strangers but a redemptive community on mission for God. For those who dare to make the journey this book provides some invaluable navigational charts for how to get there."
—Gary Brandenburg, lead pastor, Fellowship Bible Church Dallas, Dallas, TX

From **Reggie McNeal**, the bestselling author of *The Present Future* and *Missional Renaissance*, comes the third book in the series that helps to define and illuminate the popular missional movement. This newest book in the trilogy examines a natural outgrowth of the move toward a missional orientation: the deconstruction of congregations into very small Christian communities. For all those thousands of churches and leaders who have followed Reggie McNeal's bold lead, this book details the rise of a new life form in churches and the promise that they hold for greater vitality and meaning in every aspect of their ministry, their members' lives, and their impact in their communities.

REGGIE MCNEAL (Columbia, South Carolina) is the missional leadership specialist for Leadership Network. Drawing on twenty years of leadership roles in local congregations and his work over the last two decades with thousands of clergy and church leaders, McNeal counsels local churches, denominational groups, seminaries and colleges, and parachurch organizations in their leadership development needs.

MISSIONAL RENAISSANCE
Changing the Scorecard for the Church

Reggie McNeal

Cloth
ISBN: 978-0-470-24344-2

"Any new book by Reggie McNeal is something of an event, and this book is no exception. Not only is this an excellent introduction to missional Christianity, but it establishes a much-needed metric by which we can assess the vitality of this highly significant new movement."
—**Alan Hirsch,** author, *The Permanent Revolution, The Forgotten Ways, Rejesus,* and *The Shaping of Things to Come*; founding director, Forge Mission Training System; co-founder, shapevine.com

Missional Renaissance is McNeal's much-anticipated follow-up to his groundbreaking, best-selling book, *The Present Future*, which quickly became one of the definitive works on the "missional church movement."

In *Missional Renaissance*, Reggie McNeal shows the three significant shifts in the church leaders' thinking and behavior that will allow their congregations to chart a course toward becoming truly a missional congregation. To embrace the missional model, church leaders and members must shift from an internal to an external focus, ending the church as exclusive social club model; from running programs and ministries to developing people as its core activity; and from church-based leadership to community-engaged leadership.

The book is filled with in-depth discussions of what it means to become a missional congregation and important information on how to make the transition. *Missional Renaissance* offers a clear path for any leader or congregation that wants to breathe new life into the church and to become revitalized as true followers of Jesus.

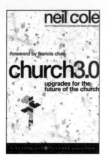

CHURCH 3.0
Upgrades for the Future of the Church

Neil Cole

ISBN 978-0-470-52945-4
Cloth | 304 pp.

"Church 3.0 is an all-in-one compass, survival manual, tool kit, leadership agenda, and imagineering workshop. It is a treasure trove that distributes the wealth of Neil Cole's rich experience and insight. I cannot imagine trying to navigate without it."
—**Reggie McNeal**, author, *Missional Renaissance*

In *Church 3.0*, Cole makes the argument that Christianity needs more than new programs, buildings, or worship formats. It needs a complete upgrade to a new operating system. The early church shifted to a more institutional form in 300 ad and has been stuck in the 2.0 operating system ever since. We are overdue for the next upgrade. Church 3.0 discusses issues such as how to deal with heresy, how to handle finances, what to do with children, and what to do with worship, rituals, and ordinances. Even the most enthusiastic proponents and practitioners of organic churches often wonder how to handle such matters in a faithful way.

NEIL COLE is an experienced and innovative church planter and pastor. He is the founder of the Awakening Chapels, which are reaching young postmodern people in urban settings, and a founder and executive director of Church Multiplication Associates. He is the author of *Organic Church* as well as *Search and Rescue, Organic Leadership*, and *Cultivating a Life for God*.

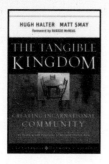

THE TANGIBLE KINGDOM
Creating Incarnational Community

Hugh Halter and Matt Smay

Paper
ISBN: 978-0-470-58023-3

"Among increasing numbers of faithful, conservative, Bible-believing Christians, an important shift is beginning to occur. These aren't wild-eyed radicals; they're solid, established church leaders and members who are asking new questions because deep within they discern that something is wrong with the status quo. Hugh and Matt have been through this shift, and offer wise counsel for a way forward."

—**Brian McLaren**, *author, A New Kind of Christian Trilogy* and *Everything Must Change*

Written for those who are trying to nurture authentic faith communities and for those who have struggled to retain their faith, *The Tangible Kingdom* offers theological answers and real-life stories that demonstrate how the best ancient church practices can re-emerge in today's culture, through any church of any size.

The Tangible Kingdom outlines an innovative model for creating thriving grass-roots faith communities, offering new hope for church leaders, pastors, church planters, and churchgoers who are looking for practical new ways to re-orient their lives to fit God's mission today.

HUGH HALTER is a specialist with Church Resource Ministries and the national director of Missio, a global network of missional leaders and church planters. He is also lead architect of Adullam, a congregational network of incarnational communities in Denver, Colorado (www.adullamdenver.com).

MATT SMAY co-directs both Missio and Adullam and specializes in helping existing congregations move toward mission. Halter and Smay direct the MCAP "missional church apprenticeship practicum," an international training network for incarnational church planters, pastors, and emerging leaders (www.missio.us).

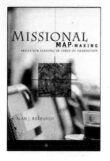

MISSIONAL MAP-MAKING
Skills for Leading in Times of Transition

Alan Roxburgh

ISBN 978-0-470-48672-6
Cloth | 240 pp.

"This important book provides insightful historical perspective toward clarifying the contours of our present landscape, while also being deeply instructive for helping reflective and courageous Christians develop skills for creating new maps toward participating more faithfully in God's mission."

—**Craig Van Gelder**, Ph.D., Professor of Congregational Mission, Luther Seminary

In the burgeoning missional church movement, churches are seeking to become less focused on programs for members and more oriented toward outreach to people who are not already in church. This fundamental shift in what a congregation is and does and thinks is challenging for leaders and congregants. Using the metaphor of map-making, this book explains the perspective and skills needed to lead congregations and denominations in a time of radical change over unfamiliar terrain as churches change their focus from internal to external.

ALAN ROXBURGH is president of Missional Leadership Institute (Mli) and has pastored congregations in small towns, urban centers and the suburbs. He has served in denominational leadership as well as on the faculty of a seminary where he was responsible for teaching in the areas of leadership and domestic missional church leadership. Alan teaches in numerous seminaries as well as lecturing (including at the emergent church conventions) and consulting all over North America, Australia and Europe in the areas of leadership, transition, systems change and missional theology.

This page constitutes a continuation of the copyright page.